THE PRICE OF FREEDOM

THE PRICE OF FREEDOM

A history of East Central Europe from the
Middle Ages to the present

Piotr S. Wandycz

London and New York

First published in 1992
First published in paperback in 1993 by
Routledge
11 New Fetter Lane, London EC4P 4EE

Simultaneously published in the USA and Canada
by Routledge
29 West 35th Street, New York, NY 10001

© 1992, 1993 Piotr S. Wandycz

Typeset in 10/12pt Palatino by Intype, London
Printed and bound in Great Britain by
Clays Ltd, St Ives plc

Printed on acid free paper

British Library Cataloguing in Publication Data
Wandycz, Piotr
The price of freedom: A history of East Central Europe from the
Middle Ages to the present.
I. Title
943

Library of Congress Cataloging in Publication Data
Wandycz, Piotr Stefan.
The price of freedom: A history of East Central Europe from the Middle Ages
to the present / Piotr S. Wandycz.
p. cm.
Includes bibliographical references and index.
1. Europe, Eastern—History. 2. Central Europe—History.
I. Title.
DJK38.W36 1993
943—dc20 93–16894

ISBN 0–415–07627–7 pbk
ISBN 0–415–07626–9 hbk

In memoriam
Oscar Halecki
and Hugh Seton-Watson

CONTENTS

MAPS

TABLES

PREFACE

This book is a survey and an attempted synthesis of the modern history of East Central Europe. A regional approach is meant to take the reader beyond national histories that can be, and sometimes are, parochial, isolated, and self-centered. A comparative regional history seeks to overcome this drawback by bringing out similarities and differences and putting national histories on a larger canvas.

Providing a necessary minimum of factual information – in the text, chronological tables, and the index – this study concentrates on broad currents and fundamental issues. Frequently, satisfying answers cannot be provided to questions that are raised; controversies are noted but not resolved. Serving as an introduction to the complex problems of the past and present, this book will achieve its object if it whets the reader's appetite, and encourages him or her to reject clichés and to probe deeper the region's complexities.

The term "East Central Europe" is used here to denote Bohemia/Czechoslovakia, Hungary, and Poland. In presenting the histories of these countries the emphasis is on states, even though there were breaks of continuity in statehood. While the three states were historically multinational, the stress is on the state or ruling nation, while the other nationalities are treated in relation to it.

The multi-ethnicity and the changing state borders have resulted in vexing linguistic problems that are likely to baffle the reader. The names of towns, for instance, differ greatly depending on a given period. How is one to realize that Pozsony (Hungarian), Pressburg (German), and Bratislava (Slovak) are one and the same city? Which form should one use throughout this book in order not to be accused of anachronism or partiality? Is the Lithuanian Vilnius, Polish Wilno, or Russian Vilna more appropriate? The Saxon towns in Transylvania with their German, Romanian, and Hungarian names, that do not even sound or look alike, present a particularly annoying problem. There is often no solution and inconsistencies are unavoidable. An attempt was made here to follow at least certain rules. If an anglicized or English form exists it is used.

Thus, we have Cracow not Kraków, Prague not Praha. The official state language of the time is also respected as far as possible. This means that for the sixteenth and early seventeenth century in Bohemia, Czech and then German names would be used; for Hungary, Hungarian and Latin; for Croatia, Croat and Latin; for Lithuania, Polish, Belorussian/ Ukrainian, and Latin. If the German name of a given town or place is used less frequently than it might be warranted by the above rule, it is because the German name has often become a symbol of deliberate germanization. Admittedly there are problems, the usage of Danzig or Gdańsk being one of them.

In a sense the issue boils down to the question of continuity or lack of continuity in East Central European history. If breaches were more characteristic, continuity was more fundamental. Then there is also the question of roots. To give but one example: Slovakia did not exist as an entity, administrative or otherwise, throughout most of its history. It corresponded merely to a number of counties in Upper Hungary where Slovaks lived. Yet to ignore the Slovak roots by refusing to use the term Slovakia prior to the twentieth century seems unacceptable.

Names of rulers are generally given in the anglicized form or its English version. Thus John not Jan, Stephen not István, Wenceslas not Václav. Only such names as Bolesław for which there is no English equivalent appear in their original form. First names of all other individuals are written in their native form and spelling, diacritical marks included. Yet certain problems still remain, notably with Croat-Hungarian or Polish-Lithuanian historic figures such as Zrinski/Zrínyi or Jogaila/Jagiełło. All this made the original manuscript a most difficult one to type, and I greatly appreciate Florence Thomas's expertise and achievement in producing the final copy. I acknowledge with gratitude the award of an A. Whitney Griswold grant from the University to cover the cost of typing.

Seeking to overcome the multitude of problems connected with a regional history that covers several centuries, I have turned for assistance to several fellow historians who were kind enough to read critically various parts of the manuscript. I would like to thank Ivo Banac, my colleague at Yale, Józef Andrzej Gierowski of the Jagiellonian University of Cracow, Jan Havránek of the Charles University in Prague, and Antoni Mączak of the University of Warsaw. I owe a special debt of gratitude to István Deák of Columbia University who read with untiring patience the entire manuscript, offered valuable criticism and insightful comments. I am also grateful to Leszek Kosiński of the University of Alberta without whose help the historical maps would not have been possible. The cartographic work is that of Jeff Lester. While acknowledging all this help, I must add that the responsibility for errors, omissions, and misinterpretations is mine alone.

This volume is dedicated to two historians of East Central Europe who deserve special recognition: Oscar Halecki, whose Lithuanian descent, Viennese upbringing, Polish patriotism, and deep Catholicism made a Great East Central European, and Hugh Seton-Watson, whose inborn and inherited interest in the region made not only a "Scotus viator" like his father, but a great interpreter of East Central Europe to the West. The two men differed greatly in outlook and temperament, but they shared a common characteristic: they were scholars and gentlemen.

New Haven, 1991

A GUIDE TO PRONUNCIATION

Accents over vowels in Czech, Slovak, and Hungarian mean that these are long vowels.

Czech and Slovak	Hungarian	Polish	
	á		ah
	a		short open o, as in top
		ą	as in French bon
ä (Slovak)			between a and e, as in fat
c	c	c	ts
		ć	soft ch
č	cs	cz	soft ch
ch		ch	as in loch
	gy	dź	as in journey
ě			soft ye
	é		as in gate
		ę	as in French main
j	j	j	as in yet
l' (Slovak)			soft l
	ly		as in yet
		ł	as in one
ň	ny	ń	as in knew
		ó (u)	as in mood
	ö, ő		as in French deux, short and long
ř (ž)	zs (zh)	rz (ż)	zh as in measure
š	s (ss)	sz	sh
s	sz	s	s as in sun
t' (Slovak)	ty		soft tj as in tune
	ü, ű		as in French punir, short and long
		w	v

xv

INTRODUCTION:
WHAT'S IN A NAME?

East Central Europe is a much neglected region. Except from specialists it attracts little general interest. Its history seems complicated and confused; it is seen as a medley of troublesome nationalities with unpronounceable names. East Central European history is neither exotic enough to arouse curiosity nor sufficiently familiar to facilitate understanding. And yet its importance is undeniable. Two world wars began in this region, as did the Cold War. The phrase of the British geographer H. Mackinder, "Who rules East Europe commands the heartland, who rules the heartland commands the world," sounded ominous in the days of Soviet ascendancy. The Polish Solidarity, which flashed suddenly over the horizon, was to many observers one of those events that shape world history. The collapse of communism in East Central Europe and its unprecedented transition to political and economic freedom carries with it hopes and dangers of great magnitude.

So one cannot be satisfied with a fragmentary and superficial knowledge of East Central Europe, developed in response to headlines. Real insights require a historical perspective, and an appreciation of what this region really is. The term "East Central Europe" is arbitrary. It arose out of a need to define a region that is neither wholly Western nor Eastern, but represents a "middle zone" or "lands in between," as some authors have entitled their works on the subject. The term is borrowed from geography, yet neither geographers nor politicians would agree on the exact contours of the region. The expression "East Central Europe" has been applied to the entire area between the Baltic, Adriatic, Aegean, and Black seas (flanked by ethnic German and Russian blocs), or some variations thereof, or to its "heartlands," to use Timothy Garton Ash's phrase, that is, Poland, Czechoslovakia, and Hungary. It is with these three countries that this book is concerned.

The frontiers of these states have fluctuated a good deal throughout history. They expanded and contracted, comprising at various times the present day Lithuania, Belorussia, and the Ukraine, as well as parts of Yugoslavia and Romania. The special standing of and involvement

1

in the region of the House of Austria, or the Habsburg dynasty, has also to be recognized.

The concept of East Central Europe is new. Indeed a distinction between a European West and East was nonexistent for a long time. In antiquity the southern Mediterranean world contrasted with the north: civilization with barbarism. In spite of the existence of a western and eastern Roman empire in the medieval period, contemporaries did not think in terms of a West–East division. It was only in the course of the nineteenth-century debate in Russia between the Westerners and the Slavophiles that this dichotomy came to the fore. Subsequently, many historians adopted a cultural-religious criterion to justify this dualist approach to Europe's past. The Byzantine Greek Orthodox heritage determined the evolution of one part of the continent; the Roman-Germanic, whether Catholic or Protestant civilization, marked the other. But what about the region that belonged in terms of religion and culture to the West, yet was generally regarded as being part of Eastern Europe? A certain ambiguity in terminology was becoming evident.

After the Second World War the term "Eastern Europe" became virtually synonymous with the Soviet bloc. What is more, the dependence of this region on the USSR received, so to speak, a historical legitimization. It seemed as if these lands, unable to stand alone, fulfilled their destiny by becoming part of the Russian-led communist empire. There was mention of "organic ties" between Moscow and its neighbors, and communism appeared as the road toward modernization of this part of Europe. It was only in the late 1980s that the region was seen as a "great co-stagnation" sphere, to use Joseph Rothschild's expression, and Soviet domination was perceived as anarchic and destabilizing.

Opposing the Eastern European terminology that tended to blur the distinction between the region and Russia, the Polish historian teaching in the United States, Oscar Halecki, came up with a novel conceptualization. It was published in his books in the 1950s and 1960s: *Borderlands of Western Civilization* and *The Limits and Divisions of European History*. He postulated a fourfold division of Europe couched in historic terms: Western, West Central, East Central, and Eastern. The term "East Central" was undoubtedly cumbersome, and although considered valid by many scholars, did not eliminate the more common "Eastern," which the Cold War had made even more current. Halecki's term was redefined and developed some twenty years later by the Hungarian scholar Jenő Szűcs, whose *The Three Historical Regions of Europe* dropped the West Central component. Roughly at the same time Czechoslovak, Polish, and Hungarian intellectuals, mostly living in the West – Milan Kundera, Czesław Miłosz, György Konrád – began to propagate yet another name, "Central Europe," because the "eastern" appellation involved a recognition of the region's forcible separation from Europe. Kundera protested against this "perfidious vocabulary" and insisted that "Central Europe represented the destiny of the West."

Indeed Bohemia (later Czechoslovakia), Hungary, and Poland did belong to the Western civilization. Christianity and all that it stood for had come to them from Rome, or to put it differently, the Western impact was the dominant and the lasting one. We must remember, of course, that Byzantium had begun the conversion of this region through the Constantine (Cyril) and Methodius mission to Moravia in the late ninth century, and that Eastern Christianity's impact on Bohemia, Hungary, Croatia, and parts of Poland was also significant in the early medieval period. But, although affected by these influences at the dawn of their history, East Central European countries became part of the West. They were shaped by and experienced all the great historical currents: Renaissance, Reformation, Enlightenment, the French and Industrial Revolutions. They differed drastically from the East, as embodied by Moscovy–Russia, or the Ottoman empire that ruled the Balkans for several centuries. "If Russia is Europe," wrote the prominent Yale Russian historian George Vernadsky, "she is only partly so." Muscovite autocracy and the subordination of the church to the state was alien to the Western tradition. So was the Ottoman system based on Islam. No wonder that historic Hungary and Poland, bordering on Muscovy and the Ottoman lands, regarded themselves, and were regarded by others, as the bulwark of Christendom (*antemurale christianitatis*). Their eastern frontiers marked the frontiers of Europe.

Yet it would be a mistake to visualize these borders as rigid and impenetrable. The "borderlands of Western civilization" or East Central Europe represented cultural crossroads. The above-mentioned influences of the Eastern, Byzantine world remained crucial in the vast eastern confines of the Polish and Hungarian states such as Belorussia, the Ukraine, or Transylvania. But there was more to it. At the time when the Hungarians or Poles appeared as the staunchest defenders of Christendom (read "the West") they underwent a significant orientalization of their culture. Even their national dress owed a good deal to Turkish influences.

While the notion of a rigid dividing line in the East is untenable, our usage of the terms "Western" or "West European" may require a word of explanation. When we speak of the West we have generally in mind such culturally and economically leading countries as France or England, and not the most western, geographically speaking – Iceland, Ireland, or Portugal. Hence the cultural-geographical-historic model of Halecki and Szűcs (West, East-Center, East) needs to be complemented by another paradigm, borrowed from economics and popularized by

3

Hungarian scholars. It is based on the notion of center, semi-periphery, and periphery, and has the advantage of showing that countries that belong to the East Central group have socio-economic counterparts in the West, South, and North. A nineteenth-century Polish historian, Joachim Lelewel, has already attempted a comparative study of Poland and Spain.

Historically, Europe has always consisted of several zones representing different levels of development. They interacted with one another, the more advanced countries (the core or center) stimulating and challenging those more backward. The nature of the challenge varied and so did the response. The relationship had been generally more advantageous to the core, but a reduction of the periphery to a "colonial dependence," augmenting its backwardness, was not always and necessarily the result of this intercourse. Some parts of the core have been known to lose their privileged character, while those of the periphery ceased, under favorable conditions, to belong among the underprivileged.

Still, it is striking that the core, which has usually been rather small and whose development and achievements were in many ways exceptional, has remained relatively stable over the centuries. Taking as criterion the density of population, some historians view as the fourteenth-century core, Italy, northern and part of south-eastern France, the Netherlands, west and part of southern Germany, and southern England. Looking at the map this can be seen as a longitudinal strip from Palermo through Naples and Antwerp to London. On both sides of this strip would be the semi-periphery: southern France, Spain, Portugal, Brandenburg, Bohemia, Hungary, and Poland. The farthest outlying zone, the periphery, would include Scandinavia, Lithuania, Russia, and the Balkans. From the mid-fifteenth to the late seventeenth century the core still comprised the Netherlands, England, northern France, and the Rhineland while other parts would be more dubious. The semi-periphery and periphery would largely remain unchanged. Taking GNP per capita as a criterion for the nineteenth century the core consisted of a somewhat expanded western region to which Switzerland and Sweden were now added. A similar map could be drawn for the twentieth century.

During all these periods East Central Europe belonged to the intermediate zone – semi-periphery – although Bohemia stood very close to the core and the eastern provinces of historic Poland and Hungary resembled the periphery. Could this model, which is generally applied to socio-economic and political history, be also useful with regard to cultural developments? Obviously culture cannot be easily, if at all, quantified, but there is some relationship, not always clear, between socio-economic status and cultural achievements. Did most of the great

4

cultural currents and movements in Europe originate in the core? Has East Central Europe been mainly an adapter and developer rather than an initiator? The question is complex, but it would be a mistake to see the Czecho-Polish-Hungarian area as a passive member of the European community, always a taker, never a giver. Its contributions in the spiritual sphere must not be forgotten: Hussitism in Bohemia, the concepts of liberty and constitutionalism in Poland and Hungary, a certain uncompromising idealism that had served as inspiration to others. Was the British historian Norman Davies partial to the Poles when he saw their country during the Solidarity heyday as "an enduring symbol of moral purpose in European life"?

Certain periods excepted, the socio-economic inequality between the core and the periphery was accompanied by feelings of cultural superiority on the part of the West. Although there were notable exceptions, many an Englishman, Frenchman, or Italian tended to look down on the nations of East Central Europe. Condescension often mingled with ignorance. On their side Poles, Hungarians, and Czechs often looked up to the West – particularly France and England – with a mixture of adoration and envy. Everything "European," a synonym for the West, seemed worthy of praise and imitation. The nineteenth-century Hungarian leader István Széchenyi characterized the laziness and backwardness of his countrymen as "Eastern traits" that had to be discarded. But this feeling of inferiority needed to be, and often was, compensated for by a glorification of national history and national uniqueness. Poles, Czechs, even Slovaks all referred at various times to their homeland as the heart of Europe. Hungarians and Poles regarded themselves as defenders of the West. Feeling unappreciated or ignored they emphasized their spiritual ideals, which they opposed to the materialistic and degenerate West. Obviously, different periods produced different reactions, but the ambiguity of this relationship, including a love–hate component, was semi-permanent.

Let us now look closer at what constitutes the distinctiveness of East Central Europe. What are the features that distinguish it from other areas, and what are the similarities and differences within the region, among the Hungarians, Poles, Czechs, Slovaks, and others? The cultural-historical concept of East Central Europe combined with the core–periphery model constitutes the starting point of our inquiry, but what approach should be emphasized? Does the key to the understanding of the history of the region lie in its exposed geographic position, landlocked and subject to outside pressures? Does the variety of nationalities and their intermingling justify an emphasis on the ethnic approach? Or does the delayed socio-economic development make the use of the modernization theory particularly rewarding? While the relevance of these and other concepts seems obvious, a word of warning

5

is necessary. Let us not be tempted to sacrifice diversity and the richness of the historical process in the region to a search for a single common denominator. The words of the French historian Fernand Braudel, although uttered in another context, appear most appropriate here: "we must visualize a series of overlapping histories, developing simultaneously. It would be too simple, too perfect if the complex truth could be reduced to the rhythms of one dominant pattern."[1]

The delayed start or cultural lag in East Central European development is clear. The region became part of the European medieval community and civilization only in the tenth century, as a result of what was the first major challenge coming from the West: Christianity. One may argue that the formation of the Polish or Hungarian kingdoms was not that much retarded. After all the French monarchy of Hugh Capet, or the England of Edward the Elder, the kingdoms of Castille and Aragon, indeed the first German kings did appear at pretty much the same time. But they were building on old foundations. In East Central Europe a certain tardiness in the acceptance of the more developed Western models and norms was accompanied by what Szűcs has called "shallow cultivation." This meant that the adoption and implementation was somewhat superficial. We shall return to this point in a moment.

The original gap between West and East Central Europe was greatly narrowed, if not fully bridged, during the first five centuries. Then the economic distance between the two regions of Europe began to increase. Features characteristic of a core–periphery relationship became more noticeable as the agrarian models began to diverge and the West moved toward proto-industrialization. The "second serfdom" marked the East Central European evolution, although it seems clear that Marxist historians, in their insistence on economic determinism, oversimplified and even distorted the importance of this process. There is no doubt, however, that the agrarian character of East Central European society proved enduring. The peasants did not transform themselves into capitalist farmers, retaining well into the twentieth century their particular ethos and conservative outlook. But, we should hasten to add, they were not unique in that respect, and shared many of these traits with the peasantry of the western and southern semi-periphery: Ireland, Spain, or parts of Italy.

Another feature of the region was that institutional developments often preceded socio-economic realities, Bohemia being, as always, by and large an exception. To put it differently, advanced forms of political organization appeared or operated in conditions that were not always ripe for them. A political democracy of the gentry functioned in Poland within an antiquated social structure. Referring to the nineteenth century in that country, a historian remarked that the "intellectual world was more in step with the West than was the condition of the [Polish] industry."[2] A certain provincialism in politics, a less developed political culture, and the absence of the consensus model (essential to American politics) seemed typical of the region, in which the gap between a highly sophisticated elite and the masses has been larger than in the West.

Constant endeavors to catch up with the more developed core have been singled out by the proponents of the modernization approach as the most important, indeed the determining, trend in the area. Even nationalism in East Central Europe is perceived as a response to its backwardness and as a means of resolving the socio-economic and psychological problems. For all the obvious importance of modernization processes, the usefulness of this approach seems to have been grossly exaggerated. A fascination with a fixed progression toward a modernizing goal (not always easy to define) has produced oversimplifications, nay distortions. A good example is provided by the Soviet-imposed industrialization drive which was taken at its face value as a modernizing process, while in some cases it led to retrograde measures: a "feudal" system of privileges and compulsory labor akin to serfdom. Similarly, attempts to draw analogies between modernization in East Central Europe and the so-called Third World produced some interesting results, but obscured very profound differences.

Turning to national and nationality problems there is little doubt that they have been particularly complex and acute in this region. Was this due solely to a large number of ethnic-linguistic groups, larger than in the West and intermingled? Surely, Italy, Spain, Britain, or even France have been also highly heterogeneous, but have succeeded in imposing greater uniformity on their inhabitants. Hence the often made assertion that while in the West the state created the nation, in the East (East Central Europe included) the nation created the state, is only partly true. The state in pre-nineteenth-century Poland or Hungary did create a nation, a "political nation" (composed mainly of the numerous gentry) that was multi-ethnic in origin, but Polish or Hungarian in its cultural-political outlook. Shortly before the partitions in Poland this nation began to transcend its noble character and to take the form of a modern nation. The term Polish had a double meaning. It referred to ethnic Poles, but was also used to include all inhabitants of the state whatever their ethnic or linguistic background, much in the way the word "British" transcends the English, the Scots, or the Welsh.

It was the interruption of statehood, in Poland's case through the partitions, that vitiated the process of nation forming along the Western lines. The result was an evolution toward a different concept of nationhood, colored by the romantic outlook, conceived in terms of ethnicity and cultural-linguistic criteria. It promoted the rise or revival of nations

7

that either never had their own statehood (Slovaks) or had lost it at early times. In that sense it was not so much the multi-ethnic character of the historic Poland, Hungary, or Bohemia, as the interrupted statehood that brought the nationality issue to the fore.

Border changes, more frequent in the last century than before, have added to a growing feeling of confusion. An individual born in Ungvár around 1900 grew up in the Austro-Hungarian monarchy (more exactly in the Hungarian part) but in 1918 he found himself to be a citizen of Czechoslovakia, his home town being called Užhorod. In 1939 he lived for a few days in a Carpatho-Ukrainian state to become again a Hungarian subject. Since the Second World War he has been a Soviet citizen. By ethnic standards he may have been a Ukrainian, a Hungarian, a German, or a Jew.

The distinction between citizenship and nationality, largely unknown in the English- and French-speaking countries, became essential in East Central Europe. Furthermore, the state often stood in opposition to society and vice versa. While the existence of a civil society has always been a distinctive mark of the Western civilization, in the East Central European region civil society acquired a strong national coloration. This was largely the result of periods of foreign rule. Sustained by native culture civil society was the mainstay of a national identity that was often endangered by the foreign ruler or foreign state. As a result of all this, civil society, which traditionally defended pluralism and its autonomy against the encroachments of the state, and in that sense could be regarded as the surest guarantor of the individual, became in East Central Europe the principal defender of nationhood. This led to a certain uniformism and intolerance in the name of a common stand against the non-national or anti-national forces. A Polish author called this a mentality of the besieged fortress.

Interrupted statehood resulted from such traumatic events as the Hungarian defeat at the battle of Mohács in 1526, the lost battle of the White Mountain in Bohemia in 1620, or the partitions of Poland in 1772, 1793, and 1795. The first of these events led to a threefold division of Hungary that lasted about a hundred and fifty years. The second endangered the very survival of the Czech nation. The last effaced the Polish-Lithuanian Commonwealth from the political map of Europe. For over a hundred and twenty years Polish lands were partitioned between Austria, Russia, and Prussia (Germany). The problem of continuity and discontinuity has thus been a major issue in East Central European history, and is distinctive for the region.

If the nations of this part of the world may have been numerically smaller than some, but by no means all, nations in the West, this was not a problem in itself. The Netherlands was not a populous state and Prussia when it began its political expansion was a small country. The awareness of being a small nation became acute among the Czechs in the nineteenth century; the Hungarians alternately described themselves as a small nation isolated among powerful foes and referred to their state as an empire. Only the Poles, even at the direst moments of their history, did not think of themselves as a small nation. It is dubious therefore if smallness *per se* led to the emergence of large conglomerate states or commonwealths that characterized the region in the past. Two of them, beginning as dynastic unions based on marriage, the Habsburg monarchy and the Polish-Lithuanian Commonwealth, played a dominant role in East Central Europe for several centuries. The Commonwealth was in reality a republic presided over by a king and it was held together by the multi-ethnic political nation in which true sovereignty resided. The Habsburg monarchy, which comprised Bohemia and Hungary from 1526 until 1918, was largely based on loyalty to the dynasty.

Another rather unique feature of East Central Europe as far as the scale is concerned, was the presence and interaction with the local peoples of the Germans and Jews. Most of Czech history, as one of the great scholars, František Palacký, put it, revolved around the issue of confrontation and cooperation between Germans and Czechs. Indeed, from the early medieval times to the final expulsion of Germans from Czechoslovakia in the wake of the Second World War, this antagonism and symbiosis permeated most developments. The German impact on Poland, while less pronounced, was still of capital importance. Its nature, however, tended often to be misinterpreted. Many Poles would emphasize the brutal and rapacious characteristics of the expansionist German "drive to the East" (*Drang nach Osten*). The Germans were inclined to stress their civilizing mission in the backward Slav lands. The reality was more complex. It included conflict and cooperation, oppression and assistance, policies of germanization and polonization of Germans. The Hungarian case was different again. Here were large groups of German settlers who enjoyed a special autonomous status, as in Transylvania, and retained their identity. The Germans at certain periods virtually made up the middle class in the country – this was true on a smaller scale in Poland – and affected its economic transformation. The Germans (that is, Austrian-Germans) played a significant role during the period of the Habsburg monarchy.

While the Germans were a group operating within the society, the Jews were both part of it and outsiders who lived in a world apart, separated by barriers of religion, language, and customs. For many centuries East Central Europe was home to large numbers of Jews fleeing oppression elsewhere. In the early seventeenth century Prague was virtually the capital of European Jewry; the Polish Commonwealth (Polin as the Jews called it) comprised the largest Jewish community

9

in the world. Nineteenth-century Budapest had a most dynamic and numerous Jewish intelligentsia whose influence was undeniable.

The Jewish-Christian relationship seemed least unhappy in East Central Europe as compared with the rest of the continent. For several centuries it was even reasonably happy in pre-partition Poland, and there were periods of satisfactory coexistence in all countries of the region. The Judeophobia that was present throughout Europe seemed less pronounced here, until it assumed the form of modern anti-Semitism in the late nineteenth century. The reasons for this development were manifold, general and local, political and economic. A tragic chapter began that found its terrible denouement during the Second World War Nazi occupation: the Holocaust. Today there are hardly any Jews in Poland, few in Czechoslovakia, and greatly reduced numbers in Hungary. Anti-Semitism, which resurfaced amidst the convulsions accompanying the post-communist transition, has no socio-economic foundations comparable to those before the war. No political trend admits to being anti-Semitic. Yet, in the unsettled conditions of hardship, the Jew – and the term is very loosely used – appears as a convenient scapegoat. Is this a transient phenomenon? It is too early to say.

Hardships are no novelty to the region, and past centuries had provided many examples of them. Kundera spoke once about the "experience of an extremely concentrated history," a euphemism for recurring struggle, oppression, and misery. At times East Central Europe has resembled a laboratory in which various systems are being tested. Adam Ulam called the region in the post-Second World War era a "laboratory of neo-imperialism." In the early 1980s Poland was described as a laboratory for political change. Indeed the laboratory metaphor could be applied to various periods in the past.

A good part of East Central European history has been filled with the struggle for freedom. Oppression came from outside because of an exposed geographic position: peripheral in the case of Hungary (as the historian Péter Hanák has suggested), open to invasions from east and west in Poland's case, or surrounded by Germanic lands as Bohemia. But in each case there was usually also an ideological element: outside absolutism versus local constitutionalism.

Defense of national freedom exacted a heavy price. Between 1794 and 1905 the Poles engaged in six uprisings and in one revolution, paying in blood, devastated country, cultural losses, and exile. Their battle cry "For your freedom and ours" invoked the solidarity of the oppressed, and the Poles seemed to epitomize the freedom fighters throughout Europe. The 1848 Hungarian Revolution was part of the European Spring of Nations, but it also followed native late seventeenth- and early eighteenth-century risings fought under the slogan

"With God for Country and Liberty." The price paid by the Czechs for their struggle against the Habsburgs in 1618–48 affected entire generations and was seen as part of a universal struggle for freedom.

Freedom was, of course, long conceived as an attribute of the "political nation" from which the peasant masses were excluded. Indeed, it is they who paid in a sense for the "golden liberty" of the nobility. A conviction that political and social freedoms were inseparable threaded its way through the nineteenth century. But what was of higher value, national or social emancipation? What if they were found to be in conflict, as they frequently were? As always, freedom had a price which had to be paid by somebody: a nation, a class, or an individual.

During the twenty years of independence between the First and the Second World Wars the countries of East Central Europe grappled with the problem of how to reconcile freedom with authority. In Poland especially resistance to foreign authority had become so ingrained that submission to native authority did not come easily. In Czechoslovakia the centralism of Prague conflicted with autonomous demands of Slovaks and political aspirations of the Germans. The authoritarian regimes in Hungary and Poland guarded national independence but restricted domestic freedoms. During the nightmare of the Second World War and of the German Nazi (and in Poland's case Soviet) occupation a heavy price was paid for national resistance. The communist rule that followed offered perhaps the greatest threat to liberty, be it individual, social, or national. Freedom once again was the battle cry in the 1956 upheavals in Poland and Hungary, in the 1968 Prague Spring in Czechoslovakia, and again in Poland in 1976 and 1980. The Solidarity ethos was largely based on freedom – "to be independent means to be oneself" asserted the "bishop of Solidarity," Father Józef Tischner.

The year 1989 saw the crumbling of the Soviet bloc and the re-emergence of an independent East Central Europe. Yet freedom had a bitter taste and the price that needed to be paid seemed exorbitant. Economically ruined, socially dislocated, corrupted, and demoralized by forty-odd years of communist rule, the peoples of East Central Europe discovered that such things as liberty, pluralism, and democracy were not a panacea but were conditions essential for building a new reality. Problems of transition in a post-communist era, whether economic, social, or political proved immense, and Poles, Hungarians, Czechs, and Slovaks have been put to what may be the hardest test in their history. Will they succeed? Will they try to go it alone or give some meaning to the term East Central Europe by practicing regional cooperation? Will they resume their old place or gain a new place in Europe, possibly a united Europe? The future alone will provide some answers, but the past may provide some guidance.

11

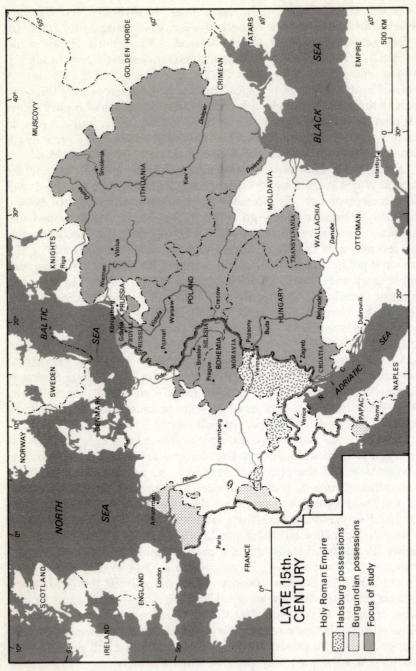

Map 1 East Central Europe in the late fifteenth century

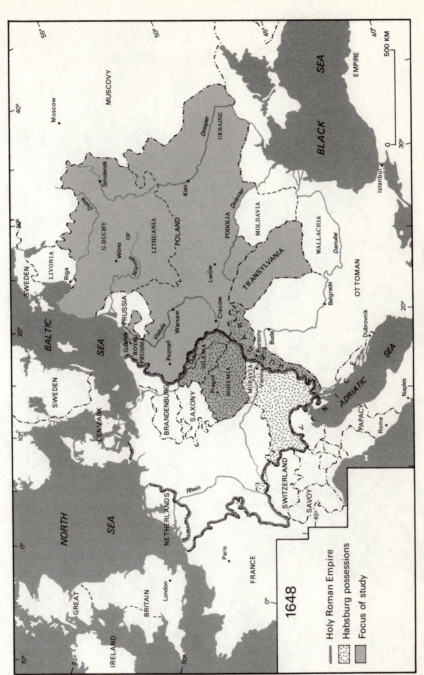

Map 2 East Central Europe, *c.* 1648

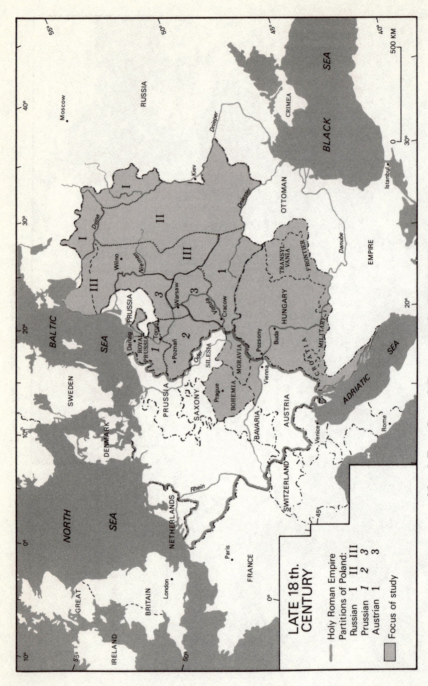

Map 3 East Central Europe in the late eighteenth century

LATE 18th.
CENTURY

Holy Roman Empire
Partitions of Poland:
Russian I II III
Prussian 1 2 3
Austrian 1 3

Focus of study

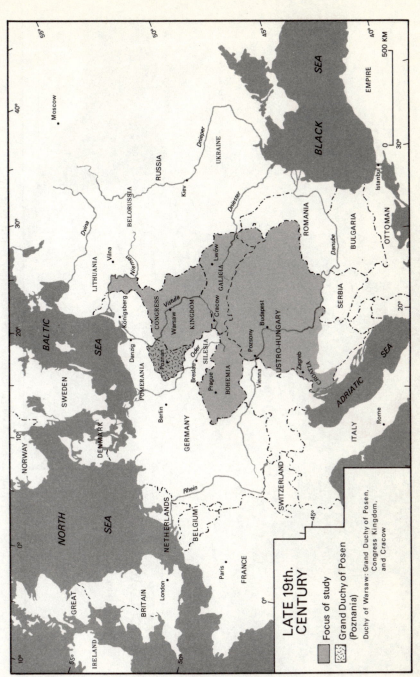

Map 4 East Central Europe in the late nineteenth century

LATE 19th.
CENTURY

Focus of study

Grand Duchy of Posen
(Poznania)

Duchy of Warsaw: Grand Duchy of Posen,
Congress Kingdom,
and Cracow

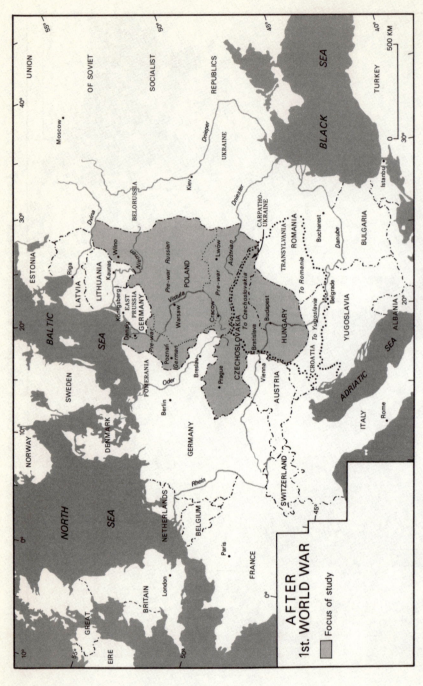

Map 5 East Central Europe after the First World War

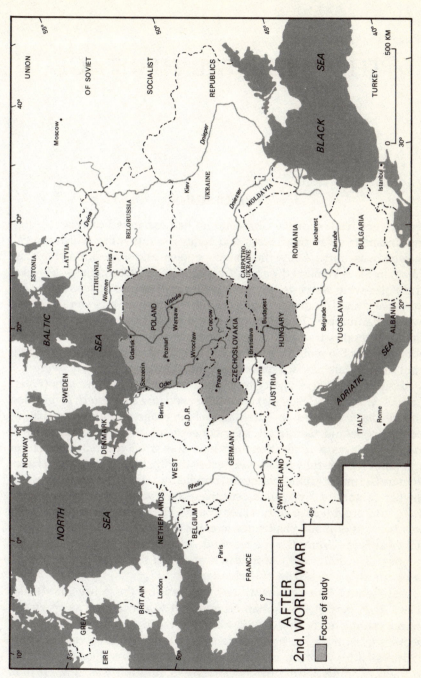

Map 6 East Central Europe after the Second World War

1

THE MEDIEVAL HERITAGE

THE ORIGINS

By the year 1000 medieval Christendom had expanded eastward, bringing under its sway most Slavs and Magyars; the entity which we call Europe was born. Only the Baltic peoples and the virtually extinct Polabian Slavs remained pagan. Czechs, Croats, Hungarians, Slovaks, and Poles were converted by Rome; Kievan Rus (out of which modern Russia and the Ukraine emerged) and the southern Slavs were baptized by Constantinople. This had long-range repercussions. The Byzantine Greek Orthodox tradition differed considerably from the Latin. While both affected the region which we call East Central Europe the predominant and lasting impact came from the West.

Acceptance of Christianity by Hungarians and western Slavs (Poles, Czechs, Croats, and Slovaks) meant the exposure to Western civilization and all that it implied: an international language and alphabet (Latin), Romanesque and Gothic art, new concepts of law, economy, government. This was a civilization that had drawn on the rich heritage of antiquity, never fully destroyed even during the Dark Ages. Here, Roman-Germanic-Celtic elements mingled in the countryside, while towns, centers of civilization, survived as seats of ecclesiastical hierarchy and provided for cultural continuity. The challenge of Christianity was the first of many challenges to come from the West. How successfully did East Central Europe respond to it? How did it develop during the next five centuries? Did it "catch up" with the West? These are the basic questions raised in this chapter.

East Central Europe was a "new" Europe in the sense that it had never been part of the Roman empire. Yet to conceive it as an empty frame waiting to be filled with content would hardly be correct. Its peoples must have reached a certain level to be able to accept, absorb, and to stamp with their own individuality the new values transmitted to them. Admittedly the process of Christianization was slow. It took up to three centuries before the new religion and all it stood for shaped the outlook and the way of life of the western Slavs or Hungarians. The initial confrontation must have been dramatic, and myths have grown around it. Some medieval chroniclers and romantic historians bemoaned the loss of innocence of the early Slavs – portrayed as freedom-loving equals living in conditions of primitive democracy – lost to or corrupted by the feudal, Germanic West. Magyar mythology glorified the alleged ancestors, the Huns, and represented their dreaded leader Attila as the "sword of God," who punished the world for its iniquities.

Our knowledge of the formative period of East Central Europe is scanty. We know little about agriculture and animal husbandry. As for the population, it lived in less advantageous geographic and climatic conditions than in the West and was lower in numbers and density.

Table 1.1 Population estimates, c. 1000

	Population (in millions)	Density per sq. km
France	9.0	16.0
Germany	5.4	10.0
British Isles	2.5	7.9
Italy	7.0	24.0
Poland	1.25	5.0
Hungary (without Croatia)	1.0	
Bohemia	1.0	7.8

Source: M. Małowist, Wschód i zachód Europy w XIII–XVI w. Konfrontacje struktur społeczno-gospodarczych (Warsaw, 1973), p. 20.

Political evolution bore some resemblance to that of the Germanic-Frankish states of the sixth or seventh centuries, but it occurred about two hundred years later. This was hardly an idyllic Golden Age but rather an age of iron, as testified by the strife that accompanied the building up of the state. The process was most likely that of progressive, often forcible amalgamation of clans or tribes under the leadership of a chieftain or duke. His ability to transform a tribal organization into a territorial unit depended largely on the armed retinue (drużyna in Polish, družina in Czech, jobbági in Hungarian) that transcended clannish loyalties and was housed, fed, and commanded by the duke himself. All the land was theoretically the ruler's property (dominium directum), while cultivated land belonged, although was not in his full ownership, to the user (dominium utile). The ducal control over the country was assured through a system of fortified places or castles in which an official administered the surrounding area as judge, tax collector, and war-leader, and tended to the ruler's domain properly speaking. He received as pay part of the latter's produce. Around some castles pre-urban conglomerations arose, in which settled the artisans who worked for the duke and his retinue. The emerging society formed a pyramid with the duke and his officials and knights-warriors at the top and various categories of free or half-free men and slaves at the bottom.

How was this society affected by contact with the West, particularly by feudalism and the position of the church and monarch? Before turning to this question let us survey briefly the emergence and consolidation of states in the tenth century. Bohemia led the way, drawing on the tradition of the Great Moravian state in the ninth century. Great Moravia, comprising most of present-day Czechoslovakia and parts of southern Poland, was exposed to Christian missionaries from Constantinople (notably Cyril and Methodius) and involved in a mostly antagonistic relationship with the Frankish state. After Moravia's fall at the turn of the ninth and tenth centuries, the political focus shifted westward to the region around Prague where the native dukes, the Přemyslids, eliminated rivals and led the process of state building. St Wenceslas (Václav) – associated with the Christmas carol – was one of the early dukes and patrons of Bohemia. A Czech princess married the Polish duke Mieszko I and was instrumental in his baptism in 966. Mieszko, the first historic Polish ruler, expanded his sway – from the northern base around Gniezno and Poznań inhabited by the Polanie tribe – in all directions, including Cracow. His armed retinue was estimated by the Jewish-Spanish traveler Ibrahim Ibn Jacob at three thousand, a formidable fighting force. He was the real founder of the Piast dynasty that ruled Poland for several centuries.

Unlike the Czechs and Poles, the Hungarians were a nomadic tribe of Finno-Ugric descent who invaded the Pannonian plain in the late ninth century, led by Árpád, the founder of the Hungarian native dynasty. For the next sixty years the Magyars raided Western Europe, penetrating deep into Germany, Lombardy, and even France. A crushing defeat, which they suffered at German hands at the battle of Augsburg on the Lech river in 955, forced them to retreat to what is Hungary today and transform it from an operational base into a state.

Did West European feudalism shape the nature and the relationships of these states? Let us first clarify the use of this ambiguous term. Strictly speaking feudalism means a system in which the entire state structure is based on contractual personal arrangements between superiors and inferiors – lords and vassals – with land being the traditional form of reward for services. The vassal, placing himself under the protection of the lord, paid him homage and was invested with land that carried with it the obligation of serving the lord in war and often also in administrative and judiciary council. Land thus held in exchange for services was known as a fief. The fief could be, and was, sometimes sub-divided (in sub-infeodation) so that a feudal pyramid emerged with the lord (or king) on top, with chief vassals below him and sub-vassals at the bottom. This pure model was by no means omnipresent and it varied with time.

The term feudalism is also used in a more general sense to denote a regime in which a landed aristocracy predominated and lived on the fruits of labor of the lowest class, the peasantry. Although there were certainly peasants holding land as tenants in a way not drastically different from that of noble vassals, basically they were villeins or serfs. Various degrees of limitation were placed on their freedom and they were burdened with obligations known as socage in England, corvée in France, and *Robot* or *pańszczyzna* in Slavic countries. Finally, Marxists use the term feudalism to describe a pre-capitalist mode of production and land ownership.

Owing to different needs and circumstances only certain forms of feudalism (in its narrow sense) penetrated East Central Europe, and only with considerable delays. Fiefs existed mainly on the highest level: dukes (later kings) of Bohemia stood in a vassal relationship to the emperor, and this was also true about certain Polish duchies. But, some exceptions notwithstanding, neither the original ducal retainers nor the knights held the land in the form of fiefs. Military obligation stemmed from allegiance to a superior, but not in the typical vassal fashion. In Bohemia knights were more interested in land held in full ownership (that is, allodial land) than in fiefs. The feudal pyramid was virtually absent, although a dependence of the lesser nobles on the lords did develop sometimes, for instance, in the so-called *familiares* system in Hungary. But it involved no investiture properly speaking, nor did it give the lords full jurisdiction over freemen.

The phenomenon of chivalry and knighthood so characteristic of Western Europe in the feudal age also took divergent forms in the East Central European context. First, there was a delayed and rather superficial reception of external forms and customs. Second, while the exorbitant cost of armor and steeds tended to keep down the number of knights in the West, in Hungary and Poland the use of light cavalry, better suited to local warfare, contributed to their growing ranks. At a later time the practice of ennobling whole villages for military prowess led to a situation where – except for Spain – Poland and Hungary had the most numerous knightly class in Europe. We shall deal with the transformation of knights into nobility (which crystallized as an estate by the fourteenth or fifteenth century) later in this chapter.

Religion and the church occupied a central position in medieval society. The church differed from other institutions by its transcendental and universal nature. It acted as the spiritual guide and leader. It supervised education, from cathedral schools to universities. At times it aspired to supremacy over temporal rulers, but at the same time it was enmeshed, as an institution and as individual clergymen, in the feudal structure of political-economic power. In the West it predated the formation of states and played a key role in the revival of the empire under Charlemagne. It came to East Central Europe as missionary and carrier of Western civilization, overawing the Slavs and the Magyars with its cultural superiority, the external splendor of liturgy, the didactic arts, and the entire system of new values and precepts. Christianity was imposed from above and was meant to strengthen the young monarchies. Perhaps this combination provoked the reaction to it, in the form of bloody pagan uprisings in Bohemia in the tenth century and in Hungary and Poland in the eleventh.

Around the year 1000 Poland and Hungary obtained ecclesiastical organizations directly dependent on the Holy See, and headed by archbishops of Gniezno and Esztergom. The bishopric of Prague was subordinated first to Regensburg, then to Mainz, and achieved a metropolitan status only by mid-fourteenth century. The subsequently developed network of dioceses and parishes, however, was more dense in Bohemia than in Poland or Hungary, although much less so than in Italy. The connection between this phenomenon and urbanization – to be dealt with later – seems obvious.

The interaction between church, state, and society was of a multiple nature. The East Central European rulers sought direct links with Rome, while seeking at the same time to limit Rome's power in domestic matters, for instance the nomination of bishops. The early patriarchal dukes or kings drew their counselors from the ranks of upper clergy and wished to have a voice in their selection. On the parish level the noble sought similar rights of patronage. Attempts to dominate the ecclesiastical hierarchy built into the state structure led to clashes, comparable, although not identical, to the great Investiture Controversy between the pope and the emperor in the eleventh and twelfth centuries. The clergy gained some freedoms and privileges during this period in Poland, and in the thirteenth century in Bohemia. Later kings would, however, reassert their rights of nomination of bishops. The church was meanwhile affected by local customs, and it is in that sense that historians speak of a folklorization of Christianity. The church in East Central Europe was influencing the development of these lands but it also came to reflect their way of life and culture.

Can one speak of national consciousness of the medieval societies of Poland, Bohemia, and Hungary? We must be careful not to apply modern concepts to the past even though recognizing certain similarities. The feeling of distinctiveness *vis-à-vis* outsiders is both ancient and basic, and "national" consciousness is thus formed in terms of the relationship to others. In the Middle Ages such terms as *natio* and *gens* appeared, lending credence to the view that just as antiquity was the time of cities and empires, so the Middle Ages gave birth to nations.

Admittedly the imprecise word *natio* did not mean nation as we understand it. At church councils or at universities a single *natio* comprised several nationalities. The criterion of "nationhood" usually comprised common descent, language, political allegiance, and territory, with shifting accents at different times. Common ancestry was invoked in the legend which makes Poles and Czechs the descendants of the two brothers Lech and Czech. The stress on a common ruler of the people was apparent from references to the dukes of Czechs and Poles, rather than to dukes of Bohemia and Poland. But the notion of territorial allegiance was not quite absent, since the ruler regarded the country as his patrimony and himself as the natural heir. The issue was, however, complicated by the fact that each son could claim the inheritance, the right of primogeniture (succession by the oldest son) being unknown in East Central Europe prior to the thirteenth century. This complication was partly overcome by the growing concept of the Crown that separated the institution of kingship from its actual incumbent. Thus, the notion of the Crown of the Polish Kingdom (Corona Regni Poloniae), for instance, served as a unifying factor, both legal and political, even if the state was fragmented into several duchies. The symbolism of the Crown of St Wenceslas in Bohemia and of St Stephen in Hungary was even more important, and the expression "Lands of the Crown of St Wenceslas" or "of St Stephen" denoted the territories respectively of Bohemia, Moravia (and later Silesia), and of Hungary, Transylvania, and Croatia-Dalmatia-Slavonia.

A Hungarian chronicler of the thirteenth century defined a Hungarian as a subject of the king, born in the country, and drawing his descent from the land. Two centuries later in Bohemia, Jerome of Prague stressed the religious element, declaring that common blood, language, and faith were the ingredients of the nation. By this time there was a tendency to restrict the term nation to "noble" or "political nation" that excluded the toiling masses. This was an important qualification.

A xenophobic attitude to foreigners, whether inhabitants of neighboring states or settlers – which often meant rivals – was an early phenomenon. Anti-Polish sentiments were prominent in some Czech chronicles and vice versa. Hungarians were not spared either. There were sporadic outbursts of antagonism of varying intensity against the migrating Germans and Jews, the two groups whose interrelation with East Central European states and societies has been of special importance for Czech, Polish, and Hungarian history. Other immigrants from western Europe, the clergymen, knights, or merchants who came at various times and in smaller numbers to the region, were more easily absorbed.

Medieval East Central Europe, especially Hungary, was multi-ethnic, although hardly more so than many states of that period in the West. The conquering Magyars found, apart from Avars and Gepides, a Slav population living in the Pannonian plain, although its actual size and importance has been disputed by historians. By the eleventh and twelfth centuries the Magyars expanded into the Carpathian regions bringing under their sway Transylvania and what was known later as Slovakia. The former retained a distinct character and regime with its own *voievod* or prince. In the twelfth century the Kingdom of Croatia became linked with the Crown of St Stephen. The precise nature of this relationship – union or annexation – has been disputed, but Croatia remained a separate entity with its own governor (ban). Thus the people of the lands of the Crown of St Stephen comprised Magyars and the related Szeklers, Vlachs–Romanians, Slovaks, Ruthenians, Cumans, Jazygi, as well as Armenians, Greeks, Gypsies, Germans, and Jews. This multi-ethnicity was acknowledged in a phrase attributed to St Stephen, namely that "a kingdom of one language and custom is weak and fragile," a sentiment that reflected less a spirit of tolerance than the belief that diverse groups of people would be useful to the ruler in the process of building up the state.

The "noble nation" (*natio hungarica*) absorbed largely what was then the elite of these peoples. But did a double national consciousness exist particularly among a number of nobles of Croatia who played a major role in Hungarian history? And what do we make of the "national" Hungarian king Matthias Corvinus whose descent was Romanian on the paternal and Serb on the maternal side, and whose preserved letters contained none written in Hungarian, although there were some in Czech. Once again, we must remember not to apply present-day criteria of nationality to this era.

Bohemia was less heterogeneous than Hungary, even though we must distinguish between Bohemia, Moravia, and the largely Polish-speaking Silesia. Most important were the Germans, moving steadily into the borderlands from earliest times. Since the Kingdom of Bohemia for certain periods ruled Lusatia and more fleetingly Brandenburg, there were times when German-speaking subjects amounted to a half of the population. Their cultural impact was enhanced by the links between Prague and the Holy Roman Empire. Indeed many a family seat of nobility bore a germanized name even though the owner was not a native German. The prominent place of the Germans in the "political nation," as lords, knights, and burghers, will become clearer as this study proceeds.

By comparison Poland was the least multi-ethnic state during the medieval period. Differences between the original tribes largely disappeared, although the Kashubians survived as a distinct group in Pomerania. This changed when in the late Middle Ages the principality of Halich (the future eastern Galicia) was brought under the Polish Crown. Its Ruthenian inhabitants differed from the rest of the people not only in language but also in their Greek Orthodox religion. The region also contained some Armenian immigrants. Throughout Poland the Germans, coming in successive waves from early times, became dominant in most towns, although (except in Silesia which passed from Polish to Bohemian kings) this did not lead to a lasting germanization, either cultural or linguistic. We shall return to the Germans in connection with the so-called colonization and socio-economic changes of the thirteenth century.

These changes, and especially the growing money economy, were intimately connected with the influx of Jews in East Central Europe, although the emigration cycles were largely determined by the developments in the West. Thus, while some Jewish presence in Hungary may have predated the Magyar conquest, and small Jewish communities may have appeared in Poland and Bohemia in the tenth century, one can speak of three big waves of Jewish exodus from western Europe since then. The first was connected with the Crusades (eleventh and twelfth centuries) and was accompanied by massacres of Jews; the second with the Black Death in the mid-fourteenth century, that occasioned anti-Jewish outbursts; the third resulted from the expulsion of Jews from Spain in 1492. The rulers of Hungary, Bohemia, and Poland (Béla IV in 1251, Přemysl Otakar II in 1254, and Bolesław the Chaste in 1264) offered the incoming Jews shelter and protection that included guarantees against forcible baptism, personal freedom, and some legal autonomy. These privileges were seemingly patterned on papal guidelines and the Austrian Fredericianum of 1244. Except in Poland, East Central European Jews were subjected on several occasions to expulsions, and eventually Poland became their largest center.

In Bohemia and Hungary the Jews were serfs of the royal exchequer (*servi camerae*), and only in the late Middle Ages were Hungarian lords also allowed to have "their" Jews. In Poland Jews were regarded as free men who were not obliged to wear distinctive garb or be confined to ghettos. Some towns, however, did not permit Jewish presence. The Jews settled largely in towns, provoking an antagonistic reaction from the dominating German burghers. The anti-Jewish sentiments which led on occasion to riots, even pogroms, were, however, sufficiently different from the later racist and ideological anti-Semitism, to warrant the term Judeophobia, suggested by Arno Mayer. It was characterized by religious fanaticism accompanied by popular prejudices about ritual murder, and alleged Jewish responsibility for plagues. Economic reasons (competition and financial dependence) were also present. Still, as their growing numbers indicated, opportunities and living conditions for Jews were better in East Central Europe than in the West.

FIRST THREE CENTURIES

The principal issue that the East Central European states came to face after their entry into medieval Christendom was the relationship to the Holy Roman Empire and the papacy. The former, based on Germany, approached these countries from two standpoints: as an empire that claimed universal dominion, and as the German kingdom whose border marches were expanding eastward seeking to Christianize and control the pagan Polabians (the term comes from Laba or Labe, the Slav name for the River Elbe). The Polabian lands constituted a buffer between Germany and Poland, which also attempted to bring these Slavs under its sway. One of Mieszko's main political reasons for baptism was to be able to treat with the empire and Germany on a different level from the Polabians.

Indeed, the acceptance of Christianity enabled Mieszko the play the papacy against the empire, at one point even placing his state under the protection of Rome. Although he was obliged at times to recognize the emperor's suzerainty – which some of his successors also had to do – the Polish rulers never accepted a permanent status of vassal of the emperor. The possibility of an advantageous relationship arose when Emperor Otto III dreamt of recreating a Roman empire based on four pillars: Italy, Gaul, Germany, and Sclavinia (Slavdom) and saw Mieszko's son and successor Bolesław I the Brave as the head of the latter. The two rulers met at Gniezno in 1000, where the emperor recognized the independent status of the Polish duke and a separate Polish ecclesiastical organization. The meeting in a sense marked Poland's entry into the European community as an independent state. But after the untimely death of Otto III, Bolesław's objectives of a Slav bloc and the royal crown had to be pursued in opposition to the empire. Bolesław's occupation of Bohemia and Moravia, when he invoked his right to the Přemyslid succession, led to a major war. A Slav bloc failed to materialize, but Bolesław assumed the royal title and made his kingdom an important member of medieval Christendom. Incidentally, the borders of his state were fairly similar to those of present-day Poland.

A decade or so after Bolesław's death, in the late 1030s, Duke Břetislav of Bohemia attempted to bring Poland under his sway. He failed, and if his objective had been to gain greater independence of the empire, he did not achieve it either. While Polish–Czech conflicts were characteristic for this early period, they do not tell the whole story of their relationship. Crucial was the Czech contribution to the developing Polish culture, as was the role of the former bishop of Prague, subsequently canonized as St Vojtěch (Adalbert), in spreading Christianity in Poland and to a lesser extent in Hungary.

Bohemia, unlike Poland, was from the beginning more directly exposed to Germanic pressure. During the turbulent process of state-building, the Přemyslid dukes recognized the feudal overlordship of the emperor, a fact that historical maps somewhat inaccurately represent by making Bohemia indistinguishable from the Holy Roman Empire. Prague's dependence went hardly beyond the duke's homage and his obligation to provide a few hundred knights for the Italian expeditions. No imperial troops were ever stationed in Bohemia nor were the imperial diets ever held there. The bishops were not princes of the empire, no lands within Bohemia were imperial fiefs, and only the legislation that emanated from Prague was valid.

Still, the association with the empire bound Bohemia more intimately with Germany, allowing it to intervene and influence developments. The price was not only a growing cultural germanization, already mentioned, but also a certain *de facto* political dependence. The emperor's bestowal of the kingly title was first *ad personam* and in compensation for loyal services. It was only at the turn of the twelfth century that Bohemia became permanently a kingdom.

The position of Hungary was very different. Like Poland the state was only fleetingly under the suzerainty of the empire, and it had already become a kingdom in 1000 when Stephen obtained the crown from Rome. Like Mieszko he allegedly placed his country under papal protection. A balancing act between the empire and the papacy, so characteristic for early Poland, was also noticeable in the Hungarian case, but it was compounded by problems that arose from a south-eastern, Byzantine direction. Constantinople was expanding in the Balkans and had designs on Hungary. The ensuing conflicts led to armed clashes, notably over Bosnia and Serbia. Hungarian interests in the region were bound with the above-mentioned union with Croatia. Initiated under St Ladislas it was consummated under Coloman when the Croatian lords recognized in the 1102 *pacta conventa* the Árpáds as their rulers. Hungary's involvement with policies in the Adriatic caused a rivalry with Venice and complex maneuvers in Rome and Norman Sicily.

With Hungary in the lead, East Central Europe was becoming drawn more intimately in the affairs of Christendom. The Árpáds, the Přemyslids, and the Piasts were intermarrying with each other and with German, French, and Kievan princes and princesses. When the earlier-mentioned great Investiture Controversy placed the emperor and the pope on opposite sides, Czech rulers generally sided with the former, those of Poland and Hungary with the latter. It was thus an irony of history when King Bolesław II the Bold, who revived the royal title that had fallen into disuse, found himself in a conflict with bishop Stanislas of Cracow and put him to death in 1079. The tragedy, somewhat reminiscent of the murder of Thomas à Becket under Henry II of England a century later, led to the king's fall and the eventual canonization of Stanislas, who became the patron saint of Poland.

It was typical for these early centuries that the vicissitudes of Poland, Bohemia, or Hungary and the changing political constellations, were intimately bound with the persons of rulers. Brief stability was followed by strife and breakdown of order, to lead again to recovery. Thus Bohemia declined politically from the strong position it had occupied in the late tenth century, and temporarily lost Moravia. Supporting the emperors in the late eleventh and twelfth centuries the rulers of Bohemia registered some gains, but then also suffered from imperial interference especially under Emperor Frederick Barbarossa. Moravia was erected into a margraviate and treated as a direct fief of the emperor. The already noted absence of primogeniture made each succession in the country a conflict between claimants.

This was a particularly acute problem in Poland where the Piasts were numerous. Another Bolesław (the Wrymouth) sought to regulate the system of succession through the recognition of divergent centers of power in the country. His last will, of 1138, divided Poland among his five sons, the eldest being designated senior and lord over the indivisible province of Cracow. He was also to be the supreme authority with regard to ecclesiastical and external affairs. The period of division thus initiated was characterized by the ever growing number of small political units warring with each other. One may justifiably speak of feudal anarchy, if one remembers the differences with the West, admitting also that local centers could and did perform certain useful functions.

Although Hungary went through a decade of successes, administrative, cultural, and financial, under the reign of Béla III (1172–96), it plunged into domestic strife after his death. The secular lords asserted their power in the counties, nominally as royal officials, but in fact as great landowners in their own right. Historians speak about the beginning of the transformation of the royal counties (*komitats*), from administrative units based on castles into nobles' counties enjoying local autonomy.

The Crusades, that great movement of the early Middle Ages, affected East Central Europe to a relatively small degree. Only Hungary witnessed the actual fleeting passage of the First (1096–9) and of the Third Crusade (1189–92) which brought numerous Western knights into contact with the country and led to some new immigration. King Andrew II actually joined the Fifth Crusade in 1218, just as the king of Bohemia, Vladislav II had taken part in the Second in 1147. Only one of the Polish dukes and probably some knights had taken the cross, but this was of marginal significance.

East Central Europe developed economically between the tenth and the thirteenth century but not in any spectacular fashion. Despite considerable natural riches there was relatively little mining. Towns, in which rudimentary artisanship played a minor role, evolved from rural agglomerations, some of them performing specialized services, into centers where goods were exchanged. The presence of Jewish, Muslim, and Greek merchants contributed to an eventual organization of production and supply of capital. Both Hungary and Bohemia were well located with regard to intra-European trade; as for Poland, the early Piasts' control over Cracow, Wrocław (Breslau), and some Pomeranian towns laid the foundations for its later involvement in international commerce.

Agriculture was not only more primitive and extensive than in the West, but differed with regard to the organization of great property. In Western Europe the manor had its reserve products worked by serfs. In East Central Europe manorial reserve was rather exceptional and most peasants paid their rent in kind, something typical for France and England only in late medieval times.

In the cultural sphere the region seemed to be absorbing the initial Western stimulus rather than making rapid progress. Still, a steady transformation under the aegis of the church was visible. Religious architecture performed through visual arts a didactic function that was essential in a predominantly illiterate population. Artistic levels of sculptures, illuminated manuscripts, and other art objects were surprisingly high as attested by recent discoveries and archeological finds. The first chronicles written in Latin by clergymen appeared in the twelfth and at the turn of the thirteenth century: the chronicle by Gallus (possibly a French monk), that by the Prague canon Kosmas, and the Anonymous chronicle or *Gesta Ungarorum*. The great church reforms in the West brought to East Central Europe such religious orders as Benedictines and Cistercians, whose role in the spiritual and material progress proved to be most important.

THE GREAT TRANSFORMATIONS

From the late twelfth century through to the thirteenth, and then again in the fourteenth and early fifteenth centuries, East Central Europe experienced far-reaching changes under a Western impact. Indeed, they could be called revolutionary for they affected the region in almost every way: economic, social, political, cultural. The first phase was linked with a western European demographic expansion into the less populous and developed areas: a veritable colonization process. The second, involving smaller numbers, stimulated a dynamic economic growth in East Central Europe that contrasted with the mounting structural crisis in the West. The final results were: a growth of money economy linked with new techniques in production and exchange of goods, a transformation of agriculture, development of mining, urbanization, and the expansion of trade both regional and intra-European. All these changes contributed to new departures in the socio-political sphere which resulted in the crystallization of estates (into nobility, clergy, burghers) and their participation in government through representative bodies.

The mass influx of settlers, mainly from Germany, that was organized by the rulers and great nobles has often been connected with the population losses suffered as a result of Tatar invasions. Indeed their major attack in 1241, which lay waste southern Poland and nearly annihilated the Hungarian state – which the invaders occupied – inflicted severe damages. But since the colonization began earlier and was rooted in economic realities, the Tatar ravages probably just intensified the process. The settlers were arriving in organized groups headed by elders, who negotiated contracts that resembled somewhat the vassal–lord relationship. They were to cultivate land and build villages and towns as free rent-paying tenants under the so-called German law, which also provided for some self-administration.

The introduction of money rents, although in some cases the system operated with payments in kind (Polish law), occurred first in Bohemia in the course of the thirteenth century. It brought about greater productivity – the peasant had to sell in order to have money for the rent – and seemed to favor the wealthier stratum. In some cases it lessened the peasant's dependence on the lord although it seemed to operate against the formation of strong peasant communes – as in the West – and generally strengthened the lord while weakening royal power.

Were the German settlers solely instrumental in the introduction of new cultivation methods that involved the heavy plow and the three-field system? Were they real pioneers of progress among the backward peoples of East Central Europe? The somewhat oversimplified view that they were has been challenged on two grounds. First, the whole process of absorbing the settlers and making them a stimulant of change implied a sufficiently high degree of local civilization. Areas in which no Germans settled shared in the general development. Second, it seems that the actual number of Germans (and they included people from Flanders and the Rhineland) was smaller than often represented. Thus a distinction between the impact of the German law and that of the ethnic German colonists appears valid.

Presiding over the colonization process the lords sought to gain tax exemptions from the rulers as well as judicial powers over the tenants. The growing power of the Hungarian magnates antagonized the lesser retainers (*servientes*) of the kings who denounced the constant alienation of royal land to the lords, and clamored for a status of nobility and a voice in the administration of justice. In 1222 King Andrew II issued the Golden Bull, which provided for tax and judicial exemptions to all the nobles, restricted their military obligations and assured their access to offices, from which Jews and Muslims were to be excluded. Compared occasionally to Magna Carta – although some historians regard it as less sophisticated – the Golden Bull also contained a clause that allowed rebellion should the king violate his engagements. The clause was officially applicable to lords only, but it came to be seen as a prerogative of all nobles.

A short digression about the terms, nobility and estate, appears to be in order at this point. In West Slav languages the word "nobility" (*szlachta*, *šlechta*) comes from the German *Geschlecht*, which means race or family and denotes the importance of descent. The Hungarian *nemesség* has a similar derivation. "Estate" means a group of people with an identical legal status, normally into which one is born, and which sees itself as a collectivity. Indeed the notion of an autonomous community (*communitas*) and of civil society (*societas civilis*) was then making rapid progress in the West both in theory and practice. It implied group rights and liberties, contrasting with the essentially individual ties under feudalism.

These developments led to the emergence of a new type of assembly representing the estates and eventually taking the form of a parliament (the diet). In Hungary in the 1260s the representatives of the noble counties came to attend the assembly. In 1278 a special assembly was convened in Bohemia, following the death of the monarch. It comprised the clergy, the higher and lower nobility, and burghers. The 1291 manifesto of Wenceslas II is usually seen as heralding the emergence of the estates-based monarchy. The diets of Poland and Hungary eventually became bicameral; in Bohemia, after some wavering a unicameral system prevailed. Their legislative powers were less than those of the House of Commons in England. While the presence of burghers became a permanent fixture in the diet (*sněm*) of Bohemia – *de facto* since the Hussite revolution in the fourteenth century – and of Moravia, in Poland towns enjoyed real representation only between the thirteenth and the fifteenth centuries; in Hungary mainly in the fifteenth. By the middle of that century, however, no legislation could be adopted without the consent of the nobility.

The growth of East Central European towns during this period of great change was one of its most important facets. Colonists went to build new towns or to rebuild old ones. Since most of the city charters were based on the so-called Magdeburg municipal law (providing for city autonomy and self-government), some historians speak of the *birth* of towns in East Central Europe in the thirteenth century. This is inaccurate insofar as towns had existed before in the region, but it denotes a quantitative and qualitative change in their character. One might observe parenthetically that Berlin's charter was dated 1230.

The nature of towns varied. There were royal and private (meaning lord's) towns. Several arose as mining communities, others as mainly commercial or administrative centers. The German presence was strong, although it seems that with some notable exceptions the Germans did not represent the majority of the urban population, and after the Black Death their immigration was greatly diminished. Yet, for a century or two – in some cases longer – the German language became the lingua franca of cities throughout the region. Together with Latin it reigned at the royal courts of Prague and Visegrád and at the princely seats of Silesian or Pomeranian Piasts. In some cases one can speak of German towns in a special sense, for instance the Saxon towns in Transylvania that enjoyed a wide territorial autonomy, to name only Kolozsvár (Klausenburg, Cluj) or Brassó (Kronstadt, Braşov).

Although estimates are tentative and controversial, the density of the urban network in Bohemia seemed comparable to that of the West, and was exceeded only by such regions as Flanders and parts of Italy. Prague, with possibly 35,000 inhabitants in the second half of the thirteenth century, could be called a large city – urban historians consider 10,000 as the divide between medium and large – but could hardly equal such metropolises as Paris, Venice, Florence, or Genoa.

According to a classification of the historical geographer Norman Pounds a town of up to 1,000 was a predominantly agricultural agglomeration of local importance. That of up to 2,500 was of regional significance; towns of around 5,000 constituted a center of commerce and crafts serving a larger area. With these figures in mind we may look at East Central European towns in the fourteenth century and toward the end of the Middle Ages. In Bohemia the mining town of Kutná Hora at one point reached 18,000. Brno had 8,000 and Cheb around 4,500. The transfer of sovereignty over Silesia from Polish to Czech rulers meant that Wrocław (Vratislav in Czech, Breslau in German) with over 20,000 inhabitants and growing, must be counted as a town in the lands of St Wenceslas. In Poland, except for Gdańsk (Danzig), again under Polish sovereignty after 1466, with over 20,000, only five or six towns exceeded 10,000. Cracow had about 12,000 in the late fourteenth century; Poznań may have counted between 5,000 and 6,000. Nearly eighty towns had 2,000 to 3,000 inhabitants. The remaining five hundred boroughs had between 500 and 1,500. In the Hungarian kingdom Buda reached some 8,000 in the fifteenth century; Esztergom

(Gran) and Szeged had about 7,500, and the capital of Croatia, Zagreb, about 1,000 a century earlier. About thirty-five towns had a population between 1,000 and 3,000. Typically, agrarian agglomerations akin to villages (500 to 1,000) without any municipal status were in the vicinity of eight hundred. The Dalmatian towns are not included in view of the relatively short period of Hungarian sovereignty over the region: 1358–1420.

As throughout Europe, towns took the initiative in the production of goods and ideas, as the French historian LeGoff put it, and they became a symbol of mobility and enterprise. The city of Gdańsk invoked the old Roman saying "one must navigate" (navigare necesse est). The awareness of burghers that they constituted a separate estate expressed itself in strivings to establish defensive inter-town coalitions and to exact corporate privileges. Polish towns proved able to do the former in the fourteenth and early fifteenth centuries; those of Bohemia and Hungary achieved the latter in the fifteenth. However, lasting coalitions based on the towns' solidarity were noticeable only in Bohemia. Elsewhere – the Transylvanian case is special – towns preferred to deal individually with the ruler who shielded them but who did not give them a place in the political power structure. The multi-ethnic character of the cities – German, Jewish, Armenian, Greek, Italian – that distinguished them from the countryside was also an impediment although not the principal cause of the towns' failure to achieve permanent representation. In the late Middle Ages the line dividing the rich burghers from the knights was not rigidly drawn. The patriciate of Cracow enjoyed a great deal of social prestige and power, but in the long run many of its members acquired land and nobility and moved from one estate to another.

The medieval saying that city air makes free expressed the custom that after a certain length of stay the personal freedom of a town dweller could not be questioned. This encouraged social mobility and strengthened the links tying town economy to the countryside.

The proceeding urbanization and economic growth in late medieval East Central Europe was closely connected with mining. Gold, silver, and copper were extracted in Bohemia and Hungary (Slovak and Transylvanian regions), and lead (essential for silver and copper melting) and silver in southern Poland. The latter also had important salt deposits. Intensive mining was largely the result of a technical breakthrough due to imported German specialists, as well as to a policy of economic incentives for mine owners. German and Italian capital was invested in these enterprises. By the end of the fourteenth century precious metals began to play a decisive role in developing trade patterns. Hungary became the main supplier of gold, with an output of possibly a third of European production. Silver from Bohemia represented comparable amounts. In the case of Poland iron production in 1340–1580 doubled per capita.

Polish medieval commerce, unlike that of Bohemia and Hungary, had been mainly of an east–west transit nature. But by the fourteenth century, the country joined in and derived profits from international regional trade. Polish lead was the most important item, and Cracow financiers were investing capital in Hungarian mines, joining with such German bankers as the Fuggers. The output of Bohemian and Hungarian precious metals not only increased currency circulation in the two countries – where the Prague silver grossus and the Hungarian golden florin became symbols of a hard currency – but allowed its export to the West. This equalized their balance of payments. Western Europe was sending cloth and other finished products, spices, wines, fruit, or salt. Some of them contended with and harmed the local products on domestic and foreign markets, although Polish cheaper cloth was competitive, and Bohemia was still an exporter of finished goods. Germany, France, and the Netherlands were their chief trading partners in the West; Rus principalities in the East.

One can speak of two distinct trading zones – the Central (Hungarian, Bohemian, and southern Polish) and the Baltic – although their hinterland was interconnected. Precious metals, as mentioned, played a key role in the former, although sheep (and wool) and cattle from Hungary and some from Poland began to gain in importance. Vienna's staple right (having goods in transit open to sale in the city) somewhat hampered this trade, which may explain the Bohemian and Hungarian attempts to control Austria.

The second zone, the Baltic, was dominated by the Hanseatic League of mainly German towns whose members and agents were scattered from London to Novgorod. Hansa acted as a middleman between regions that complemented each other economically, carrying grain, salt, fish, furs, cloth, timber, tar – all essential for the Western economy – while contributing to the growth of towns in the East. Hansa's activities involved southern Poland (Cracow was a member) and Hungary, from which it imported precious metals, although most of them went overland. This was largely a commerce in bulk commodities with relatively low investments that placed the eastern countries in a position of some dependence *vis-à-vis* the West.

An incipient division of labor will be discussed more fully in the next chapter. Here let us dwell on the growth and prosperity that had a definite bearing on political dynamism of the late medieval period. Indeed, there is much to be said for the theory that without the silver, the expansionist policies of the last Přemyslids would have been unthinkable. The greatness achieved by Hungary in the late fourteenth century was largely based on gold. The policies of the last Piast, Casimir the Great, of making Cracow the focal point of economic activities along the north–south (Baltic–Hungarian) and west–east axes corresponded to his political goals. Similarly the attempts to bring the entire region under the control of one dynasty, or at least unite the two crowns, were connected with the growing economic interdependence of East Central Europe. As compared with the population estimates for the year 1000 (see Table 1.1) there has been, three hundred and fifty years later, a definite increase in Hungary and Bohemia, less so in Poland although the density of its population did grow. The gap with Western Europe remained, although it may have diminished after the Black Death which only slightly affected East Central Europe.

Table 1.2 Population estimates, before 1348–50

	Population (in millions)	Density per sq. km
France	19–20	36.5
Germany	8.5–10	15.7
British Isles	3.3	10
Italy	9.2	under 30
Poland (within different borders)	1.5	6–7
Hungary	2.5–3	7–10
Bohemia	1.5–2	14 (c. 1300)

Sources: M. Małowist, Wschód i zachód Europy w XIII–XVI w. Konfrontacje struktur społeczno-gospodarczych (Warsaw, 1973), p. 20, and J. Kłoczowski, Europa słowiańska w XIV–XV wieku (Warsaw, 1984), p. 53.

If the data in Table 1.2 and some additional figures were represented on a map of Europe a central zone running from Palermo–Naples and Antwerp to London with more than 20 inhabitants per sq. km would emerge, bordered by a second zone with 8–15, and an outlying sphere with 2 or less per sq. km. Poland, Bohemia, Hungary, Brandenburg, southern France, Spain, and Portugal would all belong to the second, intermediate region.

What was the stage of culture reached by East Central Europe in the High Middle Ages? How far did this region develop over these centuries? The church and the court continued to be the centers and patrons of culture, but the place occupied by the towns became increasingly important. Town halls and patrician residences were built, providing fine examples of secular Gothic architecture. Stone or brick (in the north) were the building material in bigger towns as well as in castles, whose number increased greatly under the last Piast king of Poland. Terms such as Vistula Gothic or Prague Gothic testify to the original stamp put on them in the region. German influences were strong; such masters may be mentioned as Peter Parler, the Prague architect and sculptor, and Veit Stoss (Wit Stwosz) the Cracow sculptor, but Italian and French impact was felt toward the end of the Middle Ages, particularly in Hungary.

In vernacular literature, even though there is some evidence of literary composition of religious character in Czech in the tenth century, written Czech, Polish, and Hungarian appeared in the thirteenth century. Nevertheless, Latin remained the language of *belles-lettres* and chronicles. The Latin poetry of Bohemia was thoroughly "western"; such important chronicles as that of Simon Kézai in Hungary and Wincenty Kadłubek in Poland in the thirteenth century, and of Dalimil (written in Czech) in Bohemia in the fourteenth compared favorably with their counterparts abroad. Czech prose, and particularly religious verse and hymns connected with the Hussite movement, reached the highest level in the region in the late fourteenth and fifteenth centuries.

The religious and clerical element in the cultural process continued to be evident. It was strengthened by a rapid growth of convents in the thirteenth century: over fivefold in Poland, slightly less in Bohemia, and fourfold in Hungary. The most numerous newcomers were the friars – Dominicans and a little later Franciscans – whose task was to deepen the religious consciousness of the masses. Indeed, it was to this deep religiosity, as contrasting with the worldliness of the church hierarchy, that the late fourteenth-century reformers appealed in Bohemia, so opening the path for the Hussite movement. Hus's contribution to the Czech language, its grammar and spelling, is comparable to Luther's impact on the German tongue. A Czech translation of the Bible was preceded only by German and Italian, and followed by the French. Hussite influences were responsible for the first translation of the Bible into Hungarian. Unrelated to Hussitism were the renderings into Czech of Plato and the great Italian poets.

The growing political, religious, and cultural need for centers of higher learning in the region led to the establishment in 1348 of Prague university. It was conceived both as a universal and a Czech institution serving four nations: Czech, Saxon, Bavarian, and Polish. It was the first university on the continent north of the Alps and east of the Rhine. The university of Cracow followed in 1364, becoming more famous, after its renewal around 1400, as the Jagiellonian university. Its special contribution lay in the field of mathematics and astronomy, with the first chair in that discipline in Europe. A university founded in Pécs in Hungary in 1367 did not survive, and Hungarian students attended the universities of Prague and Cracow, as well as the newly created one at Vienna where the Hungarian *natio* included also Poles and Czechs.

The full impact of the Italian Renaissance and humanism was felt in

East Central Europe, taken as a whole, in the sixteenth century, and at that time the region was also affected by influences coming from the Germanic lands and the Netherlands. But its earlier, fifteenth-century humanism, which has not been given its due in the past, must not be forgotten. Characterized by a flowering of Latin literature but seeing also the first important works in the vernacular, it developed initially in the lands of the Crown of St Stephen, particularly in Croatia, which lay near and had close contacts with quattrocento Italy. Indeed, the Croat Latinist literature in the age of humanism was particularly rich and valuable. Marko Marulić may well have been the greatest writer in Latin, but his contributions in the vernacular earned him the title of the "father of Croatian literature." The type of man whom Marianna Birnbaum described as the "Hungarian Renaissance personality" whether of Croatian, Romanian, Polish, or German background, was attracted to the magnificent court at Buda of Matthias Corvinus. Under his rule Renaissance palaces appeared, even though the Gothic style would continue well into the sixteenth century. The king's magnificent library was said to have been the largest in Europe outside of Italy. Two other patrons of arts, themselves prominent humanist scholars and writers were János Vitéz, the primate of Hungary, and his nephew the bishop of Pécs, János Csezmicei (Česmički in Croatian). The latter, a famous Latin poet, known generally under the name Janus Pannonius, epitomized the high level of humanist culture reached by the country's elite.

Bohemia's connections with Italy had been interrupted during the Hussite wars; Czech heretics were not welcome in Rome. Still, in the second half of the fifteenth century there was a small number of prominent humanists, to mention only the Latin poet, Bohuslav Hasistein of Lobkovice. In contrast to Bohemia, Poland, especially Cracow, was in the mainstream of European cultural and intellectual life. The university was involved in the Conciliar movement that attempted to apply medieval constitutionalism to the government of the church. It produced a pioneer of international law Paulus Vladimiri (Paweł Włodkowic) whose condemnation of the conversion of pagans by sword attracted the attention of the Council of Constance. Jan Długosz authored several chronicles that pointed in the direction of modern history writing. The Italian humanist, Philip Buonacorsi, better known as Callimachus, also active in Hungary, maintained contact with the Neoplatonic academy of Florence.

As the Middle Ages were waning East Central European elites were becoming fully integrated in European culture. If printing is taken as an indication of progress, the following dates are meaningful: the first printing presses began to operate in Bohemia in the 1450s, in Hungary and Poland in the 1470s. The corresponding dates are the 1460s for

Italy and the 1470s for England and France. Obviously, narrow circles of people were affected, but were they much narrower than throughout most of Europe? One can argue about the originality of culture, but even here East Central Europe has put its own stamp on it. As for political developments to which we shall now turn, they indicated an élan and achievements that compare favorably with the West.

HIGH MIDDLE AGES

To summarize the chronology of the main political developments in East Central Europe over three centuries is no easy task. Perhaps a rough division into four periods may make it more intelligible. The first covered most of the thirteenth century and was characterized by fluctuations in Bohemia and Hungary, both ascending but suffering setbacks. Partial unification of divided Poland led to a dependence on Prague. Two new forces appeared in the region, the Teutonic Knights and the Habsburgs, with tremendous long-range consequences.

The second period encompassed most of the fourteenth century. This was the era of a remarkable parallelism in the three countries, all gaining power and importance. In Bohemia and Hungary, this was the Golden Age.

The third period, beginning in the 1380s and ending by mid-fifteenth century, brought Bohemia and Hungary under the same dynasty, but this powerful combination was largely offset by the Hussite wars in the Czech lands and the rising Turkish threat in the south-east. In Poland's case a dynastic union with Lithuania represented a turning point in the country's history and affected the balance of power in the region.

The fourth period, finally, covering the rest of the fifteenth century, witnessed first another round of parallel developments under the form of an East Central European version of the New Monarchy. It ended with the Polish-Lithuanian dynasty becoming established in Bohemia and Hungary as well.

Let us now follow some of these developments in greater detail. The bid for the imperial crown by the king of Bohemia Přemysl Otakar II (preceded by his expansion into Austria) ended tragically in 1278 with his death on the battlefield of Moravské Pole (Marchfeld or Dürnkrut). Some of the Polish dukes sided with the Czech king, and the Hungarians took the part of his successful rival Rudolf of Habsburg, whose appearance on the scene heralded the role to be played by that dynasty in East Central Europe. Yet Bohemia's power was not spent, and the last two Přemyslids – Wenceslas II and Wenceslas III – gained control over most of the Polish duchies and assumed the crown of Poland, in 1300. Wenceslas III also briefly bore the title of king of Hungary. That country had recovered from Tatar ravages under Béla IV, called the second founder of the state, but this spectacular recovery proved transient. After Béla's death in 1270 a period of almost complete decentralization followed, the powerful magnates defying or ignoring the successive kings. There was periodic cooperation between Hungary and the divided Poland, which retained certain elements of unity: the concept of the Crown, the senior duke in Cracow, and a single ecclesiastical organization. The southern Polish duchies had also suffered, as mentioned, from Tatar incursions; in the north the duke of Mazovia, Konrad, unable to cope with the raiding pagan Prussians, brought in the Teutonic Knights. A crusading order, mainly German, seeking an arena for its activities, it had operated briefly in Hungary but was expelled when its territorial ambitions alarmed the king. Coming to Poland in 1226, the knights conquered and converted the Prussians and established an ecclesiastical state. It was totally independent of Konrad, some of whose lands it used as a base and refused to evacuate. Thus a Germanic expansionist state arose in the colonized and conquered areas that surrounded the Poles from the north-east. Here was the germ of the future "corridor."

To turn to the second period, the extinction of the Árpáds and Přemyslids in the first decade of the fourteenth century marked the beginning of rule by foreign dynasties in Hungary and Bohemia. As far as Poland was concerned this strengthened its chances for reunification, although the new king of Bohemia claimed the Polish crown as well. The conflict with the Piast claimant, Władysław the Short, had a proto-nationalist Polish-German aspect. Władysław was facing a coalition of the German town patriciate, the rival German-oriented Silesian dukes who recognized John of Bohemia as king, and the Teutonic Knights. The long-drawn-out strife, which witnessed a Polish-Hungarian *rapprochement*, ended with the re-emergence of a united kingdom of Poland, but without two of its most developed regions: Silesia and Pomerania. The former came under the Crown of St Wenceslas; the latter, including Gdańsk, was seized by the Teutonic Knights.

The period that followed saw a curiously symmetric development in the three countries throughout most of the fourteenth century. In each case there was a father and then a son on the throne, the son reaching the summit of power: Władysław and Casimir the Great in Poland; the Angevins, Charles Robert and Louis the Great of Hungary; and the Luxemburgs, John and Charles IV in Bohemia. Under the rule of this last monarch, who was also Holy Roman Emperor, and who made Prague a great capital, the lands of the Crown of St Wenceslas rose to a central position in Europe. The debate whether Charles was acting as a German who sought to integrate Bohemia into the empire, or as a good Czech (his mother was a Přemyslid) who concentrated on developing the kingdom, seems largely anachronistic. Charles essentially pursued policies that were dynastic and centered on the Bohemian base, not unlike the Habsburgs later on, who relied on Austria. Under his reign the country went through a process of centralization and codification of laws, saw the founding of the Prague university and the establishment of an independent archbishopric. The Golden Bull of 1356 made the king of Bohemia formally the first of the imperial electors. With Silesia and Lusatia under the Bohemian Crown, the country achieved its maximum expansion. Yet as the subsequent developments were to show, the society was undermined by a brewing crisis which erupted as the Hussite revolution.

The neighboring Poland under Casimir the Great continued the pro-Hungarian policy of his father, but in internal reconstruction it seemed to follow the Bohemian inspiration. Casimir's attempt to codify Polish laws may have been influenced by the Maiestatis Carolina code. The town of Kazimierz was founded adjacent to Cracow, taking as its model the New Town of Prague; the Cracow grossus was a Polish counterpart of the Czech coin. Finally, the Cracow university was to rival the Prague institution. Casimir was unable to regain the lost provinces, and partly to compensate for their loss, partly to strengthen his position and the chances of recovery, he established his rule over Red Rus or Halich Rus (later known in history as eastern Galicia). This was the first eastward expansion of Poland, made possible by the splintering and partial Tatar subjugation of the Rus lands that had once been part of the Kievan state. It made the kingdom more heterogeneous. The thrust of Casimir's policies was to weld together the formerly independent Polish duchies and to transform them into administrative provinces. Hence the stress on centralization, unification of laws, and urbanization that was accompanied by new charters to Jews. The idea that the king was the owner of the whole land and could bequeath all or parts of it coexisted with the newer notion of an indivisible Crown. It was in virtue of the latter principle that all of Poland went, after Casimir's death, to his nephew, King Louis of Hungary.

Louis was presiding over a period of Hungarian greatness, but its foundations had been laid by his father Charles Robert. A member of the Naples branch of the French royal house of Anjou, Charles Robert favored French models and modes, and they replaced German influences during his reign. Successfully breaking the power of the magnates, who had virtually parceled out Hungary among themselves, the king sought to centralize his power through administrative reforms and the application of late feudal patterns. Charles's military force consisted of troops raised by the lords on their estates – entailed to prevent subdivisions – and of noble levies led by the county governors or royal counts (ispáns). With these lords and county units called banderias, which means banners, he established a well-functioning military system. Operating from a sound financial and economic basis, as mentioned earlier, the monarch derived a third of his income from the precious metals that the owners had to exchange in the Royal Mint (similar to that of Bohemia). Distribution of land to royal supporters, however, continued and a new aristocracy was coming into existence; the provisions of the Golden Bull were broadened to encompass the entire nobility. A new tax was imposed on the peasants.

The court of Louis the Great in the magnificent residences in Buda and Visegrád impressed his contemporaries. When Poland came under his rule (1370–82) the Angevins regarded themselves as equals of the French kings and Holy Roman Emperors. True, the union with Poland was not rooted in realities and produced little but friction. Moreover, Louis, who had only daughters, granted concessions to the Polish *szlachta* (nobles) to assure the right of their succession. These privileges issued at Kassa (Košice) in 1374 lowered the land tax to a symbolic amount and limited the obligation to serve in campaigns outside the country. This established a precedent for future Polish bargaining at times of royal succession.

The end of the Angevins opened the way for the Luxemburgs and the Habsburgs, who were intended to marry Louis's daughters (Mary and Hedvig) and control Hungary, Poland, and Bohemia. Had this happened, the surviving Habsburgs would have created an empire, including Poland, as early as the mid-fifteenth century. But the Polish lords thwarted these plans by insisting that Hedvig marry not the Habsburg archduke to whom she had been promised, but the grand duke of Lithuania, Jogaila (Jagieło). Thus Mary's husband, Sigismund of Luxemburg, became the king of Hungary (1387), Bohemia (1419), and also Holy Roman Emperor, bringing under his rule a vast array of states. Meanwhile Jogaila (baptized Władysław) and his wife Hedvig (as Jadwiga) ruled over Poland and Lithuania, another huge entity. Indeed their joint possessions occupied an area of nearly a million square kilometers – the population of Lithuania being hard to estimate. Various historians mention three, six, or even a somewhat fantastic nine million. All this revolutionized the balance of power in the region.

Fourteenth-century Lithuania was a huge country, rich but under-developed, stretching from the Baltic almost to the Black Sea and comprising most of present-day Belorussia and the Ukraine. It was thus a dual state, Baltic and Slav, and after Jogaila accepted and introduced Christianity – the Wilno (Vilnius) bishopric was founded in 1387 – it was also a Catholic and Greek Orthodox conglomerate. In the west Lithuania faced the threat of the Teutonic Knights who, preaching conversion by sword, encroached on its territory. To stop them and to preserve the vast possessions in the east, to which the rising state of

Muscovy aspired, a union with Poland had seemed the only alternative. But it did not mean that Jogaila's Lithuanian-Rus lands became incorporated into Poland, as the union act of Krewo seemed to imply. It was the dynasty and not Poland that continued to rule Lithuania. The Lithuanians – particularly Jogaila's cousin Vytautas (Vitold) who in the king's absence was governing the country – made it clear that they would not tolerate any Polish landowners, troops, or other forms of interference.

The dynastic union, based on the marriage of Jogaila and Hedvig, proved its worth when Poles and Lithuanians jointly defeated the Teutonic Knights in the great battle of Grunwald (Tannenberg) in 1410. Yet it took another fifty years before the power of the knights was broken, and only after the Prussian towns and gentry rebelled and placed themselves under the protection of the king of Poland. The so-called Thirteen Years War ended with the Peace of Toruń (Thorn). It placed under Poland about half of the knights' territory – the old Pomerania, now called Royal Prussia – including Gdańsk (Danzig). Thus the Polish route to the Baltic was reopened, which had great consequences for the future. Meanwhile a gradual process of Westernization, even polonization of Lithuanian lords and boyars was taking place. But if Lithuania succumbed to linguistic and cultural influences of Poland it did itself produce a number of leaders who played a crucial role throughout Polish history.

The descendants of Jogaila had no automatic right of inheritance to the Polish throne, but their election was assured since the Jagiellonians were hereditary rulers of Lithuania and the Poles did not want the union to dissolve. Under their dynasty the nobility, crystallizing as an estate, gained new immunities and greater control over the peasantry. In the 1420s and 1430s the *neminem captivabimus* privilege protected nobles against arbitrary arrest and confiscation of their possessions. The act, incidentally, preceded the English habeas corpus. In the 1450s the Nieszawa statutes provided that the assent of local noble assemblies (*sejmiki*) was necessary for legislation. Still, royal power remained great and so was the international standing of the Jagiellonians. A Polish-Hungarian dynastic union was briefly revived in the 1440s when Władysław III was elected king of Hungary (as Ulászló I). He died four years later in the Varna crusade. His nephew, another Władysław, became king of Bohemia (as Vladislav II) and toward the end of the century king of Hungary. At this point the Jagiellonians came to control all of East Central Europe including the vast eastern Lithuano-Rus lands. The Poles almost took these successes for granted, coming to believe that through dynastic combinations and unions they could resolve international problems and assure their country's greatness.

We must now retrace our steps to look at the developments in

Hungary and Bohemia that eventually led both countries into the Jagiellonian fold. Sigismund of Luxemburg as king of Hungary attempted vainly to stem the rising power of the magnates, epitomized by changes in land ownership. So, between 1382 and 1437 the royal domain dwindled from 15 to 5 percent; that of the nobility fell from 53 to 43 percent; the church land remained stationary at 12 percent, but that of the magnates doubled from 20 to 40 percent. Sigismund's brief efforts to rely on the towns proved ineffective. His attempt to deal with the rising Turkish threat through an all-European crusade ended with the defeat at Nicopolis. Under his reign Dalmatia had to be finally abandoned to Venice, thus ending Hungarian aspirations in the Adriatic. There were problems elsewhere. The oppressive financial and military burdens in Transylvania led to a major uprising of Hungarian and Romanian peasantry, supported at first by towns, some Szeklers, and even lesser nobles. It was suppressed and in 1437 the union of three nations, Hungarians, Szeklers, and Saxons, became the foundation of the Transylvanian regime. The Romanians were excluded.

Sigismund's troubles in Hungary paled in comparison with those experienced first by his brother, King Wenceslas of Bohemia and then by himself when he succeeded to the throne. The Hussite upheaval was variously appraised as part of an all-European crisis that surfaced first in Bohemia, or as a manifestation of specifically Czech conditions; as a pre-Reformation or Czech reformation; and as a national or a bourgeois revolution. It was perhaps the most important single development in Czech history. Both universal and native elements mingled to produce a revolution that affected religion, culture, politics, economy, and society. Even if a certain mythology grew around it, Hussitism served as an inspiration for Czech democratic tradition in the nineteenth and twentieth centuries.

The Hussite revolution was in its origins spiritual and religious. In fourteenth-century Bohemia nearly a third of the land was in the hands of the church. Its dominant position antagonized many, who denounced the corruption and worldliness of the clergy and the betrayal of true Christian values. The nobility, especially lower nobility, was envious of the church's power, and vocal in its criticism. So were the towns, where numerous schools and the Prague university had produced an articulate and sophisticated equivalent of a middle class. King Wenceslas at first sympathized with the religious fervor of the preachers who called on the clergy to change their way of life and demanded reform. One of the most successful preachers was Jan Hus who addressed the faithful in Czech in the Bethlehem Chapel in Prague. Some of the reformers did stress the Czech nature of their movement. Jerome of Prague, as mentioned earlier, defined nationality in terms of religion and blood; there was a good deal of xenophobia in contemporary writings. The demand to make the university a truly Czech center coincided with Wenceslas's wish to subordinate it to his authority as king of Bohemia. Hence, in his Kutná Hora decree he gave three votes to the Czech nation and one to the remaining three. The result was a mass exodus that contributed to the founding of the university in Leipzig. Hus became the rector, or head, of Prague university, and since the university interpreted matters of constitutional and political nature this was not merely an intellectual appointment.

Whether the nationalism of the Hussites can be defined as being of modern type or not, it undoubtedly played a major role in the strengthening of Czech national consciousness. It also broadened the concept of the political nation by the inclusion of burghers and the more articulate peasants. Yet those historians who insist that national, political, and social issues were subordinate to religious ends seem to be on firm ground. To the Hussites resistance to authority was legitimized by faith. The most important document of the period, the Four Articles of Prague, proclaimed the principle of freedom of conscience and expression and demanded the right of all faithful to preach God's word and to receive, like the clergy, the sacrament of communion under two forms, *utraque specie*; hence the term Utraquists for the Hussites. The chalice became the sign of their revolution, and a revolution it was, with its egalitarian overtones and the demand (also in the Four Articles) for evangelical poverty on the part of the church.

The breach between Hus and the king came over the issue of the sale of papal indulgences, as in Luther's case later. Like Luther, Hus went into hiding under the protection of some great nobles. Summoned, under a safe conduct from Sigismund, to the Council of Constance, Hus refused to recant his views, which were affected by the moral rather than theological writings of the Englishman John Wyclif, concerning the freedom of individual's conscience. He was then declared a heretic and burnt at the stake in 1415. A similar fate later befell some of his leading followers.

Bohemia reacted by defiance: a defenestration (throwing out of the windows) of city magistrates – a forerunner of the more famous defenestration of 1618 – and armed opposition to Wenceslas's successor Sigismund. Imbued with religious zeal and fighting fervor the hymn-singing Hussite warriors defeated one after another crusading expedition launched with papal blessings against them. Led by such outstanding soldiers as Jan Žižka, the Hussites undertook offensive campaigns that penetrated Moravia, Silesia, northern Hungary (Slovakia), and the German lands, and pushed as far north as the Baltic. Never before or after did the Czechs show such a dynamic drive and display such martial ardor. Yet internal decomposition resulting from growing divisions set in. The radical wing, the Taborites, pursuing a religious and social utopia were eventually defeated by the moderate Utraquists and Catholics in the battle of Lipany. A somewhat shaky compromise was worked out by the reform-minded Council of Basel but remained unratified by the pope.

We come now to the second half of the fifteenth century. This was the era of the native kings in Bohemia and in Hungary, and of Casimir the Jagiellonian in Poland and Lithuania. Their regimes bear a certain similarity to the New Monarchies in the West: the France of Louis XI or the England of Henry VII.

Although one notices certain parallels in the East Central European developments, the differences are also striking. In the 1450s Bohemia came under the rule of George of Poděbrady, first as a regent then as a king. The country emerged from the Hussite decades deeply transformed. The impact on native culture, especially the language, has already been noted as well as the isolation of Bohemia from Catholic Europe. Prague and its university lost their cosmopolitan character. The Czech political nation, deprived of a monarch for a generation, turned to self-government. The importance of the assembly of estates from which the clergy was eliminated (although not in the mainly Catholic Moravia) increased, and the role of the burghers, no longer dominated by the German element, was strengthened. On the other hand, the domestic balance was being upset by the assertiveness of the lords and the nobles enriched by the land confiscated from the clergy. Thus the stability after which King George, himself a magnate and a moderate, was striving was precarious. The king's insistence that he was a ruler of both the Utraquists and the Catholics – there also arose a Community of Czech Brethren exhibiting high intellectual and moral standards – did not please Rome. The papal call for a crusade against Bohemia was, however, only taken up by the Hungarian king Matthias, known as Corvinus, for reasons that had more to do with power politics than religion.

Matthias's road to power had been largely prepared by his father, the regent John (János) Hunyadi, a hero of the Turkish wars. Indeed, the Turkish threat was becoming ever more serious and direct. Hunyadi had commanded *de facto* the ill-fated crusade of Varna at which the king of Poland and Hungary met his death in 1444. But Hunyadi's subsequent victorious campaigns stabilized the situation, permitting Corvinus to consolidate and strengthen his kingdom. This was no easy task but Hunyadi had shown the way by mobilizing the resources of towns and peasants and throwing his own fortune into the venture. Matthias began his reign by defeating opposing magnates in a real civil war. But he could not immediately overcome the limitations imposed on the monarch: defense of the country to be financed by the king, no taxation of the nobility, and annual sessions of the assembly of estates.

Matthias first relied on the assembly to concede the dominance of the counties to the lesser nobility and to make the office of palatine (nador or viceroy) elective. Then, with his supporters claiming that the monarch had absolute power (*potestas*), he attempted to rule on his own. A very effective reorganization of the administration, in which burghers and even peasants served, a fivefold increase of royal revenue (largely monopolies, customs, mining taxes, but also taxes imposed on all), and the creation of a professional mercenary Black Army, restored Hungary to a great power position. The population reached 3.5 to 4 million people, and the royal income was only some 40 percent less than that of contemporary France. The cultural heights reached under Corvinus's reign have already been mentioned.

Yet instead of using his power against Turkey, Matthias Corvinus engaged on a westward expansion. The capture of Vienna and Breslau may have been dictated by economic objectives and did strengthen his financial power. But the protracted wars against George of Poděbrady on the pretext of crusading against a heretic – which brought Matthias Moravia, Silesia, Lusatia, and even the crown of Bohemia – surely exhausted Hungary and created enemies abroad. The papacy and Venice were antagonized; Poland viewed Corvinus as a rival. The explanation advanced by some historians, that the conquest of the Danubian basin was merely a means of gathering strength for a showdown with Turkey, sounds unconvincing. But even if such was Matthias's motivation, the results were the opposite: weakness and isolation. In his eulogy for the king, the great poet Janus Pannonius blamed the West for its indifference toward the Turkish threat: "France sleeps, nor does Spain care about Christ; England is ruined by rebellious noblemen, and neighbouring Germany wastes its time in endless meetings. Italy continues to be interested in her commerce."[3] Maybe so, but this was no excuse for the Hungarian unpreparedness that invited a disaster in the next century.

The contemporary of George and Matthias Corvinus, Casimir the Jagiellonian, had the advantage of dynastic continuity and more stable royal power. His long reign saw the final crystallization of a two-chamber parliament (*sejm*) and a growth of parliamentary government that produced a certain balance between the powers. Impressive cultural developments during this period have been mentioned earlier, as well as the greatest success, the recovery of Gdańsk and access to the Baltic. The Teutonic Knights, however, did not cease to be a threat, and the ambitious Lithuanian dreams of eliminating Moscow as a rival to the Russian lands proved beyond the Jagiellonian's capacity. But developments in Bohemia and Hungary seemed to offer great possibilities. Poland had taken a friendly attitude toward the Hussites, although neither Jogaila nor Vytautas could have accepted the proffered crown of St Wenceslas. Now the Poles sided with George of Poděbrady and after his death in 1471 Casimir's son was elected King of Bohemia as Vladislav II. Nineteen years later he was called to the Hungarian throne, after the demise of Corvinus. Thus, in the last decade of the fifteenth century the Lithuanian dynasty had achieved a spectacular success, ruling Poland, Lithuania, Bohemia, and Hungary. Although Vladislav (Ulászló) II proved a weak ruler, which was probably the reason that the magnates selected him, and called him Rex Bene ("King All Right"), he was a man of great culture who in that area at least made some contributions.

By the time of the waning of the Middle Ages, East Central Europe had come a long way since the acceptance of Christianity five centuries earlier. True, the region (with the exception of Bohemia proper) did not achieve equality in the material sphere with the more advanced western countries. The near parity in the cultural domain may have been more narrowly circumscribed. In spiritual and religious matters the Hussite Movement, however, was to serve as a stimulus to the Reformation all over Europe. The identities of Poland, Bohemia, and Hungary were firmly established, the multi-ethnic and composite nature (normal for this age) notwithstanding. The borders of Poland had changed most during these ages; those of Hungary least, but the continuity was assured by the concept of the Crown, and, as we move into modern times, by that of the nation.

2

THE CHALLENGE OF THE MODERN AGE

RENAISSANCE AND REFORMATION

The traditional division between the Middle Ages and modern times is largely conventional. There was nothing special about the year 1500 to justify its treatment as a milestone. Fernand Braudel wrote about the "long sixteenth century" that covered the two hundred years from the mid-1450s to the mid-1650s. Oscar Halecki saw a transition era between the medieval and modern times that encompassed the fifteenth and sixteenth centuries. Still, if we think in terms of a lengthy process on the one hand, and of a cluster of events in the decades around 1500, the traditional periodization is useful. Although in this chapter we shall not go beyond the first decade of the seventeenth century, it is important to bear in mind this long process during which "medieval" and "modern" forms coexisted and overlapped.

Several great events occurring from the second half of the fifteenth century on were initiating profound changes. The fall of Constantinople to the Turks in 1453 created a semi-permanent military threat to Europe, contributed to the rise of the Third Rome idea in Moscow, split the Balkans from the rest of the continent, and stimulated intellectual developments in the West. The date of the fall of Muslim Granada, 1492, marked the completion of the Spanish *reconquista* and coincided with the first voyage of Columbus. The French invasion of Italy two years later introduced a new phase in international relations. Luther's posting of the 95 theses in 1517 was the first step toward the Reformation. One can note a certain chronological convergence of events occurring in East Central Europe: 1466, Polish return to the Baltic; 1490s, collapse of Matthias Corvinus's centralism, the rise of a Jagiellonian East Central Europe; 1505, Nihil novi constitution; 1525 and 1526 respectively, the secularization of Prussia and the battle of Mohács. Naturally the fall of Constantinople directly concerned Hungary and Poland.

Europe was changing although only some salient developments can be mentioned here. In the cultural, artistic, and intellectual sphere the

48

Renaissance – understood as a rebirth of cultural achievements of the Greek-Roman world – and humanism as the literary movement had already reached great heights in the fifteenth century. The apogee continued and spread throughout Europe. The elitist and sophisticated ideal of the time was the well-rounded man of the Renaissance; Leonardo da Vinci may have epitomized him. The pragmatism and skepticism characteristic of humanism was apparent in Machiavelli's writings about society and politics. Northern humanists, such as Erasmus of Rotterdam, were particularly concerned with the Bible and early Christianity. Critical of the magnificent and learned, but worldly and corrupt papal court, they still stayed within the church. The Protestant Reformation broke with it, and the repercussions of this event went beyond religious matters, affecting political and socio-economic developments.

Profound changes in economy were an integral part of the entire process of Europe's transformation: maritime expansion and colonialism, a rapid demographic growth and new needs of the urbanizing community, a price revolution and emerging capitalism, an international division of labor. The old society was becoming more fluid and mobile. The invention of gunpowder and the use of professional mercenary soldiers was undermining the military monopoly of the nobility.

East Central Europe shared in the Renaissance and Reformation, making its own contributions to both. In the political-constitutional sphere there was a growing divergence between Poland, Hungary, and Bohemia on the one hand and the West and Muscovy on the other. The difference is particularly striking if we think of the overseas expansion of the West and the phenomenal overland expansion of Muscovy–Russia. The latter occupied 750,000 sq. km in 1462 and reached 2.8 million sq. km in the first half of the sixteenth century. True, in East Central Europe a tendency toward regional consolidation continued. The Jagiellonian rule over Bohemia and Hungary from the 1490s to the 1520s was superseded by that of the Habsburgs. But the Bohemian-Hungarian realms, in turn, were hardly more than an annex to the Habsburg Germanic-Spanish-American worldwide empire on which "the sun never set." The Polish-Lithuanian dynastic union was transformed into a real union in 1569, which led to an increased eastward drive. A mid-sixteenth-century Polish economist actually advocated a colonization of the Ukraine, comparing it to West European overseas expansion and to Muscovite territorial growth, but the scale was hardly comparable.

Before turning to the question of the economic foundations of developments in East Central Europe, and of the parting of the ways between the two halves of the continent, let us look at the cultural evolution. In East Central Europe the Renaissance spread mainly through direct Italian contacts. In the case of humanism, however, one should note the strong influence of Erasmus of Rotterdam on Poland and Hungary, and of the Wittenberg circles on Bohemia. In all three countries there was an obvious connection between the cultural development and the political situation, for example, the growing constitutional-religious friction in Bohemia, a national catastrophe (at Mohács) in Hungary, and the Golden Age in Poland.

The Renaissance triumphed in art and architecture in Bohemia in the late sixteenth and early seventeenth centuries, and took the form of Mannerism. The style radiated throughout East Central Europe. The Prague of Emperor-King Rudolf was a fascinating city, to which alchemists and astrologers flocked. The legendary Rabbi Löw of Golem's fame was Rudolf's contemporary. The architecture of Czech and Moravian castles made an original contribution to art, but humanist writers lacked prominence. The chief chronicler, Václav Hajek of Libočany, was little affected by the new historiography. The Kralice Bible, however, associated with the Unity of Czech Brethren – of which more later – stood out as a monument of literary Czech. Printing activity in Czech was also impressive. In the 1560s two Jesuit colleges, notably the Prague Clementinum, came into existence.

In Hungary where the early Renaissance style in architecture still mingled (as in Bohemia) with Gothic – the so-called Vladislav Gothic exemplified by the Kassa cathedral – the political vicissitudes were not conducive to art. The defeat of Hungary by the Turks at Mohács led to a threefold division of the state: the Habsburg-ruled north-western parts, the Turkish-occupied center, and a semi-independent Transylvania. During the constant wars many outstanding buildings in Visegrád, Esztergom, and other towns were destroyed. But the door and window frames and tombs as well as late sixteenth-century palaces testify to the impact of the Renaissance. In 1541 the first book in Hungarian came off the press: a translation of the New Testament. Among the writers one great name stands out, that of the first national lyric poet, Bálint Balassi.

Nearly fifty years older than Balassi was the great Croat dramatic writer Marin Držić. Both men lived under the shadow cast by the Turks, and indeed an anti-Turkish theme was the most prominent in Croatian humanist writings of the sixteenth century. The marked dependence on the Christian tradition is also considered characteristic of this literature. Because of the constant wars, Croatian literary and artistic activities flourished more on the Dalmatian coast – Dubrovnik (Ragusa) was Držić's home – and on the islands, than in the more exposed regions, particularly the newly created zone, the Military Border.

In Poland, where there were favorable political and economic conditions for the Renaissance, architecture, literature, and science reached unprecedented heights. The royal castle, Wawel, in Cracow, rebuilt in the early sixteenth century under King Sigismund the Old and his Italian wife Bona Sforza, exhibited the purest and best-preserved Renaissance features. The Sigismund Chapel is regarded as one of the finest gems outside of Italy. The style affected the building of numerous palaces throughout the country as well as of churches. The founding of the university of Wilno (Vilnius), originally as a Jesuit college, marked great strides in higher education, as did a new private academy in Zamość – a city built entirely in a Renaissance style. The popularization of the literary vernacular through printing (the first book in Polish came out in 1513) conformed to the pattern seen in the neighboring countries. The 8,000 titles published in Poland during the sixteenth century compared favorably with the 10,000 that appeared in England.

Amidst several other names in *belles-lettres*, history, or political literature, Mikołaj Rey (Rej) stood out as the father of Polish vernacular literature. Jan Kochanowski wrote both in Latin and Polish. He epitomized the age of the Renaissance in Poland and the highest achievements of artistic form. Together with the famed astronomer Nicholas Copernicus (Mikołaj Kopernik), the pride of the Jagiellonian university (as it came to be called), and the stimulating political writer Andrzej Frycz-Modrzewski, he deserved the praise of Erasmus of Rotterdam, who wrote that Poland rivaled the most glorious of European nations.

The masses may have been less affected by the new trends; the levels of literacy and the school networks were inferior to the West, but the disparities were probably not too great. The fact that the encyclopedic vocabulary of the period, the *Calepini Dictionarium*, comprised among its eleven languages Czech, Polish, and Hungarian, showed how well the region had become integrated. Its well-traveled elite was receptive to and participated in the main cultural, ideological, and religious currents of the age. One of them was, of course, the Reformation.

Lutheranism entered the region in the early decades of the century, penetrating the towns in Royal Prussia (Polish Pomerania), the mining towns of northern Hungary (Slovakia), the Saxon regions in Transylvania, and cities in Bohemia. This was understandable, for Luther wrote in German which most burghers knew. Moreover municipal autonomy made it harder to forbid or to combat the new faith. A certain suspicion of the "German creed" on the part of the Czechs was lessened by Luther's assertion that all Protestants were Hussite at heart. The writings of Calvin were in Latin, which partly explains their rapid successes in the 1540s and 1550s among the nobility and gentry of Hungary, Poland, Lithuania, and the lands of the Crown of St Wenceslas. This near identification of the new creed with these social groups made Calvinists accept the political and social ideas of the nobility. Polish Protestants, for instance, supported the "execution of the laws" noble program, of which more later (see p. 64). Only the theologically more extreme groups, such as the Unity of Czech Brethren and the Anti-Trinitarians (known also as Unitarians, Socinians, Arians, or Polish Brethren) who rejected the dogma of the Holy Trinity, developed a kind of social egalitarianism and in some cases pacifism. These revolutionary positions isolated them from the rest of the Protestants. The strongholds of the Anti-Trinitarians were in Transylvania and in certain regions of Poland and Lithuania.

The successes of the Reformation – purely religious reasons apart – were due, as elsewhere, to the criticism of the worldliness of the clergy, accusations of its undue interference in fiscal matters and of dependence on Rome. Among the more extreme demands voiced by the Protestants were those for a national synod, the use of the vernacular in liturgy, and for the secularization of the church land. The latter demand, however, did not figure among Polish grievances.

The main contributions of the Reformation in East Central Europe lay in the cultural field: national literature, education, and the growth of national consciousness. Relying heavily on the Scriptures and propagating their creed through written works, the reformers sought to reach a wide audience. Hence, the necessity of publishing translations in the vernacular. Polish, Czech, and Hungarian Protestant Bibles included the Radziwiłł or Brześć Bible (1563), the Kralice Bible, and the Károlyi Bible (1590). They stimulated in turn the publication of Catholic Bibles, for instance, the Polish translation of Wujek. While in Lithuania a Bible in the native tongue would not appear until the eighteenth century, and the Slovak Protestants used a Czech-language Bible, the Reformation stimulated publications in languages having virtually no literature of their own – for instance, Slovak. With regard to Lithuania one could say that it was through the Reformation that the country became fully drawn into the orbit of Western civilization. Polemical literature, religious and political, appeared increasingly in the vernacular throughout the region, contributing to the perfection of the literary tongue.

The reformers placed a great emphasis on education, and indeed their schools attained high standards. In Poland the most important schools were run by the Czech Brethren at Leszno, by Anti-Trinitarians at Raków, and in Transylvania by the Lutherans at Brassó. While the Reformation in East Central Europe could claim many outstanding intellectuals, it had few leaders of national stature. The Pole Jan Łaski (better known abroad where he was very active as John a Lasco), Karel Žerotín from Moravia, or Péter Méliusz, the chief organizer of the Reformed Church in Hungary, were among the best known. The Croat Matthias Flacius Illyricus belonged among the most important Protestant theologians. Yet none of them had the stature and influence of a Luther, Calvin, Zwingli, or John Knox.

The sixteenth century was the age of religious wars and such outrages as the massacre of St Bartholomew in Paris. The Holy Inquisition was striking fear in people's hearts throughout Spain and Italy. By contrast, Poland, Bohemia (especially Moravia), and Transylvania were oases of toleration. There were several reasons for it. The Jagiellonians, and even their early Habsburg successors, displayed a moderating attitude. Luther and Melanchthon corresponded with the Polish court. So did Calvin, who also addressed Hungarian and Polish magnates and dedicated one of his works to the Polish prince Sigismund Augustus, hoping for his accession to the Reformation. This did not happen, but as king, Sigismund Augustus uttered the famous remark in the *sejm*: "I am not a king of your conscience." In 1570 the Polish Calvinists, Lutherans, and Czech Brethren reached an agreement (*Consensus Sandomirensis*) to cooperate in the defense of freedom of religion. Three years later the Warsaw Confederation made toleration a *de facto* part of the law of the land. Both acts were praised widely throughout Europe.

Toleration in Poland came from the political nation rather than the ruler, and applied to Orthodox Christians, Muslims, and Jews, in addition to the various Protestant groups. But it did not apply to the masses, and it was largely up to the nobleman whether he would seek to impose his creed on the peasantry. Generally, he did not. The attitude of the Catholic nobility toward Protestants may have been summed up by one of the magnates who said that he would give half of his life that they all return to Catholicism, but would give all of it if anyone forced them to do so.

The sixteenth century saw a new wave of Jewish immigrants to Poland. While there were sporadic outbreaks against them in towns (and in 1495 they had been briefly expelled from Lithuania), the Jews fared better than in most other states. Their figures rose to some 150,000 by 1576, a fivefold increase since the end of the fifteenth century; it was due partly to migration (often forced), from Bohemia and Hungary. They achieved a self-governing status under their own assembly (*vaad*). A prominent Jew was ennobled in 1525 without having to become Christian. At that time Jews in Habsburg lands had to wear a distinctive garb.

In Bohemia in 1512 the Prague diet had already confirmed previous religious agreements pertaining to the maintenance of peace. The expulsion of the Czech Brethren, who went to Poland, was exceptional and linked with the 1457 political upheaval. In 1575 the Bohemian diet agreed on a common Protestant platform, based largely on Lutheranism. It was called the *Confessio Bohemica*. It was not recognized by the ruler until 1609, in Rudolf's "Letter of Majesty"; this restricted toleration to its adherents, among whom it included the peasantry. In a sense toleration was more all-embracing in Moravia, for it accepted the

Unitarians expelled from Transylvania in 1569–70, and gave a certain autonomy to the Jews. The Moravian estates declared that "Moravia would rather perish in fire and ashes than consent to a forced imposition of any faith."[4] Indeed, late sixteenth-century travelers reported on a multitude of religious sects operating freely in Moravia. As for the semi-independent principality of Transylvania, its regime was based on the 1571 acceptance of four religions: Catholic, Lutheran, Calvinist, and Unitarian–Anti-Trinitarian, and the toleration of Orthodox Christians, Jews, and Armenians. After some vacillations this was confirmed by subsequent diets. But no other religious denominations were allowed.

The Reformation in East Central Europe had in the sixteenth century made important strides peacefully, partly because of the originally lukewarm opposition of the Catholic Church and the rulers, partly because of its association with the gentry. The Protestants on their side lacked the fanatic zeal that distinguished them in other countries. A British historian, R. J. W. Evans, spoke of a "fuzzy-edged" Reformation in Hungary. The Polish Protestant nobility did not run any great risks or make great sacrifices to practice their faith. Little pressure was applied to them.

The Catholic Reformation, or Counter-Reformation, proceeded slowly, concentrating on education. The Jesuits, such as the great Polish preacher Piotr Skarga or the internationally known Cardinal Hozjusz, did not appear in the guise of inquisitors. The decrees of the Council of Trent were not applied in Poland nor, initially, in the Habsburg lands. If Protestantism survived in Hungary it was largely because it was associated with an anti-Habsburg stance of the nobility. It declined in Poland largely for reasons that were not directly connected with theology. In Bohemia the forcible eradication of the Reformation in the seventeenth century was tied to political developments.

ECONOMY AND SOCIETY

The impact of the commercial revolution on East Central Europe has been the object of much debate. Does the cause of the subsequent division of the continent into the advanced and backward areas lie in the developments of this period: "the slight edge of the fifteenth century to become the great disparity of the seventeenth and the monumental difference of the nineteenth"?[5]

Historians seem no longer to believe that the maritime discoveries that brought a shift of trade routes isolated the largely landlocked East Central Europe, depriving it of the advantages reaped by the West. The maritime discoveries and all they entailed did not bring a structural change into European trade relations or produce the division of labor:

Western articles of consumption versus raw materials and food from the East. Not isolation but greater association was the result, and a "price revolution" which at times doubled the prices of many agrarian products, and stimulated agricultural production and mass exports to some Western countries (for instance to the Netherlands). Did this state of affairs produce a dependence of East Central Europe, pushing it "toward a colonial destiny as a producer of raw materials"?[6] Did West European capitalism grow up on the East European market, or to put it differently, did the region pay in the long run for the growth of the West?

Constructing a model of a capitalist world economy in the sixteenth century, Immanuel Wallerstein postulated the existence of a core, a semi-periphery, and a periphery that played specific economic roles, developed divergent class structures, and consequently profited unequally from the working of the system. The emergence of a world capitalist economy was questioned by other historians, who considered it an intellectual concept unsupported by empirical evidence. As far as East Central Europe was concerned, it was pointed out that England, a country of advancing capitalism, did not import any grain from the region, but occasionally exported it itself. The Netherlands, another country of the "core" did allegedly cover a quarter of its needs by grain imports from the Baltic region, but it also seemed to engage in a speculative grain trade. Thus the market alone imposing a division of labor on various countries, appeared a debatable proposition. In any case grain exports from Eastern Europe could satisfy the needs of no more than a million people in the West.

Another historian, Robert Brenner, advanced the thesis that not trade *per se*, but the nature of property relations determined the course of economic developments. East Central Europe did not become backward because of the one-sided, agrarian type of its exports, but because its backward structure – for instance a weak domestic market – made it engage in this type of trade. This brings us to the question of the manorial, "second serfdom," economy in East Central Europe which will be discussed more fully a little later. Wallerstein's argument that it represented a specific form of agrarian capitalism is unacceptable, and the modified thesis that the landowner, while not being a capitalist himself, was a tool of the Dutch capitalist who purchased his grain, and thus part of the system, is highly debatable. Rejecting the notion of colonial dependency as the creator of the manorial system, the Polish historian Jerzy Topolski sees the latter as the landowner's response to the declining income. This was a universal phenomenon and the French reacted to it by concentration of land, the Spaniards and Portuguese by engaging in colonial expansion. Brenner's point that the landlords did not think in capitalist terms and responded to the problem with traditional means seems well taken.

What was the "second serfdom" (a somewhat misleading term) and the manorial or demesne farming system? As mentioned in the preceding chapter the agrarian structure toward the end of the Middle Ages was characterized by holdings on which peasants produced for their own consumption and sold the surplus. Part of the produce (or cash) went to the lord as rent, for the lord had only a small piece of land adjacent to the manor which he directly cultivated, usually with hired hands. This was known as the demesne. The great estates were basically agglomerations of smaller units, and by and large brought little profit in view of the low value of rents and dues. The rent-paying peasant, while burdened with various obligations to the Crown, the church, or the lord, could hardly be described as a serf in the sense of personal, economic, and legal subjection (restricted mobility, servile duties, and seigneurial justice).

The agrarian boom and favorable terms of trade contributed to the gradual transformation of the tenant economy into demesne farming (the German term is *Gutswirtschaft*, the Polish *folwark*, the Hungarian *uradalom* although the Latin *allodium* was also used), the peasants being obliged to devote some of their time to work on the lord's land. This is what is meant by "second serfdom" and the question is, how extensive did it become in East Central Europe in the sixteenth century? Were serfdom and demesne farming inseparable? Which contributed to which? Was "second serfdom" the retrograde way, a "refeudalization" that distinguished the region from the West during this period?

The theory that the peasants' mobility was restricted, their rights curtailed, and their servile obligations augmented directly as a result of the agricultural boom may be too pat and sweeping. Restrictions on peasants' freedom were also imposed to prevent a depopulation of the countryside or for fiscal reasons. Demesne farming also existed without serfs; in some highly productive branches of agriculture serfdom was never applied. There were important differences between countries and regions.

In Bohemia the first decree binding peasants to the soil had already appeared in 1497, but had very little effect. Relations with peasants during most of the sixteenth century were generally governed by the old tenurial agreements. Serf labor began to be used in fisheries, but not in breweries. The poorest and landless peasants became hired hands on the estates where wages were rising. Thus one cannot speak of serfdom as a mass phenomenon in sixteenth-century Bohemia. Also, even if there was discontent there were no peasant risings.

In Hungary the definition of a serf in 1490 did not imply personal dependence or inability to move. After the peasant uprising (led by

Dózsa) of 1514, which was a revolt of those burdened by taxes, and limited in their rights and chances of advancement, the Hungarian diet imposed "perpetual serfdom." It defined the labor obligation on the lord's demesne (one day per week), restricted the peasants' mobility, and reaffirmed the manorial court's jurisdiction. These laws, however, were not implemented, and some were actually repealed in the 1530s and 1540s. The Crown and the great landowners favored peasant mobility on economic grounds, and the chaotic conditions during the Turkish wars and the partitioning of the country made subjugation of peasants very difficult. No serfdom existed in Turkish-ruled Hungary; in Transylvania where it did, the Szeklers were never "perpetual serfs." The status of the arms-bearing free peasants and haiduks (mainly escaped serfs), fluctuated. Peasants who were winegrowers had no servile obligations whatsoever.

The emergence and enlargement of demesne farming occurred only in Habsburg-ruled Hungary, and the added land was very seldom seized from peasants. The demesne comprised not only arable land but also orchards and vineyards. Much of it was worked with hired help. The business-minded Hungarian nobles did not control viticulture or the cattle trade. The latter, however, was successfully encroached on by the Croat magnates Zrinskis or Zrínyis late in the century. But the nobles enforced their right to the pre-emptive buying of wine and the monopoly of sale, thus doubly exploiting the commoners. As long as the agrarian boom lasted the peasants' access to the market was not seriously endangered. It was only when conditions worsened that the nobles used all the means at their disposal to oppress and exploit the serfs.

In the Polish case a series of laws in the late fifteenth century, culminating with the Piotrków statutes of 1496, and followed by others throughout the sixteenth century, restricted the peasants' mobility, imposed labor obligations on them, took away their right to have their complaints reviewed by royal courts, and closed higher clerical offices to non-nobles. Frequent repetition of these provisions suggests that they were evaded in practice. While there were contemporary references to peasant misery and exploitation by the lords, the situation varied. There were peasants who were richer than small noble land-owners, and peasants who produced for the market and sent their own laborers to perform compulsory labor on the demesne. The number of obligatory days increased from one per week to three, but this may not always have been enforced. Much of our information is derived from Crown lands or big estates of the magnates, which leaves un-answered many questions about the conditions on small or medium gentry demesnes. As in Hungary, enlargements of manorial land by forcible evictions of peasants and incorporation of their plots were rare phenomena.

Even this brief survey indicates that serfdom cannot be treated as the main criterion that distinguished East Central Europe from the rest of the continent in the sixteenth century. While Bohemia and Hungary had very little of it, compulsory servile work existed in Saxony, Styria, and Bavaria. There were certain similarities between conditions in Poland and Catalonia.

Let us look now at commerce and the pattern of production in the region, which were experiencing a growth throughout most of the century. In Poland grain production was first stimulated by the domestic market. It has been suggested that out of the total output only one third was marketed and about 12 percent was exported. But that segment was governed by European prices, which in turn affected the price structure in the country. The grain trade enriched not only the exporters (and peasant grain was included in exports) but also producers who were selling at local fairs. The export of rye, which increased eightfold between 1492 and 1618, went by Vistula to Gdańsk (Danzig), the latter city serving as the middleman, the creditor, and the exporter. Its profits were disproportionately large, but there is no evidence to show that the grain export was hurting any group in the society.

While grain represented as much as 70 percent of Polish exports, cattle, exported or re-exported, and furs (mainly Lithuanian) were the remaining chief items. In the case of Hungary, cattle amounted to about 75 percent of the value of its exports in the second half of the century, although only about 2.5 to 5 percent of the total herds were affected. The numbers involved were huge. While German lands were the main custom, Venice was importing around 15,000 to 20,000 of the big longhorn Hungarian oxen annually. The cattle were bred mainly by wealthy peasants on grazing lands (*puszta*) spread around the trading towns (*oppida*). Copper and grain followed as the next two most important items, constituting together with cattle around 90 percent of all exports. Hungarian wine, particularly Tokay, became famous throughout Europe by the mid-sixteenth century, and was widely exported, especially to Poland. Looking at imports, the chief item on Poland's list was cloth (around 60 percent of all imports) and in the case of Hungary textiles (close to 70 percent). A good deal of cheaper cloth came, as before, from the lands of the Crown of St Wenceslas.

Bohemia experienced no drastic changes in its pattern of production. In the first half of the sixteenth century there was a rebirth of mining, especially of silver and copper. The town of Jáchymov (Joachimstal) suddenly rose to prominence and its silver thaler (from which the word dollar came) epitomized the hard currency of the times. In the case of Hungary, mines in Slovakia revived after extensive modernization.

Copper, as indicated, was a most important export, much sought after in the West. After the divisions of Hungary the Habsburgs encouraged the copper production for military ends. Transylvanian mines seemed to have stagnated; only their mercury was of some importance on the market. In Poland lead and to a lesser extent silver production continued. While virtually all the above-mentioned mines of precious metals in Hungary were owned by south German businessmen, the gold mines in Silesia were taken over by the great German bankers, the Fuggers. This capital withdrew in the late sixteenth century, when the Potosi silver mines began to flood Europe with much cheaper American silver. Unable to compete on international markets, the East Central European mining industry was reduced to local importance. If we remember the role that precious metals had played in the region's balance of payments with the West this was definitely a change for the worse.

The existing division of labor between Western Europe and East Central Europe was based on a one-sided development of agrarian products for export and proved detrimental to the region in the long run. But it bears repeating that under the favorable terms of trade in the sixteenth century Bohemia, Poland, and Hungary were becoming enriched, and not only the nobles but also the burghers and peasants. The "second serfdom" took a long time in crystallizing and was less the product of the agrarian boom than of the tightening market that followed. Other than purely economic factors influenced the process. Why was there no accumulation of capital derived from trade and its reinvestment in an economically productive fashion? To simplify a complex issue one can say that most of the money went into ostentatious living, purchase of luxury goods, upkeep of the lord's retainers, or his private armies. If money was invested in land that was at least partly for reasons of prestige. A rich merchant's dream was to be a noble landowner. This was also true in many Western countries, but did not bring about a divorce between a noble status and economic activity. What is more, not even Prague or Gdańsk had among its bankers or traders such potentates as the Fuggers. The latter operating as foreign capitalists in East Central Europe took their profits and withdrew when conditions were less promising. These were economic as well as social phenomena, and they may become clearer when we turn to East Central Europe's social structures.

At the beginning of the sixteenth century, according to some calculations, figures as shown in Table 2.1 emerge. Except for Hungary the region experienced a steady and significant demographic growth, which in Poland's case was connected with expansionist eastern trends. This was in keeping with the population growth throughout Europe. Yet there were important differences regarding the development of towns.

Table 2.1 Population estimates, c. 1500

	Population (in millions)	Density per sq. km
Bohemia (without Moravia and Silesia)	1.3	c. 19
Hungary	4.5	8
Poland (without Lithuania)	3	14

Source: Based on S. Russocki, "Monarchie stanowe środkowo-wschodniej Europy XV–XVI w.," Kwartalnik Historyczny 84 (1977), p. 75 and Eric Fügedi, "The demographic landscape of East-Central Europe," in Antoni Mączak, Henryk Samsonowicz, Peter Burke (eds), East Central Europe in Transition from the Fourteenth to the Seventeenth Century (Cambridge and Paris, 1985), p. 54.

Prague continued to be the only big city in the region with some 50,000 in the second half of the century. Gdańsk came next with 30,000. Cracow had between 10,000 and 20,000. Jáchymov suddenly mushroomed from 1,000 to 14,000 in a decade, only to sink again to the level of a small town, and other mining towns did similarly. Probably over 20 percent of the population of Bohemia and 25 percent in Moravia lived in towns. In Poland proper, that is, not counting Lithuania, the estimates are also 20 percent toward the end of the century. In Hungary roughly 15 percent were town dwellers. By way of comparison the corresponding figures for Northern Italy would be approximately 50 percent and for Holland 46 to 54 percent.

The relatively dense urban network in East Central Europe was made up mainly of small half-rural agglomerations which multiplied quickly. This offered a contrast to the West, where big cities grew bigger and the number of cities of over 100,000 increased. A good example of little towns is provided by the Hungarian oppida, which developed as trading posts within winegrowing or cattle country. They could hardly be regarded as cities in a general European sense. Some of the larger royal towns passed into private hands as payments by the hard-pressed monarchs.

The Mohács catastrophe and the continuing Turkish wars inflicted severe wounds on the country's population and urban network. Conservative estimates speak of a one million population loss. Buda under Turkish occupation rapidly declined and other towns were petrified at the level of medieval urbanization. Only some towns that engaged in transit trade and the little towns fared reasonably well. Many German burghers left for Germany, which contributed to a certain urban Magyarization. By and large the number of craftsmen dropped. A noted Hungarian historian may have exaggerated when he wrote that "a nation which had reached the gateway to early capitalism by the early

60

sixteenth century sank back to the level of its nomadic ancestors in a matter of a decade"[7] but a serious regress was evident.

In Poland the century represented a dynamic socio-economic development. According to some estimates the population grew faster than in the West. From mid-fifteenth to mid-sixteenth century some two hundred new towns were added to the existing four hundred and fifty. True, many of them had no self-government, guilds, or trading associations. The growing handicrafts in the countryside were competing with the towns' artisanship. Still, the growth of linen and leather industries including the rise of first manufactories in western Poland (paper mills), and the introduction of new techniques into iron smelting (great furnaces) showed that the economic development was not totally one-sided. Gdańsk, that not only handled Poland's maritime trade but also produced many goods itself (furniture, clocks, stoves), was serving as a substitute for an all-Polish market. This Baltic city with a hinterland closely resembling the Netherlands was almost a state within the state, with its own currency, vessels, troops, and diplomacy. Its patricians owned landed estates, as did the burghers of other cities in Royal Prussia. They resembled their opposite numbers in the West to a degree unequalled throughout the region, Prague excepted. Indeed some of the free towns in Bohemia owned more land in certain provinces than did the lords or knights. By way of contrast only 1.5 percent of peasant households in Hungary belonged to the cities.

The burghers had to compete both with foreign importers and the local nobility, whose products were usually exempt from custom duties, taxes, and tolls. In Poland the lords and the gentry not only gradually monopolized the most lucrative grain trade, but stood behind the laws that excluded the burghers from landownership (1538) with exceptions noted above. The nobles began to take their grain directly to Gdańsk, bypassing the middlemen. What is more, by 1565 Polish traders were forbidden to travel abroad with their wares. Motives of competition aside, it was believed that it was more lucrative to do business with foreign importers who had to sell their wares than to run the risk of buying and selling goods abroad.

The growing ascendancy of the nobility was a result of a combination of economic, social, and political factors. There were various roads taken by the noble estate throughout Europe, and one can speak of the rise of a "new" nobility; it was new in a genetic sense, in terms of a transformation of knights into gentlemen farmers, and taking into account their growing involvement in administration, courts, or standing armies. What is more, what we may call the gentry (lower nobility, knights) was playing in some respects a role similar to that of the middle classes in Western Europe. But, and this is important, it was far less dependent on and linked with the monarch. On the other hand a patron–client relationship developed, especially in Poland, between the magnate and the middle-to-small and landless gentry, a practice that was by then declining in the West. Let us also recall that the Polish gentry that may have reached 6 to 8 percent of the population, and that of Hungary, estimated at some 5 percent, were exceeded in Europe only by the hidalgos of Spain: possibly 10 to 12 percent. A large segment of Polish and Hungarian gentry was very poor, as it became customary to ennoble entire villages for valor displayed during wars. Access to this estate was not through different forms of state service as in many European countries, and in theory it was a closed group. In practice fraudulent entry into noble ranks was not easily detected, especially in Poland where no heraldry office existed. Apparently self-ennoblements or tacit ennoblements, though punishable by law, were not infrequent.

The social structure of sixteenth-century East Central Europe was, taking all the local divergences and variants into consideration, not drastically different from that of France. The magnate group was comparable, the clergy was smaller in numbers, the gentry far more numerous, the burghers roughly similar in numbers. Contrasts in dress, manners, and customs were certainly less striking than a century later.

POLITICS

The rising absolutism in the West and autocracy in the East (Muscovy) represented two distinct approaches to politics. As Jenő Szűcs put it, the West centralized while the East annihilated (for example, in Novgorod, whose citizens were deported *en masse* by Moscow in 1478). In the West the absolutist state was a compensation for the disappearance of serfdom while in the East autocracy was a device for its consolidation. In the case of East Central Europe its specific character precluded a successful initiation of the Western model. The existence of a "civil society" and a "corpus politicum" excluded the use of Eastern methods.

By the early sixteenth century Bohemia, Hungary, and Poland had all crystallized as estates-based regimes (*Ständestaat*, as the Germans call it) with parliamentary institutions. The evolution of the system was affected by a contest for power between the king and the estates, meaning the lords and the gentry, and in the case of Bohemia also the powerful burghers. In Poland the rulers made fuller use of the gentry as potential allies against the lords only late in the century, and they failed to exploit the alliance for their benefit. Consequently a specific form of gentry democracy developed in the state, a *Respublica*, meaning commonwealth.

The Bohemian and Hungarian lords achieved an ascendancy over the king in the first decades of the sixteenth century, although the lords' power was contested by the gentry, and in Bohemia the towns successfully withstood attempts to relegate them to an inferior status. In the second half of the century, the attempts by the Habsburgs to strengthen royal power produced a more balanced system. Local assemblies on the level of *Land*, District, or County (*komitat*) respectively in Poland, Bohemia, and Hungary, significantly increased their fiscal and administrative powers. The Hungarian *komitat* especially came to play a special role in the subsequent evolution of the country.

The concept of the Crown of St Wenceslas, St Stephen, or of Poland which symbolized the symbiosis between the monarchy and the political nation, was in a sense more modern than the prevalent "proprietary dynasticism." The political nation in Bohemia, we will recall, comprised the three estates of lords, knights, and burghers represented in the diet (*sněm*). The estate of the clergy continued to be included in the Moravian diet. The Royal Council failed to transform itself into a second chamber. The two Jagiellonian kings, Vladislav and Louis II, found their prerogatives as supreme executive, judge, and commander-in-chief, circumscribed in practice. The Land Ordinance of 1500 (Zřízení zemské) that provided for a more equitable distribution of offices between lords and knights further limited the royal power. The financial basis of royal power dwindled with the alienation of the king's domain and his promises not to reclaim it. The role of the diet that voted extraordinary taxes and elected rulers increased rapidly.

The Hungarian diet crystallized into a bicameral institution, and had lords seated, along with top ecclesiastical appointees, in the upper house (the table of lords). Elected representatives of counties, delegates of free royal towns (with one collective vote), and deputies of absent magnates and bishops attended the lower chamber. Thus only the nobility, high and low, dominated the diet and could rightly claim to be *the* political nation. Their claim was endorsed in the Opus Tripartitum of István Werbőczy in 1514, which although not sanctified by the king was treated as a codification of laws. The Tripartitum declared that all nobles were equal and confirmed their privileges, including the armed-resistance clause of the Golden Bull. Theoretically they could all attend the diet in person, which emphasized the fact that sovereignty resided collectively in this *natio hungarica*, that was united with the state through the Holy Crown of St Stephen. The diet of Croatia was, of course, a separate institution.

The Polish diet (*sejm*) came closer to the Hungarian than to the Czech model. The clergy was not represented in the lower chamber, and the burghers only symbolically, a result both of the nobility's reluctance to share its power and of a certain indifference on the townsmen's part. Exceptionally, in the provincial assembly of the semi-autonomous Royal Prussia representatives of the large towns balanced the nobles. The mode of election through local noble assemblies (*sejmik*) was comparable to that in Hungary. The upper house, called the senate, was not however a hereditary domain of the lords, but consisted of a number of lay and ecclesiastical dignitaries appointed by the king for life. It attempted at first to dominate the lower chamber, but succumbed to a gentry offensive. The latter operating on the platform of "execution of the laws" – linked, as already mentioned, with the Reformation – sought to strengthen the royal power but under public supervision of the political nation. Before saying a few words about this most important trend, we need to stress the place of law in the sixteenth-century Polish *Respublica*.

Based on codes known as the Laski statutes, the Polish system seemed to have a number of original features, and it functioned better than those in Hungary and Bohemia. Its main principles included the protection of property against confiscation and of personal rights against arbitrary arrest (neminem captivabimus). The Nihil novi constitution of 1505 asserted that no new laws could be adopted without the approval of the diet. The emphasis on the primacy of the law was clear. Indeed, a contemporary law book asserted that "both the king and all the estates of the realm shall be subject to the law."[8] Law was to guarantee freedom, and freedom was conceived as freedom from oppression or absolutism as well as freedom to participate in the government and freedom to resist it. One must not forget, however, that freedom also meant jealously guarded privileges of the noble nation, which, as the Polish historian E. M. Rostworowski remarked, was modern in its all-national activity, but medieval in its estate-like character. One might add, however, that the term "Polish nation" was also used in sixteenth-century writings to denote all inhabitants of the country. The famous preacher Skarga stressed that the peasants were Poles of the same nation.

To return now to the "execution of the laws" movement: it strove to weaken the magnates' ascendancy by making them return the profitable leases of the royal domain (any further alienation of it to be forbidden) and prohibiting accumulation of offices. The clergy was to share in the tax burdens; the administration of finances and justice was to be overhauled, all under the control of the gentry-run *sejm*. The movement offered an opportunity to the monarch to count on the gentry to strengthen his power, like the French or English rulers did, by relying on the middle class. Yet the analogy is not perfect. The gentry had political ambitions and appeared less predictable than the magnates with whom the kings were traditionally working. Toward the end of the century, with royal power seriously limited by *pacta conventa* and Henrician Articles (discussed later in this chapter), the magnates learned how to manipulate the noble masses for their own ends.

In the course of conflicts and polemics a new system was emerging.

A contemporary political writer commented that in "our country in some strange and unusual way a mixture of three forms of government has formed."[9] The three were monarchic, aristocratic (embodied in the senate), and democratic (represented in the lower chamber). The term *forma mixta* came into use. The system was regarded with some pride as based on checks and balances and reflecting a gentry democratic ideology. The use of the expression "democratic" may strike us as inappropriate. But to the gentry, trained in schools in which the models of antiquity were held up as an example, Polish democracy followed that of the Roman republic, a direct democracy in the classical sense. Civis Romanus, Senatus Populusque Romanus were concepts that were both familiar and relevant. If the *szlachta*, a sizeable cross-section of the society from top to bottom, claimed the right to run the state in spite of being a minority let us not forget that the political electorate in France even in the 1830s comprised less than 2 percent of the population. In England it was a little over 3 percent before the 1832 reform. True, Polish constitutionalism and freedoms coexisted with serfdom and discriminatory measures against the burghers. There was a price to be paid for the Golden Age, but was it unusual? The glory and greatness of Athens and Rome was built on slavery, and so in modern times was that of the United States.

JAGIELLONIANS AND HABSBURGS

As the century began the Jagiellonian state system covering all of East Central Europe relied mainly on the cooperation between members of the dynasty. Because of the stronger position of Poland and its monarchs the latter sought to influence Hungarian politics, or through the appointment of a Jagiellonian prince as governor of Silesia to strengthen the position of Vladislav in Bohemia. Given the Habsburg claims and aspirations to the Crowns of St Wenceslas and St Stephen, a Jagiellonian–Habsburg rivalry developed and ran parallel at times to the Habsburg–Valois duel in the West.

Seeking to exert pressure on Poland and Lithuania, the Habsburgs supported the Teutonic Knights and Muscovy. Exposed as it was to a constant Muscovite expansion, by 1500 Lithuania lost nearly a third of its territory; only the victorious battle at Orsha in 1514 temporarily stopped the Muscovite advance. In an attempt to detach the Habsburgs from the anti-Jagiellonian alliance, a congress held in 1515 in Vienna arranged for a matrimonial pact, ensuring in effect the succession of the surviving dynasty in Hungary and Bohemia. Louis the Jagiellonian married Mary Habsburg, while Ferdinand Habsburg married Louis's sister Anne. Here was an example of the policy that the Habsburgs became famous for and which contemporary lines celebrated: "Bella gerunt alii, tu, felix Austria, nube" ("while others wage wars you, happy Austria, marry").

Some Czechoslovak and Hungarian historians accuse the Jagiellonians of a willingness to abandon Prague and Buda as the price for Habsburg friendly neutrality. This is debatable. True, Hungary may at times have appeared a liability in view of its internal turmoil and corruption. An attempted crusade against Turkey resulted in the earlier-mentioned Dózsa's peasant rebellion against the lords. Its brutal suppression indicated the extent of social antagonism. In 1525–6 there was a miners' uprising in the Slovak region. Politically, the country was divided between a pro-Habsburg, mainly magnate faction, and the national party based on the gentry that refused – as in the 1505 vote in the diet – to accept foreign rulers. Werböczy was one of its leaders and the Tripartitum reflected its outlook. The voievod of Transylvania, János Zápolya (Szapolyai) who himself aspired to the crown, stood behind it. Louis II, who ascended the throne in 1516 at the age of 10 and was being depraved by his tutor, could hardly be expected to restore the powers of the monarchy or assure its defenses. Border garrisons, unpaid and undermanned, fought a hopeless struggle against the Turks. In 1521 Belgrade, in effect the southern gateway, fell. The country had sunk very low.

Sigismund the Old of Poland, Louis's uncle, vainly attempted to bolster Buda's position. Mindful that a Polish anti-Turkish intervention in the 1490s in Moldavia had produced a breach with suspicious Hungary, Cracow trod warily. Poland also could not afford to antagonize the Ottoman empire with which it would later (1533) sign a perpetual peace. Moreover, the country faced complex problems that arose after the grand master of the Teutonic Knights, who was also Sigismund's nephew Albrecht of Hohenzollern, became Lutheran. Poland had the choice of making war on the isolated Albrecht, adding his lands to Royal Prussia, or accepting the secularized Duchy of Prussia (the future Eastern Prussia) as a Polish fief. The former would require money and was risky; the latter might eventually lead to peaceful annexation, as had happened with the vassal Duchy of Mazovia after the death of its last ruler. It was difficult to foresee that a small semi-independent Prussia would one day grow into one of the great powers of Europe. Nor could one have anticipated the death of Louis II of Hungary opening the way to the Habsburg succession.

Louis II perished in August 1526 at the battle of Mohács. A hastily assembled army comprising large Czech, German, and Polish mercenary contingents, as well as the flower of the Hungarian nobility, was destroyed. The nineteenth-century poet Mihály Vörösmarty called Mohács the "great graveyard of national grandeur," and indeed it started a chain reaction that changed the course of Hungarian history.

The immediate consequence was a double election of Ferdinand Habsburg and Zápolya, who having abstained from the battle of Mohács kept his forces intact. Despite this advantage and the legality of his election he was defeated by the Habsburgs. During the highly complicated years that followed Zápolya cooperated with Poland (he was Sigismund's brother-in-law) and together with the Turks unsuccessfully besieged Vienna in 1529. After the failure of long and intricate negotiations for an eventual reunification of the Habsburg and Zápolya-held lands, Ferdinand attempted to seize all the country. The Turks intervened, and in the 1540s occupied Buda and central Hungary. Despite renewed attempts at diplomacy in which Cardinal Martinuzzi (Utišinović), the only real statesman of the time, was deeply involved, a threefold division became irreversible. The country was split into Royal Hungary, ruled by the Habsburgs and comprising the western strip with Slovak and truncated Croatian parts; a Turkish Hungary made into a province of the Ottoman empire; and the Principality of Transylvania, which although tributary of the sultan was free to run its own affairs as long as they presented no threat to Turkish interests. It was this semi-independent Transylvania, subscribing to the principle of a united kingdom embodied in the Crown of St Stephen which became a guarantor of Hungarian rights and to a large extent a depository of its tradition.

The multinational state system which the Habsburgs set out to build in East Central Europe after 1526 had a number of distinguishing features. The connection with the Holy Roman Empire – Ferdinand assumed the imperial office in 1556 – was a source of power but also of friction. To maintain their position in the empire the Habsburgs needed to strengthen their East Central European base and vice versa. Preoccupied with larger European problems, they had on occasion to neglect the interests of their kingdoms: Hungary was obliged to bear the brunt of frontier fighting, Bohemia was squeezed dry to finance wars. Yet, their position of an outpost or bulwark against the Turks had certain advantages for the Hungarians. Miklós Zrínyi's (Nikola Zrinski) heroic defense of Szigetvár built up the spirit of independence, especially of the lesser nobility in the counties, and toughened their resistance to the Habsburgs.

Desirous to consolidate their power, the Habsburgs sought to make the Crowns of St Wenceslas and St Stephen hereditary. The estates of Bohemia, Moravia, Silesia, Lusatia, Croatia, and Hungary on their side insisted that Ferdinand was their ruler because they had elected him in 1526–7 and not in virtue of the Vienna succession accord. The Habsburgs promoted the hereditary principle indirectly by holding elections of successors during the lifetime of the reigning monarchs. Simultaneously, they and the pro-absolutist "Spanish party" at court attempted to centralize and to strengthen the financial basis of the monarchy. The chancelleries of Bohemia and Hungary, while remaining powerful organs of central administration, had a mixed success. The Aulic Council (Reichshofrat), dealing with administrative and judiciary matters, never became an important institution because of Czech and Hungarian reluctance to participate. By the 1530s the Hungarian and Bohemian section ceased to function. Between 1530 and 1608 no palatine of Hungary was named and the Hungarian governing council composed of selected lords never worked as a real bridge between the monarch and the local administration. The counties largely disregarded the government. Only in military and financial matters was there real centralization with the effectively functioning War Council (Hofkriegsrat) and Court Chamber (Hofkammer). The latter had agencies in Prague and Pozsony (today's Bratislava). The latter was a seat of the diet and the *de facto* capital of Royal Hungary. Of the remaining organs, the Privy Council (Geheimrat) which dealt with foreign policy, was an exclusive domain of the ruler.

With an estimated population of 4.5 million (contemporary England had 5 million) Bohemia as a whole was a powerful state. Taxation increased tenfold between 1520 and 1600, but only a fraction of this revenue was spent locally. The monarchy also drew on foreign credits, pledging in return mines and state income. This affected adversely the local economy. In the case of Royal Hungary there were complaints about the favoring of Austrian lords and towns as well as about importation of Austrian wine. An influx of Germans, mainly nobility, but also burghers, was a result of the imperial connection. The Habsburgs were unable to base their power on any social class in the lands of St Wenceslas and they promoted German counselors and occasionally the German language. The Bohemian diet resented this development.

Attempts to have common meetings of the different diets of the Habsburg lands were made inconsistently. One difficulty was the great disparity in the type of diets; those of Tyrol and Voralberg, for instance, even included peasants. There was also a risk of promoting a united bloc of the estates likely to act against the monarchy. Nonetheless there were general diets of the lands of the Crown of St Wenceslas (Bohemia, Moravia, Silesia, and Lusatia). A conference was held in the early seventeenth century to discuss issues of common defense, and this brought together representatives of Bohemia, Hungary, and the Austrian hereditary provinces.

The two major issues of the second half of the sixteenth century were to do with economic problems and religious developments. The former were tied to defense measures against Turkey and the centralizing policies of the Habsburgs. They provoked some resistance in the estates. The latter resulted in a showdown with the towns in Bohemia, which sided with German Protestants in 1547 and lost some of their privileges. The earlier-mentioned expulsion of the Czech Brethren followed. In the 1550s, the Jesuit order was introduced in Bohemia and a few years later in Hungary. Yet, as already pointed out in this chapter, there was a good deal of toleration. The early Habsburg rulers were not religious zealots. The humanism of the dynasty in the sixteenth century "outran" its Catholicism as R. J. W. Evans put it. The balance between the rulers and the estates and between Catholicism and Protestantism may have been fragile, but it existed.

The situation was, of course, much less stable in the war-ravaged parts of Hungary. While borders fluctuated, the Habsburgs controlled the largest part – some 262–300 thousand sq. km as opposed to some 237 to 275 under the Turks and about 137 in Transylvania. Population estimates are especially difficult for the Turkish part; for Transylvania the figure of 500,000 inhabitants would represent an optimum.

In the heterogeneous Transylvania of three nations and four religions, counties coexisted with Saxon autonomous towns and lands (*Königsboden*) and with Szekler districts. The Magyars were mainly nobility, Catholic and Calvinist; the Szeklers had a large Unitarian contingent and their status fluctuated between noble, free-peasant, and transient serfdom. They constituted the biggest reservoir of fighting men. The Saxon burghers were usually Lutherans. Another group, a product of constant warfare, were the haiduks, the escaped peasants from the Turks or from noble estates who lived on plunder and adventure. The haiduks provided cheap mercenary manpower, and having assisted Transylvania at one stage of the struggle against the Habsburgs were settled on lands attached to it.

The Transylvanian regime allowed the prince to gain a good deal of power, playing one group against the other and assuring himself a sound economic base. Gold, iron, and salt mines were part of the Crown estates, and the princes were by far the biggest landholders. In 1576 Prince Stephen Báthory, having defeated renewed Habsburg designs on Transylvania, was elected to the Polish throne. Another Polish-Hungarian (Transylvanian) personal union occurred and lasted until 1586. Five years later Transylvania was involved in the Long or Fifteen Years War, an extremely complex series of conflicts in which the Habsburgs and the Turks were the main protagonists. By 1600 Transylvania briefly came under the control of Michael the Brave of Moldavia and Wallachia, who was seen by Romanian historiography as the first author of Romanian unity. Then the Habsburgs asserted their rule, against which an uprising was launched by Stephen Bocskai. Elected prince by the diet of Transylvania and that of Upper Hungary (Slovakia), Bocskai also received support from the haiduks, whom he rewarded with freedom. In 1606 he virtually imposed on the Habsburgs the Treaty of Vienna. It was implemented two years later under the pressure of the diet in Pozsony.

The treaty illustrated Transylvania's role as the protector of Hungarian rights under the Habsburgs. The rulers had to grant the diet the right of electing the palatine, as well as other concessions. Freedom of religion was confirmed. Simultaneously new provisions were passed reaffirming perpetual serfdom, including lack of mobility and subjection to the landlords' judicial power. More important was that matters related to serfdom were placed directly under the control of counties.

In these conditions, the Habsburgs could not withhold concessions in Bohemia, where a family crisis in 1609 made Rudolf issue the Letter of Majesty. It confirmed the free exercise of *Confessio Bohemica* and placed the consistory and the university under the protection of the Czech diet. Similar privileges were extended to Moravia and Silesia. A special body of defenders representing the three estates in the diet was established to watch over the implementation of the Letter. On their side the Catholic and Protestant members of the estates concluded an agreement (the Porovnaní) to guarantee the freedom of religious worship. This agreement included the right of building churches on lands belonging officially to the Crown.

The 1606–9 settlement, in which the peace treaty with Turkey signed at Zsitvatorok should be included, brought a longish period of peace to Hungarian lands. After the enormous devastations it was badly needed. A certain stability seemed to have been reached in the relations between the court and the diets or assemblies of estates, and between the Catholic and the Protestant camps. Yet the compromise was likely to last only as long as a certain balance of power prevailed. A decade later the greatest confrontation between absolutism and parliamentarianism, Catholicism and Protestantism would erupt in Bohemia, with dire regional and European-wide repercussions.

THE POLISH-LITHUANIAN COMMONWEALTH

The reigns of the last two Jagiellonians, Sigismund the Old and Sigismund Augustus covered the major part of the century. Both kings, even though elected, regarded themselves as "natural" dynastic rulers with a hereditary base in Lithuania. Yet Sigismund the Old, for all his power proved at crucial times irresolute; and his son had a tendency to procrastinate. At home the already-mentioned "execution of the law" movement occupied a central place under Sigismund Augustus, leading to a triangular contest between the king, the magnates, and the gentry. The movement was failing as the gentry – according to the Polish historian Antoni Mączak – became ever more enmeshed in a client relationship to the lords, was losing the economic battle, and lacked leaders and organization. The more prominent lesser nobles were themselves passing into the ranks of the magnates. On his side, the king failed to imitate the Western practice of paying salaries to the officials. They were still compensated by royal domain, land being the real indicator of wealth and prestige.

In foreign matters, Sigismund Augustus continued the policy of avoiding a conflict with Turkey. He compounded, however, what may have been the original error of erecting a Duchy of Prussia by extending the succession rights to the Brandenburg branch of the Hohenzollern. Their possessions now effectively flanked Poland's maritime province. The Baltic problem, the question of "dominium maris Baltici" arose, however, mainly as a consequence of Moscow's expansion in that direction. The isolated Order of Knights of the Sword (previously tied to the Teutonic Knights) operating in Livonia (that is, present-day Latvia and Estonia), was caught in the middle of the Muscovite–Polish rivalry. A series of Livonian wars waged with great cruelty by Ivan the Terrible ensued, in which Denmark and Sweden participated. The Great Master Gotthard Kettler then proceeded to secularize his order. He was unable to extend his sway to all of Livonia, so allowed himself, through an act of union with Poland in 1561, to become a vassal duke of Courland. The rest of Livonia was placed under joint Polish-Lithuanian rule.

The Commonwealth's involvement in Baltic problems increased the risks of confrontation with Muscovy and Sweden. It necessitated renewed attempts to build a navy and to convince the nobility that their economic interests were tied to the Baltic. The Muscovite threat significantly contributed to a transformation of the dynastic Polish-Lithuanian ties into a real union. Demands for such a union had been made throughout the century and figured in the "execution of the law" program. At first, the Poles meant by union full absorption of Lithuania. The Lithuanians objected and other vested interests militated against such a solution. The Lithuanian lords, who had much more power over the boyars (gentry) than the Polish magnates had over the *szlachta*, feared they would lose it. The Jagiellonian monarchs, whose hereditary standing in Lithuania assured them the Polish throne, were loath to compromise their dynastic interests. Sigismund Augustus, however, was childless and he wished to complete the work that his ancestor Jogaila had begun. Political, socio-economic, and cultural conditions had greatly evolved in Lithuania, bringing it closer to Poland. The Lithuanian gentry wished to gain the same privileges as their Polish opposite numbers and agitated for a union. As for the Greek Orthodox nobility of Lithuania (in Belorussian and Ukrainian provinces), their full equality of civic and political rights were recognized by Polish *sejm* in 1563 and 1568.

The Union of Lublin of 1569 was in the final analysis due to Sigismund Augustus who applied pressure on the Lithuanian lords by incorporating into Poland the provinces of Podlachia, Volhynia, and the Ukraine. Fearing lest he proceed to merge the entire country with Poland the Lithuanians yielded. The union established a Commonwealth of "two nations" with a jointly elected ruler, bearing the title of king of Poland and grand duke of Lithuania, a joint bicameral diet, and dual administrative offices on all levels. The Lithuanian Statutes were maintained, as was the old Belorussian language used in official acts. Eventually Polish replaced it almost as a matter of course, given the linguistic polonization of the Lithuanian *szlachta*. The two states were joined by a customs and monetary union, but retained their own treasuries. Distinct and separate armies continued, and the handling of certain foreign matters (for instance relations with Muscovy) remained the prerogative of the Lithuanian chancery. This was a federation *sui generis*, unique in a sense, which contemporary Western political writers cited as the "sole and classical case" of a union between two states.

The Commonwealth was the largest country in Europe after the semi-European Muscovy and Turkey. Its size, however, was a mixed blessing, for the great distances and poor communications adversely affected the functioning of the state apparatus and the mobilization of adequate defenses. Lithuania's contribution measured in taxes was relatively small. The disparate character and interests of the far-flung eastern provinces, in which the magnates rose to semi-independence, upset the balance between the lords and the gentry. The transfer of the Ukraine to Poland from which it differed in religion, tongue, and customs was to create major internal problems. Externally, the Ukraine under Poland's rule meant the establishment of a common Polish-Muscovite frontier. Poland was becoming drawn into Eastern problems, and exposed to Eastern influences. A certain orientalization of the country and society began.

A comparative study of the Commonwealth and the Habsburg monarchy would offer most interesting insights into these two models of regional integration. The Polish-Lithuanian *Respublica* with its semi-federalist and dualist system and a tendency toward greater legal uniformity, was more firmly grounded; it was based on a common political culture of the multi-ethnic *szlachta*. This *szlachta*, in which the real sovereignty came to lie, was indeed the mortar holding the Commonwealth together. In the Habsburg monarchy it was the dynastic principle that increasingly served as the consolidating element. While the term "Austria," as frequently used to describe collectively the Habsburg lands, was incorrect, the term "Polish" was ambiguous. Polish meant ethnic Polish in contrast to Lithuanian or Ukrainian, but it also meant state-Polish and covered the entire Commonwealth. Had a term equivalent to "British" (that covers English, Scottish, and Welsh) existed some confusion would have been avoided. Officially, the Polish part was called the Crown – every Lithuanian official had as his counterpart a Crown official – but attempts to apply the term to inhabitants of the Crown as a noun (*koroniarz*) were operative only on a colloquial, almost slangy level.

The multinational character of the Habsburg monarchy was comparable to that of the Commonwealth and so were the forces working against centralization in both. Lands inhabited by compact Polish blocs probably did not exceed 20 percent of the entire territory of the *Respublica*. Ethnic Poles were perhaps about 40 percent in the second half of the century. In the Crown (Poland) the largest group was composed of Ruthenians–Ukrainians whose distinctiveness made them into a third, although officially unrecognized, nation of the Commonwealth. The Germans, who represented an important segment of the population, were more closely integrated and undergoing some polonization after Royal Prussia was fully incorporated in 1569. Apart from the growing Jewish community, surveyed earlier, the smaller groups, mainly in towns, comprised Scots, Italians, and Armenians. Some of these people lived in the Lithuanian part of the Commonwealth. There, ethnic Lithuanians also occupied a smaller part of the state, the eastern lands being mainly Belorussian. There were also Tatar settlements, and new German immigrants from Livonia; their nobles were rapidly joining the ranks of the nobility of Lithuania.

In the religious sphere the major dividing line was between Catholicism and Greek Orthodoxy, and in 1596 an attempt was made to cement the Commonwealth through the religious Union of Brest. A complex undertaking with many dimensions, it aimed at bringing the Greek Orthodox masses of the Kievan metropolitan province under Rome and away from Constantinople and Moscow. The union, however, led to internal divisions with dire religious and political consequences. Henceforth the Catholic, the Orthodox, and the Greek Catholic (Uniate) churches found themselves in sharp opposition to one another.

The religious problems in the Habsburg monarchy, as we shall see later, were linked with the absolutist tendencies of the rulers, notably the policy of electing kings during the lifetime of their predecessors. This practice never developed in Poland, the only case being that of Sigismund Augustus. The political nation opposed it adamantly as leading toward *absolutum dominium*. The subsequent evolution took an opposite direction in each country. While the Habsburg dynasty consolidated its hold, in Poland the period of free election of kings and the resulting discontinuity weakened royal power. Still, it is interesting to observe that the *szlachta* tended to favor the members of the same ruling family as long as they were available.

The death of Sigismund Augustus in 1572 was followed by the first election with a free choice of candidates. The winner was Henri Valois, Duke of Anjou (later King Henry III of France), obliged in view of the record of the French monarchs to sign a veritable social contract with the noble nation. Known as Henrician Articles and accompanied by special provisions – to be drawn up for each successive king and called *pacta conventa* – the accord formed henceforth the basis of the regime in the Commonwealth. The king agreed not to interfere with a free election of his successor; to call biennial diets whose consent was necessary for new taxes and the *levée en masse* (mobilization) of the *szlachta*. The consent of a resident council of senators was required to declare war or to conclude peace. A breach of these articles released the political nation from its oath of obedience to the ruler. Henry had also to swear that he would observe religious toleration.

His reign of less than a year ended when, hearing of his brother's death, he speedily returned to France to ascend the throne. In the confusing and complex contest for the vacant Polish crown there ensued a double election of Emperor Maximilian II and Stephen Báthory of Transylvania. The latter ascended the throne in 1576 while retaining control over Transylvania through a special chancellery in Cracow. His eleven years' reign saw seeming stability at home and successes in foreign policy; death interrupted his long-range plans.

Batory, as his name is spelled in Poland, wanted to be a strong monarch and he was ably assisted by Jan Zamoyski, who astounded his contemporaries by his meteoric rise from a lesser noble to the richest man in the country, to be founder of the city and academy of Zamość, chancellor and great hetman (commander-in-chief). Yet King Stephen's successes were often purchased at a price. Undertaking a major campaign against Ivan the Terrible, who had struck again at Livonia, Batory traded political concessions for money. Thus he obtained sizeable credits from Gdańsk and forgave its challenge to royal authority. He let the elector of Brandenburg assume the tutelage over the sick duke of Prussia in exchange for monetary compensations. To have new taxes voted by the diet he accepted the erection of a tribunal that replaced the royal court of justice. While this last measure corresponded to the "execution of the laws" program, it was dictated by expediency rather than by larger considerations. In fact the king avoided reliance on the gentry, warning it that a quest for freedom could degenerate into license.

The victorious war against Muscovy was spectacular and extremely well prepared. The use of Szekler troops and native Polish infantry was imaginative. Livonia was recovered, and only peace saved Muscovy from utter defeat. Was King Stephen's eastern policy connected with his plans for an anti-Turkish crusade and eventual reunification of

Hungary? Did the road to Buda lead through Moscow? There has been much speculation about it. At any rate Zamoyski was able to continue the old policy of protecting Poland from a clash with Turkey by means of buffer states (Moldavia recognized Polish suzerainty in 1595) that were in Poland's sphere of influence while remaining friendly to the sultan.

Batory's death once more brought the matter of succession to the forefront. Once again a double election pitted a Habsburg against, this time, Sigismund, the son of the king of Sweden, and his Jagiellonian wife. Zamoyski assured by military means the victory of Sigismund III, but the new king did not want to be dependent on the kingmaker. A conflict between the two cast a shadow over one of the longest reigns in Polish history: 1587 to 1632.

While Batory appealed greatly to the Poles and may have been overpraised, Sigismund III Vasa owed at least part of his own downgrading to his personality and style. Although half-Jagiellonian and conversant in Polish, Sigismund III always appeared a stranger. "Taciturn, tardive, and tenacious," as seen by contemporaries, he was incapable of winning over the garrulous, often fickle and emotional *szlachta*. Married to a Habsburg, he surrounded himself with Germans. By a strange irony of history Sigismund, the victor over the Habsburgs, had great affinity with them in religious matters and ideology. Expected to bring about a pacification in the Baltic he made every effort to gain the Swedish succession. To achieve that end he engaged in secret talks with the Habsburgs, offering to cede to them the Polish crown in exchange for support. When these plans were brought to light at the "inquisition" *sejm* of 1592 they nearly cost Sigismund his throne. The prestige of the monarchy suffered an irreparable blow. It became apparent to the *szlachta* that dynastic interests of the foreign kings (Anjou, Báthory, Vasa) need not be identical with those of the *Respublica*.

Sigismund's effort to assert himself in Sweden failed. Lutheran Sweden did not want a Catholic king. At this point Sigismund decided to honor his promise of transferring Estonia from Sweden to Poland, which meant war. The Lithuanian hetman Karol Chodkiewicz won a spectacular victory in 1605 at Kircholm (Salaspils), but the war revealed serious military weaknesses of the Commonwealth. The country badly needed an overhaul of its institutions to be able to mobilize its vast potential. This was what the "execution of the laws" movement had vainly sought to achieve. The concepts of the king and his entourage diverged from them and were clearly monarchic. They involved the election of Sigismund's son during his lifetime, increased taxes to permit a standing army, a reform of parliamentary proceedings, possibly some peasant emancipation. The nobility regarded these ideas as smacking of Habsburg-like absolutism. The king needed a popular spokesman, but Zamoyski was now on the other side of the fence and busy weakening royal power. After his death a strange coalition formed against the king. It brought together the Catholic magnate Mikołaj Zebrzydowski, Protestants suspicious of Sigismund's links to the Counter-Reformation, and gentry reformers pursuing the "execution of the laws" program.

Accusing the king of breaking the law, the opponents resorted in 1606–9 to a *rokosz*. This word had a Hungarian origin and was used to denote a justifiable rebellion. The royal forces won on the battlefield, but both the king and the reform-minded *szlachta* were the real losers. In that sense the Zebrzydowski (or Sandomierz) *rokosz* marked an important turning point in Polish history. The *szlachta* democracy, instead of evolving into a truly parliamentary system, with a strong executive capable of making the huge *Respublica* a great power and tackling the abuses of serfdom, began to turn into an unruly oligarchy. Obstruction became politics. In the years to come the magnates were to gain all that had been refused to the king: a solid financial basis, a standing army, and a vast clientele of nobles.

The first decade of the seventeenth century was momentous if we think of its consequences. The Zebrzydowski *rokosz* coincided with the affair of the False Dimitri that marked a new phase in Polish–Muscovite relations. Supported by Polish and Lithuanian magnates the usurper, who claimed to be Ivan's son, ascended the throne of the tsars; the Time of Troubles in Russia began. Then the Commonwealth itself was involved and after the spectacular victory of Hetman Żółkiewski at Klushino in 1610 the Polish troops garrisoned the Kremlin. The city of Moscow elected Sigismund III's son Władysław as tsar, provided he embrace Orthodoxy. It seemed as if the Commonwealth had reached its pinnacle of power in the east, but in the long run it proved to be an illusion. The events in the Commonwealth and in Muscovy occurred almost simultaneously with the Letter of Majesty of Rudolf and the accord among estates in Bohemia. Again, the real issue had not been resolved. A confrontation between absolutism and the estates, Catholic Reformation and Protestantism (and Greek Orthodoxy) lay ahead as part of a major international crisis.

3

THE SEVENTEENTH-CENTURY CRISIS

THE TERM AND ITS MEANING

The seventeenth century was a tempestuous and turbulent age, filled with ruinous wars and bloody revolutions. In the early 1640s some English preachers and political pamphleteers spoke of a "universal shaking" that affected states from Catalonia to England and from Germany to Portugal. They observed that the struggles then waged "pierced many kingdoms," and they included among them Bohemia, Hungary, and Poland.

Profound changes were occurring almost everywhere and in many spheres of life. Historians examining new departures in warfare refer to a military revolution. Those who study sciences, as symbolized in the seventeenth century by Isaac Newton, speak of a scientific revolution. Indeed, the term has a wide application. Progress and regress, magnificence and misery seemed equally characteristic of this era. The resplendent baroque style in literature, arts, and architecture, affecting the general outlook and the way of life, appeared as an outward manifestation of the triumphant Counter-Reformation, rising absolutism, and aristocratic mentality. And yet all this grandeur seemed also designed to dispel doubts. Historians viewing the baroque in the Habsburg lands have characterized it as a "blend of insecurity and confidence" and felt that it reflected a "crisis of sensibility."

Turning to East Central Europe, the leitmotif of imperilment and even of threatening doom ran through the writings of contemporaries. Hungarian politicians, preachers, writers gave way to despair when speaking of wars, social ills, economic dislocations. In Poland the optimism of the sixteenth century seemed on the wane. Moralists would see a sign of God's wrath in the Cossack uprising of 1648 and translate the royal initials ICR (Ioannes Casimirus Rex) into "initium calamitatis regni" (the beginnings of calamities in the kingdom). The great Czech thinker and pedagogue Jan Amos Komenský (Comenius) spoke in similar terms about the catastrophe of the Thirty Years War.

His famous allegorical book, *The Labyrinth of the World*, portrayed a pilgrim's search for order and harmony in a world full of frightening contradictions. The work may be symbolic of the wider preoccupations with conflict and disintegration in culture of the time.

Recent historiography has advanced the concept of a general crisis of the seventeenth century, which is formulated in spiritual, ideological-political, and socio-economic terms. When exactly did this crisis occur, and what were its origins, nature, and outcome? Did it affect all of Europe? The British historian E. J. Hobsbawm, noting the economic and demographic boom being succeeded by stagnation and even recession, used the term to cover the entire 1560–1660 period. Wealth, he argued, had grown too fast and was used unproductively by the upper classes. The crisis was symptomatic of the break between feudal society and the capitalist forms of production, and it marked a transition from feudalism to capitalism. Several historians probing into economic stagnation, demographic decline, and recessions added findings about climatic conditions and other factors. Hobsbawm's concept was tested with regard to political developments in England, Spain, and France (by H. R. Trevor-Roper, J. E. Elliott, and R. Mousnier) and produced varying definitions of the crisis: a conflict between the "court" and "country," between the center and the regions, between absolutism and republicanism. The tentative conclusion was that one could indeed speak of an economic and political crisis in western and central Europe that manifested itself in different ways, the differences resulting from divergent social and political structures, religious institutions, and beliefs.

The Czechoslovak historian J. Polišenský sought to bring greater precision to the notion of crisis. He defined it as

> the culmination of ever-deepening internal conflicts within the infrastructure of a given society, which leads to a sudden collapse of existing economic, social, cultural and political relationships, and whose consequences will be either regression – regional or general – or on the other hand a powerful step forward in the development of that society.[10]

This definition allowed Polišenský to include the Netherlands (then in its Golden Age) and England, for which the crisis meant advancement and not decline.

The question of exact origins and of the length of the crisis troubled the American historian T. Rabb. By invoking the original use of the term in medicine, he stressed the importance of the "rising temperature" stage and of the climax which marked the discontinuity of the process. He placed the relaxation of tensions in the 1660s. Incidentally, this decade was meaningful for Poland, to some extent for Bohemia, least for Hungary. Recognizing the multifaceted nature of the seventeenth-century crisis, its economic, social, ideological, and other dimensions, Rabb concluded that if a single label was appropriate to cover such disparate manifestations it would be "a crisis of authority." Here, the basic questions would be, what constituted authentic authority? Where was it located? Where did it come from? The issues involved were: the growth of a centralized government, bureaucracy, and taxes, all threatening the freedom or autonomy of an estate or a province. The contest between Castille and the provinces in Spain, between the Crown and the nobles (and peasants crushed by taxes) in France, and the Crown and Parliament in England provided illustrations of these processes. The outcome according to Rabb was a domination of politics, society, and culture by an aristocracy associated with the central government and its institutions, and the establishment of structures recognizable as the modern state.

An attempt to test in depth the applicability of these concepts to East Central Europe would transcend the nature and the size of this book. We may note, however, a tentative model constructed by O. Subtelny on the basis of five crises in the region in the early eighteenth century. Without going any further into methodological issues, one can state that Bohemia, Poland, and Hungary were all affected in the course of the seventeenth century by a major upheaval for which the term crisis is most appropriate. In the Czech and Polish cases the results were far graver than anywhere else in the West. They marked a turning point in their history and threatened the very survival of the Czech nation and of the Polish-Lithuanian state. Chronologically, the crisis affected Bohemia in the first half of the seventeenth century, and while permanent scars remained, economic recovery was visible in the last decades. In Poland's case the relatively peaceful and prosperous 1620s and 1630s were followed by the mid-century upheaval. As the country began slowly to recuperate the process was interrupted by wars in the early eighteenth century. The crisis in Hungary, in view of its threefold division, did not affect most of the country until fairly late. Transylvania, for instance, experienced a short-lived Golden Age in the early part of the century and collapsed after the mid-1650s. Wars and uprisings were an almost permanent occurrence in the Commonwealth and in the lands of St Stephen.

Let us now look briefly at the demographic, economic, and social components in East Central Europe that bore some resemblance to those in the West, but retained their own specific characteristics. While a certain demographic stagnation or even decline was visible in many European countries the situation was nowhere as catastrophic as in East Central Europe. Historians speak of a general slowing down of European economy, but the regression in Poland was on a totally different scale. Owing to wars fought on their territory and plagues which accompanied or followed them, the population of Bohemia and Poland declined by as much as a third or even a half, depending on the various estimates. Similar figures were given for Hungary, reunited at the end of the century, although they are now being questioned as too high. At any rate this demographic disaster has been seen as decisively impeding the productive forces at a time when they were most needed. However, there are also historians who stress the growth of manorial economy and serfdom as making an economic recovery impossible. The latter view may now be less popular.

The general picture was complex and there were many factors that adversely affected the economy, in particular, the decline of the urban sector. The towns that suffered greatly during wars were also affected by a contraction of the domestic market, a result of the growth of self-sufficient magnate estates as well as of noble encroachments on municipal structures. Private towns without guilds and linked with the rich hinterland offered serious competition to free or royal towns. In Bohemia and Hungary the burghers endured increased fiscal burdens. The nature of East–West trade (agrarian products for finished goods) was in the long run harming towns, even though Silesian and Lusatian cloth and linen products, cheaper than those from England, were gaining. The wars of the 1650s destroyed the dynamic network of international fairs; other factors, such as the competition from Russian grain and Swedish copper, damaged the existing trade patterns. With falling grain prices in the West and Polish productivity registering no increase, the Baltic exports peaked in 1618 and then declined. Hungarian cattle exports suffered a similar fate, the 1620s seeing the end of the previous boom.

By mid-century East Central Europe lost its earlier significance in the international division of labor. The Polish–Dutch trade began to be replaced by British–Muscovite (and Swedish), in which hemp and tar occupied an important place. Intensive Polish–Lithuanian–Muscovite commerce, however (manufactured goods for furs and forest products) continued, with Riga playing a role comparable to Gdańsk. The Hungarian cattle trade in turn was suffering in competition with the Danish, and Hungarian copper likewise with Swedish metals. When cattle prices went up again in the 1660s the beneficiaries were mainly foreign (that is, South German) merchants. Hungarians, except for such magnates as the Zrínyis and Batthyánys, could no longer compete.

As economic conditions deteriorated, the divergence between the rich and the poor grew. Many peasants fell into the latter category, although the highly diversified character of this social class makes sweeping generalization about its economic position and legal status hazardous. While serfdom, accompanied by a growing manorial economy, was spreading during the century over Bohemia and Royal Hungary, there were borderline strata, such as the earlier-mentioned haiduks in Hungary or the Cossaks (see p. 100) in the Commonwealth. Still, two facts need stressing. One, that serfdom was becoming harsher; two, that it was not confined to East Central Europe. King John Casimir of Poland vowed in 1656 to free the people of his kingdom "from unjust burdens and oppression."[11] A contemporary Hungarian chronicle contained the statement that it was against God that "one nation should thus cripple other people of the same nation."[12]

Were peasants still viewed as belonging to the same nation as the nobles and burghers? Komenský defined the nation as a mass of people descended from a common tribe, inhabiting the same place (which they call the country), using their own tongue, linked together by special ties, and striving for common good; he saw himself as being of the Moravian nation and Czech language. But this did not necessarily mean that he spoke of the nation in terms of a conscious political-social unit. Increasingly the term political nation excluded the peasantry, even though exceptions existed. A contemporary Polish political writer, A. A. Olizarowski, opined that his country had no real democracy because the *sejm* deputies represented only *szlachta* and not the people. But his was not the typical view.

The lot of the peasantry was getting worse in many parts of Europe, which makes some historians speak of "refeudalization." In France, Cardinal Richelieu compared peasants to mules "which being accustomed to carry burdens, are harmed more by a long rest than by working." A contemporary Neapolitan economist saw the peasant as "a beast of burden."[13] What may have been different in East Central Europe was that, as mentioned earlier, the royal government had ceased to interfere in landlord–peasant relations. Also, the passing of the boom worsened the economic status of the peasants; it killed their initiative while making their compulsory work highly inefficient.

On the other end of the social scale the richest part of the nobility was increasingly distancing itself from the rest of the gentry. Wealth was the principal criterion, wealth lavishly displayed and used to fortify one's political and social position. This top group, rejuvenated by some new blood (but strikingly new and on a large scale only from the 1620s on in Bohemia), took the form of magnate oligarchy in Poland-Lithuania, and of a titled aristocracy in Bohemia and Hungary. As for the poor nobles, the decline of the Hungarian institution of retainers (*familiares*) deprived the gentry of additional incomes. In Poland the *szlachta* became increasingly dependent on the magnates, especially in Lithuania and the Ukraine, although the lords were careful to pay lip-service to the principle of noble egalitarianism. As for Bohemia, the great upheaval of 1618–48 resulted in a virtual collapse of the gentry (that is, the knights) as an independent political factor.

UNDER THE HABSBURGS

A dynastic continuity formally achieved through the imposition of hereditary rule in Bohemia after 1627 and in 1687 in Hungary during its reunification was made possible by two factors: military conquest or reconquest and the physical survival of the Habsburg family. Absolutism, however, was not tantamount to despotic or unlimited power. The ruler had to rely on certain groups in the state and to be assisted by effective institutions of executive character. In the Habsburg lands the titled aristocracy, exclusive and hereditary, was the main element of support. Unlike the Polish kings, the Habsburgs acquired virtually a free hand in awarding nobility; this included the important right of domicile, of creating titles, and of giving their assent to the establishment of entailed estates (*majorats*). From the sixteenth century on the monarchs created barons and counts (more sparingly and later, princes) in Bohemia and Hungary. A given title rather than the traditional term *pan* (lord) came into use in the lands of the Crown of St Wenceslas.

A distinction, however, must be made between the Bohemian and Hungarian aristocracies. The former drastically changed its character after the Habsburg victory at the White Mountain in 1620, a crucial date in Czech history. As a result of persecutions and confiscations, around a half of all estates changed hands. The old Bohemian lords gained 30.2 percent, the "new aristocracy" brought in by the Habsburgs and owing them personal loyalty – Piccolominis, Buquoys, Colloredos, Gallases – 68.8 percent. Their presence illustrated dramatically the Habsburgs' imperial connection. The growing numbers and importance of Germans after 1526 had been resisted by the Bohemian estates. In 1615 they passed language laws obliging all officials and all members of the estates to use Czech. All this changed after 1627. We shall deal with those developments later in this chapter.

The Hungarian magnates becoming a titled aristocracy were also pro-Habsburg but here the alliance was more fragile. Although there was a certain amount of intermarriage and close contacts with their counterparts in Austrian and Moravian lands, the Hungarian aristocrats did not yet become integrated in the Vienna power structure. Their dress, speech, and names set them somewhat apart. The one hundred or so families occupying the top of the social ladder and by now mostly Catholic did their best to ensure that the ongoing crisis would result neither in a clear-cut victory of absolutism nor in an oligarchic anarchy. After a temporary setback in the last decades of the seventeenth and the beginning of the eighteenth century a political balance, even if somewhat uneasy, was restored.

During most of the period Hungarian developments were affected by Transylvania, whose mission of watching over the interests of the Hungarian estates when threatened by dynastic absolutism had been reaffirmed by its princes. Transylvania had no native aristocracy comparable to that of Royal Hungary, and its gentry was largely composed of ennobled Szeklers, haiduks, Romanian and German "Saxon" elite. Burghers of some cities were collectively raised to a noble status. Until the late 1650s Transylvanian observers were sent to the diet at Pozsony. Two of its ruling princely families came from Hungary proper. Thus one could hardly treat Transylvania as a foreign entity. Habsburg designs on the principality met with criticism even from staunch Catholic loyalists, including the all-important primate Cardinal Péter Pázmány himself. Its separate yet very visible presence mattered a good deal for the further evolution of the lands of the Holy Crown.

Habsburg policies aiming at strengthening the royal power required, in addition to the alliance with aristocracy, a sound financial basis and an efficient bureaucracy. The monarchs no longer derived their revenue from the lands of the Crown – which accounted for little more than 1 percent of total revenue from Bohemia – but from ordinary and extraordinary taxes. The former included regalian rights and income from royal towns; the latter were based on the declared value of certain kinds of income or property. The monarchy strove to impose, increase, and collect taxes with only a nominal assent of the parliamentary bodies. It also sought to prevent the gentry and aristocracy from avoiding payments altogether. Toward the end of the century these goals were largely, although not completely, achieved.

State bureaucracy was still mainly dependent on the estates, which alone would make its germanization difficult. Still, the already-stressed presence of newcomers from the empire in administration and the army command seemed essential to assure the undivided loyalty of officials. Not all of them were ethnic Germans and many came from the far-flung Habsburg lands. It took time and effort to make the bureaucracy a distinct state organ fully controlled by the monarchy.

As the century progressed, a developing bureaucracy and a large army became the two pillars on which the Habsburg rule rested. Historians have, however, challenged the older notion that Austria (this conglomerate of states) acquired its own and separate identity as a result of wars with Turkey. Evans, for one, insists that the unity of the monarchy was fostered by the political implications of the Counter-Reformation, by socio-economic developments, and above all by a set of common habits of the ruling group. If this interpretation is accepted it means that conformity grew more out of the ethos of the aristocracy than from the constantly advancing central controls. In turn the monarchy achieved a great power status in a series of wars with the Turks, but not because of these wars.

There is little doubt that the Counter-Reformation, colored by the Spanish model, exerted a major influence on the shaping of Habsburg absolutism and its role in Bohemia and Hungary. Yet it is all too easy to emphasize its Austrian dimension while overlooking the native Czech and Hungarian aspects. After all not only Protestantism but also the Catholic Reformation had a great impact on national language and national conscience. In Hungary the great figure of Cardinal Pázmány comes to mind, for he was an important Hungarian-language religious polemist. Largely for that reason he did not achieve much renown outside of the country. In Bohemia a scion of a lesser noble family, Bohuslav Balbín, defended the Czech linguistic heritage and the use of the native tongue, but his major work could not come out in print until the next century. In Croatia the Counter-Reformation produced another important literary and political figure, Juraj Križanić, who advocated the reconciliation of churches (Latin and Orthodox) as a way of unifying the Slavs. In that sense he appears as a precursor of nineteenth-century Slavophilism. Péter Beniczky, who wrote in Slovak and Hungarian, is included in the literatures of both countries.

Pázmány and Balbín were Jesuits and indeed the Jesuits were in the forefront of the Catholic offensive throughout Europe. This was particularly true in the Habsburg lands, which lacked a sufficient number of secular priests. The successes of the Jesuits, overshadowing those of the Dominicans, Franciscans, Capuchins, Carmelites, Piarists, or Paulines, were largely in the field of education. The Jesuits gave a good deal of attention to the emotional and spiritual needs of the people and found a great response. A Jesuit university was established in Olomouc in Bohemia. Pázmány founded a college in Pozsony (Bratislava) and a university in Nagyszombat (Trnava in Slovak) in 1635. The latter, the first Hungarian university to survive, was eventually moved to Budapest. The Jesuits were gradually winning over the aristocracy while Calvinism survived among the Hungarian gentry, reinforcing their anti-German feelings.

Was the culture of the baroque in Hungary and Bohemia tantamount to Habsburg absolutism and therefore contrary to Czech and Hungarian traditions? As in the above case of Counter-Reformation this would be too bold an assertion. The first baroque church in Bohemia was built by the Lutherans. Baroque mannerisms can be found in the writings of Protestants. The writings of Komenský, particularly the most important piece of Czech seventeenth-century prose, the already-mentioned *Labyrinth*, belong to the baroque era. The same is true for the paintings of a Catholic, Karel Škreta, and a Protestant, V. Hollar. Polish Sarmatism, a specific ideology of republicanism in the baroque era, to be discussed later, strongly influenced Bohemia and Hungary as well as Croatia and Slovakia. It was not so much that references to Attila and the Scythians as ancestors of the Hungarians showed superficial similarities to Polish invocations of ancient Sarmatians. There were deeper analogies on artistic and ideological levels. Seventeenth-century Hungary has been described as a meeting place of Sarmatism, Illyrianism (understood as a Serbo-Croatian baroque humanist product), and Pannonianism. The *Siege of Szigetvár*, an epic poem by Miklós Zrínyi (a descendant of the sixteenth-century hero), is regarded as the most important literary work of the century. Written in Hungarian, it was rendered into Croatian by the author's brother. The palaces of the Zrínyis, the Esterházys, the Wessélenyis, were the centers of Hungarian culture before the aristocracy fell under the spell of Vienna and the Habsburgs. Transylvania played a major cultural role during this period. The College of Gyulaféhervár (Alba Iulia), with its German teachers brought in by Gábor Bethlen, was an important center. In the early 1650s Komenský taught for several years at Sárospatak in Hungary.

The darker side of the era was represented by witch hunting, practiced earlier in the Czech lands than in Hungary. Gypsies could be killed on sight in Bohemia. As for Jews, their privileges were confirmed in the lands of the Crown of St Wenceslas, and toward the end of the century they received territorial autonomy in Bohemia and Moravia, following the Polish model. Prague, with the largest Jewish urban population in the region – some 7,800 people around 1635, almost half of the Bohemian Jewry – was referred to as the "capital of Israel." The monarchy used the Jews during the Thirty Years War, but sought to reduce their role and numbers during the next hundred years. This proved not so simple. The estates and the Jews, needing each other on economic grounds, contracted closer ties. The attempts by towns to impose restrictions met with limited success. It was also clear that the administration extended its support to the Jews for fiscal reasons. Occasional expulsions occurred in Bohemia and Hungary alongside the familiar accusations at times of epidemics. The Counter-Reformation contributed toward Judeophobia among the masses. Conditions were better for Jews in Transylvania where Prince Gábor Bethlen freed them of the obligatory display of a distinctive mark.

THE *RESPUBLICA*

Political confrontation in the seventeenth century seemed often to result from the state seeking to enlarge its power. The reaction it provoked was usually not a social revolution, but rather a rebuttal of the pretensions of centralism. In that sense absolutism was interfering with the continuing medieval process of increasing society's share in government. This was true in both the Habsburg lands and in the Polish-Lithuanian Commonwealth, but with an important difference in the latter case. Here the formal opponent of the political nation was the ruler, but in fact the process was vitiated by an evolution toward oligarchy that was undermining the political nation. A tendency toward oligarchic rule was common to the contemporary republican regimes, such as Venice or the Netherlands, and it did not result in anarchy. But in the Polish case not only was the urban context of these republics missing, but the magnates, spread over a huge territory, were preoccupied with their particular interests. One finds no example of an oligarchic ideology or attempts to make the senate a power base. No oligarchic regime came into being in which the magnates would maintain the balance between the rulers and the *szlachta*. To the surprise of foreign diplomats the oligarchs could not impose their candidates to the throne in such elections as Wiśniowiecki's or Sobieski's. But what they lost on the diet's floor they recovered in the economic sphere, through a continuing accumulation of large estates that gradually made them almost all-powerful in the state. Regional differences remained. Many of the Polish magnates favored a mixed form of government and behaved with moderation toward the "younger brothers." It was otherwise in the Ukraine or in Lithuania, where the lords of the huge estates virtually monopolized state offices and treated the lesser gentry tyrannically. But there were limits, as the powerful Sapiehas learned in Lithuania in the 1696–1700 confrontation with the *szlachta*, who defeated them in pitched battles.

When did the evolution of the nobles' republic toward a magnates' oligarchy begin? With the end of the Jagiellonian dynasty, or with the 1609 *rokosz* with which we ended the preceding chapter? There is no unanimity of views among historians. But by the late seventeenth century the process was virtually completed, the liberum veto (see p.103) standing out as the symbol. Undoubtedly many factors entered into the making of this transition. Its essence was the struggle for sovereignty between the king and the political nation – "maiestas versus libertas" – with the magnates affecting the process in a decisive way.

Elective monarchy weakened the executive, and rulers of foreign background were suspected, often justly so, of pursuing their own dynastic interests. This was the case with Sigismund III Vasa and to some extent with his two sons, Władysław IV and John Casimir. Their attempts to regain Sweden as a hereditary base and their collaboration with the Habsburgs, the champions of absolutism and Counter-Reformation, damaged the credibility of the Vasas and raised accusations of absolutist designs. It would be a mistake to think that the Vasa kings were mere figureheads. By and large they succeeded in maintaining an internal balance of power within the complex mixed form of government and tried to become stronger. They were free in the conduct of foreign policy as long as it did not seem aggressive to the pacifically inclined *szlachta*. They still commanded some respect. However, there were numerous restraints on royal initiative and power.

The royal domain (still some 19 percent of the land) was mostly leased to magnates. Still, the revenue of the royal exchequer, separated toward the end of the sixteenth century from public treasuries of the Crown and Lithuania, was not negligible. A fifth (although called the Quarter) of the monarch's income went for the upkeep of a small standing army of a few thousand men. As a result of the almost constant warfare throughout this century about 90 percent of the state budget was earmarked for military purposes and there was constant deficit. The respective figures for Brandenburg, Muscovy, and France were 50, 60, and over 62 percent. The state revenue remained stationary from the fourteenth century, and consequently the budget of the Commonwealth was about 50 percent of that of Sweden, 5 percent of that of England, and just under 3 percent of that of France. A special effort was required, accompanied by temporary high taxes that fell mainly on the burghers and the peasants, to raise an army of 78,000 men. This maximum figure was reached once, around 1621.

Without a real standing army or bureaucracy and handicapped by the dualist administration and great distances, the king could hardly run a centralized government. Like contemporary Spain the Commonwealth had grown too big and lost its capability of translating potential power into actual strength. The kings sought to change this state of affairs by attempts to alter the mode of royal election, to create a central council, to increase the size of the army – whose upkeep would be assured through regular and permanent taxes – and to restrict the prerogatives of the *sejm*. All these attempts produced a backlash and new limitations imposed on the Crown. Between the early 1630s and mid-1640s the king was deprived of the right to grant nobility, to raise troops without the consent of the diet, and to acquire new landed estates. In the absence of popular uprisings the *szlachta* did not need a strong ruler to protect its social position. Since most of the wars were fought – until mid-century – on the borders, the monarch did not appear as the necessary defender against foreign threats. When, however, the whole country came to be occupied by the Swedes, the prestige of the monarchy suffered.

Unlike the Habsburgs, the Polish kings had few potential allies. Through powers of patronage they attempted to win over a coterie of magnates. They did not seriously try to play the gentry against the lords or to use the military potential of the Cossacks, realizing that this could lead to a civil war and endanger the very structure of the state.

Nor were towns and burghers a pillar on which the monarchy could rely. It was not that this estate was insignificant in size, but there were few big and rich cities and these preferred to promote their own interests by other means than the rough and tumble of parliamentary politics. Gdańsk and Riga could and did use bribery. Cracow, Wilno, and Lwów acquired the right in 1658 to buy landed estates and to send delegates to the sessions of the *sejm* and local diets (*sejmik*). But this did not mean an intervention in state politics. The material and population losses suffered by towns in mid-century seriously undermined their position.

There remained the Catholic Church, which during this period played a crucial role as the supporter of the Habsburg throne, but failed to pursue the same line in Poland. True, there were important churchmen who promoted strong monarchy, criticized the anarchic inclinations of the *szlachta* and even dared to attack, as Bishop Szyszkowski did, the kind of freedom that had become the "biggest oppression exerted by few."[14] But by and large the church in Poland became "Sarmatized" in the seventeenth century. Distancing itself from the Spanish model the hierarchy, increasingly composed of top families, came to identify itself with the magnates and the *szlachta*.

The Commonwealth, as the American historian R. H. Lord remarked, was "the largest and the most ambitious experiment with a republican form of government that the world had seen since the days of the Romans."[15] Still, it did not represent a strong constitutional regime based on a parliament. The sovereign, it bears repeating, was the entire noble nation, adhering to the constitution and filling it with real meaning. With the weakening of the central legislature in the seventeenth century, the local assemblies became the power centers. They were a school of politics for the provincial gentry and strongholds of republicanism, but they also presided over what the Polish historian B. Leśnodorski called "a decentralization of sovereignty." The *szlachta* claimed the direct exercise of sovereignty in moments of crisis by means of confederations. Comparable to "covenanting," the confederations were organized to remove a real or alleged threat to liberty and to defend the country. They were not illegal and they took decisions by majority vote, unlike the unanimity-bound *sejm*.

The *szlachta* treated the state as the realization of its "golden" liberty. "The fatherland," wrote a magnate in the 1620s, expressing the credo of the nobility, "consists in neither walls, borders nor riches, but in the exercise of laws and freedom."[16] The great Dutch lawyer Hugo Grotius commented in a letter to a Polish friend that "the freedom to think what you want and to say what you think is based among you on the laws of the kingdom."[17] Yet, for all its love of freedom, the gentry was becoming a closed community that exhibited a good deal of conformism. In the absence of a *noblesse de robe* (service nobility) ennoblements were relatively rare (illegal entries excepted) and the *szlachta* set itself apart as a caste more rigidly than in the past.

In the course of the century a specific cultural formation developed that impregnated the political philosophy and the mentality of the *szlachta* as well as its life-style. The term "Sarmatism" referred to alleged ancestors, the Sarmatians; the concept itself served as an ideology integrating the multi-ethnic *szlachta* and put a specific stamp on it. Sarmatism was more than a conservative landowner's outlook, anti-urban and anti-intellectual, characterized by superficial religiosity, a tendency toward economic waste and ostentatious luxury as well as arrogance of caste. Such traits were common to many a nobleman of seventeenth-century Europe. Sarmatism involved a view of Poland as a granary of Europe and a shield of Christendom against Turks and Tatars, but above all as the realization of a superior form of government inspired by the Roman republic and based on the "golden freedom." There was nothing the Poles could learn from the West, and the oriental dress they adopted from their Muslim foes was underlining their distinct and original identity. This orientalization of Poland was often through the intermediary of Hungary – the Hungarians also dressed à la Turque – and was most visible in the realm of culture.

Sarmatism, which was replacing the older criteria of the nation – country, language, and culture – was overlapping with the baroque but was not identical with it. Because of the Sarmatian connection, the baroque, which gained prominence in architecture, arts, and literature, may in a sense be regarded as a more "native" style to a good part of the region than the Renaissance had been. But although there were several important literary figures during this period – to mention only the colorful memoirist J. C. Pasek – the high levels of the sixteenth century were not attained. In sciences the Gdańsk astronomer, Johann Hevelius, a member of the English Royal Society, was above all a European, but he acknowledged also being part of the Polish world (civis orbis Poloniae).

Polish religiosity in the age of the baroque as influenced first by Spanish and then French spirituality, also became Sarmatized. The Sarmatian vision of God and the saints was that of a monarch surrounded by senators; Heaven resembled a nobles' republic. Polish piety was strongly stamped with the Marian cult and became rather superficial in its outward manifestations. It also gained intolerant traits. Sarmatian xenophobia combined with parochialism and opposition to change, and fed on struggles with the invaders: Orthodox Muscovites, Lutheran Swedes and Prussians, Muslim Turks and Tatars. Increasingly Polishness became identified with Roman Catholicism.

Here as in many other fields the mid-century constituted the great divide. Sigismund III discriminated against Greek Orthodox, and under his rule the number of Protestant senators dwindled from 25 to 5. It increased under Władysław IV, but it was a far cry from the early days of the Reformation. Indeed, scions of great families were returning to Catholicism.

Religious riots grew in vehemence in the cities although usually the offenders were brought to justice. Władysław IV favored attempts at a dialogue, and indeed a Colloquium Charitativum was held in 1645 in Toruń between Catholic, Lutheran, and Calvinist theologians. A leading political writer, Łukasz Opaliński, opined that it would be counterproductive to take measures against the heretics. Grotius commented that "to impose laws on religion is not Polish,"[18] and Komenský (then living as an exile in Poland) wrote in the famous Panegyric to Charles Gustavus of Sweden that Poland had never spilled Christian blood in religious disputes. Although bigotry was mounting, there were no dragonnades à la Louis XIV, or state-directed persecutions. The only religious group ever expelled were the anti-Trinitarians in 1658, and they were largely made a scapegoat for collaboration with the Swedes.

The number of Jews in the Commonwealth tripled in the 1576–1648 period, reaching a figure of some 450,000, estimated as 4.5 percent of the population. More than two-fifths of the Jews lived in the Ukraine, over one quarter in Lithuania, their status varying from paupers in towns and villages to rich merchants and lessees of nobles' domains and enterprises. Seen as the oppressive tools of the nobility they were hated in the Ukraine, where the 1648 Cossack uprising was also the Jewish Black Year. Thousands of Jews perished in massacres and in fighting alongside the Poles against the Cossacks and Muscovites. Suspected later of collaboration with the invading Swedes, the Jews also suffered at Polish hands. Still, they made up for the losses of life in a remarkably short time. This turbulent period saw also the proclamation in 1665 of Sabbatai (Shabbetai) Zevi as the Messiah.

FROM THE WHITE MOUNTAIN TO RÁKÓCZI WAR

The seventeenth century saw several rulers in the Habsburg lands. The last years of Rudolf II were followed by the short reign of Matthias and the interlude of Frederick, the "Winter King." Then came Ferdinands II and III, who played a major role during the four crucial decades and were succeeded by Leopold. Under his reign, covering the second half of the century, Austria acquired more of a distinct identity as Germany and Spain went on their separate ways.

An uneasy balance in Bohemia, based on the Letter of Majesty and the accord of 1609, prevailed for a few years only. In the opinion of Polišenský the structure of the Bohemian society that the estates sought to preserve guaranteed reasonable conditions for economic, religious, and cultural development. True, there were elements of tension. Bohemia, which paid more taxes and contributed more troops than other Habsburg lands, had the reputation of being rich while the state deficit was growing. The noble estate and most of the burghers, who together were predominantly Protestant, faced a vigorous "Spanish party" that believed in Counter-Reformation and stronger central power. Although moderates on both sides tried to negotiate, the extremists rejected concessions. The diet did not seek to replace the Habsburgs by a native dynasty, but it wanted to limit their authority and to that end it promoted collaboration among the Protestant majorities in the assemblies of estates in Austria, Bohemia, and Hungary. Yet though the anti-Habsburg opposition was of predominantly Protestant character, it was not exclusively so. Among the nobility that later took to arms about 16 percent were Catholics, and there were Protestants who remained loyal to the Habsburgs or were neutral.

The conflict that erupted in Prague in 1618 and triggered the Thirty Years War was largely a confrontation about royal prerogatives and the rights of the estates. It was also part of an all-European strife between the Habsburg-Catholic and the Protestant-Dutch models of government and economy. The general nature of the conflict was stressed by Komenský, who wrote later to the Swedish chancellor Axel Oxenstierna that the Czechs had borne the brunt of the Habsburg attack and thus had given the others a chance to defend themselves. The notion of Europe being split into two camps, with the Netherlands, Bohemia, Transylvania, some German princes, England, France, Denmark, and Sweden on the one side and the Papacy, Austria, Spain, Italian states, and Poland on the other, the German lands being split, was widely accepted then and later.

The conflict started over an incident concerning Protestant churches built on lands of the Crown that had been given to the Catholic Church. The estates engaged in a political demonstration and petitioned the king, who had resided since 1609 in Vienna. A hard line taken by his Prague representatives, who were known to be the pillars of the "Spanish party," was seen as a deliberate infringement of the rights of the estates. A delegation went to the castle, and after a violent altercation with the two chief counselors Vilém Slavata and Jaroslav Martinic, threw them out of the window. They survived the fall, but the Defenestration of Prague of May 23, 1618 opened a new and crucial chapter in Czech history.

The estates pretended at first that they had acted against the bad counselors of the king, not the monarch himself, but the situation changed when Ferdinand succeeded Matthias. He had been imprudently elected in 1617 despite being a known champion of

Counter-Reformation and of absolutism. In 1619 the estates declared his election illegal and chose as king the head of the Protestant League in Germany and the son-in-law of James I of England, Frederick of the Palatinate. Yet hopes for the emergence of an anti-Habsburg coalition proved vain. Even Moravia at first adopted a stance of neutrality, and Silesia partly stayed out of the conflict. Only the Netherlands extended some financial assistance and Transylvania some military help.

The objectives of the uprising could be surmised from the reforms initiated by the estates, and stressing genuine election of monarchs, the diet's consent for changes, and religious toleration. Jesuits and those Catholics who had sided with the Habsburgs were expelled. A more inspiring program was lacking; there was no unity in the country comparable to that in the Hussite days. Certain towns, such as Plzeň and Budějovice, actually opposed the estates. The army consisted of mercenaries, national militia, and troops raised by lords. It was placed under the command of Matthias Thurn and Georg von Hohenlohe, and won certain military successes that involved two advances on Vienna. Then the army of the estates was confronted on November 8, 1620 by the imperial troops and those of the Catholic League at White Mountain (Bílá Hora), now a suburb of Prague. The two armies, roughly equal in size, had in their ranks Germans and Czechs on both sides, Walloons, Italians, and Spaniards in the Habsburg regiments, and Dutch, Swiss, and Hungarians in the estates' contingent. Although accounts differ, the battle seems to have been relatively brief. As the Habsburg troops won, King Frederick fled Prague. In the words of an English observer, the army of the Bohemian estates had "fought badly for their good cause."[19]

As the conflict broadened and other powers took the field against the Habsburgs – Denmark in 1625, Sweden five years later, finally France – small-scale fighting on the Czech soil continued. Saxon troops occupied Prague in 1631, which led to a brief revival of the government of the estates. The Swedish army in which the Czech political emigration placed their greatest trust besieged Prague unsuccessfully in 1639 and 1641 and captured Olomouc. Danish, Polish, and Cossack contingents ravaged the land. The meteoric rise of the imperial general Albrecht Wallenstein (Valdštejn), a great Bohemian noble who as Duke of Friedland controlled large tracts of the country and may have had designs on the crown of St Wenceslas, briefly aroused Czech hopes. The last fighting occurred in Prague on what we know as the Charles Bridge in October 1648, but by then the fate of Bohemia had been sealed. At the Treaties of Westphalia the Habsburgs lost a great deal, but not Bohemia. For the first but not for the last time, an East Central European country allied to the winning side would find itself abandoned. "What avails us," bitterly wrote Komenský to Oxenstierna, "that you are victorious by the help of our tears, when ye, having in your power to give liberty to those of us who were rescued, are again delivering us into the hands of our persecutors." Viewing the defeat in religious terms Komenský uttered the often-cited words, "I trust God that after the passing of the storm of wrath which our sins have brought upon our heads, the rule of thine affairs shall again be restored to thee, O Czech people."[20]

What was, in essence, the nature of this catastrophe symbolized by the White Mountain and viewed as a breach of continuity in Czech history? Put in the simplest terms the Habsburg victory amounted to a destruction of the existing political nation (composed, as we know, of lords, knights, and burghers) that shaped and preserved Bohemia's culture and identity. What remained of the first two estates was a narrow and formalized stratum of aristocracy reinforced by church hierarchy and largely alienated from the people. The Habsburgs may not have "created" this aristocracy but they certainly helped in the process and confirmed it. The gap between the nobility and the bulk of the nation left the latter leaderless. This was a drastic departure from the previously existing model that was also common to Poland and Hungary, and it had long-range repercussions.

The Habsburg policies were based on the principle that a rebellious country had lost its ancient rights. Those that were to remain would stem from royal favor. In June 1621, 27 leaders of the uprising – 17 burghers, 7 knights, and 3 lords – were publicly executed in Prague. Confiscation of landed estates of escaped leaders, of those executed, and even of the politically suspect, proceeded in three waves: 1623–7, 1632–4, and 1634–7. Sales of land belonging to those who were forced to leave the country proceeded, often under duress. This resulted in the earlier-mentioned changes in the distribution of great estates. As far as the gentry (knights) was concerned, their holdings dropped from a third to a fifth of all estates in Bohemia and to a tenth in Moravia. Out of the 1,128 families that belonged to that estate only 238 remained. Taking the nobility as a whole, out of 1,174 pre-1620 families only 308 stayed on and 192 new ones were added.

The basic constitutional law imposed on Bohemia in 1627 and on Moravia a year later took the form of the Renewed Land Ordinance. It put an end to royal elections, assuring hereditary succession to male Habsburgs. The position of the top Bohemian official, the burgrave of Karlštejn, was abolished. In the assembly the clergy was reinstated as the first estate; its land was restituted in 1629. While previously each estate had one vote, now in many deliberations each member of the first three estates had one vote, the burghers retaining one collective vote. Out of 30 royal towns that had sent delegates only four remained. Legislative initiative belonged henceforth to the king, and officials took an oath to him and no longer also to the estates. The king and not the estates now granted nobility, including the right of residence (*incolat*). The German language was placed on parity with Czech for all state purposes.

With all non-Catholic religions (except Jewish) declared illegal, the Protestants faced the choice of conversion or emigration, and many chose the latter. They were joined by strictly political émigrés who had left at various stages of the war. The situation was different in Lusatia and Silesia, where limited toleration prevailed, and some of the émigrés went there. The Czech Brethren (with Komenský) went to Poland; others chose Saxony, Prussia, Transylvania, Denmark, Sweden, England, and the Netherlands. It is assumed that about 150,000 departed, a huge figure assuming that Bohemia had a population of roughly 2 million and Moravia of around 1 million. Although all these estimates contain a wide margin of error, the total population may have declined by a third; these losses, however, were largely made up in a half century or so.

Physical destruction went together with financial ruin of many a town, depreciation of currency, food shortages, and worsened conditions of life in the countryside. A mood of gloom, resignation, even despair prevailed. The baroque culture resplendent in Prague architecture had as its other side, parochialism, continuing denationalization, a decline of the Czech language and *de facto* germanization. Szűcs regarded the degradation of Bohemia into a hereditary province as a far worse fate than the total disappearance of the state – as was the later case of partitioned Poland.

The image of the post-White Mountain period as a "dark age" in which Bohemia lost its religion, its language, and its very identity can no longer be accepted without qualifications. Was Catholicism an alien, imposed creed, or did it permit the people – a carrier of baroque religiosity with the cult of St John Nepomuk – to preserve Czech historical continuity albeit on the lowest linguistic level? While germanization was a consequence of Habsburg victory, the struggle itself could hardly be reduced to a national German–Czech confrontation. The argument advanced by some historians (including E. Denis and Palacký) that a victory of the estates would either have plunged Bohemia in anarchy resembling Poland or drawn it even closer into the German orbit is debatable. But whatever the alternatives, the White Mountain shaped the direction and the nature of Czech history at least for the next two centuries, and it has remained a point of reference even today.

The uprising in Prague in 1618 had naturally affected Transylvania, whose prince Gábor (Gabriel) Bethlen was presiding over the Golden Age that continued under his successor George I Rákóczi. Their policy combined religious toleration with mercantilist tendencies in economics and a penchant for absolutism in politics. Both princes aspired to the Polish throne, a constant ambition since Stephen Batory, and had designs on Moldavia and Wallachia. In their conflict with the Habsburgs they gained only a few counties, but may have saved Hungarian Protestants from the fate of their co-religionists in Bohemia. Under one of the treaties (Linz in 1645) Transylvania gained the right for even the serfs to choose their own religion. Yet the larger objective of restoring a free Hungarian kingdom proved beyond the princes' grasp. The ambitions of the Transylvanian rulers were greater than their actual capabilities, a fact which Bethlen was realistic enough to acknowledge when he refused to assume the crown of St Stephen.

Bethlen had reacted quickly to the developments in Bohemia and extended military support to the estates. His light cavalry, the famed hussars, joined in the march on Vienna, participated in the battle of the White Mountain, and fought again in 1623, 1626, and 1643. The first offensive was checked by a diversionary action of Polish and Cossack light cavalry, which had been enlisted for Habsburg services with Sigismund III's approval. This form of indirect aid resulted from the king's pro-Habsburg policy, exemplified by the secret accord of 1613, which provided for mutual aid against rebels. The action against Bethlen, when combined with Polish moves in the Danubian principalities, antagonized their suzerain the sultan of Turkey. In 1620 the Turks inflicted a crushing defeat on the Poles near Ţuţora (Cecora). Poland redressed the situation a year later at an armed confrontation at Hotin (Chocim), which the greatest Croatian baroque poet Ivan Gundulić celebrated with the epic poem *Osman*.

Transylvania reached the summit of its international standing by becoming a signatory to the Treaties of Westphalia, and the Habsburgs had to take this fact into consideration in their all-Hungarian policies. Successes of Counter-Reformation in Royal Hungary, and a transformation of the magnate class – both mentioned earlier – played by and large into the hands of the Habsburgs. But points of friction remained alive. Economic activities based on Vienna and affecting cattle trade were deemed detrimental to Hungarian interests: the 1622 Landsverlegerische Viehcompagnia and the Kaiserliche Ochsenhandlung were set up in 1651. Fierce competition with the Zrínyis developed. Feelings that Vienna was out to ruin the Hungarians combined with criticism of Habsburg policies toward Turkey. The Hungarian political nation, or at least its important segment, was reaching the conclusion that nothing could be expected from Vienna.

The Turkish grip on central Hungary was loosening. Impoverished by wars the region could not yield enough taxes to maintain an effective administration and army. Legal matters and even tax collection had to be handled by Hungarians themselves. Landlords living in Hungary could exert more control over their estates under Turkish occupation, and they clamored for liberation policies. Increasingly the Habsburgs were being blamed for inactivity or even obstruction of plans for a total expulsion of the Turks. Germanophobia present in many Hungarian circles received new impulses.

The greatest Hungarian of this period was Miklós Zrínyi, the ban (governor) of Croatia, "a son of two fatherlands" and, were it not for Ferdinand's opposition, the likely palatine. He made the liberation of Hungary and its constitution into a free state his life goal, and he stressed religious toleration as essential for bringing together the Calvinist gentry and the Catholic aristocracy. Zrínyi's plans, however, were undermined by the collapse of Transylvania. Its prince George II Rákóczi, pursuing the Polish throne, joined in the war then raging in Poland, overreached himself, was defeated and deposed. Transylvania ceased to count as a real element of power. In 1664 the Habsburg armies smashed the Turks in the battle of Szentgotthárd (St Gothard), but the "shameful" Peace of Vasvár that followed returned all the conquered territory to Turkey. Vienna, preoccupied by its simultaneous struggle with France on the Rhine treated Hungarian interests as secondary.

The Wesselényi or Zrinski-Frankopan conspiracy – the name differs in Hungarian and Croatian historiography – then began; it was a plot to overthrow the Habsburgs, in cooperation with Turkey. The conspiracy was discovered and the government responded with reprisals comparable to those that had been meted out to the Bohemian rebels after the White Mountain. Several aristocratic conspirators were executed, the office of the palatine was abolished, non-native officials appointed, and an extraordinary tax imposed. Protestant ministers were singled out for savage persecutions; a number of them were made into galley slaves. The constitution of the country was suspended.

The brutality and the arbitrariness of the regime provoked a movement of resistance around 1672. Known as the "kuruc" (crusader), the name originally given to Dózsa's companions in 1514, the uprising relied heavily on the peasantry. By the mid-seventeenth century constant warfare had again loosened the bonds of serfdom. With the decline of private armies and the nobles' withdrawal from military service, haiduks, free peasants, and foreign mercenaries made up the bulk of soldiers. Imre Thököly, married to a Zrínyi and proclaimed prince by his supporters, assumed the leadership of the kuruc army. He promised exemption of dues to any serf joining the struggle, a promise that every subsequent rebel leader echoed. Under his leadership the kuruc fighters became in time more of a regular army than a band of social revolutionaries. France, under Louis XIV, was providing them with financial subsidies.

An approaching war with Turkey forced the Habsburgs in 1681 to restore the constitution and revert to limited religious toleration. The war began with a siege of Vienna by Turkey and its dramatic relief by Polish–German forces. But it continued for the next 16 years, almost to the end of the century. King John III of Poland tried to mediate between the Habsburgs and Thököly. Leopold was adamant, and in any case the Austrian military effort was concentrated against Thököly and his northern principality centered on Kassa (Košice), reducing the Hungarian leader to complete dependence on the Turks. In 1686 the imperial troops took Buda from the Turks; a year later the diet in Pozsony, overawed by Habsburg might, voted to abolish royal elections and the right of resistance to the ruler as stipulated in the Golden Bull. The adoption of these measures, together with the recognition of Habsburg hereditary succession, removed major obstacles on the road to absolutism.

Thus the liberation of Hungary did not mean the restoration of the independent constitutional state as it had existed some hundred and fifty years earlier. Moreover Turkish rule had changed the topography of the country and contributed to its depopulation. Not only was there a demographic drop, mentioned earlier, but the ethnic composition changed, owing to an influx of Serb, West European, and German colonists whose separate identity was deliberately encouraged. The often referred-to Habsburg policy of divide and rule found here an early application.

The Hungarians could hardly rejoice over the liberation of their country. The war costs had been high and they fell heavily on the peasantry. The cosmopolitan imperial army lived off the land and engaged in mass looting. Even the generals joined in policies of extortion. The gentry, eager to reclaim their estates in the recovered lands, found its hopes deceived by the deliberately inimical policy of the land commission (Commissio neoacquistica), an organ of the Hofkammer. Presided over by the anti-Hungarian Cardinal Leopold Kollonich, it favored pro-Habsburg aristocrats, for instance the Esterházys, and discriminated against the less loyal gentry by insisting on actual proofs of ownership. In a process characterized by much arbitrariness some free peasants were reduced to serfdom. The commission operated on the assumption that, to cite its own words, "Hungarian blood which makes people inclined toward unrest and revolution be mixed with German blood so as to assure trust and love toward their natural hereditary king."[21]

The lands of St Stephen were not reunited. The Military Border, mostly in Croatia, remained under Vienna's control. An area in southeastern Hungary called the Banat was made into a separate district. Transylvania, according to the Diploma Leopoldina of 1691, continued to be based on four religions and three nations, but the princely title went to the Habsburg ruler; a governor with powers similar to the old *voievod* was appointed; a separate chancellery and treasury were established. The impact of the Reformation and Counter-Reformation on the language and the self-awareness of Romanians in Transylvania assisted the efforts of Cardinal Kollonich to bring about a union, in 1697–1700, of the local Greek Orthodox church with Rome. The Ruthenians of north-eastern Hungary already had their Greek Catholic Church, since the Union of Ungvár (Užhorod) in 1648.

Habsburg policies raised objections on all counts: political, economic, social, religious. The oppressive nature of the system was bound to provoke an upheaval, and indeed the Tokaj peasant uprising erupted briefly in the north in 1697. In 1703, three years after the Treaty of Karlovci (Karlowitz) had formally marked the Turkish surrender of almost all Hungarian territory, the greatest anti-Habsburg rising swept the country. Originally a peasant revolt, it was transformed under the leadership of Francis II (Ferenc) Rákóczi into a war of independence. It was somewhat ironic that the greatest Hungarian landowner, a Catholic and a pupil of Kollonich should head a movement based on peasant masses and centered politically on the Calvinist gentry. Yet Rákóczi had the Transylvanian princely tradition, the blood of Zrínyis, and was Thököly's stepson. Under the banner of "With God for Country and Liberty" Rákóczi, supported by a Polish-style confederation, rose to be prince of Transylvania in 1704 and prince of Hungary a year later. In 1707 the Habsburgs were officially dethroned.

Rákóczi governed the country with a strong hand, relying mainly on lesser gentry and some burghers. Those aristocrats who supported him he confined to military posts. He taxed, not very successfully, the nobility, sought to eliminate religious and national conflicts, and promised full emancipation to all serfs who joined him. The Rákóczi war of independence coincided with two major European conflicts: the War of the Spanish Succession (1701–14) in which France and the Habsburgs were the main protagonists, and the Northern War (1700–21) in which Augustus of Poland and Saxony, Peter the Great of Russia, and Charles XII of Sweden were the main characters. Rákóczi tried early on to link the Hungarian struggle with Poland, and especially with the Franco-Austrian conflict. Louis XIV found the Hungarian diversion most useful, but save for subsidies, he never treated Rákóczi even as a junior ally. For all the international ties, and those with the Polish aristocracy were the closest, the Hungarian struggle was a lonely one, and as such doomed to failure. The imperial troops and their Hungarian allies (*labanc*) were superior to Rákóczi's kurucs, and defeats in 1707–9, accompanied and followed by epidemics, lowered the morale of the people. Despite the fairly broad social basis of Rákóczi's regime, many Saxon burghers, the Serbs in the south, as well as magnates who

objected to his peasant policies, remained pro-Habsburg. During Rákóczi's absence abroad where he was seeking aid, the deputy army
commander negotiated an honorable peace with Austria, the Treaty of
Szatmár, in 1711. Rákóczi and many of his followers chose emigration,
some 3,000 of them in Poland. The war of independence entered history
and legend, the hopeless but unavoidable struggle being celebrated in
songs and poems.

THE "DELUGE": BEFORE AND AFTER

The seventeenth century in the Commonwealth was an age of wars.
By the 1650s, for the first time in centuries, the country was exposed
to hostilities at home, indeed to foreign occupation. The term "deluge,"
popularized by a famous historical novel of Henryk Sienkiewicz, well
described the predicament. And yet the first few decades did not augur
an approaching catastrophe. The struggle with Muscovy was rendered
inevitable by Sigismund III's insistence on the tsar's crown for himself,
and ended with the truce of Dyvilino in 1619 (one year before the White
Mountain), which brought territorial gains to the Commonwealth. But
Muscovy under its new dynasty, the Romanovs, remained inimical
even though the tsar's court was deeply affected by Polish culture.

The truce allowed Poland to concentrate on Sweden, which under
Gustavus Adolphus had set out to make the Baltic into a Swedish lake.
Gustavus Adolphus attacked Livonia, captured Riga, and moved into
Ducal and Royal Prussia, threatening to cut Poland off from the sea.
At this point the Thirty Years War had already begun, and Warsaw
(Sigismund III moved the capital there from Cracow) could not escape
its implications. The already-mentioned anti-Bethlen expedition was
repaid by the Habsburgs through military assistance against the
Swedes, and the two armies jointly won the victory at Trzciana in 1629.
But the superior Swedish tactics and fire-power proved a hard nut to
crack even for the so-far invincible Polish winged hussars (they had
wing-shaped plumage attached to their armor), led by one of the best
commanders, Hetman Stanisław Koniecpolski.

The French wanted the Swedes disengaged from the Polish front so
that they would be able to intervene in Germany. King Gustavus
Adolphus was eager to comply, but did not want to leave Poland in
his rear. Muscovite preparations for an offensive against the *Respublica*
and concealed subsidies to Stockholm relieved the king's anxiety and
made the Swedish–Polish truce at Altmark in 1629 possible. The Poles
on their side feared a simultaneous war with Muscovy and Sweden
and made serious concessions: the Swedes were left in control of Baltic
ports and allowed to levy custom duties. These helped to finance the
German campaign of Gustavus Adolphus, the timetable of which seems

to have been affected by the coordination with Muscovite anti-Polish moves. Indeed, Moscow celebrated Swedish victories and bemoaned the death of Gustavus Adolphus on the battlefield. As for its own war with the Commonwealth, it ended with Muscovite defeats and the peace of Polanovo in 1634. Władysław IV gave up his claims to tsardom, and engaged in vast plans that included cooperation with Muscovy against Sweden or Turkey, as well as the continuation of a pro-Habsburg line. To that end the small Polish fleet was dispatched to Germany, where it was captured by the Swedes.

Władysław IV, an ambitious ruler and a gifted military leader, sought to link his foreign policy goals with domestic attempts to strengthen royal power. The *sejm* suspected, not without reason, that plans for an anti-Turkish crusade for the liberation of the Balkans were dictated by internal considerations, and that the king was not above provoking a conflict that would involve the Commonwealth in war. Hence his plans were sabotaged. In 1635 the armistice with Sweden was renewed at Stumsdorf on conditions advantageous to Poland, but it brought no real peace. Nor did it put an end to Władysław's various plans for complex dynastic combinations; they involved a Habsburg–Vasa family pact over a somewhat hypothetical division of future spoils at the expense of Sweden and Turkey.

Władysław IV died without having managed to gain the Swedish throne, which, after the abdication of Queen Christina, went to Charles X Gustavus. Władysław's attempt to provoke an all-out war with Turkey and the Tatars in the mid-1640s had misfired, and his death came at a moment when a big Cossack uprising in the Ukraine was posing a major threat to the Commonwealth.

The Cossacks were, not unlike the haiduks, frontiersmen, who organized themselves into a fighting community to resist periodic Tatar raids. From defense they passed to offense, and their looting expeditions on the Black Sea on occasion reached Istanbul itself. When the Commonweath was at peace with Turkey the Cossacks were a source of friction between Poland and the Ottoman Empire, but at times of crisis they constituted a reservoir of fighting men. Some 40,000 Cossacks, for instance, led by P. Konashevich-Sahajdachny, had played a significant role in the battle of Hotin in 1621. The demands of the Cossack host to be treated as *de facto* gentry were scornfully rejected by the *sejm*. The number of Cossacks placed on the royal register as enlisted troops was small. Cossacks also served in private armies of the magnates who were then colonizing the Ukraine, but they were often at the mercy of these "little kings," who tried to turn resisting Cossacks into serfs. The interests of the king and of the local magnates were often at variance, and Władysław IV, who sympathized with Cossack grievances, had a place for the Cossacks in his Turkish plans. These being thwarted by the *sejm*, the Cossacks came to favor a strong central monarchy.

The Cossack issue, with its socio-economic and political implications, became linked with religious matters. The Union of Brest, mentioned in the preceding chapter, viewed by Rome as a step toward a union of Western and Eastern churches and by Warsaw as integrating the Ukrainian-Belorussian lands closer into the Commonwealth, produced unexpected difficulties. First the resisting Greek Orthodox hierarchy was driven underground with masses remaining true to it. This left the official Uniate Church as a hierarchy without a faithful following. But as the Orthodox Church gained powerful protectors, including some Cossack leaders, it had to be recognized by the rulers. Since most of the native great magnates were then embracing Catholicism and Polish culture, the alienated masses turned to the Cossacks, who somewhat unexpectedly were cast in the role of defenders of Greek Orthodoxy and the Ukrainian people. Thus, when they rose again in 1648 to avenge past defeats and to reclaim rights which, as they believed, Władysław IV regarded as legitimate, all Ukraine was aflame.

The Cossack leader was Bohdan Khmelnytsky; contemporaries compared him to Cromwell. Elected hetman by the Zaporozhian host, the self-governing community beyond the Dnieper cataracts, he allied himself with the traditional enemies, the Tatars, and in a series of battles (at Korsuń and Piławce) defeated the armies of the Crown and of the magnates. The insurgents were joined by burghers, some small gentry, and the peasant masses, and they proceeded to massacre nobles and Jews. The magnates responded with savage reprisals which only fed the flame of the uprising. While the newly elected king John Casimir and his advisers sought peace, the "little kings" sabotaged it. The successive agreements with Khmelnytsky, whose objective changed from that of a separate Ukraine under the Polish Crown to an independent state, were mere palliatives. In renewed fighting the Poles won a major victory at Berestechko in 1651, but no solution to the conflict was in sight.

The vested interests of the nobility were preventing concessions, just as the aspirations of the Ukrainians could no longer be appeased by an enlarged Cossack register and ennoblements. The Ukraine was emerging as a political entity, and Khmelnytsky, unable to achieve a settlement with Poland, turned to Moscow. In the much debated Pact of Pereiaslav the Cossacks recognized the overlordship of the tsar; the result was a new Russo-Polish war. The Muscovite armies occupied most of Lithuania's eastern provinces and entered Wilno. Their occupation was to last for several years. The Commonwealth was thus fully absorbed in the east when Sweden struck: one army entered Poland where the noble levies capitulated, another menaced Lithuania. Janusz

Radziwiłł, Lithuania's grand hetman, deprived of Polish reinforcement and unable to gain a cease-fire from the Muscovites, decided to denounce the Polish-Lithuanian union and link Lithuania with Sweden. Branded arch-traitor by Polish tradition and seen as a true patriot by the Lithuanians, Radziwiłł was essentially an ambitious magnate whose Protestantism inclined him toward Sweden. It was not unusual in the seventeenth century for a great lord to take matters into his own hands or treat with foreign rulers.

Charles X Gustavus, having overcome the relatively slight Polish resistance, was recognized by most magnates and gentry as king of Poland. The hapless John Casimir sought refuge in Silesia. Yet the rapid and easy Swedish conquest proved ephemeral. The largely mercenary troops behaved as in a conquered country. Anti-Protestant fervor was whipped up by the successful defense of the Pauline monastery of Jasna Góra at Czestochowa. This apparently miraculous event became one of the great national symbols. Anti-Swedish resistance spread widely; even the peasantry fought against the foreign and heretical Swedes. Although the hero of the partisan warfare, Stefan Czarniecki, could not defeat the Swedish army, the Swedes could not win a decisive victory either.

The Swedish might and Charles Gustavus's inordinate ambitions aroused Europe's fears, and a vast coalition comprising Austria, Denmark, the Netherlands, Muscovy, and Brandenburg-Prussia came into being. By what may have been the greatest diplomatic blunder of the century Warsaw had granted the Brandenburg electors the succession in Ducal Prussia in 1611. Now, the Great Elector subordinated all his policy to one goal: full independence of Prussia. He pursued it relentlessly by changing sides, until by a series of treaties from 1657 to 1660 he obtained it from all the belligerents.

The Swedes had at various times enlisted as allies Prussia, the Cossacks, the Radziwiłłs, and finally George II Rákóczi of Transylvania. After a veritable pact of partitions had been concluded, Rákóczi marched into Poland. The venture, as already mentioned, ended with his utter defeat and deposition by the Turks in 1657–8.

The "deluge" was over with the Treaty of Oliwa in 1660; it was an eastern counterpart of the Treaties of Westphalia and the Peace of the Pyrenees of 1659, and brought general pacification. Territorial status quo was restored; Prussia's independence confirmed; John Casimir renounced the title of King of Sweden. But the Ukrainian and Muscovite issues were still unresolved. An attempt to create a Ukrainian (Rus) principality as a third member in the Commonwealth – embodied in the most promising Pact of Hadiach of 1658 – failed. It provoked, however, another round of fighting with Muscovy. Polish armies won victories in the 1660s but they proved to be without a political sequel.

The Truce of Andrusovo of 1667 divided the Ukraine along the Dnieper River, putting an end to Ukrainian national aspirations. Nineteen years later, when Warsaw needed Moscow's assistance, the truce was made into a permanent peace. It was a turning point.

The long decades of hostilities fought on Polish and Lithuanian territory ruined the country. Cultural losses due to destruction and looting were enormous, many art treasures ending up in Swedish collections. Wars, epidemics, and famines accounted for the catastrophic population drop. Certain parts of the country registered a loss of 60 percent of inhabitants. The towns of Cracow and Warsaw were reduced respectively by two-thirds and a half. There were great shortages of laborers, farm animals, and implements; the productivity of agriculture further diminished. With contracting markets and a dislocation of trade the economy was in deep recession. Export of grain to and from Gdańsk fell to a third of the early seventeenth-century levels. Historians sought to ascribe the slowness of recovery to the manorial system in agriculture, but the system certainly did not prevent the recovery of the ravaged Prussia. Furthermore, the attempts to replace serfdom with free tenant farming should have produced better results than they did. Others blamed the magnitude of devastations, but Muscovy had suffered equal devastations in the early part of the century without such long-range repercussions. There is much to be said for the argument that the "deluge" caught the Polish economy at the worst possible moment, making recovery so slow and incomplete. Moreover several factors must be taken into consideration, domestic and international, socio-economic and political, which were all responsible for this downward trend.

The political nation failed to draw a lesson from the catastrophes of the mid-century. Instead it came to believe that the country had been saved through divine providence and the superiority of the free political system. In the 1650s this free political system saw the appearance of the notorious liberum veto which allowed a single deputy to prevent the *sejm* from passing legislation. The liberum veto was not the cause of the country's decline but a symptom of it. The result, however, was a growing paralysis of the diet; the 1662–72 decade was particularly bad. The myth of a free people relying on 200,000 noble swords became an insoluble part of Sarmatism. But in fact, the *szlachta* was unable and unwilling to defend the country while opposing demands for an adequate army. The Polish political system had created free institutions, but it failed to devise means of protecting them. A defensive mechanism was lacking. John Casimir, assisted by his indomitable wife Mary Louise, did attempt much-needed reforms, but was confronted by a *rokosz* led by the popular Crown Marshal Jerzy Lubomirski in 1665–6. Amidst conditions growing ever more anarchic John Casimir abdicated, prophetically warning his countrymen that the country would be torn apart by neighbors unless it reformed its ways. Indeed, the neighboring states wanted to preserve Polish "golden liberty" and prevent reforms. Sweden and Brandenburg-Prussia concluded accords to that effect in 1667, 1686, 1696, Austria and Muscovy in 1675, and Austria and Brandenburg-Prussia in 1686. The Commonwealth was becoming an object of international politics and an arena of foreign intrigues.

John Casimir had hoped to make the way for a French prince, but the *szlachta* chose the colorless Prince Michael Korybut (Wiśniowiecki), whose father had won fame in the Cossack wars. As a Polish historian put it, the new king could speak several languages, but had nothing interesting to say in any of them. His brief reign was filled with domestic chaos and saw Poland's humiliation at Turkish hands at the Treaty of Buczacz, which resulted in the loss of Podolia. Michael's successor to the throne was the great military leader John III (Sobieski), perhaps the last outstanding Polish king. Working under constant limitations of magnate intrigues he was unable to fulfill his great plan against Brandenburg which was aiming to conquer Prussia with Franco-Swedish cooperation. Forced by events to espouse a pro-Habsburg policy directed against the Ottoman empire he led the victorious relief army that, as mentioned, together with the German forces, routed the Turks at Vienna in 1683. This was the last great Polish feat of arms, and in the ensuing years of the war the Commonwealth played second fiddle to Austria. Peace meant the recovery of Podolia and nothing more. The real victor was Vienna and the balance of power in East Central Europe was shifting to its advantage. By signing the 1686 peace treaty with Moscow Poland entered the road of future dependence on the Russian empire. Perhaps there was still a chance of recovery, but the first decade of the eighteenth century that witnessed the Habsburgs' victory over Rákóczi saw the Commonwealth plunged into the Northern War with its fatal consequences.

4

ENLIGHTENED ABSOLUTISM OR ENLIGHTENED LIBERTY?

THE EIGHTEENTH CENTURY

Enlightenment is the most useful single term to describe the dominant trends of the eighteenth century. A distinction is usually made between the Early Enlightenment, in roughly 1715–48, and the Mature Enlightenment, of the following decades. East Central Europe was mainly affected by the latter. In a sense "Enlightenment" amounted to a popularization of the intellectual and scientific achievements of the seventeenth century as epitomized by Locke, Descartes, and Newton. To Immanuel Kant it represented a maturing of man and a challenge to use reason. Indeed, the saying "sapere aude" (be bold to be wise) became a watchword, and belief in progress a rallying cry. With such key words as virtue, happiness, humanity, and liberty a new hope for mankind arose in contrast to the despair bred by wars and famines of the preceding age.

To its supporters, the spreading of light was a crusade against prejudice, irrational tradition, obscurantism, and oppression which they saw in the past. The world ruled by laws of nature appeared as a huge mechanism with God as the Great Watchmaker or Architect. Skepticism towards metaphysical speculations and religious dogmatism combined with abhorrence of fanaticism and often led to an anti-clerical stance, for the church was surely an integral part of the old regime. Yet for all the inclination toward secularism, even neo-paganism, new forms of religiosity arose, for instance Pietism or Deism. Just as the Jesuits had been in the vanguard of Catholic Reformation so the nascent Freemasonry became the champion of Enlightenment. Its role in East Central Europe proved particularly important, and the first lodge in the Habsburg monarchy appeared in Bohemia.

In the age when belief in reason and free inquiry was in the forefront of the intellectual movement, learning and education were seen as of special importance. Indeed, the century witnessed the rise of scientific societies, academies, and new educational systems. A growing number of publications culminating in the great *Encyclopédie* of Diderot and d'Alembert spread the new ideas. The French were in the lead and the names of Montesquieu, Voltaire, and Rousseau naturally come to mind. The appearance of Montesquieu's *Spirit of the Laws* in 1748 may be taken as the opening date of the Enlightenment properly speaking.

The eighteenth century was in many respects a glittering age that left a magnificent cultural heritage. Arts and architecture saw a transition from baroque and rococo to neoclassicism; literature developed new genres. The sophisticated and cosmopolitan society of the salons where manifestations of sensibility and sentimentalism reigned made Talleyrand speak wistfully of the *douceur* of life under the *ancien régime*. This culture was epitomized by the music of Mozart that had lost none of its greatness and appeal with the passage of time. Of course, there was a darker side. This was also a century of lax morality, corruption, brutality, and misery. In a society that was marked by decay, adventurers and charlatans like Casanova and Cagliostro thrived, moving from Paris to Warsaw and Rome to Bohemia.

The impact of the new ideas was facilitated by the existence of great unresolved problems in political, social, and economic spheres throughout Europe, and even beyond. The American, French, and Polish Revolutions appeared to contemporaries as an unavoidable denouement. Yet the European picture was characterized by a good deal of diversity. There was the demographic expansion, even explosion in many countries. The English population grew from 6 to 9 million during 1720–1801, that of France from 18 to 24 million, in 1780–9. Hungary's population doubled between 1720 and 1790 (from 4.1 to 8.5 million); the Czech lands had a 75 percent increase in 1670–1750. With the first censuses in East Central Europe in Bohemia (1754), Hungary (1784), and the Commonwealth (1791) we can speak of statistics with some assurance. But demographic trends were not everything. Toward the end of the eighteenth century the small country of England entered on its road to power with an agricultural and then an industrial revolution that widened the distance between the island and the continent. The accumulation of capital was obviously a precondition for such a take-off. Could the state assist in this process?

It seemed obvious to contemporaries that the state should serve as a vehicle of progress, but the form of its government was an object of disagreement. Montesquieu praised the English limited monarchy, believing, erroneously, that it was based on separation of powers. Voltaire advocated a strong monarchic government: the rulers imbued with the principles of Enlightenment acting as philosopher-kings. Rousseau seemed to favor a republican commonwealth, and unlike most people in the West liked the Polish liberum veto, for it truly demonstrated that the "general will" was more than a mere sum of votes.

Perhaps Voltaire summed up best the existing alternatives: "For a state to be powerful," he wrote, "the people must either enjoy a freedom based on law or be ruled by a strong and unchallenged government."[22] These alternatives seemed particularly pertinent for East Central Europe.

The region's weakness was evident, especially in the economic sphere. If we take the French state revenue as 100 in 1700, that of Austria would be 26 and of the Commonwealth 3. By 1788 the indicator for Austria was 43 while Poland showed a decline: it was 2.7. The Polish case was also striking if one turns to taxes per capita. In 1785 they were 2.9 percent of the figure for the Netherlands, 4.8 percent for France, and 8.3 percent of the Habsburg monarchy. In terms of military strength, while the European average was one soldier per 100 inhabitants, in the Commonwealth it was one soldier per 500 or 600.

Could such a glaring gap be narrowed only by a strong government, an "enlightened despotism" to borrow the expression first used by Mercier de la Rivière in 1767? The term was in a way self-contradictory, linking enlightenment with despotism. It incorporated such concepts as personal and civic freedoms, social contract and the law of nature, while making the despotic ruler a trustee and executor of the immature people, governing and guiding it for its own good, and identifying the good of the people with the good of the state. And all this not in the name of the divine origin of monarchic power, but because of its effectiveness. The government would educate the masses to their new task through schools subordinated to the regime. It would release their energies in the economic field by removing constraints and pursuing policies of state intervention through mercantilism, or its Central European version, cameralism. The cameralists strove to increase state revenue through foreign trade (conceived in rather static terms), which they regarded as the main source of wealth. By the use of tariffs they aimed to achieve a favorable balance, encouraging the export of finished products while restricting their imports. In the case of the Habsburg monarchy this policy led to a virtual division of labor within the state, by making Austria and Bohemia the purveyors of produced goods while leaving Hungary in the position of supplier of agrarian products.

It was up to the government to develop an efficient bureaucracy, to maintain a standing army, assure a uniform system of general taxation, introduce a modern educational system, preside over legal reforms, and raise the living standards in the country through increased productivity and output. Enlightened absolutism was, in the words of the Hungarian historian D. Kosáry, an attempt on the part of "states of the more backward European periphery to attain the level of the more developed part of Europe . . . while remaining in the framework of feudalism."[23] By feudalism the author means the landowning aristocratic regime based on privilege of birth. Kosáry tends to reject the interpretation according to which enlightened absolutism was either a revolutionary attempt by the bourgeoisie or alternatively a means of defense against bourgeois ambitions.

Under this scheme the conflict between the monarchy and the noble nation appears to be one over modernization, of progress versus regression. It is too easy, however, to oversimplify this complex issue. First of all, not everything that enlightened absolutism stood for can be subsumed under modernization. Second, enlightened absolutism was not the only way toward progress, for there remained the alternative mentioned by Voltaire: "freedom based on law." It may be described as enlightened constitutionalism in a monarchic or republican version, or briefly, enlightened liberty. An example of it was provided by the Polish constitution of May 3, 1791, and strivings in the same direction in Hungary.

Could a modernized and centralized state remain multinational, as all three countries of East Central Europe were? A process of discarding the truly international Latin and replacing it on grounds of greater efficiency by the dominant language or languages was bound to produce a reaction, and the beginnings of such a reaction were visible in the late eighteenth century in the Habsburg lands. Thus a promotion of enlightened absolutism under the conditions of a contest between the monarchy and the estates became complicated in Bohemia and Hungary by linguistic matters. In the Commonwealth policies aiming at greater uniformity were undermined by the territorial vastness and loose cohesion, as well as, during the first six decades, the dynastic union with Saxony.

The question whether Enlightenment in East Central Europe was an imported product has provoked some debate. The "Europeanization" of the region has suggested to some historians an analogy with Japan in the late nineteenth century or the so-called Third World in the twentieth century. This is a little contrived. Even if East Central Europe had undergone a certain orientalization and turned its back on the West in the course of the seventeenth century, even if Sarmatism and the "extra Hungariam non est vita" (there is no life outside Hungary) attitude prevailed, the region was an integral part of Europe. The stimuli it had received in the past, whether Christianity, Renaissance, Reformation, or Counter-Reformation had been fully absorbed. As the French historian L. Fabre put it, there was a fire in Poland that smouldered under the ashes accumulated during the seventeenth-century crises and the ensuing period of Saxon rule. But just a breath of air was needed for it to burst into flames. True, the socio-economic context of East Central Europe differed from that of the most developed parts of the West, but the issue was not that of transplanting foreign and

108

incompatible ideas, but rather of receiving and digesting them without risking loss of its own identity.

Enlightenment was coming mainly from France, and French, as the reformer Stanisław Konarski observed, was for Poles what Greek had been for the Romans. The *philosophes* took a keen if often critical interest in the region, which reciprocated the interest. The Hungarian readers of Montesquieu's *Spirit of the Laws* (published in Latin) appreciated his comment that monarchy without nobility degenerated into despotism. Rousseau's *Social Contract* was invoked when claims were made that Joseph II had broken his contract with the Hungarian nation. Rousseau's *Considerations on the Polish Government* were translated into Polish in 1789 and into Hungarian a year later. The involvement of French physiocrats with Polish magnates took place earlier in the century. True, such terms as "revolution," "patriot," "insurrection," as well as comparisons with the American and French Revolutions, were often distorted to suit the interests of the reformers or conservatives. The reforming zeal would lead to an imitation of everything foreign and a denigration of native achievements. "Poland is barely in the fifteenth century," exclaimed the versatile writer and politician Stanisław Staszic. "All of Europe is already finishing the eighteenth."[24] The partisans of reform donned the Western dress, and the famous quarrel between the "wig and the mustachioes" rocked the Commonwealth. At later stages, however, people would speak of absorption and integration of the new ideas into Polish culture and tradition, and of re-establishment of links with the West.

Enlightenment had a significant impact on the Jews of East Central Europe, the largest community on the continent and growing fast. By the end of the century it comprised perhaps close to 1 million in Poland, about 68,000 in Bohemia, and over 80,000 in Hungary – approaching 200,000 in the Habsburg monarchy as a whole. Enlightenment offered a challenge and a possibility of emancipation and assimilation. The Haskalah movement that originated in Berlin promoted modernization; the Hassidim who placed faith over learning and stressed separation from the gentile world were strongest in the Commonwealth. The rise of a sect called the Frankists resulted in their conversion to Christianity and subsequent merger in the Polish *szlachta*. The Jewish autonomy in Poland was weakened, however, in 1768 and attempts to work out a new constitutional arrangement were interrupted by the partitions.

In the Habsburg monarchy where Jews lived under much stricter discriminatory measures, Maria Theresa initiated some concessions although at one point she contemplated an expulsion of Jews from Bohemia and Moravia. Economic considerations played a role in the changing status of Jews. In Hungary especially the Jews were now filling the void left by the nobles in commerce and finance. The most sweeping measures came with Josephinism. Most of the restrictions were abolished, and the way opened to education, offices, and military service. Assimilation was promoted by compulsory adoption of German names in lieu of the traditional patronymics; in 1783 a Jewish school with German as the language of instruction appeared in the monarchy.

THE EARLY DECADES

Eighteenth-century Bohemia lived under the shadow cast by the White Mountain and all it stood for. Yet the notion of a dark age comparable to the Saxon period in Poland may be somewhat overdrawn. There was a steady population growth: 2.1 million in Bohemia and 900,000 in Moravia in 1754, and a total of 4 million forty years later. The population density of 40 per sq. km was similar to that of Western Europe. Towns, however, had declined, and even Prague appeared shabby to an English traveler who in 1716 noted only "some remains of its former splendour."[25]

The peasantry felt oppressed when more than 70 percent of its income was taken by the state, the church, and the landowner. The length of corvée (*Robot*) obligation was much greater than in Hungary, but after the 1680 peasant revolt in Bohemia the nobles found it harder to exact it. There were still peasant outbursts, as in 1717 and 1738 in Bohemia and in 1735 in Hungary.

The transformation of the nobility continued. By 1757 the old (pre-White Mountain) families dwindled to 87 (a 71 percent loss) and those of the 1620–54 vintage fell to 53, an even greater drop. With a steady influx of newcomers a foreign and "new" nobility constituted a majority by the middle of the century. Although some families, for instance the Kinskýs, were proud of their Czech descent, others regarded themselves merely as aristocrats of the Kingdom of Bohemia. Yet the fact that German and Italian speech prevailed did not necessarily mean denationalization, for patriotism was not really identified with language. Nor was there much to choose between the old and the new nobles regarding their social and political behavior; both groups displayed a good deal of indolence.

A certain political passivity on the part of the nobility could be gauged by its easy acquiescence in the most important document of the first half of the century, the Pragmatic Sanction, which provided for indivisibility of the Habsburg monarchy and extended hereditary rights to female descendants. The same nobility then elected Charles of Bavaria, who had challenged the Pragmatic Sanction, to Bohemia's kingship in 1741 when he entered the country.

The diet could no longer bargain over taxes. A lump sum being decreed by the government, the diet merely determined how to collect it. The executive committee of the diet (Landesausschuss, Zemský výbor) was a pliable instrument in the hands of the administration.

Important economic developments of the late eighteenth century will be discussed later, when we shall also touch on the origins of the national revival that belongs to the next chapter. At this point we may note the continuation of the culture of Counter-Reformation, the canonization of John Nepomuk marking the high point in 1729, and the steady progress of the German language. Among the few other developments one needs to stress the writings of Gelasius Dobner, in many ways the father of Bohemian historiography, and the paintings of Petr Brandl at home and Jan Kupecký aboard. As the ideas of Enlightenment entered the country, the Freemasons and Rosicrucians served as its propagators.

Hungary entered the second decade of the century under the sign of the Treaty of Szatmár, under which the Habsburgs promised to the Hungarians amnesty, religious freedom, respect of the constitution, and the calling of a diet. Yet the subsequent policies of reconstruction, which involved a transformation of the central government in the direction of greater efficiency and bureaucracy, and the repopulation of the country signally affected the course of events.

Szatmár carried full recognition of noble privileges and treated the political nation as a partner in control of the counties and the lower chamber of the diet. But already the resolutions of the diet in 1712–15 liquidated *de facto* the ineffective noble levy (insurrectio) and set up a standing Hungarian army, half of which was composed of foreigners and commanded by Austrian officers. Although the palatine was nominally the commander-in-chief, the army was subordinated to the War Council in Vienna, and financed by taxes paid by burghers and peasants.

In 1722–3 the central administration and judiciary were reorganized through the creation and transformation of main offices. The Lieutenancy Council (Consilium regium locumtenentiale) operated in Pozsony, and after 1785 in Buda. Although it was packed with loyal appointees the fact that its president was the elected palatine made it less submissive than its Bohemian counterpart. This changed toward the end of the century, with Habsburg archdukes becoming the last two palatines. The Hungarian Court Chancellery in Vienna was, unlike its Bohemian equivalent, an adjunct of the Lieutenancy Council. The third organ, the Hungarian Chamber (Camera) was in theory independent of the Hofkammer but its status was ambiguous. As mentioned, Transylvania, the Banat, and the Military Border retained their separate administrations; the diet's attempts to promote greater centralization in the lands of the Crown of St Stephen were viewed askance by Vienna. In matters of education, royal authority was firmly established.

Provisions on paper mattered less than actual practices and in that sense the authorities were on the offensive. As for basic constitutional changes the high point was reached with the Pragmatic Sanction through which the emperor-king wanted to assure the succession of his daughter, Maria Theresa, to all the Habsburg hereditary lands. The diet of Hungary accepted it in 1722, that of Transylvania a year earlier. The diet of Croatia, emphasizing its separate status, had already consented to the Pragmatic Sanction in 1721. All the lands of the Crown of St Stephen now formally became part of an "indivisible and inseparable" entity, although Hungary's special standing was confirmed.

The dominant position of aristocracy within the political nation continued, but the changes in its character and outlook became more pronounced. The enterprising and business-minded magnate of the preceding two centuries made room for the parasitic, often absentee landlord who ruined himself at the court in Vienna. Adopting French and German, he increasingly distanced himself from the gentry even in his speech. Ennobled high ranking officers and civilian officials joined the ranks of aristocracy. Most of the income of this group came now from seigneurial rights and monopolies, a great part of the manorial land being hired out to peasants. The commerce in oxen was in the hands of peasants or lesser nobles.

The gentry had passed the peak of their golden age, becoming more provincial and parochial. The exclusion of non-Catholics from public offices (1731) affected the largely Calvinist nobles. Although formally the Hungarian gentry was not banned from commerce and crafts like their Polish counterparts, the two groups had much in common. Both comprised the whole economic pyramid from landless and tax-paying gentleman to the wealthy nobleman, and both displayed a conservative and parochial mentality.

The position of the burghers whose most lucrative income came from winegrowing changed little, and if anything for the worse. The number of fairly small towns did not increase from pre-Mohács days. Some eight towns had the status of free royal cities and a population of over 10,000. In 1720 Buda had only 12,000 inhabitants and Pozsony around 8,000, and although half a century later the respective figures were 22,000 and 28,000, this was not much by urban standards of Europe. The burghers were hardly affected by political ideas coming from the West, and in that respect too the gentry was a potential or real third estate in the French sense. The lot of the peasantry grew worse, and most of the haiduks and free peasants were reduced to serfdom. More than half of the arable land was by mid-century in the hands of the nobility. Increased taxes and military obligations weighed heavily on the peasantry, contributing to such uprisings as that of the Serb peasants in 1735.

Devastations of the countryside going back to the Turkish wars and the more recent Rákóczi struggle, which cost the lives of some 85,000 soldiers and many more civilians, required policies of reconstruction and repopulation. It was fortunate that Hungary was no longer a battlefield; in the eighteenth century wars with Turkey were fought largely on Serb, Bosnian, or Wallachian lands. But wars and peace treaties of Passarowitz (Požarevac) and Belgrade affected population shifts, which were largely from the periphery toward the center of the country. Spontaneous migrations and government-sponsored settlements greatly changed the ethnic composition of Hungary. The numbers of Romanians and Serbs increased while settlements of Germans, the so-called Swabians, reached huge proportions (about 1 million people). It is estimated that the Magyars constituted only about 40 percent of the population toward the end of the century.

With the German language dominant in palaces and in the army, and with Latin at school, court, and the diet, Hungarian literature did not fare well during a good part of this period. A cultural and national revival began only in the second half of the century.

The developments in the Commonwealth showed both similarities and contrasts with Bohemia and Hungary. The ostentatious, vain, vulgar Polish and Lithuanian magnates with their huge clientele of impoverished gentry (an estimated 120,000 were landless) were ridiculed in Europe. But their power was incomparably greater than that of the Habsburg aristocrats. As for the political contest in the country, it was characterized, according to A. Kamiński, by three main trends: republicanism, constitutionalism, and monarchism. King Augustus II for his part pursued absolutist objectives.

Polish political culture of the early decades of the century had become an "exotic anachronism." Not only did the country lack a sizeable standing army, sufficient taxes, and a bureaucracy (the three ingredients necessary for modernization), but the prevalent view among the *szlachta* was that they were not needed. The vision of an anarchic society based on "golden liberty" and left in peace by its neighbors because it represented no threat to anyone was epitomized by the famous dictum "nierządem Polska stoi." It meant, loosely translated, that non-government was elevated to a system. The *szlachta* was not only losing civic virtues, but it was growing ever more bigoted and intolerant. In 1718 a Calvinist deputy was relegated from the *sejm*, and within the next twenty years non-Catholics lost the right to public offices and were permitted only a limited practice of their religion. A Catholic–Protestant riot in Toruń ended with death penalties for the Lutheran mayor and his associates; the "bloodbath" raised an outcry throughout Europe, the picture of an intolerant Poland being carefully cultivated by Berlin and St Petersburg.

These developments could hardly have been foreseen as the Commonwealth entered the eighteenth century. One could speak of its eclipse but not a collapse. Its throne was the object of ambition of both the French Prince de Conti and Augustus the elector of Saxony. The latter prevailed after a double election had taken place. A dynastic union of the Commonwealth and Saxony appeared at first glance a fortunate combination. Saxony could provide a power base for Augustus, who thought of further strengthening his position by gaining Livonia from Sweden. But Lutheran Saxony was incompatible with the huge amorphous and Catholic-ruled Commonwealth. The ambitions of the king, an alien monarch residing mainly in Dresden, aroused suspicions. His foreign policy plans courted disaster. In Rostworowski's happy phrase "the higher he aimed the deeper he sank."

Involving the unwilling Poland in the Northern War against Sweden in 1700 Augustus II miscalculated badly. Charles XII of Sweden not only defeated Peter the Great of Russia, Augustus's chief ally, but invaded and devastated Poland, drove Augustus to Saxony and forced him to abdicate. Charles's hand-picked candidate, the youthful Leszczyński, was elected as King Stanislas. By 1709, however, the situation changed drastically, as the crushing Swedish defeat at Poltava allowed Augustus to return to Poland. But it also made him dependent on Peter the Great, a dependence he subsequently tried to shake. His chances were small, as the situation in the country turned from bad to worse.

The slow process of the Commonwealth's recovery from the seventeenth-century devastations was not only halted but drastically reversed. Damages inflicted by Swedish, Saxon, and Russian troops were staggering, and the bubonic plague helped to devastate the population which sank perhaps to some 6 or 7 million inhabitants. The political picture was chaotic. The prestige of the king had plummeted and the warring pro-Saxon and pro-Swedish factions were out of hand. The hetmans (top military commanders), who had become an independent political factor in the state, were thwarting the king and engaging in negotiations with foreign courts. One could speak of the disintegration of sovereignty. During Augustus's reign 10 out of 18 sessions of the *sejm* came to naught. The king's plans to promote absolutism in the Commonwealth and to make the crown hereditary in his own House of Wettin were compromised by the defeats in the Northern War; his subsequent plans of a coup backed by Saxon troops produced a backlash. Peter the Great stepped between a powerful confederation – which to a large extent he manipulated – and the king. The "Silent Sejm" (deputies were forbidden to make speeches) held in the presence of Russian troops accepted a settlement. The Saxon troops had to go home, but a small standing army financed out of permanent taxes was set up, the power of the hetmans became somewhat limited and the local *sejmiks* weakened. Thus it may be an exaggeration to speak of a final defeat of the king or of a turning point in Russo-Polish relations. Had Augustus succeeded in his new policy of mounting a coalition to curb the growing power of Petrine Russia, the position of the Commonwealth might have improved greatly. But his motives were suspected at home, and Prussia and Russia confirmed their joint policy of maintaining the Commonwealth in a state of anarchy. Defeated, Augustus concentrated his efforts on assuring the succession of his son. The issue became pressing with the king's death in 1733.

Once again a double election took place and force decided the issue. The re-elected King Stanislas Leszczyński had much of the country behind him, but he was driven out by Saxon and Russian armies. The subsequent War of the Polish Succession was fought on the Rhine and had no impact on Poland, where Augustus III was recognized king. Leszczyński, however, whose daughter married Louis XV, was compensated with the Duchy of Lorraine as a dowry to be passed eventually to France.

Unlike his father, Augustus III was indolent and uninterested in politics. During his absentee rule none of the *sejms* completed its sessions. Poland watched powerless the annexation of the once-Polish Silesia by Frederick II of Prussia. In spite of being neutral, the country had its territory violated by the marching armies of Russia and Prussia and was inundated by debased currency. Poland was turning into a "wayside inn" for unwanted and unpaying guests.

With absolutist designs discredited and "golden liberty" promoting chaos, a constitutional program of reform seemed to offer the only chance of strengthening the *sejm*, creating a central executive, putting order into fiscal and military affairs, developing commerce and industry, rebuilding towns, and taking the miserable and exploited peasant under the protection of the state.

Leszczyński's re-election had momentarily brought some fresh air into Polish politics, and subsequently his court in Luneville became a center of early Enlightenment that radiated into Poland. The *Free Voice*, which he either wrote or inspired, attacked the Sarmatian mentality that regarded all progress as foreign. The Piarist Szymon Konarski, who was the first to use the word "Sarmatism" in a pejorative sense, contrasted Polish backwardness with the achievements of other republican regimes: Venice, Switzerland, the Netherlands, and, strange as it may seem to us, England. His *Way of Effective Counsels* even dared to denounce liberum veto itself. His writings apart, Konarski's real contribution lay in the field of education, and the medal he later received inscribed "to him who dared to be wise" stressed his pioneering role. Konarski was convinced that the Commonwealth could not overcome its backwardness unless a new elite was trained in modern ideas and civic virtues. A member of the Piarist Order, Konarski reformed their network of schools by stressing foreign languages and sciences in their curricula. The schools were among the first to introduce the ideas of the Enlightenment into Poland. The elitist Collegium Nobilium, set up in Warsaw in 1740, served as a model. Soon Jesuit schools followed suit.

There were other indications of change. In Warsaw the magnificent Załuski collection became the first public library in the country. Its manuscripts and books would eventually (after Poland's partitions) be carried off by Russia to St Petersburg to become part of its budding university.

Changes in the economy might justifiably be called a first phase of a proto-industrial development. Peace, which came to the Commonwealth after the Northern War, lasted for several decades, creating favorable conditions for economic activity. The 1720–60 period was characterized by the rise of manufactories operated mainly by serf labor and situated on magnates' estates, which produced glass, textiles, and metal objects for the internal market. Agriculture began to recover, with rising grain exports through Gdańsk benefiting the landowning *szlachta*. Foreign workers and specialists were brought into the country, mainly from Saxony, but also from France and Italy. Clearly, progress was slow and the conservative and parochial outlook still prevailed. But it was obvious to the reformers that the political system demanded far-reaching changes and that the Commonwealth had to be strengthened to be able to face Russia, Prussia, or the Habsburg monarchy, then in the process of major transformations.

MARIA THERESA AND JOSEPHINISM

In the middle of the century Europe was shaken by two major conflicts: the War of the Austrian Succession (1740–8) and the Seven Years War (1756–63). The Habsburg monarchy was not only one of the main participants in both wars, but its nature was greatly affected by them. The first conflict began in 1740 when Maria Theresa's right of succession to the Habsburg possessions was challenged by Frederick II of Prussia, who suddenly invaded Silesia. In turn Charles of Bavaria claimed the imperial throne, which Maria Theresa as a woman could not occupy, and the Bohemian Crown, and marched on Prague. A Prussian-Bavarian-Saxon agreement threatened to bring about a veritable partition of the lands of the Crown of St Wenceslas: Bohemia going to the Bavarian Wittelsbachs, Silesia to the Hohenzollern, Upper Silesia and Moravia to the Wettins. In this critical situation Maria Theresa appealed to the Hungarians, who in a dramatic scene at the diet offered their "life and blood" to the ruler. Maria Theresa never completely forgot this Hungarian support just as she never quite forgave the nobility of Bohemia the election of her rival Charles.

The hostilities, which centered mainly on Silesian and Czech soil, showed the superiority of the militarily and financially efficient Prussia over the vast Habsburg monarchy. The outcome was a loss of virtually all Silesia and it was keenly felt. This was one of the economically best developed provinces, with textile and metallurgical production that accounted for some 21 percent of the Habsburg revenue (Hungary excluded). It was also an important customer for grain and semi-finished goods as well as an outlet to, and major component of the northern trade. At this time it still had a significant Polish-speaking population. To strengthen the state after this loss the monarchy introduced a 10 percent increase in the army budget, began a tariff war designed to ruin the now Prussian Silesia, and launched a program for industrializing Bohemia while encouraging Hungary as an agrarian reservoir of the Habsburg lands.

The economic reforms of Maria Theresa and of her son Joseph II were designed not only to compensate for the loss of Silesia, but constituted a response to the mounting economic crisis characterized, among other things, by low productivity and low living standards. The desire to emulate the Dutch and the English had been already present among late seventeenth-century economists. Officials in Bohemia argued for new fiscal policies, a systematic promotion of manufactories, and the bringing in of experts from Protestant countries, which would require religious toleration. It seemed evident that the state needed to interfere in lord–peasant relations not only on humanitarian but also on economic grounds. Early attempts, such as those of Charles VI in 1723, had remained on paper.

Before turning to the developments in Bohemia and Hungary one needs to look briefly at the general character of the reforms of Maria Theresa and Joseph. By and large those of the empress aimed mainly at the preservation and strengthening of the Habsburg inheritance. Its cohesion was to be increased through centralization, greater administrative and legal unity, and educational and socio-economic measures designed to raise the living standards. Josephinism, while pursuing similar goals, was ideologically motivated and hence more doctrinaire. It represented in a way the classic case of enlightened absolutism with the slogan "everything for the people, nothing by the people." Josephine reforms were novel in the sense of seeking in the name of state interest to limit not only the political powers of the nobility but even their privileges. Rational and utilitarian motives were behind such reforms as civil marriage, equal inheritance rights for women, or the fostering of German language as a uniform vehicle of communication in administration and higher education. Joseph's zeal and haste in pushing through the reforms were politically unwise and contributed to the noble reaction and the withdrawal of many of his laws. One that remained, although circumvented in practice, was a partial emancipation of the peasantry.

The approach of the state to the peasant question under Maria Theresa was illustrated by her saying that sheep should be well fed in order to yield more wool and more milk. To make the peasantry a productive class in society, furnishing recruits to the army and paying taxes, one had to define the minimal size of serfs' holdings and the maximum amount of their obligations. This meant encroaching on the rights of noble landowners, who treated the serfs as personal and legal subjects as well as tools for the working of the estate. Through a series of so-called urbarial patents or urbaria – 1771 for Austria, 1767 for Hungary, and 1775 for Bohemia and Moravia where a major uprising occurred that year – the peasants were classified and their obligations defined and reduced. Subsequently, the *Robot* (corvée) was replaced on estates of the Crown by rent, and the personal subjection (*Leibeigenschaft*) terminated. In his 1781 decree Joseph made this last provision applicable to all landed estates. It meant that the peasant was free to marry, move, and choose a profession. Judicial dependence on the lord was replaced by a rather complex state–landlord joint arrangement. Joseph's decree was introduced in Hungary and Transylvania in 1785. In the latter country, where no urbaria had been applied, it came in the wake of a mainly Romanian peasants' uprising against Hungarian nobles in 1784, and did not prevent another outbreak in 1786. For all the benefits brought by the reforms, they were a mixed blessing, for the peasants had now to pay higher taxes and serve long years in the army, except in Hungary which remained free of military conscription.

Reforms in the administrative field, complex and changing, coupling and decoupling political and fiscal matters, cannot be presented here in any detail. The same is true for a multitude of reforms in ecclesiastical, educational, and other domains. On the all-Austrian level we must note policies aiming at the creation or reorganization of central organs in Vienna, backed by paid bureaucracy and police. By the same token the diets lost their administrative and patronage powers – a crucial development – and were now to be called at royal will. In order to avoid the restraints of the coronation oath, Joseph refused to be crowned king of Hungary or of Bohemia and had the holy crown of St Stephen taken to a museum in Vienna. Going beyond the traditional Habsburg policies of curbing the independent power of the Catholic Church, Joseph practically cut its ties with Rome in all but purely spiritual matters.

Acting on his own he taxed or dissolved "unproductive" monastic orders. In 1781 Joseph issued the Toleration Decree that granted the right of open religious worship to Protestants and Orthodox, and access to offices.

A reform of education undertaken by Maria Theresa gained momentum after the dissolution of the Jesuit Order in 1773. Under the 1777 Ratio Educationis the state strove to establish a comprehensive and uniform secular system of education for all nationalities and all denominations. While the emphasis was put on higher and secondary education, primary schools in every parish represented the greatest achievement of the reform.

Let us turn now to the lands of St Wenceslas which had lost, with Silesia, nearly half of its territory and become closely integrated with Austrian lands properly speaking. While ties between Austria and Bohemia (referred to as the "hereditary German crownlands") grew stronger, those between Bohemia, Moravia, and the small remnants of Silesia weakened. After the abolition of the Bohemian Court Chancellery in 1749, a joint Bohemian and Austrian Court Chancellery was established in 1762. Separate gubernatorial offices in Bohemia and Moravia presided over a local administration composed no longer of dignitaries drawn from the estates but of appointed bureaucrats.

The Czech language was rapidly losing ground in courts and administration as well as in the reorganized school system. By and large the Bohemian schools achieved higher standards than their Austrian or Hungarian counterparts; in the period 1779–91 the number of elementary schools doubled and that of the students tripled. Czech was still the language of instruction at these schools, but not on higher levels. At the university of Prague German was introduced; a Czech language chair existed only at the university of Vienna.

The process of economic integration was assisted by the elimination of all internal tariffs in 1775; the only barrier that remained was that between Hungary and the rest of the monarchy. Cameralist policies were applied more rigidly in the 1750–70 period and more flexibly thereafter. It was not determined whether tariffs were to be purely protectionist or designed to stimulate production, hence there were inconsistencies. The exclusion of imports of better quality merchandise contributed to the growth of domestic production, although not always of comparable standards. Trade as a whole was adversely affected. Nevertheless Bohemia now became the most developed part of the monarchy. Factories were founded, capital accumulated, and both management and labor gained experience even though the Germans of Bohemia, constituting roughly a third of the population, may have profited more than the Czechs from this development.

Textile production, based in the late seventeenth century on a

119

putting-out system and the exportation of raw linen, now entered a pre-industrial stage characterized by concentration in manufactories, although individual producers were still in the majority. About 95 percent of Bohemia's industrial workers were in textiles, but in 1775 these workers represented only 10 percent of the total population. A similar figure in England covered just the workers in the woolen industry. Another important branch of manufacturing was of glass. Mining and metal products were of lesser significance; iron manufactories and coal mining were still in their infancy.

The government sought to assist economic development by indirect means (for instance, elimination of internal tariffs and tolls), by weakening guilds and by creating inducements to producers. Governmental interventions were not overly successful with merchants and artisans. It was otherwise with the nobility, who frequently assumed an entrepreneurial role; the Waldstein woolen mills, for instance, were the oldest in the country.

While the proto-industrial sector led the way, Bohemia also experienced progress in agriculture. The three-field system was abandoned and there was increased productivity. Potatoes became the main food staple in the second half of the century. At the time of the 1791 census Bohemia, which accounted for 10 percent of the area and 14 percent of the population of the Habsburg monarchy (Galicia excluded) produced 25 to 35 percent of the revenue. Prague reached a figure of 70,000 inhabitants.

Material progress offered a contrast to the modest beginnings of a cultural Czech revival. A few aristocrats showed interest in the Czech language of their ancestors. A private learned society transformed itself in 1790 into the Bohemian Royal Society and gained support from literary German circles including Goethe himself. German was the language in which Josef Dobrovský published his pioneering *History of Bohemian Language and Literature* in 1792. Regarded as one of the forerunners of the Czech national revival of the nineteenth century, Dobrovský was pessimistic about the future of the Czech nation.

Eighteenth-century Hungary differed from Bohemia in most respects. In the economic field, the loss of Silesia early in the century and the partitions of Poland in the last decades adversely affected Hungarian trade. Tariffs introduced by the Habsburgs further shaped its character. External tariffs (in 1754–5) cut Hungary from its traditional northern export markets (of wine) and the southern ones (of cattle). A tariff barrier separated the country (including Transylvania, for the customs border between the two was abolished in 1784) from the rest of the monarchy. It favored the production of Austrian and Bohemian finished goods while encouraging Hungarian wool and especially wheat. Before the middle of the century textiles and metal products already accounted for 56.5 percent of imports; cattle and foodstuffs constituted over 80 percent of exports. Between 1748 and 1782 the export of wheat, grown mainly on large estates, increased fivefold. The ratio between cattle and cereals exports was changing: 2:1 in 1767, 1.6:1 in 1785. The process was accompanied by the modernization of the big estates, which involved crop rotation and resulted in increased yields.

Trade mainly enriched the magnates, although towns dependent on Austro-Bohemian commerce benefited too. Growth of manufactories was modest. Textile mills (the first cloth manufactory appeared in 1722), ceramic and leather workshops, gold and silver mining, and some coal extraction (1759 onwards) were all on a small scale. Hungarian industrial workers represented less than 1 percent of the total population, proportionately a tenth of the workforce in Bohemia. This period saw the beginnings of accumulation of capital among Greek, Serb, and Armenian merchants, and later on a larger scale by the rapidly expanding Jewish merchant community. Controlling the wool and tobacco trades, and penetrating into agrarian production, the Jews played a major role in the modest industrial take-off. Unable, before the emancipation, to buy land or occupy offices, they reinvested their capital in business. Here was the nucleus of a bourgeoisie, with a few families on the top acquiring noble status.

The Hungarian nobility was unable to prevent peasant reforms and growing state intervention, but it stubbornly refused to be taxed. Repeated government proposals being rejected, Vienna had little incentive in developing the noble-controlled (and tax-exempt) Hungarian economy. Joseph II, however, decided to bring Hungary more strictly in line with the other lands. In addition to certain administrative changes designed to subordinate Hungary to Vienna, he decreed the replacement of counties by administrative districts headed by appointed officials, and then the introduction of German as the official language of administration, courts, and education. Since Latin and Hungarian (only the latter in Transylvania) were official languages, this was a drastic change and received with much indignation. It appeared that Joseph's next move would be general taxation.

The unsuccessful war against Turkey and the outbreak of the French Revolution in 1789 forced Joseph to abandon his plans. In 1790 he withdrew most of his reforms, except for the decrees on toleration and the peasantry. Did enlightened absolutism in Hungary fail? Was there another alternative? How should one appraise the contest between the ruler and the political nation? To some historians the monarchy was the carrier of progress while the nobility pursued retrograde policies. Others stressed that the political nation represented a superior form of government and was the true carrier of national interest. Vienna, they said, was guided less by a program of Enlightenment and more by a desire to exploit Hungary, especially in the economic field.

Before looking briefly at contemporary attitudes and programs, a few words must be said about Enlightenment in Hungary. The ideas of Enlightenment were spreading in the country partly as a result of policies from above, for instance in the field of education, partly as a result of exposure to French political thought. French *philosophes* were avidly read in Vienna, particularly among the Hungarian guards created by Maria Theresa, and at German universities frequented by Hungarians. Freemasonry provided a channel and an organizational form for the dissemination of the new ideas in Hungary. Its first lodge was founded in 1769 – a branch of the Grande Loge de Varsovie associated with the Grand Orient. The number of lodges grew rapidly and those in Croatia, influenced later by Count Janko Drašković, acquired a distinctly political character. Eventually Hungarian and Croatian lodges separated. Joseph II was inimical to Freemasonry, in which he saw outside influences.

While French- and German-speaking aristocrats played a major role in the cultural revival, the Protestant gentry that could, after the toleration decree, enter administration and politics, often affected it in an anti-Habsburg and national Hungarian spirit. Changes in education were, of course, of crucial importance. The Benedictines in Hungary (and Bohemia) attempted to emulate Konarski's Collegium Nobilium in Poland. In the 1760s the Collegium Oeconomicum was founded. In Hungary the state-supervised system under the Ratio Educationis covered one university (by then situated in Buda), three royal academies, and some 130 colleges and secondary schools with a population of 13,000 students. Instruction on the lowest level was in Magyar, German, Slovak, Ruthenian, Croatian, and Romanian. Textbooks and grammars were published in all these languages. Epitomizing this type of universalist Enlightenment was the pedagogue Matej Bél, who described himself as "lingua Slavus, natione Hungarus, eruditione Germanus." Public libraries appeared, and there seems to have been a relatively large reading public. The first fortnightly paper in Hungarian came out in the 1780s; the first permanent Hungarian theater was opened in Transylvania a few years later.

Imbued with the ideas of Enlightenment, some members of the nobility and of the nascent intelligentsia favored Josephinism insofar as it stood for secularization of administrative and educational systems, religious toleration, and improvements in the lot of the peasants. The more radical groups viewed enlightened absolutism as leading toward the abolition of feudalism and paving the way for a bourgeois-type society. After 1790 they turned for inspiration to the French Revolution. The moderates, who deeply resented Joseph's efforts to replace the

Hungarian constitutional regime by a centralized government run by a German-speaking bureaucracy, developed an enlightened noble program comparable to and partly inspired by a similar one in Poland. Several figures of the literary world assumed the leadership of the movement. They included György Bessenyei, the "Hungarian Voltaire," whose *Tragedy of Agis* (1772) marked the beginning of Enlightenment and of national awakening in Hungarian literature. Bessenyei affirmed as a true man of Enlightenment that the world was his fatherland and the human race his nationality. But he also wrote that "every nation has become knowledgeable by [using] its own and never a foreign language,"[26] heralding the nascent modern nationalism. Ferenc Kazinczy, a poet and politician, most representative of Hungarian classicism, stimulated and inspired native literary life. Mihály Vitéz Csokonai was the most outstanding lyric poet. Gergely Berzeviczy pioneered classical economic thinking in the country, and may be regarded as the leading theorist of a program that could compete with enlightened absolutism. It opposed despotism, peasant oppression, and the fiscal immunity of the nobility, and strove to reconcile a modernization of the traditional social, economic, and political structures with the concept of sovereignty vested jointly in the nation and the ruler. Translated into a political platform of action the enlightened liberal movement reached its peak during the 1790 crisis that affected Hungary and Bohemia. It needs to be treated jointly with the events in Poland to which we shall now turn.

ENLIGHTENED LIBERTY AND ITS DEMISE

Enlightenment reached its high point in the Commonwealth after the election of Stanislas Augustus (Poniatowski) to the Polish-Lithuanian throne in 1764. The new king was related to the powerful Czartoryski clan, known as "familia." It was committed to republican constitutionalism that would place all power in a reformed *sejm* thus ending the king–*sejm* dualism. The Family came to the conclusion that domestic reforms were only possible in cooperation with Russia, but the Empress Catherine II disappointed them, first by applying brakes, second by withholding support to their candidate, and imposing her ex-lover, Poniatowski, as ruler. Being a *homo novus*, although related to the Czartoryskis, he was despised by the magnates. As a king he developed his own program of constitutional monarchism. Stanislas Augustus had not only to contend with the Czartoryskis whose tutelage he resented, but with other factions, the most powerful of which was the archconservative "republican" group, attached to "golden liberty" and led by the Potocki and Radziwiłł clans. The "republicans" placed their faith in France and Turkey standing against Russia.

The last king of Poland has been the object of controversies that have not disappeared with time. His critics see him as Catherine's tool, weak, immoral, corrupt, who ended up by betraying his country through capitulation to Russia. They cannot, however, deny that he was a man of keen intelligence, cultured, witty, charming, tolerant, and a great patron of arts and learning. Stanislas's defenders point out that he was a much more adroit politician than he was given credit for, flexible in tactics and consistent in his strivings for reform. He was not a military leader or a top diplomatist, and his weaknesses were very much those of the age he lived in. Confronted with a nearly hopeless situation, he did not display the virtues that the Poles particularly cherish: heroism till death and unblemished honor.

According to the papal nuncio the king "had the talent, the knowledge and above all the strongest desire to reform" as rapidly as possible, the state, the society, and the economy, bringing the Commonwealth up to the level of the more advanced nations. But reforms had to be accomplished through compromises and carried out jointly by the ruler and the political nation. Education in the new ideas was crucial and Stanislas Augustus established the Knights' School, the first secular college to train the country's elite. Most of the reforms which ensued had either the king's backing or were inspired by him and his associates. The newly established national theater and the national press played a major role in shaping the outlook of the leading circles. The bitingly satiric poems of Bishop Ignacy Krasicki, the greatest classicist poet, had a didactic character.

The two great ideologues of the Polish Enlightenment were Stanisław Staszic, a burgher, and Hugo Kołłątaj. The first believed that in order to overcome the country's backwardness it was necessary to go through the stage of a strong monarchy. Kołłątaj disagreed and formulated a program of new republicanism. In contrast to the old estate-based noble republican creed, new republicanism contained universally valid elements: a limited government, consent of the governed, civic rights. His writings, like those of Staszic, attained high levels of political discourse, and contributed signally to the alliance of politics and education that characterized Enlightenment in the Commonwealth.

Outstanding writers, scholars, scientists, economists, often combining various genres, included the poets S.Trembecki and F. Karpiński, the versatile J. U. Niemcewicz, and the critical historian A. Naruszewicz. The reformist movement centered on Warsaw, whose population grew from 30,000 to 125,000 between 1764 and 1792, and became a real political, cultural, and economic center. The other towns were just beginning to recover. Cracow appeared to a Scottish traveler as "a great capital in ruins"; Wilno had about 21,000 inhabitants. But the burghers who constituted about 17 percent of the population (including the 10 percent Jews) were starting to make their voice heard. The country gentry naturally regarded the urbanization of culture and the program of the reformers as ungodly and foreign. Indeed, the contrast between Warsaw and the countryside was striking. But change was in the air.

Banks, joint stock ventures, and new factories appeared. In 1764 the mint was opened and a general post office came into being. Weights and measures were standardized. Stanislas Augustus's patronage was most visible in arts, but he also displayed initiative in other areas: canal building, mining of hard coal, wool processing. An attempt to build a network of factories on royal lands in Lithuania proved largely a failure, but there was a growth of old magnate manufactories to which new ones were added, with royal and then with bourgeois capital invested in them. In western Poland a great textile center developed; artisans and hired workers replaced the serfs. When Poland was cut off from the Baltic after the first partition in 1772 a Black Sea trading company came into existence, reorienting exports toward the south-east.

In agriculture grain production increased, potatoes were introduced, and stock breeding developed. The belief that land was the source of all wealth, as preached by French physiocrats, provoked counter-arguments: surely, urbanization and industrial production would increase the volume of exchanges between town and countryside and enrich all? The need for money led to commutation of labor to rents in better developed areas and on great estates. Commutation was a limited phenomenon and it was argued that serfdom *per se* was not the cause of backwardness which stemmed from the general economic structure of the country. The home market was still in its infancy; the absence of protectionism was detrimental to new manufactories. The trade balance remained unfavorable, and although exports increased they did not reach the sixteenth-century levels. Still, for all its weaknesses the Commonwealth was evolving economically and was not behind Hungary or even Moravia. The population grew to roughly 12 million people, and while the density was about 15–19 people per sq. km, in the more advanced provinces of Poznania or south-western Poland it was 30 or even 50.

The Commonwealth continued to be handicapped by low revenue, military weakness, and the international context in which it operated. Europe was then split between two alignments: the northern system, based on the Russo–Prussian alliance and enjoying some backing from England, Sweden, and Denmark, and the southern system with Austria, France, and Spain. Berlin wished to keep the Commonwealth anarchic and hoped for territorial acquisitions at its expense. St Petersburg tried to maintain it in a state of dependence (half-protectorate, half-alliance) so as to have free hands *vis-à-vis* Turkey. Polish diplomacy had the difficult task of seeking to make its domestic reforms acceptable to its powerful neighbors.

In 1764–8 first steps were taken: a limitation of liberum veto, an attempted tariff barrier along frontiers, the Knights' School, and a medical academy. The seigneurial courts were forbidden to pass death sentences. This was a prelude; Stanislas Augustus was aiming at a comprehensive program of reform. Russia and Prussia threatened Warsaw with war if it was attempted and demanded instead complete political equality to non-Catholics (dissidents). The use of the dissident issue was a favorite stratagem to intervene in Polish internal affairs under the guise of humanitarian concerns. Stanislas Augustus was willing to risk the opposition of the church and the *szlachta* on the question of non-Catholics, hoping to obtain in exchange Catherine's blessings for political reforms. He found himself isolated at home (even the Czartoryskis abandoned him) and unable to gain anything from St Petersburg, which was checkmating him by fomenting two anti-royalist confederations: a Catholic and a Protestant-Orthodox. In a series of complex moves and counter-moves – at one point the Russians kidnapped two senators and literally forced the *sejm* to grant rights to dissidents – St Petersburg solemnly guaranteed free election, liberum veto, right of rebellion, noble monopoly of offices and landed estates, in short all that had rendered the Commonwealth incapable of reforming itself.

Worse still, the dissident affair provoked the launching of the Bar confederation, perhaps the most controversial in Polish history. Inspired by the hatred of the king, whom the confederates at one point briefly kidnapped, the Bar confederation was intensely patriotic, anti-Russian, Catholic to the point of fanaticism, and attached to freedom in the conservative Sarmatian version. It had in its ranks a number of magnates as well as lesser gentry – Kazimierz Puɫaski who later died at Savannah, Georgia, was one of the leaders – and it fought Russian troops and royal regiments for several years. The Bar confederation brought about and was influenced by such disparate developments as peasant (*haidamak*) uprisings in the Ukraine, the French help it received, and finally the sultan's declaration of war on Russia. The "eastern question" was born.

The king unsuccessfully tried to make some capital out of the war. As Russian victories over Turkey and fears of a change in the balance of power led to Austro-Russian tension, Prussia proposed a peace settlement at the expense of the Commonwealth. Austria had already furnished a precedent by annexing the Spisz region in 1769–70; now, after some hesitation on Catherine's part the treaty of partition was signed in 1772, which the defenseless Commonwealth had to ratify. Russia gained territories along the Dnieper River and in the north;

Prussia annexed the lands of the former Polish Pomerania (but without Gdańsk and Toruń, see p. 128); Austria took the southern provinces to which it extended the name of Galicia. For all the elaborate claims and historical justifications that were advanced, the partition was a clear case of victory of might over right. Edmund Burke was one of the few eminent contemporaries who condemned the operation as a very serious breach of the European system.

The Russian policies that had led to the first partition were now revised. Within the truncated Commonwealth, now exposed to the Prussian economic stranglehold, St Petersburg approved limited reforms. The initiative came from above, and as Gierowski aptly put it, the Commonwealth undertook a series of measures typical for an absolute monarchy without changing the character of the noble republic. The new constitution of 1775 introduced a kind of large cabinet subdivided into departments and called the Permanent Council. It was composed of a number of senators and deputies elected by the diet and taking decision by a majority vote. Hated as a Russian creation – and indeed it was meant to be a channel through which Russia could exert its influence more effectively – it put some order into fiscal and administrative matters. Had the *sejm* been also reformed it would have meant real political change, but the powers prevented it.

In 1773 the dissolution of the Jesuit order permitted the creation of the Commission of National Education, which shared with the Austrian Studien-Hofkommission the claim to be Europe's first ministry of education. It was responsible to the king and presided over a reconstruction of the educational system. A hierarchy of schools, headed by the reformed universities of Cracow and Wilno, with a modernized curriculum and Polish as the language of instruction, was set up. Only the primary schools remained in the hands of parishes and were somewhat neglected.

By 1774 the Polish press became more important as a vehicle of reform, the number of journals and newspapers jumping to fourteen. The new élan of cultural life, and the heights reached by literature, theater, painting, architecture, even sciences, seem to justify the use of the term the "Age of Stanislas". Yet, there were clear limits to the extent of reforms. Abolition of torture and witch trials, the creation of a police department, and modernization of a small army were tolerated. But when a major project of codification of laws was presented by Chancellor Andrzej Zamoyski the conservative *sejm*, backed by Russian power, rejected it. Stanislas Augustus seemed to have lost the initiative, and St Petersburg deemed it safe to withdraw its troops in 1780. Two years later, however, Rousseau published his *Considerations* with a motto taken from the speech of a Polish politician: "I prefer dangerous freedom to quiet servitude." The Poles were not giving in.

Rousseau's ideas about a strengthened republican regime in a Commonwealth transformed into a federation were part of the Western Enlightenment influences then affecting Poland. The Poles referred to the English parliamentary experiences, invoked the American ideas, particularly the Declaration of Independence, and listened to the message of the French Revolution, all the while debating the Commonwealth's future at the so-called Great *Sejm* (1788–92). For four years the international context was such that the Poles could breathe more freely. Russia and Austria were involved in a new Turkish war. Prussia, estranged from the two, drew closer to England. Stanislas Augustus first sought to join with Russia against the Ottoman Empire. Rebuffed, he steered in the direction of Berlin and London. The result was the March 1790 Polish–Prussian alliance whose merits and demerits have been debated ever since by historians. From Warsaw's viewpoint the alliance made sense, but the *sejm*'s refusal to pay Prussia's price for it (surrender Gdańsk and Toruń) made it of problematic value. In July Berlin reached an accord with Vienna which deprived the alliance of its *raison d'être*. Eventually, Berlin refused to remain allied to a Commonwealth that could become too strong and threaten Prussia's security.

For four years the Poles were advancing toward the May 3 constitution. Internal divisions and the need to overcome the opposition of the traditionalist noble masses precluded rapid change. It was necessary to dismantle existing structures such as the Permanent Council before constructing a new edifice. Drawn-out debates, occasionally degenerating into rhetorical contests at the *sejm* were accompanied by rich polemical literature. Basically, a threefold division existed: the die-hard conservatives (or the "false patriots"); the republican patriots; and the king. The first group wanted to make the Commonwealth a federation of semi-independent units (heaven for magnates), base the army on noble levies, and either emasculate the monarchy or abolish it altogether. The real, or republican, patriots evolved from republicanism toward constitutional monarchism, realizing that the American federal republic might be an ideal, but it was not attainable under Polish conditions. Their way of thinking was meeting that of Stanislas Augustus who favored a constitutional monarchy, somewhat on the English model, doing away with Polish-Lithuanian dualism, and extending concessions to burghers and peasants.

The burghers, as already mentioned, were asserting themselves. Parallel to the *sejm*-elected commission working on the constitution, a delegation of 141 towns was pressing for civic and political rights for the burghers. The outcome was the acceptance of the Statute of the Cities, which extended to the inhabitants of royal towns the right of protection against arbitrary arrest (neminem captivabimus), the right to own land, some representation in the *sejm*, assured municipal self-government, and easier access to nobility. Neminem captivabimus was subsequently also granted to the Jews, and Stanislas Augustus exceeded the number of ennoblements (ten annually) of Jewish converts to Christianity.

The constitution was rushed through on May 3, 1791 when many of the opposing deputies were absent. With troops placed on the alert, burghers acting as a pressure group, and enthusiastic crowds in the streets, people sensed that they were witnessing a revolutionary event. The constitution was passed in the name of the nation, and it affirmed that all authority stemmed from the nation. The peasantry was described as the "most numerous part of the nation" and placed under the protection of the government. The landless gentry that had long formed the magnates' clientele was disenfranchised when a property or financial qualification was declared necessary for voting rights. The constitution provided for full religious freedom.

The Commonwealth became a constitutional monarchy based on a separation of powers, and hereditary (after Stanislas Augustus's death) in the Saxon Wettin House. The king named ministers (who were responsible to the *sejm*), and exerted full executive powers jointly with the council. He was no longer, in his own right, one of the three elements of authority (king, senate, chamber). In fact, it was the chamber of deputies, regarded as the carrier of national will, that became the sovereign body. Twenty-four deputies from the royal cities took their seats in it. The importance of the senate dwindled. Liberum veto was abolished. Finally, a Reciprocal Warranty of Both Nations marked the evolution to a unitary Commonwealth in which the Poles and Lithuanians were assured complete equality. A standing army of 100,000, financed by a special tax, a direct tax imposed on the *szlachta*, was described as a defensive arm of the nation.

The constitution did not abandon the concept of estates, but by affirming that they all constituted the nation gave a modern meaning to "nation." The changes were undoubtedly revolutionary and hard to accept by the conservative and parochial masses. Had they been accompanied by far-reaching socio-economic reforms the whole edifice might have been jeopardized. But the reformers began work on a project of an economic constitution dealing with property relations, investments, protection of labor, and "a right of perpetual ownership" of land by the peasants. Obligations to the manor were to assume the form of contracts under governmental protection. The plan for a comprehensive Jewish reform was to follow.

The constitution of May 3 that won high praise of such men as George Washington and Edmund Burke filled its authors with pride. The *sejm*'s marshal (the speaker) declared that it had borrowed what was best and most suitable from the two "republican" governments, the English and the American, while obviously drawing on native republican traditions. Karl Marx was to bestow the highest accolade:

> Despite its shortcomings, this constitution looms up against the background of Russo-Prusso-Austrian barbarism as the only work of liberty that Eastern Europe has ever accomplished independently. And it emerged exclusively from the privileged class, from the nobility. The history of the world has never seen another example of such noble behavior of the nobility.[27]

Modern historians rated the constitution highly. R. R. Palmer reminds us that none of the neighboring states where enlightened absolutism prevailed could claim to possess an elected parliamentary body with such wide powers, a comparable municipal self-government, or similar rights for the burghers to own landed property. The German historian Jörg Hoensch has shown that the reformers were not oblivious of the socio-economic evolutionary trends, as older German and Russian historiography had asserted. The modernization of the state was carried out by parliamentary vote and not a decree from above, an unusual achievement in the age of enlightened despotism.

The constitution was obviously the work of an enlightened minority, but skillful propaganda during the next twelve months largely overcame the reservations of the gentry as the *sejmiks'* favorable resolutions indicate. It was otherwise with St Petersburg, Berlin, and a group of die-hard magnates. As soon as her army was freed from the Turkish war Catherine II decided to intervene and restore the system of guarantees that the constitution had rejected. The pretext was provided by those magnates who accused the king of violating the *pacta conventa*. They saw themselves in Rostworowski's phrase as "guardians of the magnate-republican raison d'état" and were "maddened by pride and doctrine." Led by S. Potocki, K. Branicki, and S. Rzewuski they formed a confederation, ostensibly in Targowica, but actually in St Petersburg, where Catherine drafted a manifesto. Catherine denied that a new partition was contemplated, and represented the invasion of the Commonwealth in 1792 as legitimate action on behalf of the "legal" regime that Russia had guaranteed.

The Polish-Lithuanian armies, barely half of the decreed strength, stood no chance of winning the war. Prussia refused to honor its obligations, claiming that it had allied itself with a different regime. Indeed, Prussia's leading minister called the constitution "a mortal blow to the Prussian monarchy"; he feared that a revived Poland could reclaim the land lost in the first partition. The Polish-Lithuanian troops retreated, although they had won some engagements in which the king's nephew, Prince Józef Poniatowski, and the hero of the American

Revolutionary War Tadeusz Kościuszko distinguished themselves. Regarding the situation as hopeless, Stanislas Augustus decided to join, with most of his ministers, the Targowica Confederation. The great achievement of May 3 was destroyed.

The dramatic events in Poland found a counterpart, although on a reduced scale, in the Habsburg monarchy. The death of Joseph II in 1790 brought a reaction against enlightened absolutism. The diet of Bohemia, voting as an entity and not as estates, seized what seemed the first chance since the White Mountain to demand the restitution of some of its previous rights. The constitution of the land, it was claimed, was based on a social contract (this was Rousseau's influence) and could not be arbitrarily changed. Hence the king should be crowned and a constitutional relationship between him and the nation affirmed. The new ruler Leopold II was sympathetic to certain Bohemian demands: the end of official germanization, creation of a national bank in Prague, promotion of cultural revival. But he was unwilling to issue a new land ordinance that would restore a good deal of the structures of the pre-centralization period. Still, he granted the diet the right to make representations to the king and in 1791 confirmed through the coronation act the unity of the lands of the Crown of St Wenceslas.

Hungary was in a much stronger position than Bohemia and its gentry could formulate stiffer demands. They included the calling of the diet (not summoned since 1765), the election of the palatine, the restoration of county self-government, a transfer of the chancellery to Hungary, control over royal domains, a Hungarian army, and free trade. The rising intelligentsia that had supported Josephinism added demands for the abolition of serfdom, a secularization of ecclesiastical lands, and a development of manufactories. Since Joseph II had never been crowned, the gentry claimed the right to elect a new ruler and introduce a constitution that would limit his powers and place taxation and the army under the diet. The Hungarians followed the developments in Poland and approved of the adoption of the May 3 constitution. Some of their hopes, however, centered on Prussian and possibly Turkish assistance against the Habsburgs.

A kind of civic guard (national banderia) came into being, supported enthusiastically by the landless gentry. Hungarian national dress and opposition to German language and customs were the outward manifestations of Hungarian patriotism. The enlightened nobility propagated Hungarian literary activities and generally spoke of national autonomy under the Habsburgs. It also favored improving the position of the burghers and peasants, even giving them political representation. By and large the reformist movement was one of the gentry supported by some aristocrats. The weak bourgeoisie was little in evidence; the peasants, apart from voicing grievances about corvée and landlords' abuses, were passive. An anonymous peasant declaration (the Decretum) – allegedly drafted by Leopold II – that attacked in revolutionary terms the foundations of the feudal system was an exception.

Leopold cleverly exploited fears of a potential social revolution, and he also showed interest in the demands of the Serbs, Slovaks, and Romanians. In 1791 the petition called Supplex Libellus Valachorum demanded equal rights of the Romanians with the three nations of Transylvania, or at least a national representation. Even the Transylvanian Saxons who had made common cause with the Hungarians against Josephinism came to fear an undue ascendancy of the Hungarians. The Poles in Galicia, on the other hand, hoped to exploit the ferment by formulating demands for an autonomy of the province under a planned Charta Leopoldina.

Success for the reformers hinged largely on the Austro–Prussian war that was expected. But instead, in July 1790, the earlier-mentioned accord between Vienna and Berlin intervened and took the wind out of the sails of any anti-Habsburg calculations. The Hungarians turned to a compromise. Leopold recognized the diet's assertion that Hungary was a free and independent country, to be ruled in accord with its constitution, but he prevented any attempt to transform the Habsburg–Hungarian relationship in a way originally demanded by the noble nation. As the French Revolution gained momentum the Hungarian nobility drew closer to the monarchy. The small Jacobin plot of Ignác Martinovics in 1795 only increased counter-revolutionary hysteria in the country.

The parallel rise, although asymmetrical, of enlightened liberty in Poland and the Habsburg lands was a transient phenomenon, although it formed part of the larger European "democratic revolution." The rule of the Targowica confederation was a brief and shameful episode, which was ended by the second partition of 1793. Austria, engaged in war against Revolutionary France, abstained from participation. As far as the West was concerned "Poland might be, in fact, considered as a country on the moon."[28]

The mutilated remnant of the Commonwealth could not survive, and preparations for its demise prompted an insurrection against Russia in 1794, led by Kościuszko. Assuming the title of Chief (naczelnik) he bypassed and isolated the hapless king. Warsaw crowds, however, turned revolutionary and hanged several dignitaries of the Targowica confederation. Indeed, there were traces of Jacobinism and terror in the Kościuszko insurrection, although the leader himself, "a gentle revolutionary," but a firm democrat did not endorse it. His contribution was the Połaniec Manifesto, in which he promised personal freedom to serfs and release from corvée if they joined him. Many did, such as the fierce fighter Bartosz Głowacki. The involvement of artisans, for instance the shoemaker Kiliński who rose to a colonelship, or of Jews organized by Berek Joselewicz into a fighting unit, testified to the broad base of the insurrection. Yet its military chances, especially as Prussian troops joined the Russians, were virtually nil. Hopes for intervention by Revolutionary France, to which the uprising in Poland was a most welcome diversion, proved ill-founded. After several months of struggle in which more soldiers were mobilized than ever before, Kościuszko was wounded and taken prisoner. The Russian army of Suvorov stormed Warsaw's suburb Praga and mercilessly massacred its inhabitants.

In 1795 the third and last partition wiped off the remnants of Poland from the map. In all, Prussia had gained some 20 percent of the territory and 23 percent of the population; the respective figures for Austria were 18 and 32 percent; for Russia 62 and 45 percent. The partitioning monarchs agreed to erase forever the very name of Poland.

The first partition had occurred because of the Commonwealth's weakness; the second and third took place when it was reforming itself and regaining strength. This the partitioning powers would not tolerate. The partitions grievously affected the European balance of power. On the ruins of Poland, Prussia and later Prussian-ruled Germany achieved dominance on the continent. Russia was drawn more into Europe and had now a common border with the Habsburg monarchy. From the perspective of the latter the disappearance of the Commonwealth was surely a mixed blessing. The demise of old Poland saw the rise of the "Polish question," with all the repercussions it had for Europe's international relations. While the partitions had administered a shock to the European system and epitomized the crisis of the Old Regime it would require another shock (the First World War) for Poland to re-emerge on the political map of Europe.

The partitions shaped the society of the Commonwealth, having interrupted its evolution and put the clock back, for the next two centuries. Not only the Poles but all the nationalities of the Commonwealth were affected. The Polish question served to cement the alliance of the partitioners but it also influenced their domestic evolution and international standing.

Polish and foreign historians have endlessly debated whether the Commonwealth fell because of its internal decomposition or because its neighbors were determined to pull it down. There is no single answer, since various elements entered the picture. The Commonwealth, having failed to resolve its internal problems in the seventeenth century (the Ukraine provided the best example) gradually ceased to be a factor of power and stability in the region. It had either to reform itself or fall victim to the partitioning principle then practiced. It attempted reform and demonstrated that its constitutional system was reformable. But the international constellation only *seemed* to be propitious. A decade or two later Poland might have found its place in a Napoleonic Europe, but whether this would have been advantageous for the country is another question.

Did Poland fall because it had missed and bypassed an absolutist phase in its history? This is a plausible but not a fully convincing view. Absolutism did not prevent the decay of Spain, while other "republican" regimes survived. Irrespective of its faults, Polish republicanism proved to be of great importance to the partitioned nation. Not only did the "noble nation" pass its Polish identity and values to the emerging modern "stateless nation," but the republican tradition sustained a kind of civil society that could exist and develop in spite of the foreign state that was superimposed on it. This proved vital in the process of surviving the hundred and twenty-odd years of captivity.

As matters stood at the end of the eighteenth century the last of the independent states of East Central Europe was gone, and Bohemia and Hungary seemed destined to exist only in the framework of the Habsburg monarchy.

5

THE AGE OF LIBERAL
NATIONALISM

NATION AND NATIONALISM: THE POLISH CASE

Two forces shaped the course of the nineteenth century: the French Revolution and the Industrial Revolution. The impact of the first was mainly in the political-ideological domain, although its social and economic implications were profound. The second, more than a technological breakthrough, was a combination of economic, social, and political changes that led to a revolutionary transformation of economy and society. Europe altered, expanded, and grew. In a veritable demographic explosion its population doubled.

In East Central Europe in the first six decades of the century only the Czech lands went through the Industrial Revolution. For that reason, as well as for the sake of clarity, the emphasis in this chapter will be on ideological and political developments, although such occurrences as the emancipation of the peasantry and of the Jews will be included. In the realm of culture the stress will be on romanticism, which represented a new way of sensing human experience. A departure from the rationalist and cosmopolitan Enlightenment, romanticism stressed feelings, passions, and in the case of nation and society, it explored native roots and appealed to the medieval past.

The peoples of East Central Europe made romanticism as well as the basic concepts of the French Revolution very much their own, and colored them with their native outlook, tradition, and existing conditions. In the Polish case, romanticism, as A. Walicki observed, could neither be bourgeois-liberal (in view of the social stratification) nor conservative in a stateless nation. As for the watchwords of the French Revolution, the Slav Congress meeting in 1848 in Prague addressed its manifesto to the peoples of Europe "in the name of liberty, equality and fraternity of all nations."[29] The three watchwords became respectively symbols of the movements that issued from the Revolution: liberalism, democracy-radicalism, and nationalism.

Liberalism as a term will be used here less in the sense of tolerance, broadmindedness, and humanitarian inclinations, and more as a political ideology. Thus perceived it was based on the notion of freedom, individual and societal. It opposed both conservatism and, later, radicalism and socialism. It strove toward parliamentary government under a constitution, and represented a wide range of attitudes toward revolution. Although closely associated with economic doctrines of *laissez-faire*, free trade, and the natural harmony of interests, liberalism did not remain their slave.

Liberalism was to a large extent the creed of the Western bourgeoisie which gradually stamped the nineteenth-century society with its outlook and values. This process of "embourgeoisement" was painfully slow in the monarcho-aristocratic context of Russia, Prussia, and Austria. It succeeded in Czech society, which was deprived of its native nobility; the results in Hungary and the Polish lands were slight because of the noble ethos. We shall return to this issue in the following chapter, in connection with the Industrial Revolution. Liberalism in East Central Europe was thus greatly affected by the socio-economic conditions. Although such Polish slogans as "for your freedom and ours" were deeply rooted in the liberal *Weltanschauung*, and liberalism was the reigning creed in Hungary during the Spring of Nations, the liberal ideology displayed somewhat distinct characteristics in this part of Europe.

The term "nationalism" also requires a brief elaboration. The almost interchangeable use of such words as nation and state obscures the basic difference between the two. The state is, of course, a legal and political organization; the nation is a community of people. Hence, as the British historian Hugh Seton-Watson reminded us, it is illogical to speak of "nationalization" of industry, but unfortunately there is no equivalent of the French word *étatisme*. Nationalism in English often denotes the love of one's country, a fusion of patriotism with national consciousness. But nationalism in the last two centuries has been an ideology, and it took, roughly speaking, two forms: liberal nationalism which culminated with the Spring of Nations, and integral nationalism which arose on the ruins of the liberal utopia. The former was an open creed, largely descended from the French Revolution. The latter treated the nation, conceived in deterministic terms, as the highest norm. It was often accompanied by hatred of other nations.

Modern scholarship has approached the phenomenon of nationhood along different lines. Hans Kohn and most of the historians who followed him saw the modern nation as a product of national consciousness, a spiritual phenomenon. To the Marxists the nation was a product of economic relationships, and they emphasized the existence of a national market and the bourgeoisie as determinants. The Czechoslovak historian Miroslav Hroch defined the nation mainly as "a constituent of social reality of historical origin." He stressed social relationships, among which he included national consciousness. Karl Deutsch postulated a connection between the rise of nationhood and the system of communications. To J. Breuilly, nationalism was a "particular response to the distinction, peculiar to the modern world, between state and society."[30]

If a group of people or a society is transformed under the impact of ideas into a nation, the existing conditions may facilitate or obstruct this evolution. Similarly a transition from a political nation (or geographic, or linguistic, or legal) to a modern nation depends on various factors. We may mention just two: increased social mobility, and general and uniform education. In the first half of the century serfdom in East Central Europe was a major obstacle to the former. As for education we must remember that by 1840 even in England and in France respectively 40 and 50 percent of the population was illiterate.

The *Encyclopédie* of Diderot and d'Alembert defined "nation" as a large number of people inhabiting a certain area within certain borders and owing allegiance to the same government. The French Revolution thus espoused an essentially political definition, and regarded nationalism as popular will organized in the state. The emphasis that began to appear on a community of language was mainly of a utilitarian character. This was the reason for attempted germanization under Joseph II and the promotion of French during the Revolution. In the latter case it was justified by ideologically colored language. It was said that "in a free people language must be one and the same for all." Breton was denounced as the language of federalism and superstition, German as that of emigration and anti-republicanism, Italian as counter-revolutionary, and Basque as embodying fanaticism. The speaker fulminated against these "barbarous jargons" and "vulgar idioms."[31]

The concept of nationhood acquired a very different connotation when expressed in spiritual and cultural terms by such German Romantics as Johann Gottfried Herder. Each people (*Volk*) could emerge from the state of barbarity and become a nation solely through the culture of the native tongue, he wrote. Three elements entered into this process: the consciousness of linguistic and ethnic community, a historical consciousness, and the consciousness of a historical mission. Just as freedom was essential for the individual, so it was for the social group. Nations were really individuals writ large, which looked both to their members and to humanity. Herder believed that mankind could best be served by nations, which to Mazzini were "God-appointed instruments for the welfare of the human race." As the Act of Brotherhood of Young Europe expressed it in 1834: "Every people has its special mission which will cooperate towards the fulfillment of the general mission of humanity. Nationality is sacred."[32]

Nationalism in the early nineteenth century was thus almost by definition liberal. True, a potential contradiction between the contractual element in liberalism (the notion of compromise) and the organic concept of nationalism (being born into the nation) existed, but at first it made little difference. As a Hungarian historian put it: "Freedom in capital letters is the word most often found in East European poetry, and in general terms this always meant the freedom of the nation."[33]

Several historians, influenced by Kohn's interpretations, tend to distinguish between the Western type of nationalism (in England and France) that perceived "nation" in political terms – an integrated community under the state – and the Eastern model (bearing the stamp of German romanticism), that saw "nation" as formed by language, culture, tradition, and a specific outlook rooted in the past. They opine as already mentioned in the Introduction, that in the West the state created the nation; in the East the nation created the state. In the West nationalism was predominantly a positive phenomenon, based on a relative ethnic-national homogeneity achieved prior to the nineteenth century, and corresponding to the changing social, economic, and political realities. It strove after an open and pluralistic society. Eastern nationalism was often a protest against the state (usually an alien state). Feeding on historical myths and stimulated by hopes in the future, it developed amidst ethnic diversity before a socio-economic transformation had taken place. It aimed at a monolithic community with authoritarian traits.

The above generalizations, for all the truth they contain, cannot be accepted uncritically. The stress the French put in the sixteenth century on their Gaulish ancestry, or the Dutch on their Batavian past, indicated that historic roots, real or legendary, did play a role in the formation of the Western-type nationalism. But, what is much more important, the Western Enlightenment model was, as we know, operative also in East Central Europe (late eighteenth-century Poland and Hungary) and was only partly replaced by the Eastern (German romantic) concept. The Eastern model is thus mainly valid for "non-historic nations" (we shall return to this term later): Czechs, Slovaks, Lithuanians, Romanians, Ukrainians. The Croats occupied a half-way position. The concept of national awakening or revival is applicable only to a limited degree to the Poles and Hungarians. And there is a further difference between these two.

Let us begin with the Poles. The late eighteenth-century processes that culminated in the May 3 constitution marked the beginnings of a transformation of the old noble political nation into a political nation of property owners. This corresponded to the division in France between the active citizens and the rest of the nation, and also signified an evolution from a society based on estates to a society based on classes.

To Staszic and Kołłątaj the nation was a collective sovereign, but the *szlachta* constituted only a part of it. How could the nation be made to embrace the whole population? Neither language nor religion was viewed as a criterion of state nationhood; the Commonwealth was multi-linguistic and the non-Roman Catholics probably constituted about 5 million out of 12 million inhabitants. Hence the criterion could only be cultural-political, rooted in native tradition and corresponding to ideas of Enlightenment. As Kołłątaj wrote in 1809: "None will henceforth be a Lithuanian, or Volhynian, or a Podolian or a Kievan, a Ruthene, and so on, but all will be Poles."[34] One finds similar statements throughout much of the early part of the century.

No clear distinction was drawn between nation and state at the time of the May 3 constitution. Some of the leaders noted that there was an Italian nation, but no Italian state, but generally the terminology was blurred. Even such terms as state and estate were mixed (incidentally, there is one word for both in French) and in Polish the United States were called United Estates (Stany Zjednoczone). The partitions interrupted the nation-building process, and according to Lord Acton they awakened the theory of nationality in Europe. The Poles had to confront the question of whether a stateless nation could exist, and at first views were divided. Even the marching song of the Polish Legion in Italy – later to become the national anthem – contained words that lent themselves to different interpretations. Saying that Poland was not yet lost "as long as we live" it seemed to identify nation with its living members. But a subsequent line "we shall cross the Vistula . . . and we shall be Poles" seems to point to an identification of nation and land. A pamphlet, *Can the Poles regain their independence?*, written in 1800 and inspired by Kościuszko, spoke of 16 million Poles, clearly understanding by that term all the inhabitants of the partitioned Commonwealth.

The concept of nation and nationality became refined after the Napoleonic wars, marking, in the phrase of the Polish sociologist J. Szacki, a transition from the Enlightenment conception of the fatherland to the romantic idea of nation. This process was largely completed between 1815 and 1831, although ambiguities continued to be there. A nation was represented as a historically formed community, an association of people in time and space, or, which was particularly important, as an ethical ideal. In this last sense, according to the political thinker Maurycy Mochnacki, it was a carrier of values that existed independently, although they corresponded to actual facts of national being. Hence the destruction of a nation was a loss for all. In an 1831 presentation that may be viewed as a summary of existing views on Polish nationality,

Kazimierz Brodziński called the nation "an inborn idea, which its members, fused into one, strive to realize."[35]

Romantics generally held the view that the nation realized itself through history. This was stressed by the father of modern Polish historiography, Joachim Lelewel. The myth of the early Slavs – agrarian, peaceful, freedom-loving, and subdued by brutal external force, but assisting through their sacrifice in a renaissance of humanity – played an important role in contemporary writings. One can think here of František Palacký in the Czech lands, or in a somewhat different form, of the Polish Messianic theories after 1831.

The mission of the Polish nation, according to Brodziński, lay in the cultivation of the tree of freedom and brotherhood, the development of its own personality, and representation of the Slavs. Indeed, the belief in a mission of spreading civilization and libertarian ideas among the Slavs was characteristic of Polish Slavophiles, both conservative-liberals and radical-democrats.

The emphasis placed by the Poles on language and national literature shows certain differences with developments in Bohemia and Hungary. It is true, of course, that writers throughout East Central Europe were not only artists but also national leaders. It is also true that the late eighteenth- and early nineteenth-century process of purification and enrichment of national languages was a general phenomenon throughout the region. In the Polish case the monumental dictionary of Samuel B. Linde (the first volume came out in 1806), the activity of the Society of Friends of Learning, and other initiatives provide a good illustration. But the popularization of the Polish language was undertaken before the partitions to ensure the state cohesion, and after the partitions to mobilize the people for a struggle to recover independence and sovereignty. The future Commonwealth and its "nation" was at first conceived in a unitary fashion; then the vision of a federation of the diverse peoples began to assert itself, mainly after the 1863 uprising.

Not only the Poles, but most European leaders understood under the name of Poles the inhabitants of the former Commonwealth, even as late as 1863. To Marx and Engels the revival of Poland was not to be the outcome of the application of the principle of nationality – "a Russian invention concocted to destroy Poland," as Engels wrote in 1866 – but because Poland was one of the great historic nations of Europe. It was not an ethnic community; in fact it comprised at least four ethnic communities.

In contrast to the Czechs and other nations of the region, except for the Hungarians in 1849, Polish national strivings during most of the century aimed at full independence and were characterized by national uprisings: 1806, 1830–1, 1846, 1848, and 1863. Not surprisingly the Austrian Chancellor Metternich equated Polishness with revolution.

The loss of statehood was so recent that many nineteenth-century Poles remembered the independent Commonwealth. Prince Adam Czartoryski, who was 25 at the time of the third partition and who died in 1861, may serve as an example.

Polish strivings for the reconstitution of their partitioned Commonwealth were rendered difficult by several factors. First, there was the need to absorb or at least to gain the loyalty of the non-Polish nationalities once they began to assert their separate identity. Second, in seeking to enlarge the nation so as to include the peasantry one ran into the problem that, while there were many Poles who were peasants, virtually *all* the Lithuanians, Ukrainians, and Belorussians belonged to the peasantry. Even when only ethnic Poles were concerned, a vertical integration seeking to make them consciously a part of the nation required a certain degree of economic emancipation and education. It would take time for the peasant to identify with a noble and discover ties of national solidarity that bound them together.

Polish conservatives and liberals viewed the sovereignty of the noble nation as a forerunner of popular sovereignty, and assumed that the *szlachta* would play a leading role in the transition from one to the other. The radicals who placed the masses (*lud*) on a pedestal viewed *them* as the real nation; the gentry would either have to join or be liquidated as an obstacle. The trouble was that the radicals usually belonged to the gentry themselves, and had to rely on "revolutionary nobles" in promoting their program. Finally, in this struggle for "the peasant's soul" the Poles had to confront the partitioning governments that intended to make the masses into loyal subjects of the tsar, the emperor, or the king of Prussia.

The fragmentation resulting from partitions represented, of course, the greatest obstacle to the emergence of an integrated Polish society. Certain developments, however, operated to the advantage of the Poles. The existence of a Polish army during certain periods fostered a national spirit, and one must remember that some 150,000 men passed through its ranks in 1794 and some 200,000 during both the Napoleonic period and the 1830–1 war with Russia. A partial and limited Polish administration was another asset, and it functioned in the Duchy of Warsaw (1807–14), the Congress Kingdom (1815–31), in the Republic of Cracow (1815–46), and from the 1860s in the autonomous Austrian Galicia. Polish culture was an unbroken link between the divided lands, and it is worth stressing that the Polish language was more uniform than German or Italian. Roman Catholicism came to emphasize the distinctiveness of the Poles *vis-à-vis* Lutheran Germans and Greek Orthodox Russians. In many instances Polish culture not only held its own under the regime of partitions but exerted an attraction which led

141

many Germans, some Jews and occasional Russians, Czechs, Slovaks, even Frenchmen to complete assimilation and polonization.

The modern Polish nation, as it crystallized during the century, was largely an amalgam of the *szlachta* and the plebeians, while in the West the nation arose out of the middle class and the proletariat. Yet, when speaking of a Polish or Hungarian "noble society" or "noble nationalism" two things are frequently overlooked. In many respects the Polish or Hungarian gentry was a middle class, although with a very different outlook and ethos. Second, a distinction needs to be made between a landowning nobleman and a noble-born member of the intelligentsia, and it was the latter – from Kossuth to Piłsudski – who played an increasingly important role as the political leader.

IN THE LANDS OF THE CROWN OF ST STEPHEN AND ST WENCESLAS

In partitioned Poland the patriots wanted to preserve, consolidate, and expand the nation so that it could eventually regain its statehood. Total independence and the severance of ties with Vienna was not the object of the Hungarian national movement in the early nineteenth century. True, the separation of Transylvania and other regions from Hungary rankled, but the term "state" (*alladalom*) only appeared at this time. The issue was much more the maintenance of national identity that was perceived as endangered by non-Magyars within the country and by the Germans. In the evolution from the noble "natio hungarica" to a modern nation Hungarians followed a path similar to the Poles insofar as they moved from the political concepts of the Enlightenment to the romantic vision. But there were significant differences. The hegemony of Latin had been more entrenched and all pervasive, hence the emphasis on the Hungarian language was more dramatic. The quote from Bessenyei in the preceding chapter provided a good illustration. Here let us cite the liberal magnate István Széchenyi brought up in the atmosphere of Enlightenment: "the nation lives in its language." It was a protest against both Latin and German. Rebelling against Joseph II's attempts to impose the German language, the Hungarian elite did not advocate a return to Latin, which was regarded as an antiquated, medieval language unsuitable as a medium of modern education. Furthermore Latin only accentuated the division between nobles and peasants. Latin, as Széchenyi opined, expressed the spirit of caste and the egoism of the noble estate. He himself insisted on speaking Hungarian.

The need for the modernization of Hungarian and the first attempts in this direction have already been mentioned. But it was only in the second and third decades of the nineteenth century that Hungarian literature achieved national significance. In the second decade debates between the classicists and romantics occurred, very similar to those in Poland. The publication of Mihály Vörösmarty's epic poem *Zalán's Flight* marked the beginning of Hungarian romanticism, to be continued later by Petöfi and the novelist Jokái. Realism in literature would come in the 1840s with Eötvös.

Linguistic and literary efforts were promoted through the Hungarian National Museum found in 1802, the Academy of Sciences in 1825, and the National Theater founded in the late 1830s. All of them, as most other public initiatives, were supported by Széchenyi, father and son, and connected with the growing feeling of urgency. Hungary, in Vörösmarty's words was "without companions in Europe," and Magyars constituted less than half of its population. Herder was predicting that the isolated Magyar nation would sooner or later succumb to the Slavs and Germans. Other nationalities under St Stephen's Crown were being affected by linguistic revival. The Serbs in the Banat (Vojvodina) who already enjoyed a certain autonomy on religious grounds – headed by the Greek Orthodox metropolitan – began to emphasize the language as an essential element of nationhood. The name of Dositej Obradović, a pioneer of the Serb cultural revival, needs to be mentioned. There was thought of territorial autonomy or even a future greater Serbia. The Romanians of Transylvania, where the Greek Catholic Bishop Micu had indicated the way in the eighteenth century, were experiencing a national awakening. As for the Slovaks, we shall turn to them later in conjunction with the Czech renaissance.

"Our country, from the point of view of language, is a true Babel," wrote a Hungarian liberal journal in 1841. "If we cannot change the course of things and the country cannot be united through Magyarization, sooner or later the German or Slav element will assimilate our nation and even our name will be forgotten."[36] Was Magyarization, however, to proceed through an evolutionary and voluntary process of assimilation to a higher culture, through "spiritual supremacy" and "national ennoblement" as Széchenyi envisaged it? Or was it to be furthered through legislation, as Széchenyi's protagonist Lajos Kossuth advocated, without seeing that such a policy infringed on the liberal principles which he staunchly upheld? Kossuth saw Hungary as one nation under the Holy Crown of St Stephen, and he compared the position of the Slavs and Romanians within it to that of Bretons in France or the Welsh and the Irish in Britain. This was the French Jacobin approach to nationhood at its clearest.

An ascendancy of the Hungarian language was becoming noticeable. Between 1832 and 1838 the number of books published in Hungarian increased from 127 to 216; those in Latin, German, and Slovak showed a smaller rise: respectively 71 to 82, 49 to 58, and 5 to 7. Croat books fell from 2 to 1, Serb from 12 to 6, and Romanian from 5 to 1.[37] A

Magyarization of towns, then proceeding and entailing assimilation of aliens, especially Germans, appeared essential to Kossuth in order to create a new native middle class. Once enfranchised – and some groups of professional people of the nascent intelligentsia (*honoratiores*) were granted the right to vote in 1841 – the middle class would be fully integrated into the nation. The process of forming a modern Hungarian society would be completed by the emancipation of the peasantry. Both liberals and radicals advocated it, although they differed among themselves as to the measures to be adopted. The emancipation of the peasant masses would, of course, be crucial from the viewpoint of modernization of the agrarian economy of the country.

The issue of nation and nationalism for the Hungarians was in many respects different from the national revival in the Czech lands. In Bohemia one can truly speak of an awakening or reawakening, a renaissance and conscious attempts to re-establish the broken national continuity. There was, as we know, no political Czech nation that could take the lead in the process. The nobility continued to be devoted to the monarchy (Habsburgtreu). It was German-speaking and less and less bound to the past. Out of 187 aristocratic families, 75 had settled in the 1785–1843 period; the number of oldest families was reduced to 42. True, this aristocracy was developing a local patriotism and saw itself as the elite of the kingdom of Bohemia but not of the Czech nation. It was the current leading group, not a successor of the old nobility. Its attachment to Bohemia manifested itself in some opposition to Vienna's centralist policies and in patronage of cultural, linguistic, and literary activities in the kingdom. Under these conditions Czech national revival could not take the form of expansion from the top down but had to grow from below.

The educational reforms of Maria Theresa and Joseph greatly increased Czech literacy, but did not spread the use of the language in society very much. As German continued to reign supreme in administration and trade, Czech remained an internal language in manorial offices and some town councils. Even in the 1820s, Palacký recalled "whoever wore a decent coat did not venture so readily to speak Czech in public places."[38] In schools the pioneers of the Czech language felt that it facilitated the learning of German, which they did not wish to eliminate altogether. Similarly the German-language advocates did not want to eradicate Czech but merely confine it to private life.

Early in the century the Czech–German antagonism was in its infancy. The inhabitants of Bohemia knew that they were subjects of the king-emperor, and that their country was the kingdom of Bohemia in which German and Czech were spoken. Bohemia was home to the Germans, some of whom stressed their patriotism and wrote enthusiastically about the country's past. Could a modern Czech nation have developed along bilingual lines, comparably to the Belgian nation of Flemish and Walloons? The Catholic priest and educator Bernhard Bolzano thought so, but in the early years of the century the question was not yet resolved. The two groups were unequal in most respects. Recognizing the existence of two cultural streams in Bohemia, Palacký saw the German stream as connected with modern Europe, flourishing and prosperous, while the Czech was antiquated, poor, primitive, and largely identified with the masses. Palacký opined that a good book in Czech would hardly sell more than 600 copies; one had to write in German to reach a wider audience.

How could the group of awakeners persuade the masses that they were part of the Czech nation and should be proud of it? The intellectual group was so small that in 1868 Palacký quoted a saying that if the ceiling collapsed in a room in which they were sitting this would be the end of national endeavors. No wonder that the awakeners felt, in the words of Kollár, that they were "playing a piano that had no strings as yet."[39]

The first phase that began before 1800 was characterized by an interest in Czech language and literature. It was affected subsequently by the concepts of the French Revolution, in the sense that nation was equated with the people, and then much more strongly by Herder's romantic ideas about the Slavs and their great future. In 1825 Josef Jungmann had already published in Czech his *History of the Czech Literature* and the *Czech Dictionary*. Others began to use their native tongue in scientific writings, as exemplified by the work of the great physiologist Jan E. Purkyně. Czech was also the language in which two leading awakeners (both Protestant Slovaks) Pavel Šafařik and Jan Kollár published respectively *Slavic Antiquities* and the great romantic epos the *Daughter of Glory*. The British historian R. W. Seton-Watson called the latter "an ecstatic address to Liberty" and indeed its closing lines were very much in the spirit of the age: "From the Tatra to the Black Mountain, from the Giant Mountains to the Urals, resound the words, Hell for the traitors, Heaven for the true Slavs."

Kollár sounded the tocsin of united Slavdom that was so important for the Czechs afflicted with the complex of being a small, insignificant, and backward people. It was psychologically uplifting to be part of a large and glorious Slav family. This was even more true for the Slovaks, and it was hardly an accident that heralds of Slavdom came from Slovakia. Slav reciprocity occupied an important place in the writings of the Czech journalist Karel Havliček-Borovský with whom we pass from the cultural-scholarly stage to that of patriotic agitation.

Havliček's paper *Pražské Noviny* cleverly avoided censorship by devoting much attention to the Irish demands for repeal of the union with

England; the readers understood the veiled analogy to Czech–Austrian problems. (Incidentally this was a stratagem to which Hungarian literature also resorted, in the 1850s.) The growing ascendancy of the Czech language was assisted by such institutions as the National Museum of 1818 and the Matice Česká of 1831, which promoted publication of books in Czech. Havlíček was a polonophile, and indeed the Polish input was very important for Czech national revival. The Polish–Russian struggle, however, tended to polarize Czech public opinion. Indeed, Slavophilism was much more attractive as an abstract theory, and it lost in confrontation with the reality of individual Slav nations.

Slavism was an integral element in the Czech national renaissance; the question of the meaning of national history was at its very center. Was a new nation being formed that had nothing in common with the past, or was continuity essential? Searching for lasting national values, the awakeners strove to reconcile the historical noble nation with the present people's nation by means of a somewhat selective approach to national heritage. The role of Palacký as historian, intellectual, and politician was crucial in this respect.

Palacký turned to historical research to show the richness of the Czech heritage which could bolster pride and identity. The values that justified the existence and the sense of a small Czech nation were of a spiritual nature. Influenced by Herder and Lelewel, Palacký subscribed to the belief in original Slav democracy later corrupted by alien influences. The high point of this confrontation was the Hussite period, and the Hussites were perceived as pioneers in striving for freedom and equality just as they were unique in the scale of their movement and in their victorious resistance to armed onslaught. The Hussites appeared thus as forerunners of liberalism, democracy, and nationhood, and their contribution to mankind placed the Czechs in the mainstream of European history.

Palacký's concept of the nation evolved from the territorial to the ethnic. The change in the title of his main work – *History of Bohemia* in the German original to *History of the Czech Nation* in Czech – was characteristic in that respect. The Czech–German "continual association and conflict" which he perceived as the "chief content and basic feature of the whole history of Bohemia and Moravia" illustrated in turn his principle of polarity in history. The "acceptance and rejection of German customs and laws by the Czechs" was mainly a struggle about spiritual, hence universal values. Thus the Czech past and what it stood for was something with which the reviving new nation could identify.

Palacký's vision of history, with its emphasis on the Hussite heritage, left an ineradicable imprint on the Czech outlook. It inspired K. J. Erben's poetry and later the historical novels of Alois Jirásek, and the great operas of Bědřich Smetana. Indirectly, it affected the realist literature of Božena Němcová. But, above all it served to instill confidence in the Czechs about the meaning of the past, and their destiny, indeed their mission.

What made the Czech national awakening, having started from such a low point, a success in contrast to the efforts of the Bretons, the Welsh, perhaps even the Irish? Marxists saw it in terms of the economic struggle between the German and the Czech bourgeoisie. The renaissance was a natural reaction against germanization, asserted the "awakener" Jungmann. It corresponded to the spirit of the age, opined the historian Jaroslav Goll. It was an organic development, stated his even more prominent pupil Josef Pekař. Or, as Tomáš Masaryk saw it, this was a continuation of the native religious reformist tradition brought into the open by Joseph's toleration decrees, influenced by the French Revolution and German philosophy, and evolving from a general feeling of national consciousness through the Slavic to the Czech idea as personified by the Kollár, Šafařik, Palacký trio.

The specific features of the Czech national revival stemmed from the historical context: the advent of the Industrial Revolution. It brought with it social mobility, growing communications, and the spreading of education. The role of the bourgeoisie, especially the petite bourgeoisie (the big businessmen being Germans) and of the young intelligentsia of peasant background was particularly important. In the absence of their own state, Czechs concentrated on education and economy. The nationalism that evolved was cautious, down to earth, and basically loyalist toward Vienna. It was liberal and democratic, but it differed sharply from the outlook of the Polish revolutionary noble democrats. Before 1848 it could claim hardly any martyrs. The continuing emphasis on the language as the determinant of nationality was, in the view of Hroch, due less to Herder's influence and more to the fact that it represented the only link that cut across social and even religious divisions.

Among the Slovaks the modest beginnings of a slow transition from ethnicity to nationality affected both the Hungarians and the Czechs. The latter viewed the Slovaks in terms of common Slavism or Czechoslovakism, and indeed Kollár and Šafařik appeared as the living proof of the validity of this concept. The Hungarians refused to countenance the very idea of a Slovak nation that had no history of separate statehood. The Slovaks were regarded as the Slavs of Upper Hungary, the Protestants among them using as literary language the old Czech of the Scriptures and liturgy (bibličtina). The gentry, mainly of the poorest kind, was more numerous in Slovakia than in Bohemia; in the late eighteenth century it comprised (counting only the males) 4.6 percent of the total male population in Slovakia and 0.1 percent in

Bohemia. Their highest claim was to be of "Slav language and Hungarian nation"; in fact, very few claimed as much as this.

The creation of a general seminary in Pozsony (Bratislava) under Joseph and the need for a written language led to late eighteenth-century attempts by a Jesuit, A. Bernolák, to develop a literary tongue based on educated speech. It was a failure, but a Slovak learned society did emerge in 1792 and was followed by other institutions. Still, for the next thirty years one could hardly speak of a national revival on a large scale. An attempted Magyarization of Slovak Protestant churches led to a language war in the 1820s. The Hungarian side insisted that since Poland's fall the Slav speech "ceased to be the language of freedom," and became an instrument of division in Russian hands. But the small rising Slovak intelligentsia did not give in.

In 1840 L'iudovit Štúr successfully launched what became the modern Slovak language, a move that the Czechs disliked as cultural separatism. Yet the new literary tongue resulted from a gradual shift in national identification; it was not its cause. Still, Štúr's insistence that the Slovaks were a separate nation within Slavdom drew Palacký's criticism. Practical demands of the Slovaks at this point were modest: use of the native language in primary schools, teachers' colleges, and religious classes. Slovak liberals who looked up to Vienna were thrust back into Hungarian arms, but found little understanding on the part of Magyar liberals.

Before turning to a chronological survey, some attention must be devoted to the Jews. Their distribution in the area was greatly affected by the partitions of Poland and by eastward migrations within the Habsburg monarchy. Out of the roughly one million Jews in the Commonwealth, about 150,000 came under Prussian rule, over 150,000 found themselves in the Habsburg monarchy, and the vast majority (over half a million) were included in Russia's share of the partitioned Poland. The officially established line marking the Jewish pale of settlement remained as the last trace of the Commonwealth's eastern border. In the so-called Congress Kingdom attached to Russia in 1815 the Jews constituted about 12 percent of the population; around 43 percent were in towns of which 26 percent were in the city of Warsaw.

The Jewish population in Hungary increased rapidly during the nineteenth century. While in 1787 there were 80,000 Jews (about 1 percent of the population) the figure was 185,000 (around 2 percent) by 1825. It rose to over 540,000 (4 percent) by 1869. These were largely immigrants from Bohemia, Moravia, and Austria proper, who fled the enmity and competition of German burghers, as well as newcomers from Galicia. Proportionately the number of Jews in Bohemia declined at this time and Prague ceased to be the largest Jewish urban conglomeration under the Habsburgs. Its place was now taken by Pest.

Poland's partitions were a mixed blessing for the Jews, if not an overall worsening of their position. But the age of liberalism witnessed a series of emancipation reforms, from the early Josephine legislation through the Napoleonic Code and subsequent measures in the Habsburg monarchy and Prussia. Under the "Europeanization" slogan a process of germanization was taking place in the Polish lands of Prussia, much less so in Galicia, where Hassidism was strongly entrenched. But there was also a trend among Jews of identifying with Polish patriotism and Polish national strivings. Rabbi Ber Meisels epitomized it. The Polish leaders were divided on the merits of polonization and assimilation. Czartoryski and Lelewel advocated full equality of Jews, calling them fellow citizens rather than foreigners. This movement reached its peak in the 1860s when Jews were referred to as "Poles of Mosaic faith." We shall return to this later. Opponents of Jewish emancipation included such prominent figures as Staszic, who argued that the large number of Jews, if granted full civic and political rights, might put their own stamp on society and undermine its national outlook and values. This was also the view of Széchenyi in Hungary, where somewhat similar debates were taking place, and where an increasing number of Jews identified with Magyardom. Such views, incidentally, were not exclusively East Central European for they had also been expressed at the National Assembly at the time of the emancipation of Jews in France. Anti-Jewish outbreaks occurred in Prague, Pozsony, and other cities when national feelings ran high during the Spring of Nations. But traditional Judeophobia did not assume the form of modern anti-Semitism until very late in the century.

NAPOLEONIC AND POST-NAPOLEONIC DECADES

The partitions of Poland had not only obliterated the state, but also called into question the survival of the then evolving political nation. What could be its *raison d'être*, under three monarchic regimes that relied on the nobility and protected its social position, but allowed it no share in government? The Polish *szlachta* was split into various categories, the top stratum being given the status of aristocracy, the poorest gentry reduced to plebeian level. Only a fraction of the former *szlachta* constituted the nineteenth-century landowning class, although its ethos affected other social groups. The fact of a stateless nation influenced, perhaps even shaped, Polish political culture and its outlook. Denied a normal interplay of politics many a Pole became an emigrant, insurgent, conspirator, or deportee. The term "compromise," seen as abandonment of principles, acquired a pejorative meaning and Poles often displayed an "all or nothing" attitude.

The feeling born of despair that Poland had ceased to exist for good was quickly challenged by political and military action by the Poles. As Staszic put it, "A great nation may fall, but only a base one can perish." The worst thing was that the Poles were confronted by three powers and had no ally committed to them. But, and this militated in their favor, they lost national independence at a time when the right to national independence was being loudly proclaimed in Europe. How could they proceed: engage in armed struggle, joining with revolutionaries or with powers that were at war with the partitioners? Or begin armed resistance on their own? Or collaborate with one of the partitioning powers against the others? Two trends asserted themselves. One, linking Poland's cause with Revolutionary France, led to the formation in 1797 of Polish legions in Italy. Commanded by General Henryk Dąbrowski, they constituted a visible protest against the verdict of partitions. Their song announced that they would retake by arms what had been taken away. French peace with Austria temporarily quashed the hopes of the legionaries, but their patriotism and their apprenticeship in revolutionary democracy transcended their military efforts and acquired a broader significance.

The second trend was epitomized by Prince Adam Czartoryski, who sought to rely on Russia; there, the youthful Tsar Alexander I not only befriended him but was himself imbued with French ideas, and in private called Poland's partitions a crime. Czartoryski rose to the position of Russia's foreign minister and curator of the Wilno educational district, which comprised most of the Russian-held former Polish provinces. Reorganizing and modernizing the educational system – to serve as a model for Russia – Czartoryski promoted Polish culture under tsarist rule. As a saying had it, if the light had not shone in Wilno it would have been extinguished throughout Polish lands.

Czartoryski's political plans of enlisting the tsar's support for the Polish cause in the turmoil of Napoleonic wars brought no results. No wonder then that the Poles rose in 1806, when the French troops pursuing the retreating Prussian and Russian armies entered western Poland. Taking Napoleon's side Prince Poniatowski assumed leadership over the Polish military effort, but the reward was modest. In 1807 Napoleon and Alexander agreed in the compromise peace of Tilsit to create a fractional Duchy of Warsaw (the word Polish was avoided) out of Prussia's share in the second and third partition. The duchy doubled its size and population in 1809 as a result of a victorious war against Austria, and was seen by the Poles as the nucleus of a future recreated state. Although never master of its destiny and treated by Napoleon as a pawn in his diplomacy and war strategy, the duchy at least contradicted the finality of the partitions.

Endowed with a Napoleonic-type constitution, with some concessions made to the May 3 tradition, the duchy underwent a process of modernization in which judicial, political, and social reforms coming from above largely preceded a spontaneous socio-economic transformation. Thus the peasantry was legally freed but not given any land; the Jews like all citizens were equal before the law, but their civic rights were temporarily suspended awaiting their "Europeanization." Society was laicized to some degree, particularly in the educational sphere. Many a Pole came to follow a military career, fighting as far away as Spain, where the charge of the Polish light horse guards at Somosierra became a legend. The economy of the duchy was nearing collapse under financial burdens, largely connected with the upkeep of a disproportionately large army, yet, for all the disappointments with Napoleon his legend grew, fortifying the Polish link with France and placing trust in its leadership.

Napoleon's invasion of Russia in 1812, officially called "the second Polish campaign" awoke hopes of a recreated Poland, and produced an enlistment of nearly 100,000. Polish troops continued to fight when the emperor's star began to wane, and the death of Poniatowski at the battle of Leipzig became a symbol of chivalry and loyalty. This period left behind it an important heritage. Basic reforms in the political field remained until 1831; in the administration till the 1860s; in the judiciary until the 1870s. The civil code, the Code Napoléon, survived until the middle of the twentieth century and is now being partly restored.

In 1813 the Duchy of Warsaw was conquered by Russia which wished to retain it, but the Congress of Vienna disposed otherwise of the "Polish question" two years later. Parts of the duchy (Poznania) were transferred to Prussia, and the rest, named Kingdom of Poland, was linked to Russia. Tsar Alexander became the king of what was commonly known as the Congress Kingdom. Cracow was made a free republic under the protection of the three powers. A certain reality of the old Commonwealth was recognized through the provision that assured free trade within the 1772 borders (a dead letter), and through the recommendation to the partitioning rulers to respect the Polish nationality of their subjects.

Alexander granted to the kingdom a constitution that was very liberal on the surface. But high sounding civil and personal liberties proved to be expendable, and the conservative elements dominated political society. Still, this was an autonomous state with its own parliament, government, army and treasury, citizenship and passports, and an electorate that was larger than that of contemporary France or England. At first, Alexander seemingly wanted the constitutional kingdom to be a laboratory for and a prototype of a transformed Russian empire. He considered the possibility of enlarging it by the return of the former eastern Polish provinces incorporated in the three partitions. The old Kościuszko believed that only such a sizeable Polish state could occupy a position *vis-à-vis* Russia comparable to that of Hungary toward Austria. Alexander's inability to achieve this transfer in the teeth of Russian opposition, and the "monstrosity" of a constitutional kingdom tied to a despotic empire were cited by contemporaries as the two chief causes of the November 1830 uprising. But, before it occurred the kingdom went through a decade and a half of important political, cultural, ideological, and economic developments that left their imprint for years to come.

The political spectrum in the kingdom ranged from sincere or opportunistic collaborators with the government to a liberal opposition and secret societies whose strivings for a free and united Poland were, on the surface at least, not necessarily at variance with the utterings of Alexander. But the tsar, for all the liberalism – which he shed in the years to come – was by temperament a despot who tended to resort to extra-constitutional means. The kingdom was ruled in effect by the tsar's neurotic brother Grand Duke Constantine, who commanded, loved, and maltreated the army; a special representative Senator N. Novosiltsov, a cynical intriguer; and the servile viceroy (a former Napoleonic general). The fact that this theoretically supreme post did not go to the natural candidate Prince Czartoryski adversely affected the political scene and drove the prince into opposition. Arbitrary rule, brutal persecution of opponents (which produced a martyr in the person of Major W. Łukasiński), censorship, and a police and informers' regime of surveillance, undermined the state. A contemporary analysis of the system by M. Mochnacki has a familiar ring to the student of the Gomułka and Gierek regime in People's Poland.

Naturally, there were differences. In economics, the brilliant minister of finance Prince K. Drucki-Lubecki pursued modernization, which he subsumed under a triple goal: schools, industry and trade, and armaments. He attempted to industrialize the country with the state acting as investor and producer. Industrialization was financed by heavy taxes, and the state also encouraged private undertakings. The results were mixed. The textile industry grew around Łódź (the Polish Manchester); there were achievements in coal mining, metallurgy, and banking (the Bank Polski was established). But the lack of sufficient capital and available labor, due to the obsolete socio-economic structure of the country, prevented a real industrial take-off.

Did the uprising that broke out in November 1830 occur because all the developments in the kingdom had resulted in a deadlock? The rising followed the July Revolution in France and the Belgian struggle for independence, and in a sense paralyzed the plans of Nicholas I (Alexander's successor) to intervene militarily in the West. But there is no proof that the uprising was deliberately provoked from outside. The announcement that Polish troops would participate in the intervention, as well as the realization that the secret police had discovered the Warsaw conspiracy, hastened events. The rising began as a revolutionary coup launched by youthful conspirators. The older leaders tried to exploit this "demonstration" to extract concessions from the tsar: respect for the constitution and fulfillment of Alexander's promises. Nicholas, however, refused to negotiate, and the revolution became a national uprising. It culminated politically in the act of dethronement of the Romanov dynasty in January 1831, which declared that the origin of all authority came from the nation. The struggle was a regular war fought for national freedom. While liberals, with Lelewel, asserted that this was a confrontation between constitutionalism and autocracy, and adopted the slogan "For your freedom and ours," Mochnacki saw the war as a struggle between Poles and Russians. The *sejm* wasted a unique opportunity, that of proclaiming full emancipation of the peasants; the value of this step was not that it would have helped to win the war, as the radicals asserted, but that emancipation would have come from Polish hands.

The excellent Polish army was outnumbered, but it was also badly led by generals who remembered Napoleon's defeat in 1812 and disbelieved in victory. The government under Czartoryski's presidency was internally divided. Some victories were won and the uprising spread into Lithuania attesting to the reality of the old Commonwealth. But by the autumn of 1831 the Russians took Warsaw and the rising collapsed.

Russian reprisals were severe. The kingdom had its constitution suspended, and lost a separate government, parliament, army, and even the Warsaw university which had been opened in 1816. The Polish political and military elite chose exile. A debate began abroad about the sense of the uprising and degenerated into recriminations between the radicals and the moderates. Later, the very idea of uprisings came to be questioned by those who argued that they were foolhardy and costly. The proponents replied that they sustained and prolonged the life of the nation. In the politically fragmented emigration liberals and conservatives grouped around Czartoryski; liberal democrats generally identified with Lelewel. Then there were the extremists who asserted that the road to national independence led through a ruthless social revolution.

The left emphasized the solidarity of nations, and indeed the triumphant passage of the emigrants through Germany on their way to Paris strengthened their belief that they were in the vanguard of the coming European revolution. The Democratic Society, which the historian Peter Brock called the first democratically run, centralized, and disciplined political party of East Central Europe, aimed at spreading the ideas of agrarian democracy and revolution. Marx saw agrarian democracy as a crucial Polish contribution to European revolutionary thought. On his side Czartoryski strove to gain the support of Western governments and parliaments. From the Hôtel Lambert in Paris he directed a large network that operated in Central Europe and in the Balkans, and waged a relentless struggle with Russian diplomacy. The prince did not categorically reject uprisings and social transformations, but he wished them to occur at propitious times and with a chance of success.

The emigration deserved to be called great not only because of its political activity, but on account of the prominent ideological, intellectual, and cultural role it played. Representative of the prevalent romanticism were such poetic giants as Adam Mickiewicz, Juliusz Słowacki, and Zygmunt Krasiński. These national "bards" (*wieszcze*) shaped the way of thinking of entire Polish generations. Mickiewicz's early poems of the 1820s had marked the birth of Polish romanticism. Now his masterpieces such as *Pan Tadeusz* and *The Forefathers' Eve*, and the symbolist and prophetic *Books of the Polish Nation and the Polish Pilgrim* became part of the national heritage. The earlier-mentioned ideas of romantic nationalism assumed their final shape, and found in Polish Messianism (Poland as Christ among nations) their most extreme form. Polish folklore, but what is much more important, the Polish psyche, found its reflection in the great music of Fryderyk Chopin. Two other figures whose literary and national impact proved of lasting value were the later discovered poet, Cyprian Norwid, and the greatest Polish comedy playwright from Galicia, A. Fredro.

The November uprising gained active supporters in the Prussian and Austrian parts of partitioned Poland, and it reverberated throughout Hungary and Bohemia. Šafařik called the Polish question a "sacred cause"; Slovaks in particular came into contact with Polish émigrés. Over thirty Hungarian counties made declarations in favor of the Poles, and the diet demanded that Austria extend aid to them. With the fall of the uprising voices were heard in Hungary that the Poles had committed a fatal mistake by not emancipating the peasants. Indeed, the peasant question suddenly acquired an urgency in Hungary it did not have before. The epidemic of cholera that the Russian soldiers had brought to the Congress Kingdom extended south of the Carpathian mountains. Attempts to control it resulted in a large peasant uprising that especially affected the Slovak and Romanian communities. Hungarian propertied classes were alarmed, and their fears grew when in 1846 an abortive Polish uprising in Galicia triggered a peasant "jacquerie," which was exploited by Austrian administration. It was characteristic that in the little Cracow republic, where the insurgents were momentarily successful, the peasants (earlier emancipated) did not side with the Austrians. Cracow was annexed by Austria and the lesson of

1846 was clear. Hungarian fears of a social upheaval, that Vienna would exploit, combined with the liberals' demand for change and became its important catalyst.

Hungarian agriculture had experienced a boom during the Napoleonic wars from which both nobles and peasants profited. But a fall of prices followed; Hungarian grain could not compete with that of Russia or North America. Attempts to concentrate on sheep raising did not produce immediate results. By and large the gentry fared better than the magnates, but there was a growing feeling that agricultural production needed to be transformed and modernized, serfdom eliminated, and capital made more readily available. Belief in free trade led to demands at the 1825 diet for the abolition of the custom barriers. Later there was a change of view in favor of a protective Hungarian tariff. But for the time being the Hungarians gave priority to language demands, which the Habsburgs granted in exchange for taxes and recruits for the army. Vienna was using the peasant issue as a weapon against the nobility and it simultaneously sabotaged any noble initiatives in that domain for fear of a noble–peasant alliance.

The peasant question was obviously part of a larger picture, and Széchenyi's booklet *Credit* (*Hitel*) pointed to the country's general backwardness: inefficient serfdom, entailed estates, tax exemptions for the nobles, all stood in the way of progress. Without doing away with them one could not hope to accumulate capital, activate credit, and make labor and land marketable commodities. Holding up England and Franklin's America as examples, Széchenyi wrote, "The century is on the march, but, unfortunately, I live in a country that is dragging one leg behind."[40] He stressed the need to cultivate Hungarian nationality, inter-class communications, and external commercial contacts.

István Széchenyi, "neurotic and passionate," to use István Deák's adjectives, had, as mentioned, financed institutions that promoted Hungarian language and nationality. He was also involved in most other initiatives that aimed at an economic advancement of the country and its "embourgeoisement": a bridge linking Buda and Pest, steamship navigation on the Danube and on Lake Balaton; horse breeding, the first rolling mill, and the first commercial bank. To debate current issues, a national club (Nemzeti Casino) was founded on the English model. The book *Credit* was the first of a trilogy that argued with opponents, developed concepts of Hungarian nation, and presented a stage by stage program of reform. Széchenyi, "the greatest Hungarian," dominated the scene in the 1830s, the Age of Reform. Thereafter he began to be eclipsed by the more radical Lajos Kossuth, passionate, hard working, poor, "calculating and flamboyant" – to cite Deák again.

Kossuth was a political fighter, a man who used journalism as a modern political weapon, and whose anti-Austrian stance reflected that of the gentry and intelligentsia. These groups blamed Vienna for all economic evils and formulated their demands under the slogan of "Liberty and property" in terms of liberal nationalism, although, as already pointed out (see p. 143), with a Jacobin accent. Kossuth's oppositional struggles went through three phases. In the first, journalistic, one he confronted Széchenyi, who denounced him as a demagogue, a rabble-rouser, and a Magyar nationalist whose insensitivity was goading the non-Hungarians and provoking a future life and death struggle with them. During the second phase, Kossuth, having been imprisoned, acquired the aura of political martyrdom, but the economic protectionist ideas he advocated had little success. In the final 1847 stage, when the opposition became a political party, he assumed its virtual leadership and presided over a program that would be implemented in the March–April 1848 laws. In formulating this program of sweeping reform, the Hungarians insisted that Austria, the Czech lands, and Galicia adjust their constitutional regimes to that of Hungary. This postulate would henceforth become a dogma of Hungarian politics.

FROM THE SPRING OF NATIONS TO THE 1860s

In 1848 a revolutionary tide swept across Europe. It was a veritable Spring of Nations that saw first a culmination of liberal nationalism and then its collapse amidst internal contradictions. Beginning in Palermo in January, demands for constitutional and national freedom spread to central and northern Italy; in Paris the February Revolution took place, and in March Prussia and most of Germany and Austria were aflame. Bohemia and the Polish provinces of Prussia found themselves caught in a current for a united greater Germany. If successful it would have meant the end of the Habsburg monarchy. Polish hopes arose that Austrian Galicia and Prussian Poznania might be free to join a reconstituted Poland, which German liberals wanted to be a buffer separating them from tsarist Russia.

Portentous events were simultaneously occurring on the all-German level, in Austria, Bohemia, the Polish lands, and Hungary. They interconnected and influenced each other. On March 11, in Prague, a meeting of the radical Czech society "Repeal" prepared an address to Vienna spelling out the major national demands: autonomy of all the lands of the Crown of St Wenceslas united with a common, modern parliament; guaranteed German–Czech equality and civic freedoms; emancipation of the peasantry, etc. Somewhat reformulated these demands were accepted partially and with a delay by Vienna, where the revolution had swept away Prince Metternich and instituted a somewhat shaky government. But these reforms were to be linked with the calling of a parliament in Prague, which did not occur. Nor was

Vienna prepared to grant a unification of Bohemia, Moravia, and Austrian Silesia; to this the Germans were strongly objecting. "The time has come for us to take our stand in Bohemia as Germans," wrote a poet to his friend.[41]

Meanwhile, the Vorparlament (a preparatory body) in Frankfurt, seeking to transform the Germanic Confederation into a liberal constitutional German state, invited Palacký, as a representative of Bohemia, to join its deliberations. His famous reply made two telling points. First, while Bohemia had had feudal ties with the Holy Roman Empire and then with its successor the Germanic Confederation, it was not and could not become part of a modern unified Germany. Second, Austria, according to Palacký, was performing a crucial task of protecting the smaller nations of the Danubian area, and its destruction was out of the question. Indeed, as he put it, if Austria did not exist it would be necessary to invent it. We see here the first fully articulate formulations of Austro-Slavism, which found its political expression at the Slav Congress that met in Prague in June. The congress, in fact, transcended the limits of the monarchy for the Poles who attended it represented not only Galicia but also Prussian Poland.

The events in the latter province had taken the form of a Polish movement for national separation of Poznania. It had at first the backing of German liberals and even of the Prussian state, which permitted the formation of a Polish militia. The reason was fear of Russia, for the tsar had menaced the rising nations in no uncertain terms on March 27. The Vorparlament treated the Polish statement that their land could not be incorporated in a German state with an understanding which it did not show to Palacký. The Czech leader was viewed as a secessionist. But as the danger of a Russian intervention receded, and local clashes between Poles and Germans in Poznania multiplied, even limited concessions to the Poles were withdrawn. The Polish militia was ordered to disband and its armed resistance was broken by force. As a liberal deputy at Frankfurt put it, having to choose between German and Polish interests, he opted for "healthy national egoism." This was symptomatic and it applied also to Austro–Polish relations.

Galician demands that Austria champion the cause of a reborn Poland had at first received a sympathetic hearing in Vienna. Liberal papers condemned the partitions and calmly envisaged a possible secession of Galicia from the monarchy. Encouragement came from Hungary where the diet called for the recreation of an independent Poland. From Paris Czartoryski was advising the leaders in Poznania and Galicia to await international developments, which were likely to make their provinces part of an anti-Russian Poland. St Petersburg, however, cleverly adopted a wait-and-see policy, and not only the Prussian but also the Austrian grip on the Poles tightened. Forestalling Polish preparations to emancipate the peasantry in Galicia the Austrian governor issued an emancipation decree himself. To weaken the Polish position he supported the Ruthenians, who began to insist that, after all, the Poles were not the only hosts in the province and could not speak on behalf of all. Finally, when under the influence of émigrés the radical elements in Cracow tried to seize the city, the Austrian artillery bombarded it into submission.

Hence, when the Poles met with Czechs, Slovaks, Ruthenians, and Southern Slavs at the Prague Slav Congress, they operated from a position of relative weakness. Nor was Polish sympathy for the Hungarian cause, then becoming endangered by the counter-revolution, shared by the other fellow Slavs. The congress took a stand on the right of free development of nationalities and a reconstruction of Austria along national lines. It censured the Hungarian treatment of Slavs and denounced the partitions of Poland. The congress was careful not to be accused of Panslavism, but it did not escape the ridicule that the Germans (Marx and Engels included) heaped on the ambitions of the "non-historic" nations. To Engels Palacký was a "learned German run mad" who could not even speak proper Czech. The loyalty of the Czechs received a shock when the Whit Sunday riot in Prague was brutally subdued by Austrian troops and the city bombarded on the orders of Marshal Windisch Graetz. Palacký viewed the Whit Sunday riot as a provocation meant to put an end to the Slav Congress. The latter's achievements were modest. However, in its manifesto to the nations of Europe it did go on record as favoring international cooperation, and it recalled the rights of Slavs "among whom liberty was ever cherished."

Everything else apart the chances of Czechs and Poles were severely limited by their respective confrontations with Germans and Ruthenians. The souvenirs of the 1846 Galician peasant jacquerie were also a restricting factor. Yet 1848 transformed the Czechs into a political force in the monarchy. That year was also, as a historian put it, "a year of many 'firsts' in modern Czech history":[42] first political program, first political parties, first constitutions and elections.

Hungary occupied a stronger position in the monarchy than either Bohemia or Galicia and in that sense its "lawful revolution" began as a far-reaching success. Demands voiced by Kossuth at the diet in early March and reinforced by the radical platform adopted in Pest, aimed at a transformation of Hungary, including Transylvania, into a modern constitutional kingdom with its own government responsible to a parliament elected on a broad franchise. People were to be given civic and political rights, and the peasantry emancipated. The upper house was dragging its feet, but the outbreak of the revolution in Vienna and revolutionary manifestations in Budapest on March 15 enabled Kossuth to exert pressure on the conservatives and virtually dictate terms to Austria. In the second week of April the Hungarian constitution was approved and a cabinet appointed, headed by L. Batthyány and comprising top political figures from Széchenyi to Kossuth. This victory of freedom was welcomed by the non-Magyar liberals, but soon their own national demands conflicted with the policies of Budapest.

Croatia, which from the late eighteenth century had been more closely subordinated to Hungarian central authorities, sought its own administration, greater powers for the *sabor* (diet), and the emancipation of the peasantry. It insisted on the use of the Croat language. In late March a Habsburg loyalist, Josip Jelačić, was named ban and commander of the Military Border. His choice was endorsed by the *sabor* acting in the spirit of the Illyrian program (unification of all of Croatia) and aiming at an independent Croatia linked only through a personal union with the St Stephen's Crown. "The nations will group according to their language," the *sabor* declared. Budapest reacted violently. Under its pressure the king dismissed Jelačić in June, but the latter, certain that this was a passing concession, remained in control. Indeed, as confusion increased Jelačić eventually became indispensable again. Batthyány's attempts to reach compromise with Vienna failed and the Austrian-appointed commander of the Hungarian army, General Lamberg, was killed in September by a Budapest mob. Even before Jelačić was named commander of the Hungarian army he launched his Croat troops against Budapest, but was stopped at the battle of Pákozd. The legal situation was most peculiar. The king of Croatia was battling the king of Hungary while the emperor of Austria stood aside. Of course all three rulers were one and the same person.

The September crisis marked a new phase in the Hungarian revolution, but before examining it, more must be said about the non-Magyar nationalities. The Slovaks in their "Demands of the Slovak Nation" petitioned for federalization of Hungary within which Slovakia would enjoy local autonomy. Kossuth rejected the very idea of a Slovak nation, and Slovak leaders, Štúr among them, sought refuge in Prague. There they participated in the Slav Congress. The Austrians regarded them at first as dangerous firebrands.

The Serbs, also stressing their nationality, demanded territorial autonomy, and their strivings found support across the border, in the Principality of Serbia. No wonder the Hungarians, who felt threatened by Illyrianism and Austro-Slavism, were pleased with the dissolution of the Prague Congress, and looked favorably on plans of a greater Germany, a potential ally.

While the Serbs rose in late May, and hostilities punctuated by massacres took a heavy toll, the Romanians in Transylvania demanded recognition as a nation and full religious equality. Social and political motives affected their opposition to a union of Transylvania with Hungary; Hungarian contempt for the Romanians and the vested interests of the gentry prevented a meaningful dialogue. In mid-July the diet of Transylvania voted for union, and armed clashes began. Again casualties were heavy. Kossuth appointed the Polish emigré general, József Bem, commander in this area, and he won victories in the field. But he also attempted, in accord with Czartoryski's policy, to mediate between Magyars and Romanians. He was not successful. As for the Germans they split: the historically autonomous Saxons opposing the Magyars, and the more recently arrived Swabian colonists siding with them. Thus, the April constitution, which in effect reconstituted a dual sovereignty of the king and the nation, provided no solution to the nationality problems. The Hungarian liberals could not see why collective privileges need be bestowed on ethnic groups. The Slavs and Romanians could not accept the territorial concept of the Hungarian nation reinforced by linguistic criteria. It was only in 1849, in the last stage of the revolution, that the parliament enacted a nationality law, on July 28, that granted equality to all nations (although not federalization) and proceeded to a complete emancipation of the Jews.

The nationality problem was connected with the liberation of the peasantry, which the mainly peasant non-Magyars regarded as the first, and the Hungarians as the final revolutionary step. Only the radicals, who included the poet S. Petöfi, advocated a sweeping reform without compensation to the landlords. Some of them spoke even of distribution of the nobles' land. Yet the criticism, particularly by Marxist historians, that the revolution did not go far enough seems rather unfair. After all, it was the old "feudal" diet that passed the constitution, and the parliament did not seek protection from the ruler against domestic radicals or foreign invaders.

From the start the relationship between Budapest and Vienna hinged on the resolution of the problem of the army and finances. Already in July the mounting crisis led to Kossuth's "fatherland in danger" speech and the appeal for raising a Hungarian army and collecting taxes. By September a turning point was reached, and the Batthyány government resigned. Regular war ensued, and while many ex-ministers withdrew, left the country, or broke down (as did Széchenyi), Kossuth rose to a position of supreme leadership. His main rival was General Görgey, a brilliant soldier, but a cool and difficult personality, who believed in war for limited goals. He often behaved in an insubordinate and resentful fashion toward Kossuth who in turn denied him the formal supreme command.

The Hungarians refused to assist the October Revolution in Vienna, thus wasting a unique chance of linking forces with Austrian radicals. But they clung to the dogma of the legality of their regime, which was most important to many, especially those bound by the military oath. They observed the principle of non-interference in the other part of the monarchy. In the spring of 1849, and after a series of defeats and withdrawals, the Hungarians regained most of the country. But tendencies to reach a compromise with Vienna conflicted with the insistence on Hungarian rights. The abdication of Emperor-King Ferdinand and the ascension to the throne of Francis Joseph in December 1848 had been viewed by the Hungarians as an illegal act. They naturally rejected the March 1849 centralist constitution which the new monarch proclaimed and which restored Hungary to its pre-1848 position. As for a federalist structure that had been prepared by the Austrian parliament transferred from Vienna to Kroměříř after the October Revolution, the government did not permit its completion.

On April 14 1849 the Hungarian parliament voted to dethrone the Habsburgs; Hungary, it said, was "returning to the European family as a free and independent state." Kossuth became governor-general, or regent. This was a radical departure, but neither this nor the involvement of Poles in the Hungarian revolution constituted the decisive reasons for Russia's military intervention, which now took place. As was Rákóczi a century and a half earlier, Kossuth was out of the country when Görgey capitulated at Világos on August 13. But there was no repetition of the compromise peace of 1711. The Austrian commander General Haynau, nicknamed the hyena of Brescia for the atrocities committed in Lombardy, presided over a regime of harsh reprisals. It included the execution of Batthyány and of thirteen generals at Arad. The heavy war casualties were now augmented by Hungarians who were shot, hanged, or imprisoned.

A decade of neo-absolutism descended on the Habsburg monarchy. It rested, as a wit put it, on four armies: the standing army of soldiers, the sitting army of bureaucrats, the kneeling army of priests, and the creeping army of informers. The lands of the Crown of St Stephen were split again, with new districts set up under military governors. Self-governing institutions in Croatia were abolished as was Saxon autonomy in Transylvania. In Hungary passive political resistance prevailed, with a large collaborationist wing on one extreme and the secret pro-Kossuth faction on the other. In essence all that remained of the Spring of Nations was the emancipation of the peasantry. It was finalized in Hungary in the 1850s, with loose ends remaining in the Czech lands and Galicia. The Hungarians, Czechs, Poles, and all the other nationalities had learned important if bitter lessons; as for the Habsburg monarchy, despite the reaction to the events of 1848–9, the clock could not be turned back.

After a decade, Austria's military defeats in the 1859 war against France and Sardinia forced the government to experiment with constitutional change. A "federalist" October Diploma of 1860 restored the Hungarian diet and the diets in Transylvania and Croatia. They were to be represented, together with other provincial bodies, in the all-Austrian Reichsrat in Vienna. German liberals opposed this conservative-dominated organ that hardly encroached on imperial power. The Hungarians demanded to be treated as a separate entity. The February Patent that followed in 1861 was a mixture of absolutism and constitutionalism, centralism and federalism. In the Czech lands it favored the Germans, in others the dominant nationality. Still, it did provide a quasi-federal parliamentary regime. The Hungarians refused, however, to send delegates to the Reichsrat and so did the Croatian *sabor*. From exile Kossuth appealed for a new Danubian Confederation that would reconcile the nations of the Hungarian kingdom, but was not taken seriously. In 1861 the Slovaks demanded, in a Memorandum of the Slovak Nation, a recognition of their national individuality and rather modest autonomy. This was refused in Budapest, and indeed there was no progress on other fronts. At best the Hungarians formulated general principles, but refused to discuss concrete demands.

In 1863–4 the Hungarians, together with other nations of the monarchy, watched Russia crush – in political collaboration with Bismarck's Prussia – the Polish January uprising. This had a sobering effect on many and demonstrated the high price one paid for an armed confrontation with the state.

The Spring of Nations had not affected the Congress Kingdom. Nor did the Crimean War of 1854–6, during which the Polish emigration was only partly successful in bringing the Polish question to the international agenda. At the Paris Peace Congress the Russians assured the West that the Poles would be offered amnesty, some linguistic and religious concessions, and a limited restoration of local administration, as part of reforms prepared by Alexander II. These included the all-important abolition of serfdom that finally took place in 1861.

The kingdom stood on the threshold of the Industrial Revolution. The *szlachta* was undergoing further decomposition; an intelligentsia was growing; town people were assuming a bigger role in society. The abolition of the customs barrier between the empire and the kingdom opened possibilities for economic expansion. In agriculture a process of transforming the peasant into a rent-paying farmer was proceeding, but the peasantry, supported by liberal and radical circles, wanted full emancipation and ownership of the land. A group of reformist landowners, allowed by Russia to form the Agricultural Society, gathered around the popular Count Andrzej Zamoyski, whose economic initiatives resembled those of Széchenyi. Although the leaders wanted the society to stay clear of politics, it became a platform for general discussion and a point of attraction for moderates in the country.

Zamoyski collaborated with the rising bourgeoisie of Warsaw, who were led by the great financier of Jewish descent, Leopold Kronenberg. These circles came to constitute the nucleus of the movement known as the Whites.

At the other end of the political spectrum there formed a radical current composed largely of students, younger army officers, artisans, and lesser gentry. It would eventually crystallize as the Reds. Far from avoiding politics, the Reds combined it with a social program that included the emancipation of peasants and equality of Jews. This second issue did not cause much dissent, for this period was one of the closest in Polish–Jewish cooperation. The emancipation of Jews, seen as Poland's third estate, also figured in the program of a man who was a party in himself, the Margrave Aleksander Wielopolski. A magnate like Zamoyski, Wielopolski scorned popularity and pursued his own ideas in which a low opinion of his countrymen, disenchantment with the West, and an aristocratic outlook harking back to the *ancien régime*, combined and were colored by a strong and despotic temperament. It was Wielopolski to whom the Russians turned when a mounting tension in the years 1861–2 resulted in bloody confrontation between Russian troops and the people, and the subsequent "moral revolution." Wielopolski seemed the only choice, for Zamoyski and his groups, afraid of being stigmatized as collaborationists, adhered to their demands for a restoration of the 1815 constitution.

Wielopolski, who believed that a return to 1815 was impossible and therefore stood for only limited reforms, was authorized to offer concessions in the educational sphere (the re-establishment of the university, renamed the Main School), in polonizing the administration, in emancipating the Jews, and in decreeing a rather ill-defined transformation of labor obligations into tenantry. Determined to exert full power he dissolved the Agricultural Society, warned the church hierarchy not to interfere in politics, and refused proffered help from his countrymen. As he allegedly said, one could do something *for* the Poles, but nothing *with* the Poles. Intending to break the Reds, Wielopolski decided on a particularly galling measure, namely a military conscription, so arranged that it would affect mostly townspeople, the backbone of the Red movement. Military service at that time lasted some twenty-five years, which meant an effective elimination of these people from the homeland for most of their life.

The Red Central Committee was forced into a position in which it had to oppose the draft by proclaiming an armed uprising. This it did on January 22, 1863; the longest and in many ways the most dramatic of Polish risings began. Appealing to the nations of the Old Commonwealth to take up their arms, and launching a special address to "brother Poles of the Mosaic faith," the insurgents fought for more than a year. In the spring the Whites reluctantly joined; their vast resources made it possible for the uprising to continue and expand. Still, the insurgents had to fight a hit-and-run guerrilla war without ever controlling a larger territory or a town. This prevented the National Government (as it was named) from coming into the open or enforcing its decree emancipating the peasantry. The government led the rising from its clandestine quarters in Warsaw, its seal being the only mark of recognition. The underground network was large and effective, and it says something for the patriotism and the solidarity of Poles that they obeyed the orders of an anonymous government which changed its composition several times.

The Prussia of Bismarck sided with St Petersburg; France, Britain, and Austria made several diplomatic *démarches* on Polish behalf but without any practical results. In the United States, where the Civil War coincided with the January uprising, the Northerners sympathized with Russia, making somewhat far-fetched comparisons between Southern secession and Polish attempts to free themselves of Russia. In Paris, words of encouragement (*durez!*) were proffered that included the remark that the blood of the insurgents would mark the future boundaries of Poland. Indeed the uprising spread over much of the old Commonwealth. This was the last time that the Lithuanian and Belorussian peasantry would fight alongside the Poles under the common historic banner. This was no longer true for the Ukraine, which opposed the insurgents. A wave of nationalism passed over Russia, discrediting such defenders of Poland as the popular Alexander Herzen. But the number of Russian (and even Ukrainian) volunteers in the insurgent ranks was larger than that of any other foreigners who came to struggle for Poland and freedom.

Virtually all social classes were represented in the rising, the lower clergy being more involved than the hierarchy. Although in many areas the peasants were indifferent or even actively inimical to the "noble" uprising, there were more peasant insurgents than at any previous time since the Kościuszko insurrection of 1794. The struggle was terribly uneven and militarily hopeless from the beginning. The partisans lacked arms, munitions, even experienced commanders. The last leader of the uprising, Romuald Traugutt, succeeded in prolonging the struggle until April 1864 when he was arrested and hanged, with five companions. Sporadic fighting went even beyond that date, till the autumn. The tsarist government which could not appear to be less generous to the peasants than the insurgent government, had already improved the terms of emancipation in the Lithuanian, Belorussian, and Ukrainian provinces. In 1864 it emancipated the peasantry in the Congress Kingdom. The political dimensions of this decree will be dealt with in the next chapter. Let us just recall here that the move completed peasant emancipation in East Central Europe.

The age-long dispute about the sense of the uprising and the existing alternatives is not quite resolved, but some consensus has been reached. It appears that Wielopolski, whom the Russians in fact made use of, never stood a chance of shaping the course of events. He could hardly have taken the wind out of the Red program by pushing through the emancipation of the peasantry himself, if only because St Petersburg would not have allowed it. Russian policy had been a consistent one of divide and rule. Wielopolski and the Russians forced both the Whites and the Reds into a position that left them no alternatives. In a sense the Whites had already made a choice when they refused collaboration except on their terms, in the spring of 1862. They had to join the insurrection to escape public condemnation and in the hope of giving it a moderate direction. The Reds challenged by Wielopolski's draft could only respond by resistance, even though they were badly prepared. The possibility of making free and rational calculations was illusory.

The collapse of the uprising marked the end of national revolutions in East Central Europe. A new era began. The Habsburg monarchy, having lost a war against Prussia in 1866, had to engage in drastic reconstruction. It took the form of the Compromise (*Ausgleich*) between the dynasty and the Hungarians. Austro-Hungary emerged; Galicia received an autonomy; the Czechs felt betrayed. Was compromise a real political option for the Slavs? The next decades were to bring an answer.

6

FROM COMPROMISE TO INDEPENDENCE

THE INDUSTRIAL REVOLUTION

Fifty years separated the Polish January uprising and the Austro-Hungarian Compromise from the First World War. These were the decades of the apogee of Europe and the great powers' hegemony. The Franco–Prussian war of 1870 was the last major nineteenth-century struggle fought on the continent. A shaky balance prevailed thereafter, as the center of conflicts shifted overseas. Within Europe the Balkans became, after the Congress of Berlin of 1878, the object of intense rivalry between Russia and Austro-Hungary. The European cabinets viewed this rivalry with anxiety mixed with a condescending attitude toward national aspiration in the Balkans. The world belonged to the great powers which saw themselves and were seen by others as the carriers of material and cultural progress, indeed of variously defined civilizing missions.

The Industrial Revolution was in full swing. Economic processes going back to the sixteenth century, and characterized by the production of a surplus for the expanding market (hence the search for more sources of raw materials and bigger markets) were reaching their peak. Division of labor was becoming more complex; there was a rise of a novel kind of social consciousness. Economy and society were transformed through the application of technology, combined with developments that required a broad mobilization of all resources and energies. A new type of industrial society arose that lived on perpetual growth and on expected and continuous improvement. In view of the depth of transformation and the rapidity of change, the term "revolution" still seems appropriate, all the arguments against its use notwithstanding.

The Industrial Revolution went through several phases. In the last decades of the century it extended to most of Europe, engendered new industries (electrical, chemical) and produced a new type of financial capitalism, big business organization, and imperialist expansion. The high points were followed by cyclical depressions. Throughout the nineteenth century Europe retained much of its monarchic-aristocratic and agrarian character, but the new bourgeois civilization was in the ascendancy. It stood for modernization and progress although it offered no panacea to the social ills and national aspirations of the oppressed. The contrast between the rich and the poor, between the city and the countryside, remained acute and perhaps even increased.

Modern civilization exacted a heavy price in the form of city slums, child labor, and the tyranny of the factory bell. The masses, becoming more conscious and organized, were demanding economic, social, political, and national rights. The middle class appeared as the main enemy. The radicals viewed liberalism as a screen for the interests of the bourgeoisie and accused the middle class of having betrayed the cause of the people. The conservatives regarded the liberals as guilty of having engendered political and social revolt and thus undermined the traditional system.

The liberal tenet of the natural harmony of interests was successfully challenged by concepts of class or race struggle. Social Darwinism spoke of the survival of the fittest and provided justification for integral nationalism, which found the hatred of other people more attractive than the love of one's own. Racism extolled the Aryan or Nordic myth and transformed Judeophobia into modern anti-Semitism. The Jew, whether in the writings of Charles Maurras in France, the pronouncements of Karl Lueger in Vienna, or the Russian Black Hundred, epitomized all evil.

While European society was under attack from radicals and socialists, the anarchists rejected the very notion of the state. Though electoral franchise was being enlarged, and in several cases was transformed into universal male suffrage, Russia needed a revolution in 1905 to install a semi-parliamentary regime. In the sphere of culture the *fin de siècle* produced various trends, including nihilism. Modernism sounded a call to struggle against the philistine outlook and the bourgeois system of values. The perennial truth that European civilization had two faces, one characterized by stability and prosperity, the other by malaise and rebellion, was brought out more forcibly.

Before turning to the challenge of the Industrial Revolution to East Central Europe one needs to look at the classic case study: England. In the late eighteenth century, European economy was based predominantly on agriculture, and drastic changes in that domain were needed for basic developments in industry to occur. England was the first country to go through the agricultural revolution during that century, that was characterized by the application of new techniques, changes in the utilization of the soil, and extensive and intensive farming and breeding. Production for the market increased greatly while the number of people working on the land diminished. The accumulation of capital and the existence of an available pool of labor were the prerequisites for the development of industries, whose production was revolutionized by the application of machinery. The advent of steam power heralded a new era. Cottage industries and manufactories made way for mechanized factories. Industrial towns grew; a new type of bourgeoisie developed, as did an industrial working class. Railroads created new mobility; novel types of credit arose; trade showed a phenomenal growth, increasing nine times between 1820 and 1880 and fifty times if we take the whole period from 1750 to 1913.

In the English pattern there were three phases: in the first, textiles showed a high output while heavy industries developed more slowly; during the second the latter rose rapidly; in the third a certain equilibrium between the two was reached. The brief period during which investments rose from 5 to 10 percent, and technological advances spread rapidly is usually referred to as the "take-off." In England it occurred between the 1780s and 1802; in France and Belgium between 1830 and 1860; in Germany between 1850 and 1873. Unlike in England, the Industrial Revolution and the agricultural one occurred almost simultaneously on the continent, and were accompanied by changes in credit and transportation. The delay of continental West European developments was in part due to political reasons (the Napoleonic wars) and in part resulted from structural weaknesses in agriculture or artisan production, which adversely affected the mobility of labor and free enterprise.

The response of East Central Europe (except Bohemia which conformed more to the central and West European pattern) to the challenge of the Industrial Revolution was colored by the distinctive features of its economy. Agriculture was more primitive and the gap between farming on the big estates and peasant husbandry bigger. Bohemia alone developed a strong internal agricultural market. Although individual Polish or Hungarian estates achieved a high degree of modernization they could not diffuse it more widely. The pattern of textiles leading the way in technological progress to be followed by heavy industry was either reversed in this area, or the two processes occurred simultaneously. The role of textiles as a catalyst was to a large extent played instead by food-related industries.

An unevenness of modernization was also fairly typical for East Central European developments. Modern equipment imported from abroad coexisted with obsolete tools and implements, sometimes in the same branch of the economy. Differences between sectors were also great. Finally, the cheap and abundant pool of workers did not encourage enterprises to install labor-saving devices.

According to the classic formula of A. Gerschenkron the spontaneous process of domestic accumulation of capital in England contrasted with the need for deliberate bank financing in western and central Europe, and with state intervention in Hungary or Russia without which an industrial take-off would not have been possible. The Hungarian economic historians J. Berend and G. Ránki drew a more nuanced picture. They recalled that state intervention, although indirect and occurring earlier, was also necessary to prepare the ground in England and France. Further east, state intervention was more direct, came later, and assumed a greater dimension. Railroads on the continent, for instance, began as state enterprises, then were taken over by private capital, to end in most cases by being nationalized. Hence, it

> is not the peculiar and specific role of the state, but the import of capital, promoted and motivated by state activity which may be regarded as the feature distinguishing Eastern Europe from the rest of the Continent in the modern transformation of the economy.[43]

Foreign capital was important indeed. Usually it was exploitative in weaker economies while fulfilling useful functions in more developed structures. It is worthwhile to remember that during the century virtually every country attracted capital together with advanced technology and know-how from a more developed neighbor. Toward the end of this period Britain shifted most of its investments overseas, while West European countries invested more heavily in the eastern parts. In some cases foreign capital contributed to a significant acceleration of the production processes. Among states on the "periphery," Spain is often given as an example.

Did the Industrial Revolution significantly deepen the difference between the most advanced zone (the core) and the east-central and eastern spheres? The individual regions undoubtedly differed with regard to their level of economic productivity and labor organization, social mobility and class structure, as well as the type of public authority. In all these respects the gap between the West and such countries as Hungary, and the Austrian and Russian parts of partitioned Poland, grew, all their progress notwithstanding. Prussian Poland and Moravia stood closer to the Western model. According to Marxist and New Left historians the reason that the economically weaker countries had to become relatively poorer and the stronger had to grow richer lay in the exploitative nature of trade between the two groups. The former, obliged to export foodstuffs and raw materials in exchange for finished products were perpetuating a one-sided development. Trade served as means of exploitation of the poorer by the richer.

Another explanation of the growing discrepancy dwells on political, particularly military factors, namely a competition which placed a disproportionately heavy burden on weaker economies. Another argument advanced, for instance by Andrew Janos, is couched in socio-economic terms. The growing backwardness of the "periphery" is explained by the impact of innovations and expectations on its economy. In order to satisfy the demands of the upper classes capital resources are siphoned away from investments and go into elite consumption, unrealistic economic strategies, and are dissipated through corruption. Hence, Janos concludes, patterns of consumption prove "incongruous with existing modes of production."

There is little doubt that while the European west and center responded fairly quickly to the English challenge, Polish and Hungarian economies reacted at first more sluggishly. It is also true that the west European demand for more food and raw materials exerted a pull that stimulated exports of these articles with the resulting one-sidedness mentioned above. Yet to speak of a "colonial" relationship or to draw close analogies to the Third World of today is an oversimplification. The "colonial" relationship implies that the demand by the "core" prompts investments in the export sectors needed by the "core," investments stemming largely from imported capital. The rest of the economy has no chance of real development. But in the case of at least some countries of the European "periphery" investments did stimulate processes that led to structural changes and allowed the country to become part of the "core." Thus Sweden in the late nineteenth and early twentieth centuries saw its export of wood, followed by that of iron, transform the economy to the extent that it ceased to be a "peripheral" country. In East Central Europe the transition from food to food-processed articles indicated possibilities of economic growth and transformation. But factors other than purely economic ones affected the development, being both a precondition of industrialization and a concomitant and constant complement to it. Hence, to cite again Berend and Ránki, the issue is

> not whether the export of foodstuffs and raw materials in itself leads to favourable or unfavourable terms of trade for a given area, but whether the countries of an area become trapped in the role of raw material exporters, or are, rather, able to go on from there to build up a suitable developed economic structure.[44]

The actual ability to build depends on such diverse elements as the wealth of natural resources, the network of communications, antecedents of pre-industrialization, possibilities for the accumulation of capital, governmental policies, and social-political structure of the country.

DIFFERENT PATTERNS IN EAST CENTRAL EUROPE

Industrial Revolution in the Czech lands resembled that in western and central Europe. The demographic explosion was similar – a 50 percent increase between 1848 and 1910 – and brought the population of Bohemia to over 6.7 million, that of Moravia to 2.6 million and of Austrian Silesia to 0.75 million. More important still was the decline of rural population from 71.1 percent in 1880 to 57.9 percent in 1910. Prague grew from 75,000 to 224,000. Industrial centers emerged around Brno (the textile capital), Kladno, Plzeň or Ostrava-Karvina. The emancipation of the peasantry allowed social mobility and contributed to a modernization of agriculture, although it would be a mistake to believe that emancipation *per se* led to an automatic capitalist transformation. Other factors were of importance. The fall of illiteracy to some 4.5 percent, one of the lowest in the world, needs mentioning, together with the constant growth in numbers of primary and high school students. The existence of a large market in the Habsburg monarchy in which Czech finished products had already a fairly well assured place provided another advantage. True, Bohemia was not a master of its destiny and there was a growing Czech–German antagonism which complicated the situation. On the other hand, the social structure assisting the rise of a native Czech middle class proved to be of crucial importance.

Chronologically, the incipient stage lasted roughly to the 1820s or 1830s, during which machines were introduced in some processes and areas. The first steam locomotive was built in 1815; the first rolling mill appeared in Vitkovice iron works in 1831. The second stage of growth and development lasted roughly to 1848–9. Machinery, mainly of British origin or design, was ever more widely applied. Finally, between 1849 and 1870 the revolutionary transformation of the economy was largely completed. Factory production was first predominant in textiles, then it spread to other branches, especially food processing – flour milling, brewery, and distilleries – as was characteristic for the Industrial Revolution in East Central Europe. The output of coal and iron, and steel and machine construction, expanded drastically in the last years of the century. Engineering industries and automobiles (among the first in Europe) made the Czech lands a most economically advanced region. The name of Škoda factories (founded in 1869) became world famous, especially in armaments. The role of railroads were as crucial as in the West, and their building was affected by Austrian political and strategic considerations. The first line was opened in 1832. In the 1861–71 decade tracks increased by almost 147 percent. By the end of the century the density of the railroad network was close to that of France.

The figures in Table 6.1 give an idea of the evolving economy.

Table 6.1 Shares in percentage of gross value of industrial production

	1792	1841	1880
Textiles	84	50.7	41.5
Food		14.5	33.4
Capital goods	4*	11.7*	16.1
Others	12*	23.0*	9.8

*approximate figure
Source: J. Purš, "The Industrial Revolution in the Czech lands," *Historia*, 2 (1980), p. 266.

The Industrial Revolution in the Czech lands was clearly a success. Intensive farming and an agricultural boom that lasted from the 1820s allowed the Czechs – as distinct from the Germans who dominated the textiles, glass production, and banking – to accumulate capital through food-related industries. Thus the Czechs advanced through sugar refining, for example, and the founding of their first great credit bank (Živnostanská banka, 1865–9) showed how successful they were. Foreign capital played a relatively minor role in the industrialization process. As Czech commerical banks expanded in the 1907–13 period, Bohemia not only became an industrial country, but also one in which the Czech national movement had acquired a solid economic foundation.

Between 1846 and 1910 the Czech–German population ratio changed to the advantage of the former. In Bohemia it altered from 60:40 to 63:37; in Moravia from 70:30 to 72:28. Still, the Germans held an occupational advantage. The 1910 structure of the respective work forces showed 30 percent of Germans engaged in agriculture, 42 percent in industry, and 12 percent in trade and transport. Corresponding figures for the Czechs were 44, 31, and 9 percent. In the course of the century Jews moved to towns, becoming a comfortable middle class. In 1869 they numbered 133,000; Prague itself had nearly 10,000 Jews in 1910. Their czechization was noticeable in the 1880s even though Czech anti-Semitism was there, economically and nationally motivated. Whether it was cause or effect, the fact remains that only 15 percent of Jews in Prague declared themselves Czech. Others were German-speaking and viewed as germanizers.

As in Western Europe the Industrial Revolution in Bohemia was accompanied by social problems. Workers' resistance to the introduction of machinery led to a riot in Prague in 1844. The workers' situation worsened in older branches of the economy and in regions with outdated modes of production. Later, trade unions arose, but the Czech proletariat exhibited certain features related to the artisan tradition and outlook.

In terms of transformation of the socio-economic structure of the country the Industrial Revolution was only a partial success in Hungary. It began in the second half of the century, expanded in the 1860s, reached high intensity in the 1870s and 1880s and peaked again in the early twentieth century. Hence some historians place the take-off as late as the 1890s. The population more than doubled between 1800 and 1910; in the period between the Compromise and the outbreak of the First World War it increased from 15.4 to 20.9 million. Budapest experienced a phenomenal growth from 54,000 in 1800 to nearly 900,000 in 1910, but Szeged was the only other city that exceeded the 100,000 mark. While illiteracy was reduced by more than half it still stood at 33 percent in 1910, well above the Czech average. The number of university students, however, multiplied twenty times in the sixty years that preceded the First World War.

The first signs of the Industrial Revolution appeared before 1848. Steam power began to be applied to flour mills, sugar refineries, and one could speak of an early mechanization of certain industries. Steamboats came into use, and the first railroad line was opened. Commercial and credit banks began to be established. The emancipation of the peasantry in 1848, seen as a prerequisite for capitalism in the agrarian sector, created a large landless proletariat. But although the area brought under cultivation increased, the socio-economic structure of land relationships prevented radical transformations.

Indeed, the discrepancy between technological progress and the persistence of the social and political order constituted one of the key problems. The other was the relationship of Hungary to the more advanced Austrian half of the monarchy. The lifting of the internal tariff in 1850, the subsequent customs union, and the financial accord that accompanied the Compromise of 1867 had a deep but controversial impact on Hungarian economic development. According to a now dated school of thought Hungary was placed in a position of "colonial" subservience, which prevented a full industrialization and perpetuated the predominantly agrarian character of the country. Opponents of this view see few signs of exploitation and point to the many advantages of the association with Austria, notably the large market for the fast-growing grain, livestock, and especially processed food exports. They stress the positive role played by Austrian capital. The increase in protective tariffs in 1907 clearly alleviated the lot of the Hungarian agrarian proletariat. A certain consensus seems to have been reached regarding the benefits and hardships that the association with the more developed Austria brought to Hungary. From the viewpoint of profitability and capital accumulation the advantages derived from the food processing industries outweighed the losses from the underdeveloped light industries, especially textiles. Taking industry as a whole, there were short-term advantages stemming from the Austro-

Hungarian economic partnership, but in the long run the partnership contributed to delays in socio-economic transformations.

It was agriculture and not textiles that was the major catalyst of Hungarian economic progress. While yields doubled by the early twentieth century, the growth of food processing was the major achievement. Flour milling developed on such a huge scale that Budapest became the second largest center in the world after Minneapolis. The ratio of exports between grain and flour kept changing in favour of the latter. Progress in other branches of the economy was also striking. Coal output increased over fourteen times (in 1867–1914), that of iron over five times, that of steel twice (in 1898–1914). In terms of horsepower the increase was hundredfold since the Compromise. As for industrial workers their numbers grew from 110,000 to 620,000 between 1880 and 1913.

The expansion of the railroad network was also spectacular, although at first Austrian concerns dictated the direction of the lines and only later did Hungarian interests become dominant. By 1913 the density of tracks per inhabitant placed Hungary ahead of Germany or France, at sixth place in Europe. Some economic historians regard this growth as typical for a country that lay far from the European center and needed more developed transports and communications. Non-Hungarian capital (Austrian and foreign) played a major role in the construction of railroads. Together with local capital and governmental subsidies it helped banks to flourish. Capital growth, with 1848 taken as 100, was 750 in 1867, 6,340 in 1890, and 11,380 in 1900. These were impressive figures.

In the entire post-Compromise era Hungarian national income increased threefold. The ratio of economic development between the Austrian and Hungarian parts also pointed to Hungary's relative progress: 70:30 at the beginning; 63.6:34.4 toward the end. The changes in the structure of the economy can be seen from the figures in Table 6.2.

Table 6.2 Percentages of value of total production

	Food processing	Heavy industry	Textiles	Other light industries
1898	44.1	39.9	5.0	11.0
1913	38.9	41.2	7.3	12.6

Source: Based on R. A. Kann and Z. V. David, *The Peoples of the Eastern Habsburg Lands 1526–1918* (Seattle, Wash., 1984), p. 370.

For all this spectacular growth, given the low starting point Hungary remained an agricultural-industrial rather than an industrialized country. On the eve of the First World War industry contributed only 27–30 percent to the GNP; exports comprised only 37.5 percent of finished goods (and were mostly processed foodstuffs). The majority (75 percent) of the population derived their livelihood from agriculture and 17 percent were town inhabitants (as compared with 7 percent in 1870). About 16 percent of inhabitants of the twenty-five largest towns were engaged in industrial occupations. All this showed that while the social structure of the country underwent changes they fell short of being drastic. The social pyramid remained very traditional. Titled aristocracy, owning large estates, was still at the top and played a dominant role in politics. The affluent nobility came next, but the noble class became more differentiated as the rapid decline of medium-size holdings weakened the group that had been traditionally an independent and liberal national force. This gentry might have created a middle class jointly with the non-ethnic Hungarian bourgeoisie, and such an "embourgeoisement" of society had its advocates, as mentioned in the preceding chapter. But the gentry was loath to acquire a bourgeois outlook, working habits, and values. It entered the administration or swelled the ranks of the intelligentsia, carrying to both its ethos and tradition.

The middle class that arose was largely composed of German and Jewish elements. Actively participating in economic progress as wholesale merchants, traders, or craftsmen, the Jewish population grew from 542,279 to 911,227 in the 1869–1910 period. Almost a quarter of Budapest's inhabitants were Jews, which made the anti-Semites call it "Judapest." The Jews, however, were rapidly Magyarizing, and the same was true for the Germans. While the mid-nineteenth-century Buda was a predominantly German town, by 1910 it was 86 percent Hungarian-speaking. Freed of discriminatory laws of 1867, and placed on a level of equality in religious terms with Christians in 1896, the Jews underwent massive assimilation. The Yiddish-speaking core dwindled to less than a quarter. From the ranks of Jewish bourgeoisie came top bankers, industrialists, press magnates. Over 300 top families were ennobled and 28 received baronial titles. Many completed their assimilation by embracing Christianity and intermarrying with the native nobility.

In the absence of a native middle class with ambitions of its own, and of an "embourgeoisement" of the society, the alliance between aristocracy and the bourgeoisie of German or Jewish background produced a certain ossification of the system. Some of the aristocrats approved of industrialization only insofar as it would serve the interests of agriculture, which they identified with the interests of the country as a whole. The aristocracy was flexible enough to entrust the Jewish element with a leading role in the country's economy and at times co-opted it politically as a junior partner. After all, Magyarized Jews or Germans swelled the national statistics in the lands of St Stephen. Hence the political establishment frowned on anti-Semitism, but could not prevent the appearance of a short-lived anti-Semitic party in the 1880s, or sporadic demonstrations against real or alleged Jewish separateness and exclusiveness. The traditional Judeophobia described as "a feeling of antipathy toward an ethnic group of alien and dissimilar religion engaged in pursuits unbecoming a gentleman"[45] was being supplemented by novel characteristics derived from racism or economic rivalry. The Slovak peasants hated the Jew as an economic exploiter and as a Magyarizer. This brings us to the impact of the industrialization processes on the relations between the state and the masses, and particularly the non-Magyar nationalities.

The poverty and hardship experienced by the landless agricultural workers and the industrial proletariat led to growing discontent, which was brutally checked, and to emigration. Over 1,500,000 people left the country, mainly for America. Half of them were non-Magyars. The majority of the agricultural proletariat was composed of Hungarians, but Croats, Slovaks, and Romanians belonged to the poorest stratum which made them doubly second-class citizens.

The process of industrialization affected the non-Hungarian ethnic lands unevenly. In Slovakia, seen as a distinct unit in the post-1918 borders, there was a rough correlation between its percentage of the total population (16.8) and its industrial output (18.6). There were food-processing plants, paper, textile, and iron works. The proportional share of unfinished and semi-finished products was bigger than in other parts of Hungary. In agriculture, over 80 percent of large estates was in Magyar hands. The figure was even higher in Transylvania where industrialization made relatively modest strides. Foreign capital was mainly responsible for the modernization of mining and metallurgical industries and the building of railroads. Hungarian, Saxon, and Romanian credit banks came into existence. Croatia was worse off. It had the largest proportion of people engaged in agriculture and the highest illiteracy rate. While its population comprised 12.5 percent of the total population of Hungary, it contributed only 5 percent to the total output. The direction of the railroad lines exemplified the primacy of Hungarian interests over those of Croatia. Among the masses national and social grievances were interconnected.

Turning to Poland, it is exceedingly difficult, if not impossible, to compare the Industrial Revolution in Polish lands with that of Bohemia and Hungary. For what was Poland in the nineteenth century? It was not an economic reality, its lands being part of the partitioning powers' economies. There was no Polish market, and the adjoining parts of the former Commonwealth were separated by customs barriers. The

Congress Kingdom had to import coal from the Donets basin rather than from the neighboring Silesia. Its oil came from Baku rather than from eastern Galicia. The Poles themselves could be said to be a governing nation (to some extent) only in the autonomous Galicia. After 1864 the Kingdom was reduced to the status of an occupied province. Hence their ability to shape economic developments was severely restricted. True, the Polish ownership of land was disproportionately large in the former eastern provinces annexed to Russia. But the Polish ties with the Ukraine, Belorussia, even Lithuania were weakening in the last decades of the century, and to include these countries in "all-Polish" statistics would be misleading. So in the remarks that follow we shall concentrate mainly on the Congress Kingdom, Galicia, and Prussian Poland.

In demographic terms these lands experienced an increase that was well above the European average. In the second half of the century the population of Prussian Poland grew by 60 percent, that of Galicia by 85 percent, of the Congress Kingdom by 160 percent. Differences between these three regions – cultural, and from the viewpoint of material civilization – were pronounced. The Prussian zone was characterized by modern agriculture and light industries, and its illiteracy rate dropped between 1870 and 1901 from 30 to 1 percent. But in the backward Galicia and the Congress Kingdom, then going through the Industrial Revolution, the corresponding drop was from 80 to 56 percent, and from 80 to 65 percent. Galicia could at least boast a growing university student population – 22 percent of all students of Austria – while its population amounted only to 17.8 percent.

Galicia was clearly a neglected and underdeveloped province, little affected by industrialization. Its socio-economic structure resembled that of the poorer parts of Hungary. Within its mixed Polish-Ruthenian population the Jews constituted 11.5 percent and nearly 70 percent of them spoke Yiddish. They controlled most of the local trade and small enterprises, and ranged from poverty-stricken masses in little towns to big landowners. The Galician oil production, one of the earliest and most important at the time, brought profits mostly to foreign capitalists. The building of strategic railroads by Austria stimulated the province's economy to some extent, as did subsidies for agriculture and the creation of the first provincial credit bank. Oil output increased fourfold in the 1870–90 decades and that of coal rose threefold. The population of the two main cities, Lwów (Lemberg, Lviv) and Cracow, grew respectively from 70,000 to 120,000, and from 50,000 to 70,000. This was hardly a significant increase. In 1888 a study appeared entitled *Galician Misery*, which demonstrated that the consumption level of an inhabitant of Galicia was one half, and his working capacity one fourth of that of an average European.

Such low levels of consumption and output and this economic stagnation could only be compared with the former Lithuanian-Belorussian provinces ("Northwestern Land" of Russia) where between 50 and 60 percent of manorial land was still in Polish hands. The situation was much better in the Ukraine ("Southwestern Land") which had a thriving sugar industry, 40 percent of which was owned by Poles in 1910, and where the railroads connecting the region with the Black Sea assisted production and trade. All these territories constituted the Jewish pale of settlement with a high percentage of the population (about 14 percent) being Jews. A wave of pogroms, however, drove a considerable number of them westward to the Congress Kingdom, where by 1909 they represented 14.6 percent of the total population, and made up about 32 percent in Warsaw.

The Congress Kingdom, renamed Vistula Land after the January uprising, was the only area of the old Commonwealth that experienced the Industrial Revolution. After the failure of the state-directed attempts at industrialization, mentioned in the preceding chapter, the Kingdom found itself in 1856 with a national debt that corresponded to three of its annual budgets. After the abolition of the customs barrier with Russia in 1851 and the adoption of protectionism, new opportunities arose. There was demand for agricultural and industrial products, which the building of railroads greatly assisted. The state sold its mines and metallurgical plants to private capitalists, who undertook a construction of the Warsaw–Vienna railroad (opened in 1845). An estimated 39 percent of the industrial capital was foreign, or 69 percent in terms of value of industrial production. It was attracted to the developing industries producing for the huge Russian market, but in the 1850s it was the Kingdom's domestic market that acted as the main catalyst and permitted an accumulation of industrial capital. In the ensuing decade the eastern markets offered great opportunities for exports and 70 percent of production went to Russia. The center of textiles, the mushrooming town of Łódź, became a "promised land" for enterprising businessmen: there was a new influx of foreigners, especially Germans. Łódź itself was a Polish-Jewish-German amalgam with its own distinct character. Many of the Germans became polonized. Among the Jews often placed in the awkward position between the Russians and the Poles, some of the bourgeoisie assimilated, the great banking and industrial families (Kronenbergs, Blochs, Poznańskis) becoming Christian and intermarrying with Polish nobility.

The technical revolution – using as a yardstick a more than 50 percent mechanization of a given industry – began around 1850. Sugar refining was affected first, cotton following around 1875, metallurgy around 1890. Steam engines, which had been used sporadically in various Polish lands in the second decade of the century (the first one was introduced in 1817), multiplied twenty-five times in the 1853–88 period. Between the mid-1870s and 1890s the value of industrial production increased ninefold.

Textiles led the way, being followed in order of importance by coal – a tenfold increase between 1870 and 1890 – and only a slightly lesser growth in machinery and food processing. The urban population (in towns over 10,000 inhabitants) doubled between 1870 and 1910, rising from 9 to 18 percent. This was still a low level of urbanization, even if the loss of urban status by some towns may have lowered this figure. Warsaw, however, which had 100,000 inhabitants at the beginning of the century and 151,000 by 1870, exceeded 872,000 by 1910. Yet all this development did not make the Kingdom an industrial country. Not only was the urban sector weak and the percentage of industrial workers relatively small, but society was only partly transformed as a result of economic change. True, the role of the aristocracy was less dominant than in Hungary, and the growth of the middle class was slightly bigger, but by and large the Congress Kingdom stood closer to the Hungarian than to the Czech model. It offered a good example of Industrial Revolution in the region, which while bringing important changes, differed quantitatively from Western developments, included a special role for foreign capital, and stopped short of, or at least delayed a structural socio-economic transformation.

In that sense Prussian Poland followed more of a Western path albeit concentrating on the agrarian and light industrial sectors. In 1882, 65 percent of the population was engaged in agriculture, but it was an agriculture that was technically modernized and it relied, as in the Czech case, on local credit, cooperatives, and self-aid associations. Competing with the local Germans, who were prominent in banks and bigger enterprises and enjoyed the backing of the Prussian state, Poznanian Poles had to increase their standards of production and outdo their competitors. Food processing, breweries, crafts, and smaller industries made steady progress. A Polish middle class was making its appearance on a scale unknown in other parts of the partitioned country. Numerous Germans and Jews, facing stiff competition and attracted to opportunities in western Germany, emigrated. Consequently the Jewish population, which accounted for 2.5 percent in 1890 dropped to 1.2 percent by 1910, the lowest figure in any of the Polish lands. Prussian Poland became almost a Western-type province with many similarities, economic and social, to Bohemia.

The role of the railroads in Polish developments was distorted by the fact of partitions. The railroads were built to connect Prussian Poland to Prussia and Germany, the Congress Kingdom to Russia, and Galicia, except for the strategic east–west line, to Austria. In that sense they promoted the integration of the economy of the individual Polish lands into the economic fabric of the partitioning powers. The density of the inter-Polish network was low; complementary and adjacent regions were frequently unconnected by rail. The saying that Poland had "missed" the nineteenth century found a good illustration in the story of railroad construction.

FROM THE 1860s TO 1890

One might distinguish three periods that followed the Compromise and the January uprising: the early decades, characterized by a search for accommodation and socio-economic advance; the increasingly politicized and radicalized years after 1890; and the First World War.

The Compromise was an accord between the dynasty and the Hungarians led by Ferenc Deák, a seasoned politician, unassuming, persevering, and realistic. The Hungarian parliament adopted it in May 1867 and it became law by Act XII. The monarchy was transformed into a dualist state. The Austrian part, or Cisleithenia (the River Leitha divided the two) was officially known as Kingdoms and Lands represented in the Reichsrat; it could hardly pretend to be a homogeneous country. Hungary (or Transleithenia), now encompassing all the lands of the Crown of St Stephen, insisted officially on being a "unitary national state," and allowed a sub-dualist arrangement only to Croatia. Austro-Hungary, ruled by the emperor-king, had a common army, foreign policy, and finances, but separate treasuries existed as well as equivalents of a home guard or national guard (in the American sense), called Landwehr in Austria and Honvéds in Hungary. Cabinets, parliaments, and administrations were either Austrian or Hungarian. An economic accord concluded at the time of the Compromise was to be renegotiated every ten years.

"The nation," wrote an outstanding Hungarian historian, "did not want the compromise, but neither did it want . . . to renew the fight against Vienna and the dynasty."[46] The Compromise, he argued, restored to a large extent the sovereignty the country had enjoyed before Mohács and during the 1848 Revolution. But the fate of Hungary was now tied to Vienna. Kossuth regarded this as fatal and he prophesied from his exile that Hungary, no longer master of its own destiny, would go down with Austria. Deák and his supporters thought otherwise. They wanted to strengthen the Austro-Hungarian empire, because its disintegration would not benefit the Hungarians. Isolated between inimical Germans and Russians, they would be considered "raw material, to be used for the erection of other buildings."[47]

The Compromise marked in many respects a Hungarian political dominance in the empire, including external policies under the foreign minister, Gyula Andrássy. It seemed the only realistic arrangement at the time, and the Hungarians considered it essential to preserve the traditional character of their state. This entailed a reluctance to promote social reform or offer concessions to the nationalities. Indeed, one might argue that the dualist regime prevented a further evolution, notably a federalization and democratization of the monarchy, and in that sense had adverse results for all concerned.

Under a complicated franchise that gave voting rights to an average of 6.1 percent of the population (around 3 percent in Croatia and Transylvania), Deák's party (called the Liberal Party after 1875) remained in control until 1890. Based on aristocracy, wealthier gentry, and upper bourgeoisie the cabinet of Kálmán Tisza enjoyed virtual monopoly of power. Tisza kept his partisans in line, outmaneuvered both the conservatives and the radicals, and pursued policies of "let sleeping dogs lie" in social matters and of dominance over the nationalities. To enforce unpopular policies, and to keep peace and order, a special force, the gendarmerie, which had its counterparts in the West, came into existence in 1881.

Friction with Vienna over the working of the Compromise centered on military and economic matters. Demands were made for a national army; Hungarian opposition, the "agrarians," argued for a looser association with Austria, while the governmental "mercantilists" advocated the contrary. In 1868 the parliament passed the Nationalities Act, based on the affirmation of a "unitary Hungarian political nation." The authors of the Act, especially József Eötvös, recognized the presence of non-Magyar peoples and wanted to eliminate discrimination and assure them legal equality. The cultural rights of nationalities, including the use of their language on lower levels in courts, administration, and education, were to be protected. They were to be free to form cultural and political associations. But corporate rights of non-Magyar peoples, especially in the form of autonomy, were denied, and from the 1870s the liberal spirit of the Act was evaporating and its letter twisted, through policies of forceful Magyarization. Tisza believed that the assimilation of as many non-Magyars as possible (they constituted some 46 percent, excluding Croatia) was essential in case of a future emancipation from Vienna.

By virtue of the 1868 accord (*nagodba*) Croatia had the status of an "associated country under the Crown of St Stephen" with autonomy in matters of justice, interior affairs, education, and religion. Defense and economic matters were in the hands of Budapest, and the presence of some thirty Croatian deputies in the parliament as well as a minister for Croatian affairs in the cabinet did not provide for real controls. As for the ban, he was named by the king and could only be impeached by the *sabor*. The Croats wished to change the nature of their relationship with Budapest. Their most prominent political and cultural personage was Bishop Josip Strossmayer (instrumental, among others, in the foundation of the Academy of Science and the University of Zagreb). Pursuing a final goal of Illyrianism (spiritual unification of the South Slavs) he advocated the transformation of the monarchy into a three-way partnership with South Slavs as the third element. The nomination of the tough Magyar ban Károly Khuen-Héderváry in 1883 meant that Budapest was opposed to any change or even a meaningful dialogue.

Romanian, Slovak, or Serb leaders were hardly satisfied with the right to draw up petitions in their native languages. But their wishes for limited autonomous arrangements stood no chance of being granted. Cultural and linguistic Magyarization proceeded. In 1874–5 Slovak high schools and their cultural foundation (Matica slovenská) were closed. By the early 1880s the Hungarian language reached elementary education, and extremist organizations such as the Upper Hungarian Cultural Association (FMKE) advocated total Magyarization of Slovakia. The two or three Slovak deputies in the Budapest parliament were powerless. Slovak–Czech contacts were reduced to a minimum for fear of reprisals.

The Compromise was a heavy blow to Czech political aspirations. Palacký's bitterness was reflected in his saying that the Czechs existed before Austria and would still be there after Austria was gone. Palacký and the Old Czechs he headed argued in 1868 that the rights of the Crown of St Wenceslas were the same as those of St Stephen. This may have been sound history but was naive politics. By defining Czech aspirations in historical terms the Palacký camp found itself in a blind alley. Vienna was not likely to sacrifice Germans to Czechs as it had sacrificed non-Magyars to Hungary. But insisting on historic rights Old Czechs seemed willing to give up the idea of a union with Slovaks. By cooperating with the aristocracy – Palacký was a liberal not a democrat – the Old Czechs seemed to adhere to an anachronistic program. Their political tactics, such as Palacký's travels to an ethnographic Slav congress in Russia, made them vulnerable to the cry of panslavism. Their pro-Russian stance antagonized the Galician Poles.

After an unsuccessful boycott of the Reichsrat, the Czechs tried an accord with Vienna in 1871. They proposed a general Bohemian-Moravian-Silesian diet and autonomy in judicial, administrative, and educational matters. The accord fell through largely because of Hungarian opposition. The Czechs resorted to a boycott again, but the local diets were weakened by the introduction of direct elections to the Reichsrat in lieu of indirect ones through them.

Political failures during the Old Czech predominance contrasted with the continuing socio-economic development and achievements in the process of Czech national revival. As early as the 1860s the gymnastic society Sokol became a powerful propagator of language and native culture. In 1868 a foundation stone was laid under the Czech National

Theater (opened in 1883) which was to bear the motto "The nation to itself." In 1882 Prague university was split into a Czech and a German institution. The political scene began to change with the appointment of the first Czech cabinet minister, and a mounting domestic crisis between the Old and the Young Czechs. It reached its climax in 1890, marking, as in Hungary and in the Polish lands, a new phase.

Polish policies during the post-1860 decades were strongly influenced by the traumatic experience of the January uprising and the virtual disappearance of the Polish question from the international agenda. In Galicia the Compromise initially provoked a reaction similar to that of the Czechs, but fairly quickly the conservative politicians perceived the advantages of a direct deal with Vienna. Their motivation was not purely opportunistic, nor did it just reflect vested class interests, but was caused by a re-evaluation of the Polish past, recent and ancient. Galician conservatives, many of whom had supported, despite their better judgement, the 1863 uprising, now condemned it as utter folly. To the rising Cracow historical school, the conspiratorial activities of the nineteenth century were a logical sequel of the "republican" tradition lauded by Lelewel and his school. "Liberum conspiro" was inherent in liberum veto. Józef Szujski and his colleagues blamed the anarchic nobility for the partitions and deplored the decline of the monarchic power in the old Commonwealth. To the "optimistic" libertarian-republican interpretation they opposed a sober "monarchic" thesis.

The conservatives believed that the Poles needed to be educated in political wisdom and discipline, and they saw Austria as providing the opportunities for such an apprenticeship. In a controversial address to the throne the conservatives expressed their belief that Austria had inherited Poland's mission of a shield against the East, and declared their determination to stand by the emperor. Vienna responded by piecemeal concessions rather than iron-clad commitments, but they were significant. The subdivision of the province (which the Ruthenians, now increasingly calling themselves Ukrainians, supported) was ended in 1867 and the Polish language was made the official language, higher education included. This meant a polonization of Galicia and its transformation into a Polish Piedmont. As a result Polish–Ukrainian relations deteriorated, the Poles becoming the ruling group. There was increased assimilation of Jews into the Polish establishment, even if most of them remained orthodox and alien.

The Poles became a politically privileged nation in the monarchy. Their loyalty was to the Habsburgs not to Austria, and this loyalty was valid only as long as there was no independent Poland. In the final analysis the Polish question could not be resolved within the monarchy, but only through the undoing of partitions. But before that happened the Poles found their association with Vienna mutually advantageous. There would be cabinet presidents and ministers from Galicia. The Austrian parliamentary system could hardly function without the support that the Polish circle in the Reichsrat lent to the successive governments.

Galicia paid a certain price for the rule of the Cracow conservatives. They did not prove good economic managers and their policies bore the imprint of their landowning, clerical, and somewhat limited outlook. Those whose pro-Habsburg zeal appeared too great, such as the viceroy Agenor Gołuchowski, were accused of contributing to "triloyalism." The term referred to a process in which loyalty to the three partitioning powers was offered in the hope of winning concessions. But, as critics said, the result could be a deepening of the existing divisions between the lands of partitioned Poland that would inflict permanent damage to the all-Polish program.

No concessions could be expected from Russia, which pursued policies of national oppression toward the Congress Kingdom. The emancipation of the peasantry in 1864 on conditions more favorable than in Russia itself aimed at making loyal subjects out of the peasants and preventing their becoming conscious members of the Polish nation. The latter was seen as consisting of nobles and priests, hence, as a Russian journalist put it,

> There will be no Polish question from the moment the Polish nationality loses not only its material but also its moral authority over the Ruthenian and Lithuanian nationalities in the Western Land, and when the enduring might of the peasant communes in the Kingdom of Poland smashes . . . the old ideals of the Polish gentry.[48]

As events were to show the Russians did not win over the peasantry; governmental measures against the Polish language and the Catholic religion, combined with a direct contact between the peasant and the tsarist official, drove the masses toward Polishness.

The Polish response to the shock of defeat was affected by the Industrial Revolution. Thwarted politically, society channeled its energies to economic and social endeavors. Repudiating uprisings as romantic folly, and placing their faith in reason and progress, the positivists (the name was derived from the terminology of Auguste Comte) developed a program of "organic work." Previously tried in Prussian Poland it amounted to a pursuit of modernization, catching up with the industrialized West and preserving and expanding the nation's well-being. There were some similarities between positivism and the Hungarian program of "embourgeoisement," except that the Polish gentry was barred from administrative and political careers. The poorer

184

groups reinforced the ranks of urban middle class, intelligentsia, or even the proletariat.

The positivist program was preached in novels and periodicals; its leading exponent was the writer Aleksander Prus. The positivists were in a sense a Polish version of Western liberals, although in the existing conditions they could hardly subscribe unequivocally to *laissez-faire* and bourgeois attitudes. To some of them free development of industry and commerce, as in England, was the panacea. Others were critical of plans of rapid industrialization of the Kingdom, seeing industrialization rather as a culminating point of a gradual process based on modernized agriculture. The Łódź cotton industry built by German entrepreneurs, using American raw materials and producing for the Russian market, seemed hardly the ideal development from a national Polish viewpoint. While the capitalists sought to represent the *"enrichissez-vous"* slogan as highly patriotic, and the conservatives invoked traditional values, the positivists put their trust in popular education, free associations, and careers open to talent. The realization of these hopes, however, was thwarted by policies of Russification and discrimination.

In the Lithuanian, Ukrainian, and Belorussian provinces the tsarist authorities strove to replace Polish influences with Russian. The elimination of the Polish language, restrictions or even dissolutions of local self-government, virtual prohibition of land purchases by the Poles, were all meant to serve this purpose. In 1875 the Union of Brest was abolished and the Uniates absorbed in the Orthodox Church. The extent to which the government was willing to go to sever the links with the Latin world was shown by the imposition of the Cyrillic alphabet on the Lithuanian language.

Russian policies contributed to a growing estrangement between Poles on the one side and Lithuanians, Ukrainians, and Belorussians on the other. But they did not cause it. A national awakening of the masses was bound to be directed against a landowning class that was Polish, although in many cases of Lithuanian or Ruthenian descent. At the same time the Russians regarded the Ukrainian national revival as a Polish intrigue. As for the Lithuanians their national awakening entered a new phase with the publication (abroad) of the journal *Auszra* (*The Dawn*). Its sponsor Jonas Basanavičius is often called the father of modern Lithuanian nationalism.

In the Ukraine the poetry of Taras Shevchenko showed the effectiveness and sophistication of the written Ukrainian language. The work of U. Drahomaniv (Dragomanov) indicated that the cultural renaissance was taking a clearly political direction. Its chances of success under Russia were virtually nil, so Austrian Galicia also became a Ukrainian Piedmont and an "open window" to the outside world. Among the leading writers the name of Ivan Franko stands out. The more far-sighted Polish conservatives diagnosed the Ukrainian revival in Galicia as a social movement with a national content. They favored a policy of conciliation, but as the century drew to its close passions were running too high for reason to prevail. In general the Poles viewed the Ruthenian–Ukrainian movement as an Austrian instrument. The Ukrainians were divided as to whether to strive for the status of a separate Crown land within the monarchy or pursue the long-range vision of a union with the Russian Ukraine. An anti-Polish attitude was present in both concepts.

Poles under Prussia, unlike their countrymen in the other two partitions, faced a special situation of relentless struggle against the Prussian government and then against the Germans as such. With the creation of the German Empire in 1871 the Polish question became an imperial concern. Chancellor Bismarck singled out the Poles as a disruptive element in the new Reich, and invoked the Polish threat to justify his action (Kulturkampf) against the Catholic Church and particularist interests. But the distinction that the Prussians drew between the nobles and the clergy (seen as pillars of Polishness) and the masses (regarded as Polish-speaking Prussians), was becoming obsolete. Polish society was becoming increasingly modernized, nationally integrated, and socially solidaristic. The Kulturkampf was hardly a Prussian success despite temporary gains by the government. The subsequent confrontations assumed by the mid-1880s the characteristics of a national German–Polish struggle. Seeking to germanize the Polish provinces Berlin expelled thousands of Poles and Jews who could not prove their Prussian citizenship. It also encouraged the creation of a colonizing commission that was endowed with a fund to buy out land from the Poles and promote German settlements. The response was a closing of Polish ranks and socio-economic counteraction. What is more, a Polish national revival began in Upper Silesia and in parts of East Prussia that had not been part of the pre-partition Commonwealth. This development was symptomatic of the broadening of the social base of political and national movements in the region.

FROM 1890 TO SARAJEVO

The 1890s saw the rise of mass political parties and a growing radicalization, social and national, throughout East Central Europe. In Hungary the long rule of Kálmán Tisza ended in 1890, and subsequent developments were the formation of a Hungarian Social Democratic Party (which held its first congress in 1894 and adopted its program in 1903) and a Smallholders Party in 1909. A small but increasingly vocal National Bourgeois Radical Party represented the voice of urban intelligentsia. Oszkár Jászi was one of the leaders; the magnate Mihály

Károlyi gravitated toward it. None of these movements could successfully challenge the succeeding governments, which excelled in manipulations combined with occasional reprisals, and increasingly emphasized Magyar nationalism. The celebrations of the Millennium in 1896 saw its veritable outburst. "Never did we talk so much of our being Hungarian,"[49] commented a leading historian. The semi-mythical ancestor, "the Turanian rider," fearless but realistic, an observer rather than a discoverer, was represented in various literary heroes as the embodiment of the national characteristics. The Magyar spirit was distinguished by love of one's native land, rejection of servility, and creativity in politics. Students in Budapest vowed to wear only national costume; landowners subscribed to an agrarian program and fulminated against big business that was "international" and "cosmopolitan." They opposed to it a program of national and Christian politics. Although there were anti-Semitic undertones in the new, integral nationalism, many Jews eagerly participated in the Magyarization campaign. Articles in the press which they often owned or influenced prophesied that in forty years' time there would be 17 million Magyars as against 7 million non-Magyars. Indeed, spontaneous and forced Magyarization resulted in an increase of Hungarians in the 1867–1914 period from 40 to 48 percent in all the lands of the Holy Crown.

Nationalism was a weapon used against democrats, socialists, and radicals, and even the Catholic Church, in a Hungarian version of Kulturkampf in 1892–6. But the chief battles were fought in the Magyar versus non-Magyar confrontations. The resistance of some nationalities stiffened visibly. Subject to pressures and manipulations and finding a common front with the Hungarian opposition difficult, the Croats were driven into cooperation with the Serbs (the Fiume 1905 Resolution). The Zagreb trial in 1908 and then the Balkan wars intensified the tensions. The Croatian constitution was suspended in 1912 and 1913. Although various deals still intervened, the Croatian political program was departing from the trialist (Austro-Hungarian-South Slav) conception and moving toward a Yugoslav system.

Romanians and Serbs, by virtue of their Greek Orthodoxy (or Greek Catholicism) were largely immune from Magyarization in the religious sphere. They could also look to Bucharest and Belgrade for support. Still, the Romanian Memorandum trial of 1894, to mention only one of the political persecutions, pushed them toward cooperation with the other nationalities. The results were a Budapest congress in 1895 and the emergence of a club of nationalities in the Hungarian parliament in 1906. The Slovaks were worst off. Linguistic Magyarization made new inroads (such as the Lex Apponyi in 1907) into education and Protestant churches. The Hungarian Catholic hierarchy supported by the state battled with Slovak parishes. An incident at the Černova church resulted in some fifteen people being shot by the gendarmes. A Catholic political movement took shape in the Slovak People's Party in 1905. Its leader, Father Andrej Hlinka, had some hopes of cooperation with the new Hungarian Catholic People's Party. Similarly the Slovak social democrats organized themselves within the Hungarian social democratic movement. Another group associated with the periodical *Hlas* looked to Prague's progressive circles for inspiration and guidance. The situation appeared desperate to Slovak leaders. Mass following was lacking. The feeble Slovak culture and national consciousness could, if the worst fears were justified, succumb in a generation or so to complete Magyarization. As it was, the percentage of the Slovaks in the region declined between 1880 and 1910. The hard life and a feeling of hopelessness drove nearly 500,000 of them abroad as emigrants.

The relations between Budapest and Vienna were not free from friction. The remark of Count Gyula Andrássy that through the Compromise the Hungarians had sacrificed their material interests to the idea of liberty reflected a feeling of dissatisfaction with various aspects of coexistence with Austria. The question of the army remained particularly sensitive, and demands for a national army set off a crisis that reached its high point in 1905. The governing liberals lost the election, a rare occurrence, and dualism itself was threatened.

The year 1905 was a year of revolution in Russia and its Polish lands. Strikes and unrest spilled into the Habsburg monarchy. After intricate political maneuvers in which the bait of universal suffrage was used by all sides to the conflict, so as to gain the support of the masses, Francis Joseph prevailed. Universal manhood suffrage was introduced in Cisleithenia in 1907 but not in Hungary. The liberals reorganized themselves and assumed power under a new name and under the undisputed leadership of István Tisza. Did it mean that dualism was safe and Hungary firmly wedded to it? Or did it mean that on the eve of the First World War none of the real problems was resolved in the lands of the Crown of St Stephen, be they socio-political, or to do with nationalities, or with relations with Vienna? It is difficult to give a definite answer, for nationality problems contrasted with a relative stability, and popular grievances with material progress.

In culture lights shone brightly. Three universities in addition to that of Budapest represented high levels of scholarship. The capital was a glittering city in which radically inclined intellectuals were playing an important part. European readers were familiar with the novelist Ferenc Molnár and the earlier-mentioned Mór Jókai, whose impact in Hungary was comparable to that of Jirásek among the Czechs and even Sienkiewicz among the Poles. Less well-known abroad was the greatest poet of the early twentieth century Endre Ady, the "prophet of Hungarian destiny." The fame of the historical painter Mihály Munkácsy reached the West; the rising genius of Béla Bartók in music would later be generally recognized. As the war approached Hungarian civilization was in no way inferior to that of the West, and some of its cultural or artistic figures were international giants.

Shifting one's sights from Hungary to Bohemia one is struck by certain parallel developments, although contrasts dominate. The 1890s also saw a reorientation of Czech politics that reflected a democratization and a radicalization of society. It was accompanied by conflicts about the direction which the nation should take to promote its objectives. The Centennial Exhibition in Prague in 1891 testified to the enormous material advancement that made the country the leading province, economically and in terms of its social program, of the monarchy. Yet political gains did not follow economic achievements. The 1890 agreement (the Punktace) on a German–Czech linguistic compromise in schools and in the courts was not acceptable to the Young Czechs, who came to the fore as the leading force in the country. The agreement was realized only in Moravia; in Bohemia the Young Czechs, representing liberal, anti-clerical, and radical nationalists, adopted policies of confrontation that lasted for the next four years. But student riots in 1893 that led to the so-called Omladina trials demonstrated the futility both of such demonstrations and of the martial law which followed.

A new cabinet in Vienna led by Kazimierz Badeni tried reforms. In 1896 it added a fifth curia of voters which comprised all adult males hitherto denied voting rights; this represented more electors than in the four existing curias (great landowners, chambers of commerce, towns, and villages) combined. Badeni also introduced language reforms which would have put Czech on a par with German. The Young Czechs, reverting to more opportunistic tactics, cooperated with the Badeni government; the Germans engineered its fall which prevented the realization of language reforms. Disappointed, the Young Czechs pursued policies of filibuster and obstruction in the Reichsrat. Their goal remained Austro-Slavism: a federalized monarchy and diplomatic reorientation away from Germany and toward France and Russia. In 1908 Karel Kramář launched Neo-Slavism with a congress in Prague, in which both the Russians and the Poles participated. But Kramář, who considered the idea of Czech independence an illusion and Slavdom "our last ultimate" refuge, really concentrated on current politics in the monarchy. Moreover, the Young Czech monopoly of power was being undercut by the emergence of mass political parties, a consequence of the electoral reforms of 1896 and 1907, and by the appearance on the Czech scene of Tomáš Masaryk. A new generation educated in Czech schools was now entering public life, and Czech modernism was challenging not only arts but also the prevalent view of society, nation, and politics.

The oldest Czech mass party, the social democrats, in 1896 gained a far-reaching autonomy within the all-Austrian party. Those who put more stress on nationalism and less on Marx established the National Socialist Party two years later. Its program carried some anti-Semitic overtones. The middle-of-the-road agrarians came into being in 1899; the forerunners of the Catholic Party also joined the political spectrum. Of all these groups and parties only the small Progressive State Rights Party openly advocated the destruction of the dual monarchy and an independent Czech state. Masaryk, who headed another tiny party of Realists, never went that far. But when he wrote to Kramář, "You are fighting for Austria! I am not!" he expressed a novel approach and a new philosophy of Czech politics.

Masaryk turned to history for inspiration, and he largely followed in the footsteps of Palacký. Rejecting futile lamentations over the catastrophe of the White Mountain, he insisted that the strength of the Czech nation was derived from spiritual values. These, which he termed profoundly humanistic, he traced back to the Hussites and the Czech Brethren. They, much more than the Enlightenment and the French Revolution, were in Masaryk's opinion the catalyst of the nineteenth-century Czech national renaissance. Although, as mentioned in the preceding chapter, the historian Pekař disputed Masaryk's interpretation of the Czech past and rejected the concept that the nation was a carrier of a single idea in history, Masaryk's ideas had a wide resonance. Being a moralist to philosophers and a philosopher to politicians, Masaryk was above all seen as a sage, an intellectual, and a moral giant. This did not mean that he escaped criticism, even bitter attacks. His defense of the Jew Hilsner, accused of ritual murder, and his exposure as forgery of some cherished Czech medieval documents earned him public disapproval. His call for action through moral regeneration was not fully appreciated; his universalist approach to the Czech question ("The Czech question was either a world question or no question at all") was not fully comprehended.

Indeed, a kind of national schizophrenia reigned in Bohemia with simultaneous displays of rebelliousness and loyalism, both tinged by a petit bourgeois mentality. The constant talk about a small nation and small possibilities resulted, in the opinion of the historian Kořalka, in a cult of the average little Czech. "In no way do we lack gold and silver in our conflict with Vienna," commented a prominent contemporary figure, "but we lack manliness and courage, perseverance and self-sacrifice in political struggles."[50] Masaryk himself castigated Czech politicians who unable to be lions turned into foxes, and unable to be heroes turned into lackeys. In a sense it was convenient for the nation to be without its own statehood, for it could derive benefits from the economic, cultural, and political life of a state for which it bore no responsibility. True, there were the customary two Czech members of the Vienna cabinet, but they were hardly representative of national aspirations. Still, the Czechs, as a leader affirmed in 1911 in parliament, had a real interest in the survival of the monarchy. Had the Austrians handled them more cleverly they could have, as a Czech writer put it, "wrapped the Czech nation around their little finger."[51]

Although the 1905 strikes shook Bohemia the country was hardly an oppressed province. True, a certain political deadlock existed as German intransigence made a genuine federalization of the monarchy impossible. But not only economic, but also cultural life was thriving. The two giants in music, Bĕdřich Smetana and Antonín Dvořák died respectively in 1884 and 1904, but their impact remained. Modernist Czech painters worked chiefly in France but the tradition of the romantic, national paintings of J. Mánes was very much alive. Prague was the centre of a special Jewish-German culture of which Kafka was in many ways a symbol and an embodiment.

Turning to the lands of partitioned Poland, the 1890s saw the rise of a challenge to Warsaw positivism and "triloyalism," perceived as degenerating into policies of vested class interests and servility toward the government. The challenge came from the left and right: from the nascent forces of socialism and the national democratic movement. Somewhat later populism arose. All these trends were assisted by the broadening of the political and social base, especially after the 1905 Revolution, and they stressed an all-Polish character transcending the borders of Austria, Prussia, and Russia. They were sustained by a single Polish culture.

The national democratic movement grew out of the Polish League, founded in Switzerland in 1887. Its program rejected passivity or reconciliation with the partitioning powers and sought to mobilize Poles for active struggle for independence. Transformed into a National League in 1903 with headquarters in Warsaw, the movement developed an ideology that was shaped largely by the ideas of Roman Dmowski. A natural scientist by training, and coming from a poor urban milieu, Dmowski became a herald of integral nationalism in Poland that represented a drastic change in Polish political thought.

Regarding the nation, "a living social organism," as the supreme value, and its interests as transcending those of the individual and humanity, Dmowski denounced the old noble nation for having compromised national interests. Furthering its own advantages, he wrote, it had promoted an eastern expansion which diluted and weakened the ethnic Polish core. By relying on Jews the *szlachta* had ruined towns and prevented the rise of a middle class. Tying the Polish cause to liberalism, revolution, or humanitarian sentiments, the Poles had engaged in foolhardy uprisings counting on the non-existing solidarity of peoples. Dmowski saw politics in terms of social Darwinism, as a struggle in which national egoism was the norm and survival the object. He wanted to mold a modern Polish nation out of its healthiest and strongest elements, namely the peasantry. In practice this meant waging a largely successful educational action of promoting national awareness. But it entailed a conflict with non-Polish nationalities: Ukrainians, Lithuanians, Belorussians, and Jews. The first three groups Dmowski sought to polonize, but according to him only individual Jews could be assimilated. Anti-Semitism, enhanced by the growing number of Jews in the Congress Kingdom and the economic competition with the Polish middle class, played an ever increasing role in Dmowski's ideology.

Dmowski considered that on political grounds Polish and Jewish interests clashed. While to the national democrats Germany was the most dangerous enemy and Russia a potential ally, the Jews believed exactly the opposite. Dmowski pointed to the visible Jewish presence in the socialist movement that was increasing his anti-socialist stance. An important characteristic of the Polish League and the national democrats was that they did not look upon themselves as representing a political trend, but rather, the very basic interests of the nation. Hence their tendency toward political-ideological monopoly and intolerance of other programs.

The year 1893 saw the rise of another challenge to the existing political and socio-economic order, namely the appearance of the Polish Socialist Party (PPS). Its most forceful personality was Józef Piłsudski. An impoverished member of the Lithuanian gentry, brought up in the cult of the January uprising, Piłsudski believed in the tradition of the old Commonwealth and saw Poland's way to emancipation through the collapse of the tsarist empire. PPS combined Marxist tenets with Polish national objectives, and invoked Marx to claim that the role of socialism in Poland was to be a rampart of the progressive West against the reactionary and backward East. Piłsudski insisted that the social oppression of the Polish workers was intensified by the oppression of the whole nation. He regarded the industrial proletariat in much the same way as Polish radicals had once viewed the peasantry, namely as an indispensable force to carry on the old struggle for national liberation and social justice.

The program of PPS was rejected by the leftist, "internationalist" Social Democratic Party grouped around Rosa Luxemburg and Feliks Dzierżyński, which by 1918 would provide the nucleus for the Communist Party of Poland. The social democrats (SDKPiL) argued that for the Polish proletariat national independence (most unlikely in any case on economic grounds) would mean regression and not progress. The socialist fatherland was as real to Rosa Luxemburg as Poland was to Piłsudski. But what form and shape could a future Poland take? PPS came to favor a federalist approach that recognized the national rights of Lithuanians, Ukrainians, and Belorussians and hoped for their voluntary union with the Poles. The growth of nationalism among these nations, however, was making such a program highly problematic.

The 1905 Revolution in the Russian empire brought the national democrats and the socialists in the Kingdom to an open confrontation. When at the height of the Russo–Japanese war in 1904 both Piłsudski and Dmowski had gone to Tokyo, the first argued for a Japanese-supported insurrection in the Congress Kingdom, the latter opposed it. Tokyo opted for caution. In the Kingdom the PPS fighting squads were already battling the Russians and engaging in semi-revolutionary activities; the national democrats clashed with the socialists. Dmowski, insisting on the need for peace and order, tried to gain concessions from St Petersburg, both then, and subsequently at the Duma (parliament) when it was called into existence. By 1908 the policies of Dmowski had failed to bring any concessions from Russia, and the attempts to raise the Polish–Russian dialogue to an international level through the Neo-Slavist movement proved unsuccessful. Thwarted in another electoral bid to the Duma, Dmowski blamed the Jews and in 1912 launched a boycott of Jewish businesses. Feelings ran high.

Piłsudski's increasingly insurrectionist-type actions produced a split in the PPS, and Piłsudski transferred his headquarters to Galicia. There he embarked on the preparation of a Polish military force that could show the Polish flag in the international war which to many seemed imminent. By necessity this force would have to be on the Austrian side, contrary to Dmowski's view, which had put the place of the Poles on the side of France and Russia against Germany and Austria.

Austrian Galicia witnessed a wave of émigrés from Russian Poland after the 1905 Revolution. They colored the political life of the province. On an earlier date Dmowski had also operated from this Polish Piedmont. The rule of Galician conservatives was constantly challenged from the right and the left. The earlier-mentioned electoral reforms in the monarchy did not apply to local Galician elections, which explains why the conservatives could still maintain themselves in power. But the fifth curia and then universal male suffrage helped the growth of the Social Democratic Party of Galicia, of national democrats and later of the peasant party, "Piast," and of similar groupings on the Ukrainian side. The Ukrainian–Polish tension grew and in 1908 resulted in the assassination of the Polish viceroy. Attempts to achieve some form of compromise were interrupted by the outbreak of the First World War.

Shifting one's sights, Prussian Poland continued its economic progress, especially as Chancellor Caprivi's government gave the Poles a respite which allowed them to strengthen their national position. But the germanization onslaught continued and it gained impetus with the German militant organization known as Hakate (HKT). Children at Wreschen (Września) who refused to say the Lord's Prayer in German were flogged; land expropriations occurred under flimsy pretexts. No wonder that the local Poles espoused the national democratic program, and the Silesian leader W. Korfanty joined the National League.

Although the partition borders had deepened division among Poles and even affected their mentality, Polish culture continued to be the surest and strongest national link. Poles everywhere were under the spell of the historic novels of Sienkiewicz, and saw their past through the eyes of the Galician painter Jan Matejko. Modernism in the "Young Poland" version added new elements to national expression. Whether it was the plays of S. Wyspiański or the works of S. Żeromski tinged with social radicalism, they all had a ringing national message. The reality of peasant life was masterfully represented by W. Reymont. Literary and art critics, journalists, prominent scholars, to mention only the historian S. Askenazy, or great musicians like the virtuoso I. J. Paderewski, contributed to the maintenance of high levels of Polish culture.

THE FIRST WORLD WAR

The assassination of Archduke Francis Ferdinand on June 28, 1914 in Sarajevo triggered the Austrian-Hungarian ultimatum to Serbia and then hostilities that quickly assumed all-European dimensions. To begin with Hungary, it could hardly expect anything from the conflict and Premier Tisza opposed war until overridden by the emperor. As in the case of virtually all belligerent nations, the Hungarians temporarily settled their political differences. But hardly anyone among them was prepared for the long duration of the conflict and the untold sufferings it would bring. Indeed, the cost of the war proved staggering. Almost one and a half million people were killed, wounded, or taken prisoner. Shortages of basic commodities and a rampant inflation made life miserable. From 1915 the social democrats began to oppose war; by 1917 the group of Károlyi and Jászi came out with demands for peace, universal suffrage, and somewhat ill-defined projects for the federalization of Hungary. The political establishment headed by Tisza resisted, and it took a great deal of pressure from the new ruler, Emperor-King Charles, for Tisza to resign, in June 1917.

By this time the war had entered a clearly ideological stage. The two revolutions in Russia reverberated throughout the world as did President Wilson's proclamations in favor of national self-determination. In Hungary socialist agitation increased among the war-weary masses; on May 1, 1917 there were massive demonstrations; the culminating point was reached with the general strike in Budapest in January 1918. The efforts of Charles to extricate the monarchy from the war through a separate peace misfired. His last-minute attempt to federalize the empire in October 1918 made Budapest declare the end of the Compromise. Only a personal union briefly linked Austria and Hungary while Károlyi formed the Hungarian National Council. A subsequent revolutionary upheaval brought to the fore a Károlyi government. Tisza, seen by many as responsible for the country's misfortune, perished from an assassin's bullet.

Károlyi's government represented an independent Hungary that would be drastically transformed through universal suffrage, land reform, and democratization. His government sought to retain the allegiance of the non-Magyar nationalities through some form of federalist arrangements, even by making Hungary part of a Danubian United Nations. Distancing himself from the past Károlyi hoped to have Hungary treated by the Allies as a "new" state, and by concluding a separate armistice at Belgrade protect its territorial integrity against its neighbors' encroachments. These proved to be unrealistic expectations.

True, in the early stages of the war the Croats, whose troops fought well, might have been satisfied with a trialist (Austro-Hungarian-South Slav) solution. In 1917, however, the Yugoslav émigré committee (representing the monarchy's Croats, Serbs, and Slovenes) concluded the Pact of Corfu with the government of Serbia. It called for a common kingdom of Serbs, Croats, and Slovenes. In October 1918 the *sabor* officially dissolved the union with Hungary and joined the newly created state. The Slovaks and Transylvanian Romanians were passive in the early war years; there were hardly any desertions from the army. But the Allies promised Transylvania to Romania in the secret Treaty of Bucharest of 1916, and when the war ended *faits accomplis* in the province placed Transylvania and adjacent territories in Romanian hands. The Allies ordered Hungary to evacuate Slovakia. Thus before the Paris Peace Conference met Hungary had been reduced to the core of its prewar territory and was open to further encroachments by Czechoslovakia, Romania, and Yugoslavia. With the French army behind them, Budapest was powerless. Károlyi resigned in March, and as the communists took over, Hungary's future was a question mark.

The story of Czechs and Slovaks during the First World War was completely different from that of the Hungarians. The latter were trying to salvage their state in the midst of a conflict into which they had been drawn much against their will and interest. The former two were bent on creating their own state out of the ruins of the Habsburg monarchy. This was a bold undertaking and the Allies had to be persuaded of its merits.

The Czech nation was not politically prepared for war and all its possible consequences. The program of independence was taken up by Masaryk, who despaired of any other solution and went abroad toward the end of 1914. He was joined later by E. Beneš and assisted by M. Štefánik, a Slovak who lived in France. These men became the leaders of the "struggle abroad" movement, as distinct from the "struggle at home" trend associated with Kramář. The latter initially placed his hopes in the liberation of Czech lands by the tsarist armies and thought of some connection between Bohemia and Russia. But he also cooperated with Masaryk and Beneš through the political group known as the Maffie. The difference between the two trends was largely a matter of emphasis (with the West or with Russia), but it became magnified and affected domestic politics after 1918.

Masaryk and Beneš had a difficult task. The Czech question was viewed as an internal matter of the Austrian monarchy, which the Allies had no intention of destroying. Masaryk and Beneš seemed isolated, for the major Czech political parties followed pro-Habsburg policies out of loyalty, fear, or opportunism. Even as late as January 1917 they disavowed Masaryk's and Beneš's activities abroad. It was only when the specter of a German-dominated Mitteleuropa began to haunt the Allies in 1916 that plans for a "new" East Central Europe replacing Austro-Hungary received serious consideration.

Under the impact of the February and October Revolutions (actually of March and November 1917) in Russia, and the growing hardships at home, the Czechs began openly to demand a federalization of the monarchy. A self-governing Czechoslovak state would be part of it. The Slovaks, incidentally, could thus far play no active role, for they had no contact with Prague until April 1917.

The Czechoslovak National Council (its name varied) presided over by Masaryk and established in Paris in the spring of 1916 now stood a greater chance of having its demands for national independence recognized by the Allies. The issue of a Czechoslovak army came to the fore. The Russian Provisional Government declared in favor of an independent Czechoslovakia, and a Czechoslovak brigade formed in Russia fought a victorious battle at Zborów in July 1917. But the outbreak of the bolshevik revolution complicated matters. The Czechoslovak leadership sought to avoid any involvement of the Czechoslovak legion in the Russian civil war, and wished to bring the troops to France. But the situation got out of hand and the legion found itself struggling against the bolsheviks in its Siberian "Anabasis." Some 50,000 Czech soldiers controlling the trans-Siberian railroad were performing a service to the Allies disproportionate to their size. Although the story is complex and Masaryk's role controversial, it is certain that the legion greatly assisted Czechoslovak efforts to secure Allied official recognition.

This goal was not reached easily. The organization of Czechoslovak troops in France and Italy (out of Austrian prisoners of war), the Congress of Oppressed Nationalities in Rome – a major anti-Habsburg demonstration – and Beneš's skillful diplomacy were, however, paving the way. The Pittsburgh Agreement was concluded in Masaryk's presence by Czechs and Slovaks in America in favor of a common state, and was a significant move. But in the final analysis the fate of Czechoslovakia depended on the Allied attitude toward the maintenance of the Austro-Hungarian monarchy. In January 1917 the Allies spoke vaguely of a "liberation of Czechoslovaks from foreign domination." Wilson's Fourteen Points insisted merely on the "freest opportunity of autonomous development" for the Czechs. The situation underwent a change in the spring of 1918. The Epiphany declaration of Czech deputies for complete self-determination and for Czechoslovakia's participation in a peace conference showed how far the process of disintegration had gone. In October 1918, Charles's federalist manifesto came out simultaneously with Masaryk's declaration of Czechoslovak independence. On October 28 independence was proclaimed in Prague and a day later by the Slovaks.

A new state arose, already recognized as a belligerent ally. It was shortly in control of most of the territories it claimed: the lands of the Crown of St Wenceslas and Slovakia. Its borders were yet to be drawn officially, but President Masaryk and the foreign minister Beneš could count on Allied support. Indeed, this point was stressed when Masaryk spoke of bringing to the Czechs "independence on a plate," although he later also said, "Our independence was truly bought with blood."[52] This was a reference to the struggles of the legion in Russia and to sacrifices at home. Kramář, who was at one point charged with treason and sentenced to death, insisted that without these actions the diplomacy of Masaryk and Beneš would have been vain. Here were the germs of a controversy that has not abated to the present day.

Polish strivings for independence during the war were much more complex than those of the Czechs. The fact that Poland was divided among three powers made it potentially an international issue, and with two partitioners (Germany and Austro-Hungary) facing the third (Russia) there was some hope and room for maneuver. Yet the victory of either side would still be a victory by an oppressor. What is more, an average Pole could hardly imagine that after 120 years of partitions a free and independent Poland could re-emerge.

Dmowski's conviction that Germany was Poland's main enemy led him to tie the Polish question to the Franco-Russian alliance. The manifesto of the Russian commander-in-chief, Grand Duke Nikolai Nikolaievich, promising the Poles unity under the tsar's scepter, seemed encouraging. But deeds did not follow words. When the German–Austrian armies drove the Russians out of the kingdom in 1915, Dmowski left for the West. There he went beyond his original advocacy of Poland's unification, and spoke openly of full independence. The Allies were cautious. Poland, they felt, was Russia's business, and Petrograd resented outside interference. Moreover, Dmowski represented but one of the main Polish trends, the second being the anti-Russian and by necessity pro-Central Powers current of Piłsudski.

To Piłsudski and the Polish left, Russia was the main obstacle to independence, although full independence could only come with the collapse of all three partitioning powers. Dmowski viewed such a contingency unrealistic; Piłsudski ruminated that the Central Powers might first defeat Russia and then succumb to the West. In any case war would so weaken the partitioners that even a small Polish armed force could play a disproportionately large role. Insisting that the Polish sword must not be absent from the combat, Piłsudski headed the legion operating out of Galicia. Although this placed him on the side of the Central Powers, Piłsudski (unlike Galician conservatives) treated the cooperation with Vienna as tactical. When the Russians were forced out of the Kingdom, Piłsudski escalated his political demands when negotiating with the Austrian and German authorities, and requested maximum concessions. Emphasizing that the Poles could fight only under their own flag, he sabotaged the creation of a Polish army sponsored by the Central Powers, and proceeded to build up a clandestine Polish Military Organization (POW). On November 5, 1916, Berlin and Vienna issued the Two Emperors' Manifesto announcing the establishment of a free Kingdom of Poland. Its borders as well as the form of its association with one or both Central Powers were left unspecified. Russia denounced the manifesto as a breach of international law, but had, in the tsar's order of the day, to promise on its side freedom and unity to the Poles.

The Central Powers set up a Polish Temporary State Council in the Kingdom within which Piłsudski pursued his own aims. With the outbreak of the revolution in Russia, he opined that the Central Powers had now replaced the former tsardom as the main threat to Poland. A conflict was unavoidable, and in the summer of 1917 the Germans imprisoned Piłsudski in the fortress of Magdeburg. The legions were disbanded and partly interned. The Central Powers, however, proceeded with the creation of a Regency Council and a rudimentary Polish administration, judiciary, army, and education in the Kingdom.

These developments provided Dmowski with the argument that unless the Allies did something for Poland the Germans would be able to make use of all Polish resources for their own ends. While Dmowski was active in Paris and London, setting up in August 1917 a National Polish Committee as a spokesman in the Allied camp, Paderewski was propagating the Polish cause in the United States. Through Colonel House he gained access to President Wilson. In January 1917 Wilson had already affirmed, in his Peace without Victory address, that statesmen everywhere were in favor of a united and free Poland. In late March the Russian Provisional Government and the Petrograd Soviet came out for Polish freedom, yet it seemed clear that Russia meant to keep Poland within its sphere of influence. All this changed with the bolsheviks gaining control and the separate peace with the Central Powers in Brest Litovsk in March 1918. The West not only lost its Russian ally, but felt threatened with a social revolution from the East. A Polish state appeared under these circumstances not only a matter of justice but of interest to the Allies, particularly to the French. As for those Poles who pursued pro-Central Powers policies, the Treaty of Brest Litovsk (which injured Polish interests) marked the end of their hopes.

A Polish army composed mainly of volunteers from America and commanded by General Józef Haller came into existence in France. It was placed under the political authority of the National Polish Committee. In January 1918, the thirteenth of Wilson's Fourteen Points affirmed the need for the creation of an independent Poland, composed of an indisputably Polish population, and with a secure access to the sea. On June 3 the Inter-Allied Conference confirmed that such a Poland was one of the conditions of a just peace. Events now moved fast. With Austro-Hungary crumbling and the federalist manifesto of Charles coming too late to save it, the Poles of Galicia regarded themselves as part of a rising Polish state. The government of the Congress Kingdom sought to emancipate itself from the Regency Council and declared independence. The parties of the left in turn proclaimed in Lublin the government of a People's Poland. On November 10 Piłsudski, released by the Germans, arrived in Warsaw. Both the Lublin government and the Regents handed over to him all political and military powers. Piłsudski was thus in control of the Kingdom (which he succeeded in peacefully clearing of German troops) and of the western part of Galicia. In eastern Galicia, where the Ukrainians had proclaimed an independent republic, fighting began. All other borders were in flux, with clashes occurring; and from the east the bolshevik threat loomed large.

Paris wanted to recognize Dmowski's Committee as Poland's government, and although the British and the Americans prevented it (mainly because of its rightist character), the Committee remained a rival to Piłsudski. By January 1919, however, a compromise occurred. Piłsudski remained head of state, Paderewski became premier, and Dmowski would represent Poland at the forthcoming Paris Peace Conference. It was up to the Allies to draw the definitive borders of Poland, Czechoslovakia, and Hungary, but a new and independent East Central Europe was already in existence, although it was tumultuous, ravaged, and internally divided.

7

THE DIFFICULT INDEPENDENCE

INTERNATIONAL RELATIONS

The First World War brought the collapse of the conservative monarchies in Europe and a victory for democracy and national self-determination. This victory, however, was neither complete nor permanent. The triumph of bolshevism in Russia meant not only the end of tsardom, but also the elimination of the nascent parliamentary regime. A way toward totalitarianism was opened under Lenin and reached its heyday under Stalin. In Italy a totalitarian creed of the extreme right came to prevail with the victory of the fascists in 1922. The advent of Nazi Germany in 1933 meant the addition of stringent racist doctrines. A formidable challenge arose which the Western democracies faced somewhat passively. The Great Depression called into question the very nature of capitalism. It radicalized the masses and brought new arguments and new recruits to the anti-democratic camp. Indeed, there came about a profound crisis of parliamentary democracy as derived from nineteenth-century liberal ideas, political and economic. In the West only Britain, France, and the smaller states of Scandinavia, Switzerland, Belgium, and the Netherlands successfully withstood the assault on their institutions. In East Central Europe, buffeted by the totalitarian gales from east and west, and struggling with economic problems worsened by the Depression, only Czechoslovakia was able to retain until 1938 a democratic parliamentary regime and economic stability. But even in this case one can speak only of a relative success.

The principle of national self-determination which the peacemakers, especially President Wilson, adopted as a guide for the reconstruction of East Central Europe, was to correlate state borders with ethnic divisions. In view of the existence, in many cases, of inextricably mixed areas, and the need to take into account economic, strategic, and historic factors, it was virtually impossible to draw absolutely equitable borders. True, fewer national minorities would be found after the First World War than before, but in the age of rampant nationalism they posed insoluble problems. The ensuing instability was worsened by the fact that although Germany had been defeated it did not cease to be a great power. Similarly, the weakening of the Russian colossus through revolution and civil war was of a temporary nature. Both states, discontented, revengeful, and isolated, posed a threat to the new East Central Europe, particularly to the Polish state.

Poland recovered its independence as a result of a combination of many factors. War had broken the solidarity of the partitioning states, and Russia had been forced out of the Polish lands by the Central Powers. They in turn were defeated by the Allies, while the two revolutions in Russia, the upheaval in Germany, and the disintegration of the Habsburg monarchy created a power vacuum. It was filled by the will and determination of the Polish nation that had never abandoned its struggle for freedom. Polish borders with Germany were drawn by the Paris Peace Conference, although the Poles were not mere spectators, as witnessed by the 1918–21 uprisings in Prussian Poland. The new frontiers denied to Poland its historic harbor Gdańsk, which became the Free City of Danzig, and they split, after a plebiscite, Upper Silesia. The Germans did not accept the existence of the "corridor" (as they called it) linking Poland with the Baltic Sea and separating Germany from East Prussia. They denounced it as an artificial monstrosity, although ethnically it was predominantly Polish and had been part of Poland before the partitions. Polish-Czechoslovak frontiers were easier to establish except for a small part in Silesia (Těšín, Cieszyn, Teschen) which the Czechs seized by force in 1919. The subsequent division of this economically rich district was deeply resented by the Poles, and it contributed to the bad blood between the two countries.

The Peace Conference could not effectively establish Poland's eastern frontiers given the chaos prevailing in the former Russian empire and the absence of Russia's representative in Paris. The advancing detachments of the Red Army, seeking to carry revolution westward, clashed with the Poles claiming the lands that had belonged to the old Commonwealth. In former eastern Galicia an armed confrontation between the Ukrainians and the Poles lasted until 1919, when the Polish side took over the entire province.

Dmowski and the Polish right demanded the borders of 1772 as corrected by ethnic changes that had occurred in the course of the nineteenth century. This meant a certain expansion in the west (Silesia) and a contraction in the east (roughly the line of the second partition). In the latter region the Polish minority was strong culturally and economically and Dmowski believed in the possibility of assimilating the Ukrainians and Belorussians. Piłsudski and the left favored a "federalist" approach that would lead – after the withdrawal of Russia from all of the lands of the old Commonwealth – to the creation of a bloc of federated or allied countries: Poland, Lithuania, Belorussia, and the Ukraine. The Dmowski–Piłsudski controversy over Polish eastern policies was not lost on the great powers, although they, as well as the borderland nations, often suspected that both trends disguised Polish imperialist designs.

The Peace Conference did not unequivocally side with the Poles against the bolsheviks, politically or militarily, but it did not recognize the bolsheviks or try to make peace with them either. Procrastinating and zigzaging the conference in late 1919 proposed a minimal Polish border in the east, known later as the Curzon Line. This was no solution, and Allied preference for a policy of neither war nor peace with the bolsheviks was unacceptable to the embattled Poles. Piłsudski believed that peace could only be achieved after a military victory. Gaining the support of the Ukrainian leader Petliura, he launched an offensive in the spring of 1920 that resulted in the capture of Kiev. The Red Army attacked in turn and reached the outskirts of Warsaw. The entire postwar settlement was suddenly at stake. Poland and perhaps even Europe was saved through the "eighteenth decisive battle of the world," as a British diplomat termed the Polish victory. Piłsudski's opponents, trying to belittle his achievement, called it the "miracle of the Vistula." The bolshevik rout opened the way to negotiations. The Peace Treaty of Riga of 1921 split the ethnically mixed, but largely Ukrainian and Belorussian borderlands between Poland and the Soviets. As for Vilnius (Wilno) and its region – historically Lithuanian, but ethnically Polish-Belorussian-Jewish – it was seized militarily by the Poles. Piłsudski was willing to give this region to Lithuania but only if the old Polish-Lithuanian Commonwealth were recreated. This, the Lithuanians, bent on independent national existence, were unwilling to accept. A wall of enmity arose between the two nations.

As compared with all the complexities of the Polish territorial settlement, the drawing of Czechoslovak borders was far less dramatic. The old frontiers with Germany remained unchanged, the Allies having no intention of applying the ethnic principle to them or to Austria because it would have resulted in a Germany stronger than before the war. Hence the Sudeten Germans, as they came to be known, vainly sought to detach the border regions from the new Czechoslovak state. While the peacemakers endorsed the historic borders of Bohemia and Moravia – in Silesia the above-mentioned controversy with the Poles flared up – they accepted borders in Slovakia that were a mixture of ethnic, economic, and strategic compromises. Several almost purely Hungarian-inhabited regions were included in them. Further east, the region known as Carpatho-Ruthenia or Carpatho-Ukraine, was transferred from Hungary to Czechoslovakia mainly on strategic grounds, to establish contiguity with Romania. The Hungarians' bad record of minority treatment was also invoked in this settlement. Thus, except for some extravagant claims, virtually all Czechoslovak territorial demands were granted, making the country highly heterogeneous. Somewhat ingeniously Beneš drew comparisons with Switzerland; critics said that a near replica of the Habsburg monarchy had been created.

Czechoslovakia was the darling of the Entente; Hungary was its *bête noire*. All the efforts of Károlyi to win Allied sympathy for the new state after the disintegration of historic Hungary were in vain. The subsequent short-lived Soviet Hungarian republic only increased antagonism toward the Hungarians and delayed the peace treaty. When signed in 1920 with the counter-revolutionary regime of Admiral M. Horthy, it proved to be the harshest of all treaties that followed the First World War. Not only was the ethnic principle used everywhere against Hungary, but it was also violated when operating in Hungary's favor. Plebiscite demands (with one exception in Sopron) were refused. In virtue of the Treaty of Trianon Hungary (excluding Croatia) was reduced territorially by two-thirds and in terms of population by three-fifths. Almost every third ethnic Magyar found himself now living under Romanian, Czechoslovak, Yugoslav, or Austrian rule. Hungary was fully independent at last but under conditions that amounted to a national disaster. Small wonder that extreme bitterness prevailed and the cry "nem, nem, soha" ("no, no, never") reverberated throughout the truncated land. The Hungarians became obsessed with a revision of Trianon, revisionism shaping to a large extent Budapest's external and domestic politics.

The new international order that arose out of the postwar treaties was to be based on the League of Nations. Yet from the outset its main pillar, the United States, was absent, and the support of the remaining two, Britain and France, was weakened by their mutual differences. The French were intent on the fulfillment of Versailles, preservation of the status quo, and prevention of a German comeback, by force if necessary. The British wished to eliminate the causes of German revisionism by satisfying German grievances through peaceful change. As time went on, France became increasingly dependent on Britain. This had dire consequences for France's Eastern allies, Poland and Czechoslovakia, whose fate was closely associated with the preservation of the postwar system.

The international situation and the foreign policies of the three East Central European states exerted a great impact on their domestic evolution and vice versa. Poland, recreated albeit in a different shape after one hundred and twenty-odd years of partitions found itself between the German Scylla and the Russian Charybdis, or as it was said at the time, between the jaws of a gigantic pair of pincers which when closed would crush it. Poland could not, without jeopardizing its independence, side either with Germany against Russia or vice versa. Hence, Warsaw's foreign policy came to be based on the twin principles of balance and alliances with France and Romania. It was not always easy to reconcile the two.

Unlike Poland Czechoslovakia had no declared enemy among the great powers. Identifying closely with the new international order, Prague relied in its foreign policy on three elements: the League of Nations, with which it cooperated very closely; the alliance with France, whose protégé it became; and regionally the Little Entente, composed of Czechoslovakia, Romania, and Yugoslavia. In the mid-1930s a pact with the USSR was added. As for the Little Entente, designed to keep Hungary in check, it was above all a diplomatic instrument operative against revisionism, a Habsburg restoration, or a union (*Anschluss*) between Germany and Austria.

The international standing of the defeated and truncated Hungary was obviously very different from that of the victor states. With an area of 92,963 sq. km Hungary was much smaller than Czechoslovakia with 140,493 sq. km and Poland whose territory comprised some 388,634 sq. km. Poland was the sixth largest state in Europe; Czechoslovakia was only thirteenth, but it made up for the difference in economic might. Hungary was by far too weak to think of altering the Trianon settlement by force, and it pursued its revisionism through diplomacy. Budapest's foreign policy oscillated between cooperation with Rome and with Berlin, while seeking also to exert some influence in London. Its options were obviously limited. Hungarian enmity centered on Czechoslovakia, the loss of Slovakia being particularly resented, and here Budapest and Warsaw found some common ground. The Polish card was never a trump in the Hungarian diplomatic pack, but it had its use, and it reinforced the traditional friendship between the Hungarians and the Poles.

While many reasons seemed to dictate Polish-Czechoslovak cooperation the two states never closed ranks. Prague did not want to jeopardize its position by siding with Poland, which was threatened by both Germany and the USSR. When in the mid-1930s the situation changed to Czechoslovak disadvantage, Prague's advances met with a cool reception in Warsaw. Hungarian, Czechoslovak, or Polish external preoccupations, whether they were a desire for change or the fear of it, affected domestic developments, political and economic. Concern for security necessitated heavy military expenditure by both Poland and Czechoslovakia. Hungary, of course, was disarmed under the Treaty of Trianon.

ECONOMY, SOCIETY, CULTURE

Many traditional socio-economic and cultural features remained unchanged in interwar East Central Europe. But there were also new phenomena. With the merger of Bohemia and Moravia with Slovakia and Carpatho-Ukraine within the Czechoslovak state, the country as a whole offered more parallels to Hungary and Poland, becoming more truly East Central European. Still, it was the most advanced of the three; Hungary came second; Poland was a poor third.

As can be seen from the figures in Table 7.1, the population of the three countries increased; that of Poland much more rapidly than that of its neighbors. Czechoslovakia remained the most densely populated country, and the number actively engaged in the rural population was high throughout the area. In fact, it was higher than needed on economic grounds. The result was, to use current terminology, hidden unemployment.

While roughly as many people in Italy or Germany were actively engaged in agriculture per ha of arable land as in Czechoslovakia or Hungary, the average figures for Britain and Denmark were much smaller: 15–17 persons. As regards totals deriving their livelihood from agriculture the average for Western Europe would be between 20 and 40 percent of the entire population.

Table 7.1 Population and agriculture in interwar East Central Europe

Total population	Czechoslovakia	Hungary	Poland
Increase (%)	14.0	14.2	29.9
Total population increase in millions	13.6–15.2	7.9–9.1	26.8–34.8
Density per sq. km	110.4	98.0	89.7
Dependent on agriculture (%)	34.5*	51.8	60.6
Active persons per 100 ha of arable land	34.7	29.6	45.5

*In Bohemia-Moravia 25.6 percent; in Slovakia-Carpatho-Ukraine 58.5.
Sources: J. Żarnowski, "Authoritarian systems in Central and South-Eastern Europe 1918–1939," in J. Żarnowski (ed.), *Dictatorships in East Central Europe 1918–1939* (Wrocław, 1983), p. 22; Z. Landau and J. Tomaszewski, *Polska w Europie i świecie 1918–1939* (2nd, rev. edn, Warsaw, 1984), p. 36; M. C. Kaser and E. A. Radice (eds), *The Economic History of Eastern Europe 1919–75*, vol. I (Oxford, 1985), pp. 75 and 82.

The number of hectares of arable land per tractor (in 1939) showed that Czechoslovakia with 920 and Hungary with 829 were somewhat behind France (700) and a long way behind Germany (227). The figure for Poland was exceptionally low: 8,400. One must remember, however, the war devastations in the Polish lands, which were responsible for almost halving the cattle herds, leaving large portions of land fallow, and crippling the system of transportation through the destruction of bridges, railroad stations, and rolling stock.

To remedy the existing problems it was essential to change the structure of agriculture, modernize production methods, and relieve the rural overpopulation through land reform and industrialization. Land reform *per se* was no panacea, but it was important on political and psychological grounds, and all three countries adopted it. In Czechoslovakia roughly 16 percent of arable land formerly owned by Germans and Hungarians was distributed, in Poland about 10 percent (although about 25 percent of large estates were affected), in Hungary about 4 percent (but the figure for large estates was only 10 percent). Thus, in the Hungarian case there was no real transformation of the countryside and old conditions and relationships survived.

While agriculture had been a cause of economic dynamism in the nineteenth century, now only Bohemia and some parts of western Poland produced surpluses of agricultural capital. In Hungary the owners of the large estates mainly consumed theirs. Some accumulation of industrial capital occurred in the Hungarian case in the Budapest region, or in Polish Silesia. But there was need of more foreign investments, and indeed foreign capital played a significant, if not always a beneficial, role in interior East Central Europe.

Foreign investments in Poland (with the United States and France leading) reached a high point of over 40 percent of capital in the Polish joint stock companies. They were placed in the key branches of the economy: oil, heavy industry, electricity. Foreign capital was often of a speculative kind, seeking quick profits that were not reinvested in the country. There was a good deal of friction and mutual recrimination. The situation was rather different in Czechoslovakia where foreign capital in industry, representing 20 percent of the total investments, was much better integrated in the country's strong economy. French and British capital was particularly important. The presence of foreign investments was less striking in Hungary where, however, foreign loans were much larger than in the other two countries: $95 per capita as compared to $27 in Poland and $14 in Czechoslovakia.

To turn to industry, the output of iron in the former Congress Kingdom fell in the wake of the First World War to one-tenth of the pre-1914 production; the Łódź textile industry regressed to its 1870 levels. The total industrial output (mining excluded) of Poland in 1920–1 was 35 percent of that of 1913. The corresponding figures for Czechoslovakia and Hungary were 84.9 and 80 percent.

After achieving a certain degree of economic recovery and financial stabilization in the mid-1920s, East Central Europe was hit by the Great Depression on a scale unparalleled elsewhere. While European industrial production (USSR excluded) fell by 27 percent, in Poland the drop was 41 percent. In the period 1929–33 Polish national income declined by 25 percent. Unemployment affected 43 percent of the working population. Even Czechoslovakia, which overcame the Depression earlier than its neighbors, had not reached its 1929 level of production by 1937.

The necessary condition of industrial growth was a strong and expanding domestic market, in terms of consumption and investments, and this was not realizable in Poland. Attempts were made, however, to tackle the problem of industrialization through state intervention, particularly in the late 1930s. As it was, the Polish state controlled about 16 percent of national wealth. Out of the total investment in the industrial sector the state owned 58 percent in 1928 and 63 percent in 1939. In Hungary the state share was much smaller, only about 5 percent. Thanks to the involvement of the state and French credits, the Poles built their harbor, Gdynia. Its architect, Eugeniusz Kwiatkowski, in 1936 launched an imaginative project of a Central Industrial District (COP) involving the construction and development of steel mills, chemical industries, and armament factories. A comprehensive six-year plan followed, aiming at a radical restructuring of the economy. While Polish means were insufficient to achieve it, there was a 28 percent increase in industrial production over a two-year period. The incorporation in 1938 of Teschen, which produced 52.2 percent of Poland's coke, 67 percent of its pig iron, and 38 percent of its steel, was a powerful boost. Were the chances of a self-sustaining economic take-off real? Experts are divided. The launching in Hungary of a somewhat comparable Györ program of industrialization did not achieve a similar upsurge. Hungarian economic expansion was mainly in consumer, not investment, goods. By and large, the country progressed least, comparatively speaking, toward sustained capital accumulation.

Historians have characterized the relationship between agriculture and industry in Hungary, Poland, and Slovakia as dual economy. They mean that the agrarian sector revolving largely around local markets and operating along traditional ways, was as it were divorced from industry. The peasantry was too poor to buy industrial products; the industry, deprived of an expanding market, could not develop cheap mass production. A "price scissors" opened wider between the rising prices of the industrial goods the farmer had to buy and the farm products he had to sell in order to survive at near-subsistence level. There was a vicious circle.

In 1936 industrial workers constituted 44.6 percent of the actively working population of Czechoslovakia, 21.8 percent of that in Hungary, and 18.5 percent of that of Poland. The ratio between population and industrial output was about 1:1 in Czechoslovakia, 2:1 in Hungary, and

3:1 in Poland. By way of comparison, we can note that in Germany the ratio was 1:2. Production per capita, taking the European averages in 1936–40 as an indicator, amounted to roughly 67 percent in Czechoslovakia, 43 percent in Hungary, and 20 percent in Poland. These figures represented an increase over 1913 in the first two countries, and a slight decrease in the Polish case. Should we thus speak of stagnation or even a decline of the interwar Polish economy? While new branches were developed, for instance chemical and electrical industries, and pre-1913 levels were surpassed in hard coal or iron ores, to mention just two, there were instances of stagnation or even regression in many areas of the economy.

New frontiers naturally affected economic developments in East Central Europe. Postwar boundaries were generally advantageous for Czechoslovakia. Although the disappearance of the large market of Austro-Hungary caused problems, the country as a whole adapted its production and trade structure to the new situation. Czechoslovakia figured among the first ten industrial producers in Europe. Internally, however, Slovakia suffered from the severing of its natural (in terms of geography and communications) ties with Hungary. Trade and population movements were adversely affected, and within Czechoslovakia the Slovak lands underwent a certain "deindustrialization." As for the small banking system it passed from German and Hungarian to Czech hands. The 1913 levels were passed only by 1937.

The disappearance of the geographic unity represented by the Crown of St Stephen produced at first dramatic difficulties for the Hungarian economy. After Trianon the country retained some 55.5 percent of its industrial production value, about 50.9 percent of its industrial labor, and 49 percent of its factories. Losses were particularly heavy in the timber industry (84 percent), and iron ore production (89 percent). Those in the machinery industry, printing, and clothing were relatively light. By and large post-Trianon Hungary was a more industrialized country than the historic Kingdom.

Problems faced by the Polish economy were of an entirely different nature. Here a single economic unity was created out of three distinct parts, which for more than a century had operated in the context of different economic systems. In trade, the loss of the Russian market and a dependence on Germany called for new departures. Indeed, all of East Central Europe faced the complex problem of reorientation of its foreign trade. Without entering into all the intricacies one may just observe a retraction of regional commerce and an overall decline. While this was true for interwar Europe in general, the three countries experienced the fall in value more strongly than many other states. Table 7.2 shows the regional decline.

Table 7.2 Foreign trade in dollars per capita

	1925	1929	1938
Czechoslovakia	128	138	42
Hungary	59	72	30
Poland	32	37	14

Source: Based on Z. Landau and J. Tomaszewski, *Polska w Europie i świecie 1918–39* (2nd, rev. edn, Warsaw, 1984), p. 227.

The social structure of the region underwent no basic changes, although some issues became more acute. In Hungary, the highly visible aristocracy now comprised the refugees from Transylvania and Slovakia who had lost their land. Birth was still more important than wealth, and an official annual publication dutifully recorded titles, ranks, and precedence. Szeklers had their noble status verified and many others laid a claim to nobility; a hereditary "Order of Valiants" was established by the Regent. Within the political elite, however, a larger proportion of commoners than in the past was noticeable.

The intelligentsia doubled proportionately through an influx of refugees from the lost lands, but the old distinction between the Christian or "historic" middle class (the gentry) and the other part in which Jews or people of Jewish origin were dominant, remained valid. The post-Trianon borders contained only half of the former Jewish population, and its numbers continued to decline. But proportionately it stayed at the 5 percent level, and became if anything more bourgeois and Budapest-centered. While 82 percent of Magyars belonged to the poorest stratum, only 24 percent of Jews (of which 3 percent were in agriculture) did. By contrast, the Jews constituted over 40 percent of great industrialists and nearly 20 percent of big landowners. The phenomenon of a split middle class, a cultural gap between Budapest and the countryside, and the unresolved problem of an agrarian proletariat, contributed to the socio-economic backwardness of the country.

As in the past Polish and Hungarian societies had many similarities. The gentry tradition and ethos continued to dominate over a bourgeois outlook, or at least it constituted a certain ideal to which other social groups aspired. True, Polish aristocracy could hardly rival their Hungarian counterparts in political importance. Officially all hereditary titles were abolished. The landowning gentry struggled hard to maintain its traditional way of life on the heavily mortgaged estates. If upward social mobility was relatively modest, social relations seemed to have been more democratized and modernized than in Hungary. The percentage of the petite bourgeoisie increased slightly (11 to nearly 12 percent) and those of the workers rose from 27.5 to 30.2 percent. The intelligentsia, estimated at 500,000 people and composed of white-collar workers and free professions, continued to gain in numbers and importance. The largest single group was the peasantry, about 70 percent, but figures would be different if we took into account the multi-ethnic composition of the total population.

The Poles, according to the 1931 census, accounted for 69 percent of the inhabitants of interwar Poland. The Jews who, unlike in Hungary, were officially counted as a national minority, were numerically the third largest group (after the Ukrainians) and amounted to roughly 10 percent. Around 90 percent of them were unassimilated, and distinguished themselves by dress, mode of life, and the Yiddish language. They lived in a world apart, as the novels of Isaac Bashevis Singer demonstrate so well. Only thirteen individuals were great landowners, and members of the grande bourgeoisie were hardly numerous. Two-thirds of Jews belonged to the petite bourgeoisie, especially small traders and craftsmen, which was increasingly pauperized. They were visible among the white-collar workers (about 14 percent) and constituted nearly 50 percent of the free professions, virtually dominating medicine and law. Not only was the occupational structure of the Jewish community different from that of the Poles and other minorities, but they were also unevenly distributed throughout the country. The Jewish population ranged from tiny groups in western Poland to majorities in the small towns of former eastern Galicia and Russian Poland, and constituted nearly 30 percent of the population of Warsaw.

By way of contrast the Ukrainians and Belorussians were a "territorial" minority living in fairly compact blocs in regions adjoining those inhabited by their countrymen across the border in the USSR. Nine-tenths of the Ukrainians – who according to statistics numbered below 4.5 million, but were probably well over 5 million – were peasants and agricultural workers. Virtually all the Belorussians (ranging between 1 and 1.9 million) belonged to this category. The German minority had a much more balanced structure: around 24 percent in mining and industry, and close to 60 percent in agriculture. The Germans, comprising some 800,000 people, led the other minorities in economic and social standing, not to mention educational and cultural standards. More than half of them lived in the regions that had been formerly under Prussia.

Czechoslovakia was even more multinational than Poland. Czech and Slovaks constituted (according to the 1931 census) jointly 66.9 percent of the population; the Czechs over 50 percent, the Slovaks over 16 percent. The Germans with 23 percent came in fact second after the Czechs; the Hungarians amounted to some 5 percent and the Ukrainians to about 3.8 percent. The social structure of the Bohemian-Moravian-Silesian lands differed greatly from that of Slovakia and even more so from Carpatho-Ukraine. Czech society, characterized by upward mobility, had a large middle class (20 percent of the economically active population), a growing working class (about 30 percent), and a well integrated peasantry that resembled western European farmers. The country's elite was drawn from the grande bourgeoisie (some 5 percent of the total population) as well as from the middle class (often one generation removed from the villages) and the prosperous peasants. The practical and down-to-earth Czech continued to represent bourgeois values, and he had more affinity with his hard-working German neighbor than with a member of the Polish intelligentsia or a Magyar nobleman.

In Slovakia, the vast majority of people were peasants. Owing to a high birth rate and economic dislocations, a large number fell into the category of destitute rural proletariat. The small industrial and commercial sector was largely dominated by Germans and Jews, and a portion of the landed estates was in Hungarian hands. Still, a relatively small number of Slovak families controlled a significant part of the country's wealth. A tiny Slovak gentry often intellectually Magyarized, and a growing intelligentsia which showed traces of the age-long Hungarian connection, but was now in the forefront of Slovak activities, completed the picture.

The Jewish issue as a socio-economic problem existed in Slovakia where the Jews constituted 4.8 percent, and in the backward Carpatho-Ukraine around 12 percent. Only about half of all people of Judaic faith defined themselves as being of Jewish nationality. This represented 1.3 percent of the total population of Czechoslovakia. In Bohemia and Moravia the figures were much smaller – 0.2 and 0.6 percent – for many persons of Jewish faith regarded themselves as Czechs or as Germans.

Religious, national, and social issues were frequently interconnected, and the standing of the church in society was high in various parts of East Central Europe. In Hungary 65 percent of the population was Roman Catholic and 27 percent Protestant. Bohemia, Moravia, and Silesia were predominantly Catholic although adherence to Catholicism was often nominal in Bohemia and among the middle classes in general. The Germans were mostly Catholic. In Slovakia the division between the Catholic majority (69 percent) and a Protestant minority (18.7 percent) had social and political connotations. By and large the Slovak Protestants were closer to the Czechs and represented the wealthier element; among Germans and Hungarians there were Lutherans and Calvinists. All this made Slovak nationalists tend to consider only Catholic Slovaks as genuine Slovaks.

This tendency to identify religion with nationality was pronounced in Poland where the nationalists stressed the Pole equals Catholic equation. Interwar Poland consisted of 63 percent Roman Catholics, 11 percent Greek Catholics (Uniates), 11.5 percent Greek Orthodox, and 3.2 percent Protestants. (Jews who have been mentioned above are not included in these figures.) Although Poles were predominantly Catholic there were also some Polish Protestants. Ukrainians and Belorussians were either Greek Catholic or Orthodox. There was a Catholic minority among the Belorussians and the Germans, the latter being mainly Protestant.

The social, economic, and national position of the Catholic Church in Poland was traditionally high. But this does not mean that anti-clericalism was non-existent, particularly among the leftist intelligentsia. The clergy inclined to a tactical alliance with the political right. The Archbishop of Gniezno was the primate of Poland, and his standing was probably even more elevated than that of his Hungarian counter-part, the Archbishop of Esztergom, given the influential Protestant section in that country. In Poland, Slovakia, and often among the Ukrainians priesthood represented social advancement and prestige. The Slovak Father A. Hlinka or the Ukrainian Metropolitan A. Sheptyts-kyi were both father figures and national leaders.

Even the briefest overview of the independent East Central Europe must stress the importance of culture, for this was a rich period in intellectual, artistic, and scholarly activities. Polish poetry reached new heights with J. Tuwim, K. Wierzyński, and A. Słonimski; prose was dominated by women writers. The pioneering theater of S. I. Witkiewicz was later to achieve world-wide recognition and this was also true for a few avant-garde authors. The name of K. Szymanowski, the foremost composer, deserves mention. In the case of Hungary the music of Bartók and Z. Kodály was known throughout the world. The prose of Mihály Babits and Zsigmond Móricz as well as the poetry of Attila József gained a high place in the literature of the country. The name of Jaroslav Hašek, from Czechoslovakia, became known throughout Europe, but the impact on literature and on Czechoslovak politics of Karel Čapek was of special importance. Kafka's earlier-mentioned works transcended the Czechoslovak framework.

The traditional importance of arts and *belles-lettres* must not make us forget the great achievements in learning. Among the many disciplines for which the region was renowned let us just mention the Polish and Hungarian schools of mathematics and philosophy, and the Prague center of structural linguistics. In the interwar period Poland had 24 institutions of higher learning, Czechoslovakia 17, Hungary 13. As throughout Europe, universities were elitist and had relatively few students from the lower classes. Still, one could speak of an overpro-duction of intelligentsia and a scarcity of white-collar positions. Did interwar education foster nationalism? After the long period of foreign rule which often produced a depreciation of national values a reaction was understandable. The government used the schools and the army as instruments of national integration. While illiteracy was very low in Bohemia and Hungary (respectively 2.4 and 8.8 percent) it was still significant in Slovakia and Poland (15 and 23.15 percent). As nationalism became more stringent in the 1930s, and the Great Depression produced hardships, universities and even high schools became politicized and students were often driven to extreme positions: nationalist or, less frequently, communist.

East Central Europe could boast doctors, lawyers, engineers, scholars, and intellectuals who were second to none in Europe. There were also highly qualified technicians, artisans, and blue-collar workers. None the less a gap, least visible in Czechoslovakia, between the cultural aspirations and the means to satisfy them was characteristic of the entire region. The vast majority was poor, and the leading class, the intelligentsia, often suffered privations. The fact that the membership in the elite (the intelligentsia) was determined by educational standards rather than by economic status as in the case of the middle class symbolized the difference between East Central and Western Europe.

POLITICS

Interwar politics in the region were naturally affected by socio-economic and cultural structures and relationships. In the pursuit of a stable constitutional-political model Poland moved from a weak parliamentary regime to a contested authoritarian system. Authoritarianism also prevailed in Hungary, where an essentially conservative regime was gradually yielding to the challenge of a radical right. Czechoslovakia alone was relatively successful in its parliamentary system.

Political institutions were shaped by native traditions, when they existed, and by West European models. At this time, parliamentary democracy in the West operated either on the British two-party or the French multi-party system. The latter seemed to correspond better to East Central European theory and practice of politics. In the West a professional civil service assured a relatively smooth functioning of the administration. The "new" states of the region had to create their own bureaucracy, often inspired by or inherited from the Habsburg monarchy. Throughout most Polish lands, the tradition of a native civil servant was lacking.

In Poland the interwar period was characterized by a quest for a political model which led all the way from the French-inspired 1921 constitution to the *sanacja* constitution of 1935. A turning point was Piłsudski's *coup d'état* of 1926, which made the marshal the real master of the country. The parliamentary system failed largely because of the gulf that separated the mainly socialist left from the national-democratic-led right. Except for short periods of national emergency the two could not form common cabinets. This restricted political maneuver to right-center or left-center coalitions, and the center (mainly populist) although numerous did not effectively play the role of a balancer or a bridge. The left–right rift was enhanced by the Piłsudski–Dmowski conflict which was colored even more by outlook and mentality than by doctrine.

Piłsudski and his followers, but not the left as such, came to govern Poland. In a way they became a center, not so much in terms of ideology, for their "state ideology" was somewhat nebulous, but through a pragmatic approach that transcended party politics. Most of Piłsudski's men were former legionaries, now high-ranking officers. Hence people talked of a "colonels' regime." Yet, it would be a mistake to imagine a militarization of Polish politics along the lines of a South American junta. The army in reborn Poland was too young to have created its own establishment, and these officers were not so much professionals as men who through the force of circumstances had to fight for the rebirth of their country in uniform.

Piłsudski's principal adversary Dmowski never governed Poland, but he exerted a sway over the minds of many a Pole, particularly of the younger generation. Increasingly uninterested in parliamentary politics he steered his followers in the direction of a "national revolution" as exemplified by Mussolini's Italy or Salazar's Portugal. Historians who speak of Dmowski as a nationalist and apply the same adjective to Piłsudski confuse the doctrinaire nationalism of the former with the ardent patriotism of the latter. The difference was basic and it could be observed when examining attitudes of nationals and patriots toward national minorities. It is true, however, that there were times when it was blurred in practice.

Poland, as a German historian put it, was "a multi-national state with a uni-nationalist ideology."[53] Or, to express it differently, it was perceived by Poles as a national state although having a large number of minorities. Originally, Piłsudski and the left favored concessions to non-Poles provided they were good citizens. But passions ran too high on both sides. Neither the Poles who denied autonomy to the Ukrainians in eastern Galicia and resorted to reprisals, nor the Ukrainians who made use of terrorism could find an area of agreement. At times the practice of the government came dangerously close to the program of the integral nationalists who wanted to cut drastically the rights of the minorities under the slogan "Poland for the Poles."

The stringent anti-Semitism of the Dmowski camp, particularly of its extremist splinters like Falanga, was translated into demands for the elimination of Jews from politics, the economy, and culture. Piłsudski, to whom anti-Semitism was completely alien, never tolerated such positions. After his death, however, some of his followers began to borrow the nationalist slogans (anti-Semitic ones included), largely for tactical reasons. Condemning the use of violence as practiced by extreme nationalists, the post-Piłsudski government admitted the legitimacy of economic boycott and explored possibilities of gradual Jewish emigration. The latter also figured as a possible solution in centrist and leftist programs and was supported by Zionist groups. No anti-Jewish legislation was, however, adopted by the interwar Polish republic.

Having experimented first with a "sejmocracy" and then with a "pluralist authoritarianism" or limited dictatorship, Poland offered a very different picture from Hungary, which looked to its prewar past for political inspiration. A Habsburg restoration did not prove a real option for domestic and external reasons, but Hungary remained a kingdom, be it only to retain claims to the lands that had been historically part of St Stephen's Crown. Admiral Miklós Horthy, a former aide-de-camp of Francis Joseph, became regent. His original position of holding the kingdom for its rightful ruler was little more than a sham. Horthy's Hungary, however, revived much of the past. The electoral reform of the initial postwar period was abandoned and the suffrage limited to some 27 to 29 percent of potential voters. Open ballot was restored in the countryside. The upper house also re-emerged, although in a somewhat changed form. All these provisions ensured the rule of the so-called Unity Party, which was an instrument for administration rather than a union of like-minded people. While opposition parties were tolerated in the parliament they had no possibility of going beyond their status of a permanent minority.

The interwar Hungarian model was largely worked out during the 1921–31 decade of I. Bethlen's premiership. It was a neo-conservative system reminiscent of that under István Tisza, based on the manipulation of the electorate and administrative pressures. Its actual practices were more important than the nationalist ideas that had accompanied the counter-revolution and were characterized by xenophobia, anti-urbanism, and anti-modernism. The extremists regarded liberalism, socialism, and bolshevism (seen as a sequel) as essentially un-Hungarian. They emphasized their attachment to the past and to Christianity and they preached various forms of anti-Semitism.

Horthy himself was an anti-Semite, which did not prevent his political establishment from making deals with the top Jewish grande bourgeoisie. In that as in other respects the ruling conservatives, often drawn from the aristocracy, differed significantly from the radical right which ranged from nationalist extremists (but still operating within the system) to openly Nazi-type mass movements like the Arrow Cross. The latter did not gain power, but made those in power come closer to their views. This was evident in the anti-Jewish laws of the 1930s, the last of which in 1941 resembled the racist Nuremberg Law. Conservative Hungarians strongly objected to them as they objected to the rabble-rousing and crude Hungarian Nazis who defied their notion of gentlemenly behavior in politics.

It was ironic that it was the Hungarian Jews, many of them ardent Magyars and Magyarizers, who were singled out for these discriminatory measures, even though there were exceptions and loopholes. But in the near ethnic Hungary the Jews suddenly became the only *de facto* national minority. They were no longer needed as allies, and the high visibility of Jews during the communist episode helped to turn popular feeling against them. The other national minority, the Germans, also largely Magyarized, was by contrast a privileged group with a tradition of military service. Some Germans, although it is debatable whether they were a majority, proved susceptible to the attraction of Hitler's Germany. This seemed to be valid for certain members of the officers' corps who played an important role in politics.

The contest between the conservative and the radical right constituted the essence of Hungarian politics in the interwar period. The left had been badly discredited by its association with the communists. There existed a "third road" group, which opposed both capitalism and communism. Its heralds preached populism as a value system that was least corrupted by the ill effects of industrial society: materialism, atheism, cosmopolitism. With its Christian and patriotic – although bordering on nationalist – watchwords, the third road populism belonged to a transition zone between practical politics and political thought. It never had a direct impact on major political developments.

Turning to Czechoslovakia, its political system, operating under the 1920 constitution, seemed patterned on the French model. Yet unlike the latter it was characterized by great stability. Coming close to the "directed democracy" concept, vainly pursued by the Poles, it was based on three pillars: the castle (*hrad*), meaning the president and his associates; the governmental coalition; and the financial and economic establishment. Presidential powers, not inconsiderable in themselves, became much greater in the hands of Masaryk, who until the early 1930s appointed and dismissed premiers at will. The image of the "president-liberator" was consciously cultivated by his admirers. He was, like the former emperor, a father figure: the "old gentleman," as he was familiarly called. Only a minority strongly opposed Masaryk and questioned his fundamental ideas and the use he made of them in politics. Was Beneš, the second president, Masaryk's spiritual heir or merely his pale reflection? Opinions differed sharply, and the philosopher Jan Patočka passed the severest judgement on Beneš when he called him "an ambitious, diligent, talkative mediocrity." It was a tragedy, Patočka wrote, that Beneš had to "decide upon the future moral profile of the Czech nation" and that "he chose smallness."[54]

Masaryk's rule, as a historian put it, was a dictatorship based on respect. The president believed that a dash of dictatorship was essential in a democracy that was not yet fully mature. There were instances of governmental handling of opponents in Slovakia (Hlinka or Tuka) or in Bohemia (Gajda) when the law seemed to have been stretched a bit. As for the Czech bureaucracy it continued the Austrian tradition of combining moderate effectiveness and honesty with some harshness.

The governmental coalition, an informal semi-permanent fixture, was at the very heart of the Czechoslovak political system. An author called Czechoslovakia a multinational parties' state. The five major political parties: the agrarians, social democrats, national socialists, populists, and national democrats (hence the term *pětka* (five)) acted as shareholders of power and beneficiaries of spoils and patronage. Governed by a strict discipline that precluded the possibility of rebellion in the ranks, the parties made the parliament little more than a forum for debate. No cabinet was overthrown by a non-confidence vote in the chambers, for all real decisions were made by the party leaders. The concern for an inter-party balance assisted the Communist Party – the only one that operated legally in East Central Europe – for even the rightists feared that banning it would unduly strengthen the socialists and thus destroy the equilibrium.

Cabinets assumed various forms, going beyond the five or contracting below that number. From 1926 Sudeten Germans were represented in the government. The largest party, the agrarians, was present in all political cabinets, and their leader Antonín Švehla deserved more credit than he usually receives for making the system work. National democrats led by Kramář were mostly in opposition, and the challenge to the regime from the right in 1926 and 1935 proved a failure.

Characterized by a low degree of polarization, the system was occasionally criticized as somewhat mechanistic and uninspiring. More serious was the accusation of inner incompatibility between the proposition that the Czechoslovak republic must be a democracy with equal political and civil rights for all its nationalities, and the assumption that it must express Czechoslovak national culture. In other words, was real democracy and multi-ethnicity reconcilable in twentieth-century East Central Europe?

Masaryk did not think in terms of a Czech national state, but there was no clearly visible alternative program, and the administration, especially on the local level, promoted Czechization. Prague's centralism was supported by Masaryk's Slovak associates who thought it necessary to de-Magyarize, secularize, and modernize Slovakia. In the absence of trained Slovak cadres there was a need for Czech administrators, teachers, and specialists, but while some of these people were dedicated, others were arrogant and viewed the Slovaks as poor and backward Czechs. The government's policies were often unimaginative and insensitive. The Czechs spoke of losing money in Slovakia and taunted the Slovaks with the question of where they would go if they left the republic. The Austrian tradition of avoiding change unless forced by circumstances had left its imprint on the Czech administrative style.

The argument that the Slovak problem resulted from divisions among Slovaks is only partly correct. True, the largely Protestant pro-Czechoslovak establishment – the twenty families that ruled Slovakia, according to Beneš – confronted the populists, Catholic and autonomists. The latter all too frequently claimed that they spoke for all Slovaks, but their strength and the prestige of their leader Father Hlinka was undeniable. To represent him as a disgruntled office seeker was a political mistake. Prague's role was hardly that of a disinterested observer of inner Slovak divisions, and the rejection by the parliament of the thrice-introduced bill for Slovakia's autonomy only aggravated matters.

The Slovak question was basically a constitutional problem – after all the republic was a state of Czechs and Slovaks – but it also appeared as a national minority issue. The German question belonged more to the latter category, although the Germans viewed themselves as natives of Bohemia and wanted the position of co-rulers or associates in the multinational state. Their short-lived secessions in 1918 somewhat compromised this position, as did the Czech reaction to the German "rebels." Even Masaryk once called the Sudeten Germans "immigrants." But it was clear that some arrangement was necessary, and as mentioned, the Germans came to be represented in the cabinet, the only minority in East Central Europe to enjoy such a privilege. Was this a token arrangement, and was the subsequent worsening of Czech–German relations unavoidable? Or could their demands for autonomy have been satisfied, since even in 1939 a third of Sudeten Germans did not oppose the Czechoslovak state? There are no easy answers. We must remember, however, not to divorce the evolution of German–Czech relations from the rise of Hitler and his policy of making the German minority an instrument for the destruction of the republic.

THE TWENTY YEARS 1919–39

Turning to a chronological overview we must go back to the proclamation of the Czechoslovak state on October 28, 1918 in Prague. It marked a bloodless transition which preserved legal continuity with the defunct monarchy. The constitutional process of building the state was the work of Czechs and Slovak centralists; the Germans and other national minorities were not involved. Kramář became briefly premier, and his national democrats pursued anti-inflationary policies that spared the country the first postwar economic and financial chaos that prevailed elsewhere throughout the region. Under the presidency of Masaryk, who would be re-elected twice more, and with Beneš as the perennial foreign minister until 1935, the state became stabilized internally and externally. The formation of the Little Entente and the alliance with France (in 1924) were the major achievements in the international field.

The "castle" successfully weathered the 1926 crisis in which the right and especially the small but vocal fascist group promoted General Rudolf (Radola) Gajda as the leader. His removal from the army and his later trial, as well as Beneš's victory over the rightist faction among the national socialists showed the futility of a challenge to the system. A "gentlemen's coalition" under Švehla comprised not only German ministers but briefly even Hlinka's populists. But the cooperation with the latter broke down over the arrest and trial of a Slovak populist leader Vojtěch Tuka, accused of treason. It was a bad omen for the future.

The Great Depression hit the German-inhabited regions as well as Slovakia particularly hard. In the atmosphere of radicalization, nationalist and extremist political trends came to the fore. The rise of Hitler had a direct impact on Czechoslovakia. Thus far Prague's relations with Germany had been correct if not friendly; now the thrust of the Nazi program menaced the Czechoslovak republic. The dissatisfied German minority became receptive to extremist slogans. In 1933 an organization arose under the leadership of Konrad Henlein that assumed its final pro-Nazi form two years later as the Sudeten German Party. In the 1935 general elections it captured two-thirds of the German vote. By that time Hlinka's populists had also strengthened their position, and the 1933 celebration of the founding of the first Christian church in Nitra in Slovakia turned into a demonstration in favor of Slovak autonomy.

The mid-1930s represented a turning point. The international situation grew more tense. The signing of the 1935 pacts between Paris, Prague, and Moscow only increased German and Italian accusations of Czechoslovakia as an advance guard of communism. The main Western ally, France, became increasingly weak and indecisive. A tension with Poland grew as Warsaw fanned the grievances of the Polish minority in Teschen, flirted with Slovaks and found itself on the opposite side to Prague in international counsels. The Hungarian anti-Czechoslovak stance grew bolder. There was unintended irony in the wish extended to Beneš on his succession to Masaryk in 1935 that he become the "president unifier." Lacking Masaryk's stature and fighting spirit, Beneš was more adroit in external than domestic politics. M. Hodža, the moderate Slovak agrarian who became prime minister, was not equal to the deceased Švehla.

It was an isolated and domestically undermined Czechoslovakia that entered the fateful year 1938. Demands of the Sudeten German Party for far-reaching autonomy were voiced in the Karlový Vary (Karlsbad) program and were meant as escalating demands. When Beneš, whose position was weakened by the British mediatory mission under Lord Runciman, satisfied (in his fourth plan) virtually all the German demands, the response was an uprising and Henlein's flight to Germany. It was now a showdown between Hitler and Beneš, with the Western powers anxious to avoid war and willing as arbiters to sacrifice Czechoslovakia. Should Beneš have defied all pressures, united the country in resistance to Hitler, and risked a war in isolation that was bound to be lost? This is a question which has been preoccupying many a Czech and Slovak as well as historians. The risk was enormous and Beneš felt he had no right to sacrifice an entire generation. The recollection of the catastrophe of the White Mountain was present in his mind. Nor did Beneš wish to appear in Western eyes as the man who recklessly plunged Europe in war. So, he chose to capitulate, and the price in terms of national morale was heavy. A "Munich complex" would henceforth haunt Beneš and his people.

The Slovaks, deprived of Hlinka, who died in August 1938, were now led by the discordant Tiso–Sidor team. The two negotiated with Prague, and Sidor did appeal for the defense of the common fatherland. But Beneš proved unwilling or unable to open a new chapter in Czech–Slovak relations. Slovak leaders made secret overtures to Warsaw for a Polish–Slovak union, but generally they felt uncertain and vulnerable.

The fate of Czechoslovakia was decided by the German-Italian-British-French dictate at Munich. Czech western provinces were annexed to Germany. Subsequently, under the so-called First Vienna Award (by Germany and Italy) parts of southern Slovakia were transferred to Hungary. As for the contested Teschen, Poland gained it (and a little more) through a direct ultimatum addressed to Prague. Czechoslovakia lost some 30 percent of its territory, one-third of the population, and two-fifths of its industrial capacity, not to mention the strategic and fortified borders. Beneš apparently hoped that the truncated country might survive until the outbreak of the general war that he believed imminent. But he was forced to resign, and the Second Republic arose under the colorless president Emil Hácha. It was called Czecho-Slovakia and under the Žilina accord it was a state of two equal nations with their own parliaments and administrations. Carpatho-Ukraine received an autonomous status. All this proved to be a transient arrangement. The German shadow fell on the country, which had to adjust its internal system to Nazi demands. Berlin closely watched Czech–Slovak friction and when matters reached a high point it summoned Tiso and persuaded him to declare Slovak independence on March 14, 1939. Simultaneously Hácha was called in by Hitler and overawed by the threat of a German bombardment of Prague unless he accepted the status of a German protectorate of Bohemia and Moravia. On March 15, German troops marched into Prague. Roughly at that time Hungary, assisted by Poland, occupied Carpatho-Ukraine, which had also declared its independent status. The Czechoslovak state was no more.

Interwar Hungary lacked both the achievements and the dramatic denouement of Czechoslovakia. A threefold periodization seems appropriate: first, the initial revolution of the left in 1919, second the decade of Bethlen, and third, the post-1932 "revolution of the right." The initial revolution was indeed an upheaval, a double one in fact begun by Károlyi and his supporters who sought to create a democratic system based on universal secret suffrage, land reform, an eight-hour working day, and civic freedoms. Károlyi's idealism – the only land distributed was his own – hardly sufficed to install such basic changes in the war-ravaged and partly occupied country. If the Allies had been willing to help this experiment it might have succeeded, but their policy toward the ex-enemy was devoid of sympathy. Driven to despair by constant demands to vacate more territory to be occupied by the neighbors' armies, Károlyi's government fell in a bloodless revolution. The bolsheviks led by Béla Kun were in power. Based on communist–socialist cooperation and fed by the initial military successes of the Red Army against its Romanian and Czechoslovak neighbors, the Republic of the Soviets lasted for over four months. It alienated the peasant masses by its anti-religious propaganda and the nationalization (rather than distribution) of landed estates. The industrial proletariat, although significantly increased during the First World War, provided an insufficient base of support. Kun's faith in a universal revolution and in a joining up with Russian bolsheviks made him dogmatic and unimaginative. He sought to promote a dictatorship of the proletariat and frightened the other classes by threats of a bloodbath. In fact, the Red Terror claimed far fewer victims than those who later perished during the White Terror.

When the Red Army began to disintegrate under the Romanian advance, which resulted in the occupation of Budapest itself, the Hungarian bolsheviks lost all chance of survival. The leadership fled the country. The significance of the communist episode lay in discrediting the political left, accused of "Godless bolshevism," and the Jews whose visibility among the leadership (beginning with Kun himself) was high, even though the majority of Hungarian Jews did not support the revolution.

A counter-revolutionary political and military movement, formed in the French-occupied Szeged and Arad, and eventually led by Admiral Horthy, exacted a heavy toll from their opponents. Horthy promised to punish the "sinful city" of Budapest, and reprisals ended only when the new regime needed to gain respectability to win Allied recognition and negotiate the peace treaty. The January 1920 elections, from which the socialists abstained and the communists were banned, gave victory to a conservative rightist party. Under the name "Unity Party" it was to exercise power for the next quarter of a century. In a monarchy without a king, for the two attempts by Charles Habsburg in 1921 to regain his crown were defeated by Horthy, the legitimists had to reconcile themselves to the banning of the old dynasty.

Count István Bethlen, as mentioned, built and operated the political system. Abhorring demagogy and conscious of the fact that the radicalism of the counter-revolution constituted a threat to property and order, Bethlen steered a middle course. He neutralized the Smallholders Party by promises of land reform. He struck a deal with the social democrats, permitting their activities although only in towns and without political strikes. The earlier-mentioned restrictions in electoral practices and the restoration of the upper house of the parliament completed Bethlen's work. His regime succeeded in bringing Hungary out of international isolation. A much needed loan materialized under the auspices of the League of Nations. Needless to say, the moderate and aristocratically tinged policies of Bethlen did not appeal to the radical nationalists who, like Captain Gömbös, had played a leading role in the Szeged movement.

As the Great Depression struck Hungary, contributing as elsewhere to radicalization of politics, Bethlen withdrew but remained a power behind the scene. In 1932 Horthy named Gömbös premier who adopted a program in which extreme nationalism, anti-Semitism, and some fascist-like trappings were prominently displayed. Hungary became more polarized than before. An ill-assorted alliance of Habsburg legitimists, Bethlenites, Jewish capitalists, some anti-Nazi populists, trade unionists, and bourgeois liberals faced the "Christian middle class," some army officers, certain members of the aristocracy, and the intelligentsia. Gömbös was driven to make compromises with the wealthy Jews and the conservative aristocracy, promising not to bring any sweeping changes. There is a question as to whether he would have kept these promises or proceeded toward a totalitarian model, but he died in 1936. In any case the "revolution of the right" was in full swing, even though Horthy tried to restrain it. He was more successful in keeping out of power the growing mass movement of the openly Nazi Arrow Cross, led by Szálasi. This was possible only because of the electoral geometry as practiced at the time, but even so the Arrow Cross and its allies in 1939 registered a spectacular increase in votes.

They were successful in the working-class districts of Budapest and around it, in areas dominated by agrarian radicals, among Protestants and Catholics, Germans, and the lower classes.

The impact of the Third Reich was increasingly visible under Gömbös, the first foreign statesman to visit Hitler officially, and under his successors. By 1939 Hungary's economic dependence on Germany was expressed by 50 percent of all exports and 26 percent of imports. One half of all foreign capital was German. The Nazi example served as inspiration for the anti-Jewish legislation, which the conservative upper house vainly opposed. The pro-German line earned Hungary the already-mentioned territorial gains under the Vienna award in 1938 and in Carpatho-Ukraine in 1939. The anti-Trianon stance was present throughout all these years, the post-1920 Hungary being treated as a truncated and mutilated fatherland and not a permanent state that could be taken for granted and identified with.

The history of interwar Poland fell, like that of Hungary, into clearly delineated periods, the divisions being even sharper. The initial phase of building up the state ended in 1921 with the adoption of the March constitution, the Upper Silesian plebiscite, the treaty of Riga with the Soviets, and the alliances with France and Romania. During the first three months Piłsudski had virtually dictatorial powers and then he acted as a constitutional head of state. He refused, however, to be a candidate for the presidency under the 1921 constitution that placed all power in the *sejm*. The latter's composition at this point showed a rightist plurality (36 percent) with the center slightly below that figure and the left having some 27 percent of deputies.

The election of G. Narutowicz as president in 1922 opened a new phase. The right vehemently protested against his choice, calling him a president imposed by the national minority vote which had allegedly swung the balance. A nationalist fanatic shot Narutowicz, a murder that shocked the nation and deeply affected Piłsudski. The new president Wojciechowski, although elected by the same majority, was more acceptable to the right, and assumed office without difficulty. As a right-center coalition came into being under the premiership of the tough, pragmatic populist leader Witos in 1923, Piłsudski withdrew from politics and the army. The three years that followed were characterized by frequently changing cabinets – seven months' duration being the average – and grievous economic problems. The hyper-inflation of 1923 was, however, brought under control by the Grabski reforms, which introduced a stable currency. But there was a growing discontent among the masses and fears about the future. Germany waged an economic war on Poland, and rejoining European counsels through the Locarno treaties in 1925 it did not hide its revisionist anti-Polish objectives.

Projects for constitutional and political change became more current. Those on the right showed a growing fascination with Italian fascism and proposed to curtail the presence of national minorities in the parliament. The left spoke of a threat to democracy, and the Jews in particular were alarmed. The eyes of the left were turning toward Piłsudski as the only savior. He was fulminating against unbridled parliamentarism and irresponsible politicians, calling for "cleansing" (*sanacja*) of the entire system. He had devoted supporters among his former legionaries in and out of the army, and in May 1926 he led a few regiments on Warsaw. This was designed as an armed demonstration that would force the president to dismiss another center-right cabinet of Witos. The unexpected resistance of Wojciechowski led to a clash and bloodshed. After three days of fighting Piłsudski's forces, supported by the entire left, prevailed. A new period began.

After 1926 the powers of the president were somewhat increased, but Piłsudski refused the post. While his associate Mościcki became president, Piłsudski commanded the army and was twice premier. But he was the real master. A born leader and a complex personality, comparable in some respects to Charles de Gaulle, Piłsudski rejected fascism, but did not seek cooperation with a chastized *sejm*. Trying deliberately to discredit it along with the political parties, he wanted the cabinet to govern and the *sejm* merely to control its activities. Piłsudski disappointed the left by insisting that he wished to remain above parties, and his supporters, ranging from socialists to conservatives, organized themselves into a Non-partisan Bloc of Cooperation with the Government (BBWR). They became the largest group in the *sejm* after the 1928 elections.

Piłsudski was growing impatient with what he regarded as sterile opposition. He responded to some acts of Ukrainian terrorism by ordering brutal reprisals ("pacifications") in 1930. When the center-left consolidated bloc accused the government of destroying democracy, Piłsudski had the leading politicians arrested, mishandled, and imprisoned in the Brześć fortress and tried in 1931. The sentences were light, for Piłsudski's objective of overawing the opposition had already been achieved. It was tragic and paradoxical that Piłsudski, who genuinely believed that force "does not educate but destroys" felt obliged to use such high-handed methods. His main concern, as always, was with the security of the country, and he devoted most of his attention and energy to foreign policy and the military. In 1932 Poland signed a non-aggression treaty with the USSR and two years later a similar declaration with Nazi Germany. The jaws of the pincers were seemingly pried further apart. Under Józef Beck as foreign minister, Warsaw pursued a policy of balance. There was really no alternative, for Poland's tragedy, as a French historian remarked, was that it was reborn too weak to be a power and too strong to be reconciled to the role of a client state. A certain defiant style and occasional sabre rattling earned Polish diplomacy severe criticism that a more powerful state might have been spared. While Marshal Piłsudski's health declined and he became a tense, intolerant, almost neurotic recluse, his followers passed a new constitution through dubious parliamentary tactics. The April 1935 constitution was of a presidential-authoritarian type that dispensed with the traditional division of powers. The president was placed above all branches of government, the judiciary, the legislature, and the army. But the constitution that was made for Piłsudski became an empty shell when he died in May of the same year.

Piłsudski's legend could not be bequeathed and his supporters' constant invocation of his name was no substitute for policy. Torn by personal rivalries and contradictions, the Piłsudski camp began to disintegrate. A democratic wing was opposing those who, observing the successes of dictators and the shortcomings of parliamentary democracy, stood for an authoritarian regime. President Mościcki steered his own course, but he was challenged by the new commander-in-chief, Marshal Śmigły-Rydz who was being represented as the true successor of Piłsudski. To enlarge the basis of governmental power a new political movement, the Camp of National Unity (OZN) replaced the defunct BBWR. Its ideology, as a wit put it, was a cocktail: 40 percent nationalism, 30 percent social radicalism, 20 percent agrarianism, and 10 percent anti-Semitism. It proved a soulless body. Under the existing conditions Poland could either evolve toward a semi-totalitarian model for which Dmowski's nationalism would be needed as the cement, or return to parliamentary democracy. Since the political parties boycotted general elections, because of a new law that discriminated against them, only the local elections held in 1938–9 provided some indications of the political profile of the country. In larger towns the government gained about a third of the vote, but was followed closely by the socialists and the nationalists. The opposition grew in strength with the united Populist Party (SL) and the newly formed Christian Democratic Front Morges, so-named after Paderewski's residence in Switzerland. What direction would Polish politics have taken if peace had prevailed for another decade or so? It is impossible to say.

As the threat of war loomed large, the governmental camp refused to share power and responsibility with the opposition. It persisted in this attitude when Germany launched the attack on Poland on September 1 that started the Second World War, and it went down with Poland in the military catastrophe that followed.

The point has sometimes been made, especially in the West, that the interwar East Central Europe was a failure. It has been suggested that the discrepancy between an advanced political model and the backward socio-economic context in which it operated precluded any chances of success. The fact that it was the most advanced country, Czechoslovakia, that achieved the greatest stability seems to argue in favor of this thesis. But it leaves unexplained Prague's inability to resolve either the Czech–Slovak or the Czech–German problem. In the case of Hungary it is true that its interwar record and achievements did not compare favorably with those of the preceding century of semi-independence. But then the shock of Trianon and the ensuing revulsions were partly responsible for it. Looking at the big neighbors, surely the Bethlen middle-of-the-road model or the post-1926 authoritarianism of the Piłsudski camp compared favorably with what was happening at that time in Italy, Germany, or the USSR.

In a sense each of the three states emerging after centuries of dependence or partitions was a half-way house and faced problems of overawing magnitude. That they did not resolve them in twenty years time is not all that surprising. Czechoslovakia and Poland had national minorities that they could neither absorb nor conciliate through federalist solutions, although autonomous arrangements were a possibility that the intensely nationalist atmosphere made virtually inapplicable. Hungary, and also Poland, operated with an amalgam of a free market and a planned economy, but for social reasons did not go far enough in the directions of reforms. The Czechoslovak parliamentary system proved unusually successful; those of Poland and Hungary did not, but they still retained enough traditional pluralism to preserve their civil societies. During those twenty years the national cohesion of Poles, Czechs, Slovaks, and Hungarians was strengthened. The spiritual and moral value of independence was great for peoples who had been deprived of it. If excessive nationalism was the price, it still allowed them to survive the trials of the Second World War and of forty-five years of communism that followed. The resources of Czechoslovakia and Poland were insufficient to protect them against Nazi Germany and the Soviet Union. The fact that they succumbed tells more about the system of international security or lack thereof, and of the guardians of the post-Versailles order than about the states of East Central Europe. Munich and later Yalta testified only to the vulnerability of the region, not to its inability to survive in freedom.

THE SECOND WORLD WAR

Germany attacked Poland on September 1, 1939, but while it met with stiff resistance the outcome of the struggle was never in doubt. Britain and France declared war on Germany three days later, but brought no effective aid to the outnumbered and outgunned Poles. On September 17 the Red Army acting in collusion with Germany (the Ribbentrop–

Molotov pact) struck from the east. There were hardly any Polish troops available to oppose the entering Soviets.

A new partition of the country placed western lands under direct German rule, their Polish and Jewish population being deported into a central region called the General Gouvernement. There the Poles were to be reduced to the lowest material and cultural levels, and the Jews shut in ghettos and then liquidated. A similar fate awaited most Gypsies. The General Gouvernement thus became the scene of one of the most horrible developments in history, the Holocaust. The Auschwitz (Oświęcim) concentration camp together with the death camps of Treblinka and Sobibor was grim testimony to the Final Solution. Occupied Poland, dotted with Nazi camps, came to be the cemetery of Polish and much of European Jewry. Jewish resistance was hardly possible, although it did flare up in the Warsaw ghetto uprising in April 1943. The death penalty for harboring Jews (nonexistent elsewhere in Europe) discouraged assistance on the part of the Poles, whose attitudes ranged from passivity to the two extremes of denunciation and active help. The Polish underground, the largest and most effective in Europe, the resistance movement in Yugoslavia excepted, extended some help and tried in vain to alert the West to the terrible plight of the Jews.

Life under the German occupation was a continuous nightmare. Arrests, hostage-taking, mass executions, were all meant to terrorize the Poles, who were denied secondary and higher education and whose elite and heritage were systematically destroyed. The eastern lands suffered comparably under the Soviets, who sought, however, to cloak their actions under the mask of pseudo-legality. Thus "elections" were held that produced the usual figures in the 90 percent range in favor of incorporation into Soviet Ukraine and Soviet Belorussia. Undesirables were "resettled," that is, deported under inhuman conditions into various provinces of the USSR. Although exact figures may never be known over one and a half million Poles, Ukrainians, Jews, and Belorussians – men, women, and children – were involved. Most of them never returned. In all, some six million Polish citizens perished in the Second World War; about half of them were Jews.

The Poles did not surrender after the lost campaign of September 1939. A Polish government which represented a legal continuity of the Polish state was constituted, mostly out of prewar opposition leaders, in Allied France. After the French collapse in 1940 it moved to England. Under the presidency of W. Raczkiewicz, General Władysław Sikorski became premier and commander-in-chief of the armed forces, which were composed of Poles who lived abroad or succeeded in escaping from the occupied country. These troops distinguished themselves in virtually every European theater of war and in North Africa. Polish pilots played a disproportionately large role in the Battle of Britain. The small navy was often cited for bravery. The military underground in Poland, the Home Army, was also under the orders of the government in London.

When Germany invaded the Soviet Union in June 1941, the Sikorski government found itself in a singular situation. The new ally in the anti-German coalition had so far been an accomplice of Hitler in the invasion and partitioning of Poland. It was difficult to view it suddenly as a friend. Succumbing to British pressures and wishing to free the deported Poles, Sikorski signed a pact with the USSR on July 30. It restored Soviet–Polish relations, provided for an "amnesty" to Poles in the Soviet Union, and permitted the organization of a Polish army there. Although the accord annulled the Ribbentrop–Molotov pact it did not explicitly restore the prewar borders. Henceforth, the Soviets would insist on retaining their territorial acquisitions by invoking the fake elections of 1939. The Polish government was split on the wisdom of such an imprecise accord, but Sikorski felt that no viable alternative existed. So he journeyed to Moscow to sign an agreement with Stalin on the Polish army in Russia, which was placed under the command of General Anders. But mutual suspicions lingered. The Poles did not trust the Soviets, and indeed friction over the troops ensued. Eventually, they were evacuated to the Middle East, and fought later under British command, gaining a major victory at Monte Cassino.

Sikorski realized the vulnerability of Poland facing in effect two foes: Germany with which a life-and-death struggle was being waged, and the Soviet Union, which had hegemonic designs on East Central Europe. He sought to obtain the backing of the United States (during the three Washington visits) and of Britain. He tried to strengthen the position of postwar Poland and of the entire region by planning, jointly with Beneš, a Czechoslovak-Polish confederation. But neither Roosevelt nor Churchill wished to wreck their cooperation with the USSR on the Polish rock. Churchill believed that if the Poles reconciled themselves to territorial losses in the east, Russia would not interfere with their domestic freedoms. This sounded logical, but was in reality misleading. Stalin wanted a "friendly" postwar Poland that would subordinate itself to the USSR. Only a government controlled by the communists could guarantee such behavior. Moreover, Sikorski could hardly sign away half of the country, the home of many of his soldiers, without being accused of treason. Thus the situation began to look hopeless as the Red Army stemmed the German tide at Stalingrad, and began a westward advance that would bring it to the heart of Europe.

In April 1943 the Germans announced a discovery in the Katyn woods of mass graves of Polish officers who had been captured by the Red Army in 1939. The Soviet authorities, when pressed by the Sikorski government, had hitherto professed complete ignorance as to the fate of these officers. Now that the Polish government asked the Swiss Red Cross to investigate the allegations of a Soviet massacre, Stalin accused the Poles of playing into German hands and broke off diplomatic relations with them. The Polish position deteriorated with the mysterious death of Sikorski in a plane crash, and the arrest by the Gestapo of the commander of the underground Home Army (AK). The new premier, a populist leader S. Mikołajczyk, and the new commander-in-chief General Sosnkowski, lacked Sikorski's standing. Worse still, they strongly disagreed with one another.

The hope that Soviet–Polish relations could be restored through actual cooperation in the field was dashed. The Red Army had been accepting the aid of the Home Army against the Germans, but once victorious it proceeded to arrest Polish officers and incorporate the other ranks into its own communist-led Polish units. From May 1943 a Polish division, later expanded, was organized in Russia under the command of General Berling. Its political umbrella was the communist-led Union of Polish Patriots in Moscow. Meanwhile a small communist-directed partisan movement developed in occupied Poland as a rival to the main underground. A pro-Moscow National Committee of the Homeland (KRN) was constituted toward the end of 1943, and a Polish Committee of National Liberation (PKWN) was installed in the Soviet-occupied town of Lublin in July 1944. As the Soviets were driving the Germans out of Poland they were establishing their own military and political structure in the country.

The Western Allies felt that they had limited means of influencing the course of events. They virtually conceded all prewar Polish eastern lands to Stalin at the Conference in Teheran in 1943. The Poles were to be compensated at the expense of Germany. The British pressed Mikołajczyk to accept and the premier went to bargain in Moscow in August 1944. Simultaneously Warsaw staged a massive uprising against the retreating Germans, hoping to clear the city of them in time to act as host to the advancing Red Army. But the Germans were still too powerful, and the Soviets withheld their aid, regarding the uprising as politically directed against them. Therefore, even British and American planes flying rescue missions were denied permission to land at Soviet airports. In the course of the next two months of fighting the elite of the Home Army perished alongside 200,000 inhabitants of Warsaw. The city was reduced to ashes. Whether the rising was necessary or avoidable is still debated.

The Warsaw uprising was perhaps the most dramatic event of the war and it left permanent scars. Mikołajczyk's subsequent efforts to preserve Poland's independence at the price of some territorial concessions proved futile, and he resigned. His successor, the veteran socialist T. Arciszewski, was merely tolerated by the Allies; his government was that of national protest. The fate of Poland was decided independently of the Poles at the Yalta Conference. There the Teheran border deal was endorsed and a formula found for recognizing the already functioning communist government which was to be enlarged by the addition of a few non-communist Poles like Mikołajczyk. It called itself the provisional government of national unity. What bitter irony!

The Red Army was in control of Poland and the communists were in power. The Berling-led troops constituted the fighting force. Sixteen leaders of the underground, lured into talks by the Russians, were arrested and flown to Moscow to be tried. The remnants of the dissolved Home Army were hunted down. Under these conditions the "free and unfettered" elections promised in the Yalta accord were hardly a realistic proposition; Poland was destined to be a Soviet satellite.

The dramatic story of Poland offered a contrast to wartime developments in Czechoslovakia. Its two parts, the Protectorate of Bohemia and Moravia, and the formally independent Slovak state, in turn differed greatly from one another. The protectorate was treated as an economic base and a reservoir of the German Reich, free from Allied bombings, its inhabitants exempted from military service. It contributed 9 to 12 percent of the total German industrial output. Although the Czech intelligentsia faced persecutions – universities were closed – and the Jews were gradually liquidated, workers and farmers were actually courted. Much of the administration was in the hands of the Czechs, although under strict German control, and Protector Constantin von Neurath was a moderate compared with his sadistic successor in 1941, Heydrich, and the governor of Poland, H. Frank. Under these conditions the Czechs sought to survive without unduly provoking the Germans, and avoided provocations and reprisals.

This did not mean that they willingly adjusted to the Nazi regime. There was an underground and a range of resistance groups. But they practiced rather passive resistance and economic sabotage. A tough line was taken by Heydrich: imposition of martial law and the execution of Premier Eliáš, who was accused of contacts with Beneš's government in London; it called for a response. A team of Czechoslovak paratroopers sent from London killed Heydrich. By way of reprisals the Germans razed to the ground the village of Lidice, shot all the male inhabitants and deported women and children, many of whom died. Advertised by German propaganda in order to overawe the Czechs – unlike massacres in Poland that were often concealed – Lidice became a symbol of Nazi brutality. It was psychologically easier to feel for and identify with a hundred or so villagers than with millions being systematically exterminated. After a certain point these just became statistics.

The post-Heydrich terror leveled off in the remaining years of the war. All in all, although the estimates vary, some 55,000 Czechs perished in the Second World War alongside some 70,000 Jews who represented three-quarters of the total Jewish population.

The Germans at first treated Slovakia as a show piece of the Nazi "New Order." For the Slovaks this was their first chance to enjoy the attributes of a national state of their own. The price, however, was heavy: an accommodation to Nazi Germany in a material and spiritual sense. Most industries came under German control; some Slovak troops joined in the war against the Soviet Union; anti-Jewish measures resulted in the deportation and death of three-quarters of Slovak Jewry. Slovakia was established as a one-party state under a constitution of July 21, 1939 that followed Austrian and Portuguese corporationist models; it was headed by Father J. Tiso as President, and after 1942 as Leader. He tried to curb the pro-Nazi extremists but enjoyed the support of Berlin, which wished to preserve a certain stability in the country. Slovak freedom of maneuver was greatly restricted. Attempts to strengthen its position *vis-à-vis* Hungary by cooperation with Romania and Croatia were opposed by Germany. Contacts with the Allies had to be most circumspect and were channeled through the Vatican. It was actually under the pressure from the papacy, as supported by some Slovak bishops, that Tiso halted the deportations of the Jews in the 1942–4 period.

Turning to Czechoslovak activities abroad, Beneš had in 1939 already begun to agitate for the creation of a political center that would be recognized by the Allies and to obtain an official repudiation of Munich. Prevailing over potential rivals, especially Hodža and those who insisted on a Czecho-Slovak federative structure after the war, Beneš in July 1940 gained Britain's recognition for his provisional government. After the German invasion of the USSR a full recognition from the three big Allies followed. By 1942 Britain and the Free French repudiated Munich, which implied the restoration of prewar frontiers. Subsequently Beneš obtained a somewhat reluctant Allied approval for the postwar deportation of the Sudeten Germans from Czechoslovakia. It was evident that Beneš attached great importance to collaboration with the USSR, which he saw as the liberator and the dominant power in East Central Europe. The role of Czechoslovakia, as he put it, was to be a bridge between the West and the East. Beneš's rather optimistic vision contrasted with that of the Poles. Under Moscow's pressure he abandoned plans for a Czechoslovak–Polish confederation, and further distanced himself from the isolated Poles by signing an alliance with the USSR in December 1943. While in Moscow he urged Stalin to eradicate "feudalism" in postwar Poland and Hungary.

As the Soviet armies neared Czechoslovakia, and Romania switched sides from the Germans to the Russians, an underground Slovak National Council, comprising democrats and communists and endorsed by Beneš, was getting ready to stage an uprising. Part of the army joined in. The uprising, precipitated by an attack by Slovak partisans on the Germans in late August 1944, lasted for two months, but received no real Soviet aid. Its collapse was followed by the German occupation of the country and harsh reprisals. The uprising is still hotly debated. Was it a communist-inspired operation or was it a Slovak national struggle against the Germans and the satellite regime? Did it constitute (from the Slovaks' standpoint) national redemption or treason? Was it manipulated by the government seeking to maintain independent Slovakia? Be what it may, the rising was, except for military operations of small Czechoslovak units on the Western and Russian fronts, the only great battle fought against the Germans. To say that is not to dismiss the brief uprising in Prague in May, another much disputed event.

As the Red Armies were entering Czechoslovakia Beneš flew to Moscow, where he presided over an agreement with Czech and Slovak communists to form a new government. This was much more than an enlargement of the London-based ministry. From the liberated town of Košice a program was announced on April 5, 1945 that was to serve as the basis of the new Czechoslovakia. The underground in Prague, seemingly encouraged both by communists and the Košice government, decided to rise on May 4. It was a somewhat confused affair. Czech communists did not wish the American troops of General Patton to help liberate the city; this honor was to be reserved for the Red Army. Besides, Patton had orders not to encroach on the Soviet sphere of activities. The underground was not strong enough to win militarily and was paradoxically saved from a massacre by the anti-Soviet Russian units of General Vlasov who turned against the Germans. In spite of the fact that Germany surrendered to the Allies on May 8, the local German troops were still able to negotiate their withdrawal with the Czechs. On May 9 the Red Army officially "liberated" Prague although it is not clear from whom. The entire operation cost about 2,000 Czech lives.

Unlike the Polish government, Beneš could return to Prague in triumph, but the picture was not as rosy as it seemed. Postwar Czechoslovakia no longer comprised Carpatho-Ukraine, which had been seized rather high-handedly by the USSR, and the new regime bore only a seeming resemblance to the prewar model.

The wartime story of Hungary differs sharply from that of the Poles,

Czechs, and Slovaks. Driven by the constant urge to recover its former place and undo the Treaty of Trianon, an urge colored somewhat by ideological preferences, Hungary entered the Second World War on the side of Germany and Italy. First, in April 1941, acting under Berlin's pressure the Hungarians joined in the attack on Yugoslavia. The act was considered shameful by Premier Teleki, who committed suicide. Then after an incident at Košice (Kassa) that was probably manufactured, Hungary declared war on the USSR in June. There was little that Hungary could gain from this war. As mentioned earlier, Budapest had regained parts of Slovakia in 1938, annexed Carpatho-Ukraine in 1939, and received half of Transylvania under the Second Vienna Award made by Germany and Italy in 1940. Hungary reclaimed Bacska in Vojvodina from Yugoslavia after the campaign in 1941. As a result of all these territorial changes the state almost doubled its size and population. But the durability of gains depended largely on Germany, and Budapest felt that it had to compete with Romania in particular for German support. Thus the country became ever more dependent on Berlin, politically and economically, and it had to send troops to fight on the eastern front.

The Hungarians tried to convey to the British that it would be a mistake to place them in the same category as Hitler's Reich. Indeed, they harbored Polish military and civilian refugees and did not fire on Allied aircraft. The latter in turn did not bomb Hungary until the German troops occupied it in March 1944.

During the course of the war Horthy tried to continue his policies of slowing down or moderating an evolution to the right, and keeping the local Nazis on leash. This proved increasingly difficult, given the growing dependence on Germany, and resulted in political zigzags. The shock over the atrocities committed by Hungarian military, among whom the rightist radicals played an important role, in occupied Novi Sad in Yugoslavia, which claimed thousands of Serb and Jewish victims, contributed to a change of premiers. L. Bárdossy, who had been subservient to the Germans, made room for M. Kállay. The latter was well aware of the Hungarian dilemma of being caught between Nazi Germany and Soviet Russia, and he explored ways of getting out of the war through secret overtures to the West. The débâcle suffered by the Hungarian army at Voronezh reinforced those who wanted peace. In the meantime a drastic curtailment of active war effort took place. All this was not lost on Hitler.

On March 19, 1944 German troops occupied Hungary. Kállay had to take refuge in the Turkish embassy; Bethlen, who had been using his influence to stiffen Horthy's resistance to the Germans, went into hiding. The regent gave in, and a new government was named that complied with German demands for mass deportations of Jews. Horthy prevented, however, the inclusion of those living in Budapest. While yielding to Berlin, Horthy had not abandoned his plans to bring Hungary out of the war. As Romania switched sides in August, Horthy authorized an armistice with the Russians, a maneuver which was clumsily executed and left him unprotected. This time the Germans forced him to name the Arrow Cross leader Szálasi as premier, and then removed the regent from Hungary to Germany.

The Hungarian Nazis at last tasted power and they proceeded to deport Budapest Jews and to intensify the Hungarian war effort. In September and October, however, the fighting moved on to Hungarian soil, and under the aegis of the Red Army a provisional government came into existence in Debrecen in December. It comprised three Horthyite generals, social democrats, populists, and communists under the premiership of General B. Miklós. The government signed an armistice with the Allies and declared war on Germany. On April 11, 1945 it was installed in a Budapest ravaged by a long siege. Both Hungary and Romania were now on the Allied side and they vied for the control of Transylvania. Would Hungary return to its post-Trianon shape, making war and all the sacrifices needless and vain? The price paid by the country, maneuvered into war, was high and the future seemed uncertain. It was clear that a new era was dawning, but it held in store many dangers and few hopes.

8

THE HARD ROAD TO FREEDOM

THE POSTWAR ERA

The Second World War, or rather its outcome, reversed the course of history of East Central Europe. Traditionally a borderland or a semi-periphery of the West, the region became a westward extension of the Soviet East. Czechoslovakia, Hungary, and Poland found themselves in a semi-colonial relationship of dependence on the USSR which was culturally, socio-economically, and politically more backward than they. At first, the communist-imposed transformation appeared as a modernizing process. The elimination of direst poverty and remnants of illiteracy, a certain equalization and democratization of society, and an all-out industrialization pointed toward progress. But the Soviet-style industrialization with its obsessive emphasis on coal and steel, which was no longer the driving force of modern economy, became increasingly anachronistic. Rigid central planning promoted waste. Inefficiency reigned supreme. Disregard for the environment opened the way to an ecological catastrophe. East Central Europe had to pay a heavy price for the forty-odd years of communist experiments, and the costs included an atomization and demoralization of society that escape quantification.

For the first time in history the Russian shadow fell not only on Poland but also on Hungary and Czechoslovakia. As long as Soviet might and willpower appeared intact, all that East Central Europe could do was to try to ease the yoke and try it did. This led at times to dramatic developments, as in 1956 in Poland and Hungary, in 1968 in Czechoslovakia, and in 1980 in Poland again. But it was only when reforms in the Soviet Union and the Soviet-dominated bloc became inevitable that native forces in the three countries could sweep communism aside in the miraculous year of 1989.

The symbol of the postwar division of Europe was Yalta. This wartime conference of the Big Three was in a sense an experiment in world government in which the United States and the Soviet Union were to play the leading roles. But the West did not envisage the Soviet sphere of influence as a closed bloc, and Churchill expressed dismay over the Iron Curtain that descended, separating East Central Europe from the rest of the continent. Still, the ensuing decades of peace in this bipolar world came to rest on a balance between the two blocs and their formidable nuclear arsenal. It was regrettable that a hundred million or so East Central and South Eastern Europeans were subjected to an oppressive regime. Their resistance insofar as it weakened the Soviet colossus was welcomed, but not to the extent that it might rock the boat of West–East coexistence and endanger peace. There was a certain inherent hypocrisy in American policies toward the area, whether they went under the name of Containment or Liberation.

Was Stalin's conquest of East Central Europe the result of a master plan that involved a timetable, or of exploitation of opportunities as they arose? This type of question, reminiscent of the controversy over whether Hitler had been a fanatical conqueror or a cool tactician, is somewhat naive. Surely one cannot eliminate the pragmatic factor from either Stalin's or Hitler's policies, just as one cannot fully understand these policies without stressing ideology. In the communist case the conviction about the inevitability of socio-economic change resulting in a permanent transformation of the world was real enough. So was the faith in the Communist Party; it was viewed as more than a sum of its members, and as embodying the true ideology and the power of the working class. It had to be always right even if individual leaders could be wrong. Finally, the belief that history was on the side of communism constituted a powerful component of Marxism-Leninism.

The First World War had brought a victory of communism in Russia; the Second was likely to spread the revolution throughout the continent. But, come what may, Stalin was determined to retain all the territorial acquisitions made in collusion with Hitler, and he rounded them out by the addition of the northern part of East Prussia, of Finnish Karelia, and Carpatho-Ukraine. As for Poland, Hungary, and Czechoslovakia, Moscow expected their gratitude, for the Red Army had not only liberated them from the Germans, but also "saved" them from their own history: feudal, bourgeois, clerical, and fascist. According to Soviet views they were ripe for change in 1945, and the USSR was going to bring it about. Stalin, however, was astute enough to make allowances for local conditions. The region was different from Russia and it would first have to go through the stage of coalition governments – real or bogus – and then take the form of People's Democracies before graduating to the truly socialist status.

Moreover, Soviet policies of shaping East Central Europe were operating within a changing international context. The two original Soviet assumptions of a continuing postwar cooperation between the Big

Three and of a successful ideological penetration of Western Europe, had to be drastically revised in the 1945–7 period. With the beginning of the Cold War the former grand alliance was falling apart. French and Italian communists proved unable to gain power, and massive American aid in the form of the Marshall Plan (and the birth of Containment that restricted communism to its bloc) dispelled Soviet hopes for a westward extension of its ideological and political might. In response to this evolution and in accord with its own goals Moscow began to apply ever tighter screws on the regimes it had either installed or temporarily accepted in Poland, Czechoslovakia, and Hungary.

East Central Europe emerged badly scarred from the Second World War; Poland having suffered most, Czechoslovakia least. The Soviet "liberation" was accompanied by mass looting and rapes as well as by arrests and deportations. In Hungary, where some 400,000 people perished in the war, a quarter of a million were deported to the USSR, among them István Bethlen. Even the Swedish diplomat Raoul Wallenberg, who had been saving Hungarian Jews, was taken to Russia. Budapest had suffered greatly during the siege, and destructions elsewhere were sizeable. The Soviets, acting under the guise of the Allied Control Commission, and ignoring weak protests of their colleagues, arbitrarily collected reparations by dismantling factories and using slave labor. In March 1945 Hungarian production stood at 30 percent of its prewar level; the total national wealth was calculated as having dropped by 40 percent.

The figures for Poland tell an even more tragic story. Population losses were proportionately the highest in Europe, and they comprised wartime dead, postwar deportees to the USSR, and the political emigration in the West. In comparison with the prewar 35 million, Poland's population within the new borders in 1945 stood at 24 million inhabitants. The loss of $625 per capita, the destruction of 85 percent of Warsaw and some other cities, enormous cultural losses, all caused Poland to hold a number of grim records.

Territorially, Hungary returned to its prewar shape through the peace treaty of 1947; its hopes for retaining a part of Transylvania were dashed. Czechoslovakia, as mentioned, lost only Carpatho-Ukraine and gained a small bridgehead near Bratislava. The biggest and most profound changes occurred with regard to Poland, which lost nearly one half of its prewar territory to the USSR, and acquired, largely as compensation, the former German lands of Silesia, western Pomerania, and southern East Prussia. Its new territory of 311,730 sq. km was one-fifth smaller than before the war but it included a broad access to the Baltic sea with the ports of Gdańsk (Danzig) and Szczecin (Stettin). Polish coal resources doubled; those of lead, zinc, copper, and iron ores significantly increased. Postwar Poland was thus potentially a richer country than before, even though the Soviets had shamelessly dismantled factories and engaged in massive looting in the former German lands that were transferred to Poland. Furthermore the USSR forced the Poles to deliver coal at below world prices. The Poles did, however, escape joint ventures with the Soviets, which were introduced in Hungary. The devastated and dislocated Polish economy badly needed assistance, but little was forthcoming. There was some help for the population under the Allied UNRRA schemes and some direct from the United States, but the question of how to help the country without strengthening the communist regime arose early, and proved impossible to resolve.

Territorial and demographic changes amounted to a veritable socio-economic revolution, that was accelerated by communist legislation. Expropriation of estates eliminated the aristocracy and landowning gentry; gradual nationalization of industries led to the disappearance of the bourgeoisie; the intelligentsia (its Jewish component largely gone) suffered grievous losses. Deportations, migrations, and repatriations resulted in over a third of the Polish population living elsewhere than in 1939. National minorities, after population transfers that particularly affected (apart from the Germans) the Ukrainians, have become minuscule as compared with prewar times. There remained a few hundred thousand of Ukrainians and Belorussians in Poland, although their presence has been officially acknowledged only in the last few years. There is a small but active Lithuanian minority there and a Polish minority in Czechoslovakia. Hungarians in spite of some transfers in Slovakia still constitute a sizeable group. The greatest change on the ethnic map of East Central Europe, however, has resulted from the drastic reduction, in some cases disappearance, of the Germans and Jews.

With a grudging Allied blessing some 3 million Sudeten Germans, regarded as collectively responsible for treason toward Czechoslovakia, were expelled to Germany. There were Czechs who regarded this as a Pyrrhic victory, at least from a moral standpoint, but it was only after the collapse of communism in 1989 that President Havel publicly acknowledged the feeling of guilt. Indeed, many innocent people died in the "transfer" from Czech lands to Germany. The Poles, emerging from the trauma of the Nazi occupation, found it much harder to feel compassionate toward the millions of Germans who fled, perished, or were brutally expelled from lands now coming under Poland's rule. Communist propaganda represented the Soviet Union as the only guarantor of the new German–Polish border along the Odra–Nysa (Oder–Neisse) rivers and successfully played on Polish fears of German revisionism. Thus when the Polish episcopate declared in 1965 in an address to the German bishops that the Poles forgave and asked for forgiveness, this came as a shock to many people. It is only now that the tragedy of the Germans begins to appear in the Polish eyes as an issue that needs to be faced.

The exact number of Germans living in present-day Poland is disputed and so is the definition of a German. The highest estimates put the figure at about 750,000, which represents about 2 percent of the total population of Poland. There are only some 50,000 Germans in Czechoslovakia, that is, 0.5 percent. In Hungary, after the expulsion of roughly a quarter of a million, another quarter million remain (2.1 percent).

The Holocaust was followed in Poland's case by the emigration of most of the survivors, the Kielce pogrom in 1946 and the anti-Jewish purge carried out by the Party in 1968 providing the impetus. As a result the number of Jews dwindled to some 0.03 percent. The same percentage is valid for Czechoslovakia; it is 1 percent in Hungary. The traditional, orthodox Jewry disappeared altogether; those who remain can best be described as of Jewish origin. In these conditions anti-Semitism, which has been resurfacing since 1945, often under the guise of anti-Zionism or anti-cosmopolitism, has differed considerably from the prewar phenomenon. The economic grounds and the external forms of separatedness have disappeared. True, the old term of Judeo-communism has retained its appeal in certain quarters, and the anti-Semitic weapon has been used in intra-party conflicts. But the church hierarchy has generally combated the religious motivation of anti-Semitism, which Pope John Paul II explicitly condemned as contrary to Christian beliefs. Finally, none of the major political figures or trends today openly admits to being anti-Semitic.

Let us now turn to East Central European society emerging from the Second World War, and facing, for the first time, communism as an all-pervading phenomenon. The communist appeal was especially directed toward the workers. In Hungary their numbers increased from some 688,000 to 919,000 in the 1938–43 period, and they constituted a potentially important force. Those in the Protectorate of Bohemia and Moravia who had received a somewhat preferential treatment under the Nazis had high expectations, and tended to evolve toward the extreme left. In Poland, one can speak of a certain social radicalization of the masses, but more important perhaps was the mental climate. War and the occupation lowered the respect for life and undermined norms of moral behavior. A certain fanaticism coexisted with cynicism. A Polish writer tried to sum up a fairly widespread attitude: "the bolsheviks are in the country, the communists are in power, Warsaw is burnt to the ground, the legitimate London government is abandoned. Nothing worse can happen to us, we lost the war and should look after ourselves."[55]

The attitude of the intelligentsia was especially important. It also underwent radicalization, especially the younger generation, and tended to see matters in black and white. As a Czech writer put it, for many of his contemporaries this attitude was translated into an eager acceptance of a simplified scheme: progressive communism versus obsolete reaction. Not only those intellectuals who had inclined to the left, but also some former rightists embraced communism. Ambition, conviction, fear, despair, opportunism all figured in the complex motivation that Miłosz described in his *Captive Mind*. Those who withstood all temptation, who resisted and rejected the new ideology, were not all that numerous. A person had to live, and as the communists proceeded to destroy those components of the civil society that stood between the people and the state, the lonely individual was helpless before the omnipotence of the Party.

Before we turn to a chronological survey of the communist seizure of power in 1945-8 and the triumph of Stalinism, let us look first at the character and position of the communist parties, and at those who stood in their way to power. The communist parties of Poland and Hungary were publicly seen as alien, and they were re-emerging from virtual oblivion. The Béla Kun episode and the part played by Polish communists in the Soviet–Polish war of 1919–20 were liabilities rather than assets. Moreover, the Polish communists never lived down the "error of 1926" when they had supported Piłsudski's coup, and the ignominy of having been dissolved as a party by the Comintern on the trumped-up charges of infiltration by counter-revolutionary elements. Most leaders perished in the great purges in the USSR; the survivors served mainly as Comintern agents. Similarly, Hungarian communists mostly vegetated at home or followed Soviet orders in the emigration.

The revival of the Communist Party of Poland, under the less offending name of Polish Workers' Party (PPR in Polish) took place in 1942. It had a "Muscovite" and a "domestic" wing. Bolesław Bierut, J. Berman, and H. Minc belonged to the former, Władysław Gomułka to the latter. PPR had roughly 20,000 members in July 1944, but by April 1945 it grew to 300,000, and by April 1947 to over 500,000. This rapid increase, stemming largely from opportunistic motives, was also characteristic for Hungary. There the Party (MKP) reappeared officially on Hungarian soil in September 1944 with some 2,500 members and reached the figure of 864,000 in December 1947. The leadership consisted mostly of those who had returned from the USSR, notably the foursome (of Jewish origin) Mátyás Rákosi, E. Gerő, M. Farkas, and J. Révai, plus Imre Nagy. "Domestic" communists comprised L. Rajk and J. Kádár.

The Communist Party of Czechoslovakia (KSČ) offered a contrast to its Polish and Hungarian counterparts, insofar as it had been a legal prewar party with a large following. Originating from a split in the Social Democratic Party, it underwent a bolshevization in 1929 under Klement Gottwald, and became an arm of the international revolutionary operation directed from Moscow. During the Second World War the communist underground, more important that those in Poland or Hungary, identified itself with the liberation struggle in the Czech lands, and with national aspirations in Slovakia. A separate party of Slovakia arose with Husák and Clementis as its leaders. The top echelons of the KSČ were in Moscow, headed by Gottwald and his deputy R. Slánský. The postwar growth of the party was even more spectacular than in the neighboring countries, in 1947 passing the one million mark.

The communists constituted a minority in the Czechoslovak and Hungarian coalition governments, which were about to build the postwar reality in accord with, respectively, the socially moderate Košice and Debrecen programs. But they held key positions in those governments, controlling the police and the economy. The situation was different in Poland where the communists openly dominated an essentially bogus coalition. The Lublin Manifesto, however, was similar in its moderate language and the absence of communist slogans to the Czechoslovak and Hungarian programs. The major forces that the communists had to contend with and destroy, in order to gain full power, were grouped around the populist (peasant) party in Poland and the Smallholders Party in Hungary. In Czechoslovakia the non-communists looked up to President Beneš and placed the real burden of decision and responsibility on his shoulders.

A closer look at the political scene permits us to see further similarities and differences in the three countries. In Czechoslovakia, the prewar right and center parties – the national democrats and the agrarians – were not allowed to re-establish themselves. The same was true for the Slovak populists. Social democrats were heavily infiltrated by communists and fellow travelers, which left the national socialists (Beneš's party), the Catholic populists, and the Slovak democrats to watch out for communist encroachments. Their leaders thought in terms of prewar coalition and parliamentary practices, failing to appreciate the nature of communism. A certain Czech–Slovak tension allowed the communists to drive a wedge between the democrats of both nations.

Beneš held fast to his assumption that while the USSR would be the dominant power in the region it was unlikely to interfere in domestic Czechoslovak affairs, regarding the country as a constructive factor in the region and as a bridge between the West and East. Beneš also believed that domestically his country would amalgamate what was best in the Western democracy and Eastern socialism. As for the communists, they appeared to him willing to participate loyally in a parliamentary system, being quite satisfied with moderate social reforms. In fact the communists were consolidating their strength in the cabinet, in the national councils in the provinces, and most important, in the factories.

Hungarian communists, like their Czechoslovak counterparts, also stressed a willingness to cooperate with all the democratic forces in the country. The latter comprised the Smallholders Party, which re-emerged in November 1944 under the leadership of the Calvinist pastor Zoltán Tildy, Béla Kovács, and Ferenc Nagy, the national populists and the social democrats. The Smallholders appeared from the beginning as the main rivals and opponents of the communists, while the other parties contained people who listened to communist wooings and weakened their parties' internal cohesion. Apart from the obvious fact that the Hungarian communists relied on the support of the army, the police, and the Communist Party of the USSR, they tried and did emulate the Smallholders' agrarian program. The communists' insistence on drastic land reform and other revolutionary economic changes found a response among the masses who otherwise opposed communism as such.

In Poland the communists ran the government and the populists represented by Mikołajczyk and a few of his associates had to choose between adjustment or open defiance. Mikołajczyk joined the Provisional Government of National Unity as a result of Western pressure, and many Poles believed that he also had the assured support of the US and Britain. He was determined to challenge the communists through the "free and unfettered elections" agreed upon at Yalta. He succeeded, unlike others, in quickly re-establishing an independent populist party (PSL) which outnumbered the communists and their allies. The latter consisted of more or less truncated socialist, democratic, and labor parties from which the old leadership had been eliminated. The large prewar National Democratic Party was outlawed.

For the Polish masses Mikołajczyk personified genuine national independence. To the remnants of the wartime underground, hunted down by the communists, he represented a hope for survival, and indeed he helped to save many of them through the two amnesties passed by the government. The communists portrayed Mikołajczyk as the tool of the West and the embodiment of all forces of reaction and anti-Sovietism in the country. As elsewhere at this stage the Polish communists tried to cultivate an image of social moderation. They denied any plans of collectivizing agriculture and argued with the populists (as in Hungary) merely about the size of peasant farms. They also spoke of a native way to socialism. Paying lip service to Catholicism they were careful not to antagonize the Church unduly or offend Polish religious sentiments.

The Catholic Church was hardly prepared, in ideological or practical terms, for a confrontation with communism. In Hungary the church (the Catholic–Protestant division notwithstanding) had been a great landowner, built into the socio-economic and political structure of the country perhaps even to a larger degree than in Poland. It also reacted more strongly when stripped of its privileges by the communists; the primate Cardinal J. Mindszenty publicly condemned Marxism. In all three countries, the church had a tradition of cooperation with the political right which was now held against it. In Slovakia, especially, accusations of "clerico-fascism" leveled against the wartime regime could not be easily refuted. But there is another side to the story. In Poland the church's stand against the Nazis led to mass persecutions of the clergy. Many bishops and priests had been sent to German concentration camps and Father Kolbe, later canonized, died for a fellow prisoner. This greatly enhanced the church's moral authority. In Czechoslovakia, Bishop Beran of Prague had been a camp inmate; in Hungary Cardinal Serédi openly defied the Nazis, and the Arrow Cross arrested Mindszenty.

COMMUNIST SEIZURE OF POWER AND STALINISM

The years 1945–8 saw a transition from coalition governments, more or less genuine, to complete communist controls and the establishment of a totalitarian state. The road leading to this end was diverse in each country. In Hungary the communists applied the "salami tactics" of slicing off their opponents' base of power. In Poland Mikołajczyk's refusal to become a junior partner of the communists resulted in an open confrontation. In Czechoslovakia a governmental crisis was transformed by the Party into a showdown that had some features of a coup.

The Soviets maintained the troops in Hungary to guard the lines of communication with their zone in Austria but were at first prepared to be more flexible *vis-à-vis* the Hungarians than toward the Poles. The weak position of Hungarian communists in mid-1945 had something to do with that. Municipal elections in Budapest produced an unexpected victory of the Smallholders, who gained 50 percent of votes against the communist–socialist bloc of 42.6 percent. In the general elections held in November 1945 the communists fared even worse and the Smallholders emerged with a 57 percent majority. These were to be the last free elections in Hungary for almost half a century.

Tildy became president of the republic and Ferenc Nagy (not to be confused with his better known communist namesake) premier. But by virtue of the pre-electoral accord the communists remained in the cabinet and working from within systematically undermined their

244

opponents. Under László Rajk as interior minister non-communists were removed from the administration, and mass trials of war criminals and political opponents took place. Nationalization of the economy proceeded on a wide scale. Using rumors of a nationalist plot as an excuse, the communists successfully discredited some of the Smallholders' leaders, especially Béla Kovács, who was arrested by the Soviet police. The weakened Smallholders became isolated and vulnerable. Nagy was forced to resign and stayed in exile. The communists gained more votes than the Smallholders in the August 1947 rigged elections (22.3 percent as against 15.4); exposed to a constant pressure the non-communist parties were disintegrating. The social democrats merged with the communists and the Hungarian Workers' Party (MDP) came officially into being. Tildy's resignation of the presidency marked the end of an era. Although the Party's secretary-general, Rákosi, also became prime minister a few years later, one can say that his "reign" had already begun in December 1948.

A complete communist take-over in Poland was more rapid and possibly even more brutal than in Hungary. The other political parties, infiltrated by and dominated by the PPR, had very little room for maneuver, and a confrontation between Mikołajczyk and the communists had already reached a high point in 1946. The issue was a popular referendum. Trying to compensate for the fact that the elections prescribed at Yalta were being constantly put off, the Party announced a referendum in which the voters were asked three questions: Did they approve of the socio-economic reforms? Did they endorse the Odra–Nysa frontier? Did they agree with the abolition of the senate? These were in reality non-questions, for there was a large consensus in favor of these three proposals. The current economic plan, based on public, social, and private sectors, reflected socialist rather than communist thinking. The border with Germany was seen as a major gain. The abolition of the senate was not a problem. Nevertheless, Mikołajczyk, regarding the referendum as a trial of strength and a challenge, instructed his supporters to vote "no" on this third question. This may have been a political mistake, for it revealed the extent of actual anti-communist opposition without allowing it to score a point. In an atmosphere of intimidation, and even actual murders, of populists and their allies, a fair referendum was not possible. Furthermore, there is every indication that the final results were falsified. Only in certain areas, inadvertently or to publicize the enemies' strength, were the real numbers of nays revealed.

The campaign of terror and slander intensified, Mikołajczyk's name being constantly linked with the underground units that continued an armed struggle against the communists. In these circumstances Mikołajczyk's stiff conditions for participation in a common electoral front with the communists were hardly realistic, and his tactics of confrontation began to be increasingly questioned by his supporters. What was he counting on? Surely the communists were not likely to hold a free election or to yield power. Indeed, the elections of January 1947 proved to be as fraudulent as the referendum. The communist-led electoral bloc gained 394 seats; Mikołajczyk's party only 28. Thus the populist attempt to wrest power from the communists proved a total fiasco, and in October Mikołajczyk, fearing for his life, escaped from Poland. In June 1948, in a greatly changed international atmosphere, PPR absorbed the socialist party and adopted the name Polish United Workers' Party (PZPR).

The course of events in Czechoslovakia also resulted in a communist victory, but the story differed in many respects. As mentioned, postwar Czechoslovakia superficially resembled the first republic. The president's extensive powers imposed special burdens on Beneš, and indeed the land reform, the nationalization of industry, and the prosecution of "traitors" were all done by presidential decree. In dealing with the Soviet leaders Beneš continued to be deferential, anxious to please and be accommodating.

The first elections, held in March 1946, made the communists the largest party (with 38 percent of the vote, 40 percent in the Czech lands and 30 percent in Slovakia). The national socialists trailed with 18.2 percent, the remaining parties having obtained between 12.9 and 15.6. Gottwald was named prime minister, and the communists appeared to be satisfied with the status of the first among equals. In 1947, however, the situation began to change. As the Cold War was beginning, the offer of the Marshall Plan was first accepted by Prague and then turned down on express orders of Moscow. The foreign minister, Jan Masaryk, for one, realized that Czechoslovak independence was illusory. This came as a shock. The Kremlin berated the Czechoslovak communists for their timidity, and they concentrated their activity on Slovakia, where the local autonomous authorities (Board of Commissioners and the Slovak National Council) were dominated by democrats. The wartime experiences had not made Czech leaders more understanding of Slovak national aspirations. Beneš failed to use the presidential pardon with regard to the collaborationist President Tiso, who was tried, condemned, and executed in April 1947. This was a political error. When the communists proceeded arbitrarily to eliminate the Slovak democrats from power, there was no outcry among non-communists in Prague.

By late August 1947 the Party was put on "fighting alert," and the stress put on extra-parliamentary means should it come to a showdown with the non-communists. Such a showdown was in fact brought about by a move, reminiscent of prewar parliamentary tactics, in February 1948. Protesting against the arbitrary measures of the communist minister of police, the non-communist ministers submitted their resignations, hoping that Beneš would either refuse to accept them, or dissolve the parliament and order new general elections. It was typical of the indecisive leadership of the non-communist parties to place all the burden of responsibility on the ailing president. His decision to stand above the conflict, as he put it, amounted to a capitulation. While the communists mobilized the factory workers and the minister of defense General L. Svoboda neutralized the army, the non-communists were not prepared for a physical confrontation. The isolated and overawed Beneš accepted the resignation of the ministers, making it possible for Gottwald to fill the vacancies with his own appointees.

The "victorious February," as the communists called it, was a coup only in the sense of the ever-present threat of violence that accompanied the event. Soviet involvement, which included encouragement and the possibility of armed intervention was real. Still, the Gottwald cabinet was regularly appointed by Beneš (who resigned a little later) and it received a parliamentary vote of confidence on March 10. Czechoslovakia slid into communist rule in a manner which made the Czechs think of Munich and the heavy price paid for non-resistance. Even the death of Jan Masaryk in March can no longer be be ascribed with certainty to foul play, and seems to have been suicide caused by despair. As in Hungary and Poland communist consolidation in Czechoslovakia involved the absorption of the socialists. As in Poland two token non-communist parties (three in Hungary) were preserved as junior partners.

The events in Prague shocked Western public opinion and were seen as proof of communist determination to annihilate democracy. The United States had been willing to accept a Soviet sphere of influence in East Central Europe, provided it would be open to commerce and a flow of ideas. A closed bloc of satellite states appeared unacceptable. In these conditions Containment, which seemed to have written off the region, came to be regarded as timid and inadequate. The new doctrine of Liberation arose. Espoused by President Dwight Eisenhower and Secretary John Foster Dulles it did not aim at freeing the region through a crusading war. Its object was to feed the flame of freedom among the oppressed nations, through propaganda and support of political émigrés, and to undermine Soviet controls. But as defined in 1949 "the satellite question" was "a function of our [American] main problem – relations with the Soviet Union."[56]

From 1948 communism in East Central Europe began to assume its extreme Stalinist form, characterized by rigid uniformity in following the Soviet model and in subordination to Moscow. "Love of the Soviet Union does not tolerate the slightest reservation," said the Czechoslovak *Rudé Právo* on May 25, 1952. A network of treaties, going back to the Soviet–Czechoslovak alliance of 1943 bound all the countries to Moscow and to each other. A reorientation of trade toward the USSR represented a drastic change from the prewar situation. In 1949 the Council of Mutual Economic Assistance (CMEA or Comecon) was set up in response to the Marshall Plan, but remained inactive for more than a decade. Its subsequent role of integrating the satellite countries through a division of labor led to friction and failed to produce desired results. Finally, in 1955 the Warsaw Treaty Organization arose, as a counterpart to NATO. In fact, its main function came to be containing, policing, and stabilizing the region itself.

This new trend was heralded by the organizational meeting of the Cominform in 1947 at Szklarska Poręba in Poland. The Cominform, Moscow's instrument for ideological control, was used a few months later against Marshal Tito. The breach between the USSR and Yugoslavia became the first chink in the Stalinist armor, but it also intensified the offensive against the "nationalist deviation" as represented by Titoism. A rigid ideological uniformity, embracing all walks of life, came to be associated with the name of its arch-priest Andrei Zhdanov.

Does the adjective "totalitarian" most adequately describe Stalinism? By striving to dominate the totality of man and by claiming to represent the power governing all reality, the system was totalitarian in theory, although not always in practice. One of its characteristic elements was a total rejection of truth as an absolute: hence, the big lie that the Party decreed to be the truth. The adulation of Stalin, the final authority and the final arbiter, was part of the system. The cult of personality permeated the entire communist ladder of power, but as Gomułka later put it, the cult of the lesser leaders was only "a borrowed light. It shone as the moon does." This was true for the dominant figures of this era: Bierut, Gottwald, and Rákosi.

There was a basic similarity in the developments in Hungary, Poland, and Czechoslovakia in the late 1940s and early 1950s. In the economic sphere rigid planning patterned on the USSR resulted in full nationalization of enterprises and virtual destruction of the prosperous private sector. Emphasis was placed on the development of heavy industry. Collectivization of agriculture ran into stubborn resistance in Poland, where only 10 percent of peasant land was collectivized, and produced tensions in Hungary where a restructuring of agriculture by 1953 bankrupted agrarian production. The situation was different in Czechoslovakia, where 90 percent of agriculture was collectivized and the country's strong economic base was less visibly affected.

In an increasingly atomized society the church represented the only spiritual and in a sense political power. Hence the Party switched now from conciliatory to openly aggressive policies toward it. The communists sought not only a separation of church and state, but a subordination of the former to the latter. The church was to be confined to the altar and the confessional; religion was to be eliminated from schools and religious orders deprived of any social functions. The relations with the Vatican were interrupted. In essence this was a contest not over God, but over man and his dignity. The attack went against the Christian roots and traditions of East Central European culture.

In Hungary, where the communists exploited the division between the Catholic and Calvinist churches, as well as in Czechoslovakia, the attack came earlier and was more brutal than in Poland. The defiance on the part of Cardinal Mindszenty led to his arrest and a show trial in February 1949, at which he confessed to all unlikely charges. Other bishops and clergymen were executed or imprisoned. The religious orders were suppressed in Hungary and in Czechoslovakia, but not in Poland. In Czechoslovakia and Hungary the Party sought to undermine the church through so-called Catholic Action and a Peace Movement (Pacem in Terris), and it also struck against the respected Archbishop of Prague, Beran. He was first isolated in his residence and then transported to a monastery. By 1951, exposed to relentless pressure, nine out of thirteen bishops and most of the lower clergy had sworn loyalty to the regime. Others were imprisoned.

The situation in Poland differed insofar as the church was stronger, and the primate, Cardinal S. Wyszyński, was a man of great calibre who knew how to combine a rigid adherence to principle with flexibility of tactics. In 1950 he signed, largely on his own, a *modus vivendi* with the state which committed the church only to "respect of law and state authority." An accord signed the same year by the Hungarian church hierarchy engaged the church to "support the state system." For the communists these agreements were temporary arrangements. In Poland they sponsored the so-called Patriots-Priests and supported the Pax organization. Set up by a prewar extreme rightist, Bolesław Piasecki, Pax aimed at finding a common Catholic–communist platform that would enable the group to share in governing the country. The resistance of the church to these attempts, designed as they were to undermine its cohesion and impose further concessions, led to reprisals. In 1951 Bishop C. Kaczmarek was arrested and two years later given a severe sentence. The climax was reached in 1953, when even after Stalin's death, Cardinal Wyszyński himself was arrested and interned.

The struggle against the church was part of the Stalinist offensive in the realm of culture. It ranged from an imposition of "socialist realism" on art, through making Lysenko's theories binding on natural sciences, to elevating Stalin's own views on linguistics into a dogma. Anything that diverged from these doctrines was eliminated; the ideological terror reigned supreme.

Political evolution was officially reflected in the passing of Hungarian and Polish Constitutions of 1949 and 1952 that were modeled on that of the USSR. The countries became known as People's Republics or People's Democratic Republics. Constitutions filled with high sounding principle were little more than a façade. Behind it arbitrariness reigned supreme with law as a political instrument, judges as obedient executors, and the police as a state within the state. In Poland communist terror was first applied on a major scale against the wartime underground and Mikołajczyk's supporters. It also claimed numerous victims among the anti-communists in Czechoslovakia and Hungary. After the Titoist schism Party purges followed. In Hungary the tough interior minister Rajk was arrested in May 1949, confessed in a show trial to being an "agent of imperialism," and executed. In the ensuing purges some 2,000 people perished and 150,000 were imprisoned. This represented an incomparably larger figure than of the victims of the Horthy regime. Among ranking communists Kádár was jailed, and Imre Nagy withdrew from public life.

This orgy of judicial murders, with a free use of torture, was duplicated in Czechoslovakia. Assisted by expert Soviet advisers, a veritable witchhunt began for "Trotskyites," Slovak bourgeois nationalists, Zionists, class enemies, and spies. The victims included such dignitaries as Clementis, Husák, and the secretary-general of the Party himself, Slánský. After a mass trial in 1952 in which the prosecution made ample use of anti-Semitism, eleven of the fourteen accused being of Jewish background, Slánský and his co-defendants pleaded guilty and were executed.

In contrast to Hungary and Czechoslovakia there were no show trials in Poland, and Soviet suggestions to resort to anti-Semitic pronouncements in purges were resisted. While terror claimed new victims, notably high-ranking army officers, several of whom had returned after the war from abroad, the nearest Polish equivalent to Rajk or Slánský, namely Gomułka, was never brought to trial. Although much more than they a believer in a native road to communism, hence vulnerable to charges of nationalist Titoism, Gomułka was expelled from the Party and arrested with a number of his associates in 1951. He stayed in prison while a case against him was being prepared, long enough to outlive Stalin.

THE RISE AND FALL OF REVISIONISM

Stalin's death in March 1953 brought a succession crisis and a transient regime of collective leadership. Rigid dogmatism sustained by terror was no longer tenable, and the Soviet leaders launched a "new course" in economics, and eliminated Lavrentii Beria, the dreaded head of the secret police. The repercussions were quickly felt in East Central Europe because of the ties between the security apparatus there and in Moscow. In 1954 a Polish police colonel, J. Światło, escaped to the West and his revelations publicized the inner workings of the system of terror. Dismissals and arrests of high-ranking "accomplices of Beria" followed. Gomułka was quietly released; Imre Nagy became premier and for three years tried to de-Stalinize Hungary. His name became associated with a flexible policy in agriculture, revision of legal abuses, and respect of national rights. Eventually he was pushed out by Rákosi, who regained an upper hand. In Czechoslovakia, following Gottwald's death in 1953 Antonín Novotný became first secretary and A. Zápotocký president. Both were mediocrities who did their best to prevent change and to go slow on de-Stalinization.

In the Soviet Union Nikita Khrushchev made a denunciation of Stalinism in the secret speech of January 1956 at the Twentieth Party Congress, which was leaked out to the outside world. In an atmosphere which the Soviet writer I. Ehrenburg compared to a "thaw," intellectuals and artists long stifled by Stalinist dogma engaged in massive criticism. In Poland Adam Ważyk's "Poem for Adults" blasted socialist realism; the international youth festival in Warsaw heralded the end of complete isolation from the West. In Hungary the writers found themselves in the forefront of an anti-Stalinist campaign.

In June 1956 the workers in Poznań demonstrated and the riot turned into an uprising which had to be suppressed by tanks. The event was a shock for Poland and communists everywhere. After initial confusion, the Polish leadership, deprived of Bierut who had just died, refused to stigmatize the rising as counter-revolutionary, and blamed past Party practices which had made it possible. The Kremlin decided then to intervene in the power contest within the Polish politbureau and prevent Gomułka's elevation to the position of first secretary. A high-ranking Soviet delegation led by Khrushchev himself suddenly descended on Warsaw; Soviet army units stationed in Poland began to move on the capital. In a dramatic confrontation Gomułka called the Soviet bluff and won. Amidst great popular enthusiasm – for the first time since the war a popular movement converged with developments within the Party – Gomułka was hailed as the new leader of Poland. He proceeded to denounce the past period of "errors and distortions" and stated that the communists had no monopoly of building a socialist Poland. He allowed the collectivized farms to disband and stopped the Stalinist terror. Poland's blatant subordination to Moscow came to an end; contacts with the West began. Realizing the importance of the church and desirous of its support Gomułka ordered the release of Cardinal Wyszyński. These were indeed revolutionary changes, and the term "Polish October" became current in contrast to the Russian

October of 1917. Many Poles hoped that they were witnessing the first step in an evolutionary process of regaining independence.

The events in Poland acted as a catalyst on developments in Budapest. The Soviets made the hated Rákosi step down, but his successor Gerő was no improvement. The differences between him and the recalled premier Nagy amounted to dualism, which was fatal for Hungary. Gerő was already blamed for a major clash in the capital between the demonstrators, who manifested solidarity with Poland, and the secret police and Soviet troops. Many people had been killed and wounded. Gerő had to resign in favor of Kádár, an inmate of a Stalinist prison. The government–Party dualism receded into the background, as all Party and state institutions, including security units (AVO), the army, and the police disintegrated. The Soviet troops were defeated. Nagy may not have initiated it, but he came to preside over a process that involved a restructuring of administration, raising a new army, permitting a multi-party system, releasing Cardinal Mindszenty, and finally declaring Hungary neutral under the United Nations' protection and leaving the Warsaw Pact. Did this last move trigger the second Soviet intervention and the armed suppression, with the use of eleven divisions, of Hungary's freedom? This is a common, but not necessarily the only explanation of Moscow's move.

It seems likely that the Soviet decision, and it was not an easy one, was taken earlier. It was affected by such favorable circumstances as an explicit denial of any American aid to Hungary, and the Anglo-French action in Suez which threw the United Nations and the NATO allies into disarray. Noticing Soviet preparations for an invasion Nagy felt betrayed, for he genuinely worked for a political solution acceptable to Moscow. His repudiation of the Warsaw Pact and his dramatic message on the radio that the Hungarians were resisting the Soviet troops came after the die had been cast. Nagy never used the term war, for he was frightened of the very idea of an armed struggle between two socialist states. Yet according to official figures, which may well have been lowered, the hostilities claimed the lives of 3,000 Hungarians and left some 13,000 wounded.

Kádár had switched to the Soviet side, and in the years that followed became Khrushchev's protégé. Nagy was singled out as the principal object of vengeance, and was executed with his closest associates. He did not cease to believe that history would vindicate him and condemn his murderers. This was also the view of many to whom Kádár was the arch-villain.

The "Polish October" succeeded while the Hungarian revolution failed for a number of reasons. Gomułka, coming on the wave of a reformist crest, had no rival who could, like Gerő or Kádár, effectively undermine his position. The Polish Party never lost control and the eruption of popular sentiments never spilled over. After the dramatic confrontation between Gomułka and Khrushchev both sides played a very cautious game. The Russians presumably became convinced that Gomułka was needed to save communism in Poland. Cardinal Wyszyński, acting as an arbiter between the Party and the nation counseled restraint; Cardinal Mindszenty appeared as the standard bearer of the right and he resumed his previous defiant posture. After the Hungarian revolution collapsed, Mindszenty was to spend many years as a refugee in the American embassy in Budapest until finally allowed to leave the country.

In a sense the Hungarian revolution greatly helped the Poles, but not vice versa. It is likely that the Soviet leadership, having made concessions in Warsaw, was less willing to make them in Budapest. The lesson of 1956 was manifold. It showed that a communist regime could be overthrown from within, but it also showed that the Soviets would intervene to prevent it. Were they mainly concerned with the loss of a satellite in East Central Europe or with ideological implications? The two aspects may well have been inseparable. As far as the "Polish October" was concerned it seemed to indicate the possibility of evolution of communism and a gradual self-liberation process. While the events in Budapest exposed the illusory nature of the American doctrine of Liberation, Gomułkism seemed to offer a chance for assisting domestic change toward greater freedom. American economic aid began to flow into Poland.

The twelve years between 1956 and 1968 were dominated by Kádár, Gomułka, and Novotný. In the USSR the Khrushchev era, characterized by somewhat erratic attempts at reform, lasted until 1964. The last four years were those of his successor, Leonid Brezhnev, who stood for orthodoxy and a freezing of the system.

The Kádár rule in Hungary began with harsh reprisals. Some 2,000 Hungarians were executed, ten times as many imprisoned, and 200,000 chose the road of exile. The Party underwent a drastic transformation with only 37,000 members remaining out of the original 900,000. Yet once the opposition was crushed the regime loudly proclaimed "never again" and did not seek to turn the clock back completely. A policy based on the notion that he who is not against us is with us differed considerably from the Stalinist paradigm. The power and authority belonged to the Party, which made it clear what it supported, tolerated, or prohibited, but everyday life was gradually depoliticized and rendered more tolerable. Educational and cultural activities became much freer than before; rather than jail the opponents the government encouraged them to leave the country. Just as the pre-1956 regime based its legitimacy on ideological correctness, and that of 1956 on popular consensus, Kádár placed the emphasis on economic progress. This was a "goulash" communism directed toward the consumer, in fact bribing him to acquiesce in the regime.

Kádár himself was a folksy populist rather than a dogmatic theoretician, a man of ideas as far as the ultimate goal was concerned, but also a pragmatist. He had few illusions about the Soviet leaders. A historian compared his attitude toward the Kremlin with Horthy's attitude *vis-à-vis* Hitler. Perhaps. Hungary's economic progress, assisted by the post-Second World War discoveries of bauxite and uranium deposits, was becoming visible. The 1957 treaty with the USSR improved the nature of economic relationship and brought in some Soviet loans. Agriculture was forcibly recollectivized between 1959 and 1968, but this was accompanied by a certain market-oriented flexibility. In 1968 the New Economic Mechanism, which abolished compulsory plan directives and gave the managers more freedom, was introduced. We shall return to the lights and shadows of Kádárism in the subsequent section dealing with the seventies.

Gomułka's Poland presented a rather different picture. It witnessed the rise of hopes for a revised form of communism, and indeed the leading philosopher Leszek Kołakowski envisaged the possibility of a political democracy developing under socialism. In the general elections held in 1957 there were more candidates than seats, and one could speak of a consent election rather than the Stalinist formal exercise. Cardinal Wyszyński agreed with Gomułka that to cross out communist candidates might endanger Poland's very existence, and thus lent a powerful support to Gomułka's policies. A small Catholic representation entered the parliament. In an atmosphere of de-Stalinization that saw a rejection of stifling dogmas in art and literature, the release of political prisoners, and the toleration of religious instruction (at first even in school buildings), the gains of October were real enough. The theater of Mrożek exposed and ridiculed the absurdities of totalitarianism.

Hopes placed by revisionists in Gomułka proved, however, unfounded. The man was an idealist, nay a puritan in public life, but he was also a tough fighter, a self-educated man with a distrust of the intelligentsia. Steering a middle course between the revisionists and the dogmatists who wanted a return to sterner methods, Gomułka cracked down on both groups. He also restricted the educational role of the church. Was this departure from the October ideals really surprising? If we assume that Gomułka's object had been to bridge the gap between the Party and the nation, and thus legitimize the Party, he had no interest in a further evolution that could weaken communism. Virtually the entire Party apparatus opposed change. Furthermore, the early *rapprochement* between Gomułka and the West, and his proposals for a nuclear-free zone in Germany and East Central Europe, began to weaken as the USSR and the United States entered a collision course over Cuba and Berlin.

Gomułka's "little stabilization" came to an end in the mid-1960s. A Party–church confrontation over the celebration of Poland's millennium centered on the role of Christianity in Polish history. The episcopate took the initiative in matters affecting the nation, for instance the earlier-mentioned address to the German bishops. This infuriated the Party, which accused the church of being unpatriotic. Nationalism was a handy weapon in a frustrated society, and the so-called partisans' wing in the Party led by M. Moczar quickly seized it. The Six Day War in June 1967 had created pro-Israeli feelings in many Polish (and Polish-Jewish) circles, and Gomułka allowed himself to be maneuvered by the partisans into a major "anti-Zionist" campaign. It led to a purge of people of Jewish origin in the leadership of the party, the army, and the administration. Gomułka, who was not an anti-Semite himself, tried to apply brakes, but found his authority challenged by political rivals. An incident – possibly a provocation – over the banning of a classical play by Mickiewicz because of its anti-Russian lines resulted in a showdown between the hardliners in the Party and students and intellectuals. At this point many Poles eagerly watched the reformist trend in Czechoslovakia; their slogan "all Poland waits for its Dubček" appeared most dangerous to Gomułka; he was also anxious lest Germany, then embarking on its *Ostpolitik*, come closer to Czechoslovakia and isolate Poland. The crackdown on the students, courageously defended by Catholic deputies, and the mass exodus of Jews, almost hounded out of the country, belonged to darker pages of Polish history. They were further blackened by Poland's participation in the Soviet-led intervention in Czechoslovakia.

There was no counterpart to Nagy or Gomułka, or indeed any leader of stature in post-1956 Czechoslovakia. Its stand toward the Polish and Hungarian developments of the year had been negative. With economic stability the prevailing de-Stalinization was confined to such minor gestures as the removal in 1961 of Stalin's monument in Prague. Seeking to weaken the church, the authorities made use of Archbishop Beran's journey to Rome, where he received the cardinal's hat, to prevent his return. His successor František Tomášek proved, however, a worthy successor. The leading role of the Party was inscribed in the 1960 constitution; it proclaimed that the country had progressed to the socialist state, hence the new name, Czechoslovak Socialist Republic (ČSSR). The constitution virtually emasculated all provisions for autonomy in Slovakia, deepening Slovak resentment over the slower development of their country's economy and the dominance of Czechs in the Party. Novotný's insensitivity to Slovak national feelings indicated that there was no change of heart in Prague.

In the years 1963–6, however, the Slovak Party went through a revolt against Novotný's men, gained the rehabilitation of some of the Slovak victims of purges, and obtained, at least in principle, a restitution of local bodies affected by the new constitution. A new leader emerged, Alexander Dubček, a young, shy man with a long apprenticeship in the Soviet Union and the Party apparatus, yet open to ideas of reform and aware of Slovak interests.

While the Slovak issue was among the principal causes of the approaching Prague Spring, one must also stress the economy, badly in need of substantial change, a deepening conflict between the Party apparatus and the intelligentsia, and the "metaphysical" issue of rule of law versus rule of fear. It was necessary to dissociate the political system from the past terror. The shadow cast by the cruel and arbitrary trials of the 1950s had to disappear and the victims amnestied or posthumously rehabilitated. Lawyers, writers, and journalists took an increasingly large part in a campaign that aimed to achieve this goal. Novotný, a living symbol of Stalinism, maladroitly tried to maintain himself in power, even by resorting to a coup, but he became isolated and was slighted by Moscow. Dubček, in whom both the hardliners and the reformers placed great hopes, was chosen first secretary. He was a communist who believed in the leading role of the Party and in Moscow, but who also felt that the system could be revitalized through Czech humanist traditions and a new model created. The general "Action Program" of April 5, 1968 indicated the direction in which he wanted to proceed; it was summed up by the slogan "Socialism with a human face."

Could Dubček's program of economic and political reform, involving a real federalization of Czechoslovakia, be kept within bounds now that public support for it was being enlisted and certain institutions were to be emancipated from Party control? The Prague Spring became a great public debate, based on freedom of speech, in which public opinion played an increasingly large role. A civil society was reborn with the emergence of youth organizations, political debating clubs, and church-sponsored activities. The role of radio and especially television in disseminating ideas and acquainting the people with emerging leaders could not be overstressed. The atmosphere was, in the words of the British ambassador, "intoxicating" and he added that "for the first time in 350 years the Czechs found themselves in a heroic role."[57]

An illusion of unity obscured conflicting tendencies. Party-led reformism was not identical with the intelligentsia's goal of a socialist democracy. The radical youth advocated far-reaching changes. The "Two Thousand Words" statement, published in June by the intellectuals, was meant to strengthen the reformist trend in the Party, but it was also seen as a call to action from below, hence a threat to Party leadership. Was this a reform movement or a revolution? The object was not a destruction of socialism, but its transformation was to be so drastic that it appeared revolutionary. That is how the leaders of East Germany, Poland, and the Soviet Union perceived it.

Dubček was caught between Soviet demands to contain the popular movement and restore full Party control, and the demands of Czechs and Slovaks for freedom and democracy. He seemingly believed that he could reconcile the objectives of the Kremlin and of the people, and to rule through the Party with a genuine consent of the population. Why and when did Moscow decide to intervene, justifying its military action by the Brezhnev doctrine of "aid" to a socialist country threatened by counter-revolution? As Brezhnev told the Czechs later he could not tolerate policies that had no prior consent from Moscow. Czechoslovak borders were also Soviet western borders and nothing must be allowed to affect the postwar settlement in Europe. Probably the scheduling of an extraordinary meeting of the Czechoslovak Communist Party to formalize a new statute departing from Leninist principles was the last straw as far as the Soviets were concerned. In a series of complex moves and counter-moves in July and August, the Czechoslovak leadership was pressed to reverse the process and it was threatened with military intervention. The last round of negotiations at Čierná seemed to provide some modicum of understanding and it created a false sense of a lull. The actual invasion on August 20–1, in which Polish, Hungarian, Bulgarian, and East German (but not Romanian) forces joined the Red Army, caught Czechoslovakia unprepared and stunned Dubček.

As on similar occasions in the past the dilemma of resistance versus surrender came to the fore. No military preparations had been taken, although as a Czech philosopher, Ivan Sviták, argued, two thousand tanks would have been more effective than two thousand words. The chances were that the Soviets could be reasonably sure that they would not meet with any armed resistance. But, was it necessary to countersign the death warrant – again earlier analogies come to one's mind – as Dubček and his colleagues did, admittedly under duress, in Moscow? The accord they signed meant tearing up the reform program with their own hands, and this, to cite Sviták again, "broke the back of the nation" for at least twenty years to come.[58]

There were similarities and profound differences between the Hungarian and Czechoslovak revolutions of 1956 and 1968. The former was bloody while the latter was relatively peaceful and complicated by a national (Slovak) angle. Initially, political, social, and economic objectives were similar. The political evolution went much further in Hungary, with its multi-party government and attempts at neutrality. The Party as well as the army and security had disintegrated in Hungary;

in Czechoslovakia they survived and presided, to some extent, over the process of change. While intellectuals and students were in the forefront of both revolutions, in Czechoslovakia the role of the workers and the input of the economists was more noticeable. The year 1968 marked the demise of revisionism, which fell victim to Soviet tanks rumbling through Czechoslovakia and to rubber truncheons and anti-Zionist slogans in Poland. Was communism reformable at all? This question preoccupied many people in East Central Europe. In Czechoslovakia an additional issue claimed attention: the perennial "Czech question," which acquired a new meaning and a new urgency. How was a small nation to survive in the late twentieth century? How essential was state independence for this survival?

TOWARD SOLIDARITY AND THE COLLAPSE OF COMMUNISM

Under the heavy hand of Gustáv Husák, who replaced Dubček as first secretary in 1969 and became president six years later, Czechoslovakia experienced no bloody reprisals comparable to those in Hungary after 1956. But mass purges and oppressive measures were carried out systematically, and they affected an entire generation. The intelligentsia especially was hit hard, with many members dismissed from their positions and forced to do manual work. Fear of change was the cement that held together the leadership in which former victims of Stalinism sat next to ex-Stalinists. The country was bitter. For the first time Russian soldiers had carried out an invasion of Czech lands; this was a new page in the history book. Czech Russophilism was seriously damaged.

Perhaps the only lasting product of the Prague Spring was a formal federalization of the state. Implemented in January 1969 it provided for a bicameral federal parliament – although its actual location led to a joke that it was something between a theater and a museum: two governments (in additon to the federal executive) and a constitutional court. Czechoslovakia was declared to derive its legitimacy from the right of self-determination of the two nations and their will to live in a common state. This was important from the Slovak point of view even if Prague's centralism did not disappear in practice and the Party's rule rendered some of the new provisions theoretical. Similarly the actual working of the Law of Nationalities that recognized the existence of national minorities: Hungarian, Polish, German, and Ukrainian, left much to be desired.

The Czechoslovak economy, assisted by the USSR, for instance by oil deliveries at cheaper prices, performed fairly well until the mid-1970s, even though basic structures deteriorated and quality of products declined. Internationally Prague obtained the West German recognition that the Munich dictate of 1938 was null and void from the inception. Two years later, in 1975, the Final Act of the Helsinki Conference on Security and Cooperation in Europe (CSCE) reaffirmed the inviolability of the existing borders in Europe. The Final Act also included a formal engagement on the part of the signatories to respect human rights. This proved to be of great importance for the rise of a new type of opposition in East Central Europe. In Czechoslovakia, partly inspired by similar developments in Poland, it took the form of the Charter 77 signed by around 1,000 people. It was followed in 1978 by the Committee for the Defense of the Unjustly Persecuted (VONS). Both were firmly anchored on the provisions of the Helsinki Act and the Czechoslovak constitution – which paid lip service to human rights – and constituted themselves as monitoring bodies of the actual adherence to these laws. Operating in the open, the Chartists insisted that their activities were absolutely legal; the authorities responded with harassment. A leading Chartist, Václav Havel, spoke of the "power of the powerless." This was more than a seeming paradox and harked back to the notion of civil society.

While Husák's Czechoslovakia was a product of the Brezhnev era, Hungary under Kádár still reflected the Khrushchev heritage. The regime was a kind of paternalistic dictatorship promoting limited democratization, seemingly offering people as much as was possible under the circumstances. Around 1979 the New Economic Mechanism was revived with a price reform, greater amounts of self-management on the collective farms, and more freedom of decision in industrial enterprises. Smaller units were encouraged, competition promoted, and the profitability stressed. Private initiative was permitted in agriculture, retailing, and services. Yet the system remained essentially a half-way house in which the Party's grip was arbitrarily tightened or loosened, and in which the economy, heavily dependent on foreign trade, could not fully react according to the law of the market. There was not enough domestic capital and Hungary began to borrow. A debt of $1 billion in 1970 rose to $15 billion in the late 1980s. The country was the "best barrack" in the Soviet camp, a fact recognized at home and in the West, but it was also becoming an expensive barrack to live in. Prices were rising and many Hungarians needed to have two or even three jobs to make ends meet.

The initial hatred for Kádár turned into a grudging acceptance by many people. Cultural and artistic life was freer than elsewhere in the bloc and contacts with the West more regular. The United States' approval of the Hungarian evolution was symbolized by the return of St Stephen's crown, which had been captured during the war. Intellectuals such as György Konrád spoke of their goal of "anti-political politics."

There were some superficial similarities between Hungary and Poland as it entered the decade under the new first secretary Edward Gierek. Gomułka had scored his last success in 1970: a treaty with West Germany that recognized the Odra–Nysa frontier. He was toppled by a major strike in the Baltic harbors of Gdańsk, Gdynia, and Szczecin. This December 1970 upheaval was bloodily suppressed, and it showed that the workers could cause the fall of a communist leader, but could not choose his successor. Still, Gierek, a pragmatist with West European experience, appealed directly to the workers to help him modernize the country's economy and raise living standards. Initially he met with a positive response. Cleverly exploiting the West–East détente, which the Soviet invasion of Czechoslovakia had not really damaged, Gierek brought into the country large Western credits and technology. The mounting debts were to be repaid by exports. But after a few years the program ran into insoluble difficulties.

Gierek's consumerism raised expectations and produced hopes that could not be fulfilled. The incoming capital and technology were largely wasted by a badly thought-out and uncoordinated expansion, inefficiency, and corruption. Without basic structural changes the experiment could not work; an external factor, the worldwide oil crisis, dealt the finishing blow. The strategy of investments and trade was in a shambles and Gierek kept borrowing to cover the mounting debts.

Within society the gap widened between Gierek's "red bourgeoisie" (which had never liked Gomułka's austere style) and the masses, exposing the supposed communist egalitarianism. A secular outlook spreading throughout Poland in the 1960s was in turn losing to a religious revival, which the efforts of Cardinals Wyszyński and K. Wojtyła infused with a new spirit and dynamism.

In 1976 the Party miscalculated badly, assuming that improved living standards would permit new price increases. The workers responded by strikes. There were attacks, as in 1970, on Party committees and brutality on the part of the riot police. Then developments came that later served as an example for the opposition throughout East Central Europe. The idea was that a civil society could exist outside of and in defiance of the totalitarian state. As one of the dissident leaders, Jacek Kuroń, put it: do not burn Party committees, let us create our own. In 1976 the Committee for the Defense of Workers (KOR) came into being, at first to assist the penalized and persecuted workers, later to become an organism for social self-defense. KOR was a bridge between the intelligentsia and the workers which hitherto had acted separately or even at cross-purposes. Other committees (for instance the Movement for the Defense of Man and Citizen – ROPCiO) followed. The church spread a protective umbrella over their activities: cultural, educational, or self-aid. This was also a novelty, connected with the overtures of the leftist intelligentsia (heavily represented in KOR) to the church. Abandoning their traditional anti-clericalism, people such as Adam Michnik stressed the common ground between the church and the leftist opposition: concern for freedom and human dignity. The governmental harassment of the dissidents and church-related groups was selective and relatively restrained. In the era of détente Gierek had to tread cautiously.

The anti-communist movement in Poland acquired a new dimension with an event that took place in Rome in late 1978: the election of Cardinal Wojtyła as Pope John Paul II. A year later the Gierek regime agreed to his visit to his homeland. The visit, in which huge crowds participated, endowed the intelligentsia–workers–church alliance with an all-national, patriotic, and ethical dimension. People also realized their strength *vis-à-vis* the Party and state apparatus which could do little beyond minor chicaneries. During the papal visit Poland was a free and different country. The stage was set for a major upheaval.

A strike began as a minor one in the Gdańsk shipyard but spread like wildfire through the country. The government was obliged to sign an official accord with the strikers, who were led by an electrician with an uncanny political flair and personal charisma: Lech Wałęsa. The August 1980 accord, composed of 21 points, was economic and political. It belied the thesis that the workers were concerned only about their narrow material interests. It showed that people realized that economic changes were impossible without a political transformation of the country. An "Independent, Self-governing Trade Union Solidarity" (Solidarność) grew to comprise 10 million members.

Solidarity represented the most important development in East Central Europe since the Second World War, perhaps even earlier. A Czechoslovak historian called it

> the only spontaneous and genuine working-class revolution which had ever occurred in history, directed against the "socialist" state governed by bureaucrats (in the name of, but in reality against the working class) and carried out under the sign of the cross and with the blessing of the Pope.[59]

Unlike the 1956 and 1968 revolutions it began outside the Party and was not a political movement in the sense that it fought principally for the creation of a civil society, and did not aim to govern the country. At the same time it had to fulfill a political function whether it liked it or not. In broader ethical terms, as J. Tischner put it, Solidarity stood for a dialogue and rejection of violence, for the dignity of work and the worker, and for national consciousness as ethical consciousness. Garton Ash characterized Solidarność as a social crusade of national rebirth which constituted its strength and attraction.

The Solidarity movement lasted for over fifteen months before it was banded by the introduction of martial law. Was the government determined from the beginning to destroy it, the question being simply of means? Did Solidarity sign its death warrant because it grew too radical and could not be satisfied without the demise of communism? Or was it doomed because it turned out to be a "self-limiting revolution" that refused to make a bid for power? Volumes have been written on these and other controversial points. Paradoxically every success as well as every failure brought Solidarity closer to defeat. Having only one real weapon at its disposal, the strike or the threat of a strike, it was driven into an ever more confrontational position. The ruling establishment was provoking Solidarity by refusing or delaying concessions and seeking to destroy the movement. Yet we must remember that the Party and the government were internally divided and did not follow a single and consistent line. There were also differences between the central authorities and the lower echelons. Solidarity was not a monolith either. It was pulled in diverse directions, even if we dismiss the role of provocateurs, and was obliged to fulfill various functions. Finally, as a historian put it, "Solidarity played the main role in the spectacle, but as in a Greek tragedy, fate directed events."[60]

Gierek did not survive the birth of Solidarity and made room for Stanisław Kania. In February 1981 General Wojciech Jaruzelski became premier and moved to the center of the stage. He made a contrast to the preceding leaders in many respects: in social background (gentry), profession (military), even the stiff external manner that made him look inscrutable behind the habitual dark glasses. Since he had lost his parents in Russia from where he was deported as a boy, people asked themselves whether he could be a true communist.

The 1980–1 winter was hard, and Soviet armed intervention appeared at times imminent. Solidarity had to fight for every governmental concession, step by step. In March an anti-Solidarity incident in Bydgoszcz – possibly a provocation – brought Poland to the brink of a general strike and open confrontation. Solidarity refused to take the step, but it could not go along with Jaruzelski's proposal of a moratorium on strikes. The situation in the country was growing chaotic. On December 13, Jaruzelski, who had become first secretary in the autumn, proclaimed martial law; this took Solidarity and everyone by surprise. Was this move dictated by the fear that otherwise the USSR would intervene and invade Poland? This motive has been advanced by Jaruzelski's defenders. He himself mentioned the threat of an armed confrontation with Solidarity, the deadlocked talks with Cardinal Glemp (Wyszyński's successor) and Wałęsa, and Soviet economic pressure.

The martial law which paralyzed all the country was brutal, yet if one thinks of Solidarity as a revolution, its suppression resulted in few victims. But the nation felt its humiliation deeply, and would find it difficult to forget and forgive in the years to come. Under the martial law the role of the Party, already weakened by dissent and resignations, dwindled. The martial law was in a sense an admission that the Party could no longer govern. A Military Council of National Salvation (WRON) assumed all power. Later attempts to broaden the basis of the regime by the creation of a patriotic front and a consultative body proved unsuccessful. With most of the Solidarity leadership in internment camps or prisons, an underground Solidarity, led among others by Z. Bujak, continued their resistance through clandestine publications, even broadcasts, and other activities. In 1982 Wałęsa, who had become the symbol of Solidarity, was released from confinement, and a year later martial law was formally lifted. Jaruzelski and his associates may well have been a cut above the previous ruling teams in postwar Poland, but they achieved nothing positive through the law or the measures that followed. A long-range strategy seemed absent, especially in the economic field where conditions steadily deteriorated.

During this period the stature of the church grew perceptibly, although on May 26, 1981 it had lost Cardinal Wyszyński, and two weeks earlier it nearly lost Pope John Paul II, who was seriously wounded by an assassin's bullet. The pope recovered and in 1983 again visited Poland. But if the visit was to show that the country was stabilized, this object was not achieved. The papal message was one of hope and encouragement and both were badly needed. In 1984, under circumstances still not fully elucidated, the secret police arranged the assassination of a popular young priest associated with Solidarity, Father Jerzy Popiełuszko. For the first time in communist history the policemen involved were arrested and tried. Did this indicate that the assassination had also been aimed at Jaruzelski and his policy of seeking some accommodation with the opposition? Be that as it may, the Polish situation appeared to be a stalemate. Few people realized then that the election of a new general-secretary of the Soviet Communist Party, Mikhail Gorbachev, in 1985, was opening a new era in the history of communism, the Soviet Union, and East Central Europe.

The entry of the Western world into what Zbigniew Brzezinski called the technotronic age, characterized by high technology, especially in information and communications, dramatically widened the gap with the Soviet bloc. While the armaments race was straining the Soviet economy, the inherent backwardness and anachronism of the communist system could no longer be conjured away by ideological incantations. The absence of market mechanisms encouraged arbitrariness in economic policies; the negative selection of Party cadres weakened the leadership and encouraged graft and favoritism; the absence of corrective political mechanisms resulted in factionalism and made elections a farce and a change of leadership an upheaval. The system in which there were no clear limitations on responsibility fostered irresponsibility. Society was becoming demoralized, indeed ill. Discontent mingled with cynicism or apathy.

Gorbachev realized the need for a drastic reconstruction (*perestroika*) of the economic base and the political superstructure. It was to come from above, but in order to overcome the vested interests of the nomenclatura and the inertia of the masses, people had to be enlisted in an open process (*glasnost*) of democratization. This was a bold program that involved the risk of awakening forces long suppressed, political and national. It had also to affect the whole bloc, East Central Europe included.

Reformers in the region could now view Moscow as an ally: a drastic change from the past when the cold winds blowing from Russia had frozen or destroyed the developments of 1956, 1968, or even 1980. Gorbachev was willing to push his policies even at the cost of diminishing the role of the Party. This was of crucial importance for East Central Europe, because it undermined the communists' claim of having a monopoly in cooperation with Moscow. While the rule of law, democratization, and especially reforms in the direction of market economy were the principal ingredients of change, the Russian and the East Central European contexts were, as always, different. Far-reaching changes in the region could result in the collapse of communism. This Gorbachev may not have realized, nor was it foreseen by sovietologists who had tended to dwell on common features of communism in the bloc, and not on the distinct features of East Central Europe. What was the region like in the mid-1980s?

The four postwar decades had seen many changes. The population had greatly increased in Poland, from roughly 24 to 38 million, and in Czechoslovakia, from 12 to 15 million. It remained stationary in Hungary at 10 million. The percentage of urban or industrially employed people grew significantly in Poland and Hungary, but urbanization and industrialization had not always meant progress. Czechoslovakia dropped from its prewar presence among the first ten industrialized countries in the world to perhaps a thirtieth place. It was well behind Austria and France. It was still the most advanced in the region, with $10.140 GNP per capita as compared to Hungary's $8.660 and Poland's $7.270, but the distance behind the United States ($19.770 per capita) was telling. Moreover Czechoslovakia, as well as the more industrialized parts of Poland and Hungary, was paying a terrible price with an ecological catastrophe. And, as many people feared, the national spirit of the Czechs seemed broken.

The Polish economy was in a shambles; the national income was falling. The Solidarity period and the martial law added to the financial burdens. Western, mainly American, sanctions against the Jaruzelski regime, while necessary on moral and political grounds, deepened the slump. In 1988 Polish indebtedness of $38.5 billion ($1,030 per capita), Hungarian of $18 billion ($1,820 per capita), and even Czechoslovak, officially estimated at $6 billion, although probably double that amount, showed the economic plight of the region. For all the progress achieved under Kádár it was marred by inefficiency, inflation, and the stagnation of large enterprises. Hungarians were asking why Austria or Finland, whose position was comparable, were so much better off. The credibility of Kádárization was in doubt. The Party, though internally divided over tactics, sought to preside over a controlled liberalization. This involved an improvement in state–church relations. It was characteristic throughout East Central Europe, although it was most striking in Poland, that religion, far from being the opium for the masses, as Marx had asserted, has been the "best guarantor and promoter of their freedom," to cite John Paul II's utterance in 1990.

POSTCOMMUNIST EAST CENTRAL EUROPE

The deadlock between the regime and the outlawed Solidarity was broken in Poland by the round-table talks, held, with the church acting as intermediary, between February and April 1989. The final accord provided for the legalization of Solidarity and for free elections to the newly established senate and to a limited number of seats in the lower chamber. The unexpected landslide for Solidarity in June gave it all the contested seats and eliminated the leading Party figures. After a series of complex maneuvers another compromise occurred. The presidency went to General Jaruzelski and the premiership to a close Wałęsa associate, Tadeusz Mazowiecki. His cabinet was based on a coalition with the populists and the democrats, the two satellite parties of the communists which had defected and joined Solidarity. This was the first non-communist-led government in East Central Europe, a great event that started a chain reaction. By January 1990 the Party dissolved itself and a drastic economic program was begun by the deputy premier Leszek Balcerowicz. Its object was the restitution of market economy. In June 1990 local government elections took place, and once again the Solidarity candidates swept the field. But a serious rift, of which more later, pitted Wałęsa against Mazowiecki. It destroyed the unity of Solidarity and injected much bitterness into the presidential election, which was held in November–December 1990 and returned Wałęsa as president. The future will show whether unity will be restored along different lines, and political-economic evolution continued.

Developments in Hungary indicated at first that the Party was more adroit than in Poland while the opposition was still in an embryonic stage. The largest groups, the Democratic Forum and the Free Democrats began to organize themselves only in 1987. Kádár's fall from power in May 1988 and his death roughly a year later marked the end of an era, but no great personalities emerged on either communist or opposition side. A period of fluidity followed. The solemn reburial of Nagy and his associates in June 1989, attended by huge crowds, represented a rehabilitation of the Hungarian 1956 Revolution and of its leaders. Talks between the government and the opposition, somewhat resembling the Polish round table, led to an accord in September that put an end to the communist monopoly of power and provided for presidential and general elections. These events coincided with the opening of the Hungarian border with Austria and a mass exodus of East Germans, leaving their country via Hungary and Austria for West Germany. This development shook the foundations of communism in East Germany and played a major role in a rapid course of events that culminated in the demolition of the Berlin Wall in November 1989. The issue of German unification suddenly appeared on the international agenda, and, in the months to come turned out to be the object of intensive East–West negotiations. An agreement was reached in October 1990. But would the unified Germany respect the Odra–Nysa border with Poland? The Mazowiecki government insisted on iron-clad commitments, and even at one point spoke of retainment of Soviet troops on Polish soil as a reinsurance. This stand contrasted with firm Hungarian and Czechoslovak demands for a speedy evacuation. On November 14, 1990 a final and solemn German–Polish treaty was signed, followed by one on good neighborliness on June 19, 1991, hopefully opening a new era in the relations between the two countries.

To return to Hungary, parliamentary elections in April 1990 resulted in a victory of the Democratic Forum which formed a coalition with a revived Smallholders Party. J. Antall became premier. The Free and Young Democrats constituted the opposition and they improved their standing through local elections held in the autumn.

Poland and Hungary had outdistanced Czechoslovakia in their quest for freedom. Throughout the first half of 1989 communism seemed unshaken. "Solidarity is promising Poland a future that is about as realistic as posthumous life in paradise," jeered the Bratislava paper *Pravda* on June 1. Nothing seemed to have changed since the resignation of Husák in 1987 or Gorbachev's visit to Prague the same year. The Charter continued to serve as a lightning rod for reprisals and persecutions. Contacts between Chartists and Solidarity resulted in arrests. It was a crime to bring a Bible to Slovakia. But the upheaval in East Germany coming after Polish and Hungarian changes finally isolated communism in Czechoslovakia. Mass demonstrations began in August and October 1989, and the police brutality in dispersing them increased popular anger. The November 17 demonstration led to a crisis. Intellectuals and students were joined by workers, who proclaimed a brief general strike; unrest spread throughout the country. The communist government resigned and the Party abandoned its power. The Civic Forum in the Czech lands and the Public against Violence in Slovakia group came into being as the leading anti-communist forces. Havel was elected president: the veteran of the Prague Spring, Dubček, became the speaker (president) of the Czechoslovak parliament.

The events in Czechoslovakia were so rapid and relatively painless that people spoke of a "velvet revolution" and boasted that while it took the Poles ten years and the Hungarians ten months to do away with communism, the Czechs and Slovaks did it in ten days. Naturally, this speedy victory was only possible because everything around the country was crumbling. If the collapse of the communist pillar, East Germany, gave the final push, the earlier examples of the northern and southern neighbors must not be forgotten.

After the Hungarian general elections and before the local elections in Poland, Czechs and Slovaks went to vote in June 1990. The Civic Forum and its Slovak counterpart emerged victorious, although the communists gained a respectable vote. In Bohemia-Moravia they were the second largest party. While the name of the Party was changed, as in the Polish and Hungarian case, it continued in its new guise as a significant political factor. This was again apparent after the local elections held in late November. The Civic Forum led with 35.6 percent in the Czech republic, and the Christian Democrats with 27.4 percent in the Slovak republic. But, the communists still scored 17.2 percent in the former and 13.6 in the latter. The government moved cautiously in economic matters, submitting the first blueprint for reform in September 1990, and taking the first concrete steps in January 1991. The Czechs hoped to proceed toward a free market economy and privatization much more gradually than the Poles.

East Central Europe rejected communism, as a body rejects a transplant, because it was contrary to freedom, and because it was foreign. While liberty has once again become the most cherished value, there have been fears that it might degenerate into license. Democracy is not a panacea but, as Churchill put it, a system that is less bad than any other. The same is true for market economy. In the present convulsions that accompany the birth of a new era, "it would be tragic indeed were liberty to be identified . . . with unacceptable economic deprivation," in the words of an American economist.[61]

A common struggle against communism had provided the chief bond among the various groups of the opposition. The ethos of Solidarity, or Havel's "power of the powerless" had been the banner in the struggle for ideals; now the anti-communist revolution has reached the second stage, the struggle for power. The effect it has on the relationship between ethics and politics worries Polish leaders; Havel deals with the same issue in his remarks on the anatomy of hatred.

Then there is the question of the communists who made up a sizeable percentage of the population: 10.9 percent in Czechoslovakia, 7.7 percent in Hungary, and 5.8 percent in Poland (in 1988). Embedded in the society and its economic structures they controlled most walks of life and have been related to many more people in the country. Both the Havel and the Mazowiecki governments, and to a large extent that of Hungary, have rejected the idea of massive purges and witch-hunts. This course may have been the only alternative, but it has raised the danger of the communists' survival and even retention of power. A grim joke that the communists have gained their goal of being a leading force through free elections reflects a prevailing malaise. Similarly, many members of the nomenclatura transferred their activities to business and underwent a metamorphosis from communist bosses to capitalist entrepreneurs. There is a mounting pressure for punishing communists, outlawing the neo-communist parties, and confiscating all their assets.

The demand for "acceleration," a battle cry of the Wałęsa camp, has combined with criticism of the Mazowiecki government as being too lenient and too elitist. Wałęsa, his own ambitions apart, has been stressing the need for a strong leader, a demand heard also in the neighboring countries and implying that East Central European society is not yet ready for parliamentary democracy.

There has been a good deal of talk about a left–right struggle in East Central Europe; the left being associated, or represented to be, with the discredited communism. This distinction belongs more to partisan polemics than to cool analysis. An intellectual of the "leftist" pro-Mazowiecki camp somewhat snootily remarked that his group stood West and not left of the Wałęsa supporters, implying that the latter were Eastern-type populists. True, the urbanist–populist dichotomy seems to have resurfaced to some extent in Hungarian politics. Also, the Forum may be more genuinely right-centerist and the Free and Young Democrats more leftist than the corresponding groups in Poland. In the Czech case a recent meeting of the left showed that the word does not have the same unfavorable connotation in that country. Still, the old historic parties, be they of the left or right, have not been able to re-emerge in any other than marginal form so far. Although parties, movements, and groups multiply, there is a certain political vacuum in the three countries. In Czechoslovakia, where the Civic Forum has largely disintegrated, only two parties are considered to be really well-organized: the communists and the Slovak Nationalists.

The constitutional model still remains to be worked out by the parliaments, and the relationship between the executive and the chambers determined. Neither the French presidential paradigm nor the British (or German) system in which the prime minister (or chancellor) is the key figure are likely to be adopted. In Czechoslovakia the process has been complicated by the Czech–Slovak issue. It has led to a dualist structure of the state, the Czech and Slovak Federal Republic (ČSFR), with limited powers of the federal authorities. Even so, the demands of Slovak extremists for complete independence have not entirely disappeared and may yet prevail.

The unprecedented transition from a communist-type to a free market economy has so far been boldly tackled only by the Balcerowicz plan in Poland. It succeeded in stopping the hyper-inflation and gaining at first a trade surplus. But reorientation of trade and finding new markets after the loss of Soviet and East German ones remains a great problem. So is a decline in production that proved to be larger than anticipated. The virtual wage freeze and a stabilization of currency *vis-à-vis* the dollar cut into the standard of living of many; the peasantry felt especially bitter about the discrepancy between prices of agricultural and industrial products. The Mazowiecki government's economic policies have not been above criticism, and hardships are real. However, a sweeping economic reform in Poland, as in Czechoslovakia and Hungary (bearing in mind that these last two were better off to start with), is unlikely to succeed unless the mentality of the population changes drastically. For over four decades people had become used to a system in which bribes, connections, bypassing of laws and lack of interest in quality work and expertise were accompanied by low wages and low performance. An overnight change into honest entrepreneurs, dedicated managers, and conscientious workers is virtually impossible. Working incentives while undoubtedly crucial have to be accompanied by a new working ethos. To create, or to recreate, it is a lengthy and painful process which can only take place in an atmosphere of at least some confidence and stability.

The role of the church could be very important in this respect. Having been the mainstay of opposition to totalitarian communism and a protector of freedom, national and individual, the church must now become the great educator of the alienated nation, teaching it good citizenship, communal solidarity, and tolerance. This concern permeates the encyclicals and utterances of John Paul II. His visit to Prague, which Havel termed a miracle, infused the papal message into the humanist Czech tradition. But the abortion issue and reintroduction of religion in schools (in Poland) brought forth criticism of undue interference by the church.

The frequently used phrase, East Central Europe's "return to

Europe," refers to a multitude of issues on diverse levels. There is the question of being oneself again. Wishing to obliterate the communist half-century, Poles, Hungarians, Czechs, and Slovaks have engaged in a massive restoration of old symbols of independent statehood. The Polish eagle is crowned again and the Hungarian flag displays its ancient emblem. Monuments to communist leaders, foreign and domestic, are disappearing together with street names that had honored them. Interwar history is being rehabilitated if not glorified. Does all this mean that East Central Europe is returning to its pre-1939 identity which, as Joseph Rothschild opines, has survived in a remarkable fashion the communist decades? Chief elements of this identity were, as he perceives them, extreme nationalism, a non-democratic tradition, a rule of elites alienated from the masses, and a "balkanization" in interstate relations.

Nationalism and populism have indeed re-emerged, but largely as a reaction against the trampling over and the manipulation of national sentiments by the communists and their failure to satisfy demands for social justice. An intolerant attitude toward national minorities and a largely verbal, although nasty, anti-Semitism are also visible. At the same time efforts to overcome this xenophobia are more serious than in the past. Moreover, the prevalent trends in Western Europe, which had always affected the region, are now toward internationalism and integration, and this is a drastic change from the pre-1939 decades.

Since 1945 East Central Europe had been cut off from democratic processes which have produced a highly successful West German system and effected a transformation of Spain. The interwar crisis of democracy has been replaced by a new democratic élan. Once again, the East Central European region will have to catch up with and learn from the West. If historical analogies exist they would (in the Polish case at least) be of the eighteenth-century "modernization" versus the old regime's anarchic tendencies. Such key works as pluralism and democracy that arose as ideals in opposition to imposed uniformity and totalitarianism, have to be adapted to real conditions of everyday life. Hence the unavoidable clash between lofty ideas and practice, between the intelligentsia's political concepts and the down-to-earth needs of the man in the street. Yet a revival of the "strong man" ideal and authoritarianism modeled on the 1930s is likely to be a transient phenomenon.

The traditional difference between the elites and masses, more deep-seated than in the West, has, all appearances notwithstanding, been permanently affected by the postwar leveling down, upward mobility, rising educational standards, and social intermixture. The traditional leadership of the intelligentsia is being successfully challenged by new forces that in the long run are likely to resemble those in the West.

This has not yet been fully understood by the intellectuals who speak disparagingly of populism.

The lifting of the communist lid over the boiling cauldron has fully revealed the existing conflicts between nations and states in the region. The Czech–Slovak controversy has resurfaced although its character is very different from that of the prewar republic. The issues of the Hungarian minorities in Transylvania and Slovakia have created an outcry among the Magyars. There are tensions between Poles and Lithuanians, Ukrainians, Belorussians, and Germans. Extreme nationalists draw maps which display expansionist appetites. Yet, as mentioned earlier, the size of national minorities has shrunk dramatically, and near ethnic purity was achieved (but at what price!) through the region. Possibilities for resolving controversial issues appear far greater than before the war. The talk about a perennial "balkanization" of this region is hardly helpful, and in many instances misleading. Again the international context of these conflicts is very different in the Europe of today that has abandoned war as a means of resolving disputes.

If one concludes that all the similarities notwithstanding East Central Europe cannot simply return to its prewar past, its present and future relationship to the West also exhibits quite novel features. The "return to Europe" is affected by contradictory hopes and apprehensions. What kind of Europe does the region want to return to? There is the West that had always been an inspiration and the stark day-to-day real Europe with inequalities, its rich and its poor, with Spain, Portugal, Ireland, or Greece representing the old periphery. The hope, indeed the absolute need for Western capital is mingled with fears of becoming a sphere of exploitation, a poor relative whose assets are all in foreigners' hands. East Central Europe cannot progress economically unless the debts that stifle it and discourage foreign investors are eliminated, and outside capital poured in to assist the reconstruction of the entire economy. The first encouraging signs, however, grew dimmer as the whole international situation underwent changes. West Germany, the most likely investor, became absorbed in a rehabilitation of the former German Democratic Republic, the costs being much higher than anyone had imagined. The Middle Eastern crisis of 1990–1 not only affected oil deliveries – Iraq had been paying Poland with oil – and cost the Polish economy a few billion dollars, but it turned the world's attention away from East Central Europe and its problems. The ongoing disintegration of the USSR has alerted the West, especially Germany, to the necessity of assisting the Soviet economy. Indeed, the Soviet situation with its far-reaching ramifications looms large. Western aid in order to be effective needs to be linked to political democratization, evolution toward market economy, and the transformation of the USSR into a new Commonwealth of Independent States. The Baltic republics refused to join, but the relationship of the Ukraine and Belorussia to the Commonwealth is ambiguous and remains to be worked out. All this affects East Central Europe. Soviet troops have already left Hungary and Czechoslovakia but they linger on in Poland. The tendency in some Soviet quarters to retain maximum influence in East Central Europe may have largely collapsed as a result of the anti-Gorbachev coup, Yeltsin's victory and the formal demise of the USSR. One hopes for good relations with the successors, but there is uncertainty. In these conditions economic aid to ex-Soviet republics could take the form of credits for the purchases of East Central European goods, thus assisting both economies. Polish and Hungarian leaders and most recently Czechoslovakia's President Havel have outlined such a plan in some detail.

There are other problems connected with the USSR that could assume gigantic proportions, namely mass exodus of people from the East and into the West. Already the first trickle of Russians, Ukrainians, Romanians, and Gypsies has alarmed the neighboring states. Unless the economy of the eastern part of the continent of Europe be reconstructed and its inhabitants assured a decent life at home, migratory problems might get out of hand. The Iron Curtain must not be replaced by a "gold curtain" that divides a prosperous West from a prostrated East, and impedes a European integration that modern technology makes inescapable.

Some version of a new Marshall Plan for the eastern part of the continent seems imperative. Will the West have enough imagination and willpower to propose and carry it out? Will East Central European states assist it by cooperating among themselves? Addressing the United States Congress in February 1990 President Havel said that he hoped to coordinate Czechoslovakia's return to Europe with that of the other countries, above all Poland and Hungary. Subsequent meetings of the leaders of the three states at Bratislava, Warsaw, and Visegrád have shown both a willingness to cooperate and the existence of differences in perception and approach of international issues. A certain solidarity and a convergent policy has been in evidence *vis-à-vis* the Soviet Union over matters concerned with trade and the dismantling of CEMA and the Warsaw Treaty Organization. There has been less unanimity, at least at first, in dealing with the West concerning such matters as debts, the accession to the Council of Europe, and the transformation of the Conference on Security and Cooperation in Europe (CSCE) into a more effective organization. Let us not forget that the three states are at this point neither in the Warsaw Pact nor in NATO.

Efforts toward regional collaboration encouraged by the West and partly successful have been noticeable more among politicians and intellectuals than on the popular level. An average Czech, Slovak, Hungarian, or Pole has little consciousness of a regional community of interests and experiences. Regional cooperation has not taken any systematic or organizational form as yet. Italy has been promoting a pentagonal grouping (with Czechoslovakia, Hungary, Austria, and Yugoslavia), recently joined by Poland. The group's future appears uncertain. Warsaw, mindful of its eastern connections, has its eyes turned toward Moscow, Vilnius, Kiev, and Minsk. But how to proceed so as not to antagonize Russia, nor alienate Lithuania, the Ukraine, and Belorussia? A hard task for Polish diplomacy.

Post-communist East Central Europe has taken, as in all revolutions, a leap into the unknown, and it would be hazardous to try to predict the course of future developments. Yet, the region remains molded by the heritage of its history. To appreciate it properly one has to approach it in Braudelian terms of "longue durée." For centuries challenges coming from the West and an ambivalent relationship with the West constituted an essential element of East Central European history. The center–periphery pattern has become established. There was continuity even in exceptions, the Czech lands being more advanced than the rest of the region in the fifteenth as well as in the twentieth century.

In the past the contributions of East Central Europe have been more spiritual than material. From Hus's insistence on freedom of conscience to Masaryk's "Christ not Caesar," from Paulus Vladimiri's rejection of conversion by force to Solidarity's ethos, from Gábor Bethlen's fight for freedom and religion to Hungarians dying in 1956 for "Hungary and for Europe," the liberty bell has tolled in East Central Europe for generations. It would be pretentious to maintain that freedom means more to Poles, Czechs, Hungarians, or Slovaks than to other nations of Europe. It is just that history has forced them to defend and to fight for it more frequently than in many other lands. But freedom, as everything else, has a price and its nature varies. At present the price seems largely economic, but it has other dimensions. Freedom is not an absolute in itself, but a condition of meaningful existence of individuals and society. It must be self-limiting in order not to become license and lead to oppression of others. Freedom in East Central Europe has been gained at a high price and must not be lost. As John Paul II expressed it in his Encyclical Letter "Solicitudo Rei Socialis" of 1987, "Each [nation] must discover and use to the best advantage its *own area of freedom*. Each must likewise realize its true needs as well as the rights and duties which oblige it to respond to them." Thinking about the past and pondering about the present and the future, these deceptively simple words need to be remembered.

NOTES

1 Fernand Braudel, *The Mediterranean and the Mediterranean World in the Age of Philip II*, Vol. II (New York, 1975), p. 392.
2 J. Jedlicki, *Jakiej Cywilizacji Polacy potrzebują* (Warsaw, 1988), p. 10.
3 Cited in A. Kadić, "Croatian humanists at the Hungarian court," *East European Quarterly* 12 (2) (1988), p. 132.
4 Cited in J. Mezník, "Religious toleration in the 16th century," *Kosmas: Journal of Czechoslovak and Central European Studies*, vols 3 and 4, nos 1 and 2 (1984–5), p. 111.
5 I. Wallerstein, *The Modern World System: Capitalist Agriculture and the Origins of the European World-Economy in the Sixteenth Century* (New York, 1974), p. 99.
6 F. Braudel, *Civilization and Capitalism, 15th–18th Century*, Vol. II (New York, 1981–4), p. 267.
7 S. Domanovszky, cited in I. T. Berend, "The Place of Hungary in Europe," unpublished conference paper, Ráckeve, September 10–11, 1988, p. 30.
8 M. Kridl, W. Malinowski, J. Wittlin (eds), *For Your Freedom and Ours: Polish Progressive Spirit Through the Centuries* (New York, 1943), p. 32.
9 Cited in J. Pelenski, "Muscovite Russia and Poland-Lithuania 1450–1660," in J. Pelenski (ed.), *State and Society in Europe from the Fifteenth to the Eighteenth Century* (Warsaw, 1985), p. 113.
10 J. V. Polišenský, *The Thirty Years' War and the Crisis of the Seventeenth Century* (Berkeley, Calif., 1972), p. 5.
11 Cited in A. Jobert, *De Luther à Mohila: La Pologne dans la crise de la Chrétienté 1517–1648* (Paris, 1974), p. 102.
12 Cited in P. Hanák (ed.), *One Thousand Years: A Concise History of Hungary* (Budapest, 1988), p. 63.
13 Cited in F. Braudel, *Civilization and Capitalism, 15th–18th Century*, Vol. II (New York, 1981–4), p. 262.
14 Cited in W. Czapliński, *O Polsce siedemnastowiecznej* (Warsaw, 1966), p. 83.
15 C. H. Hoskins and R. H. Lord, *Some Problems of the Peace Conference* (Cambridge, Mass., 1920), p. 160.
16 Cited in H. Wisner, *Najjaśniejsza Rzeczpospolita* (Warsaw, 1976), p. 234.
17 Cited in Jobert, *De Luther*, p. 9.
18 Ibid., p. 185.
19 Cited in Polišenský, *Thirty Years' War*, p. 131.
20 Cited in M. Spinka, *John Amos Comenius, that Incomparable Moravian* (Chicago, 1943), pp. 113 and 118.

21 Cited in H. Hantsch, *Geschichte Österreichs 1648–1918*, 2nd edn (Graz, Vienna, Cologne, 1955), p. 58.

22 Cited in F. Stern (ed.), *The Varieties of History: From Voltaire to the Present* (New York, 1956), p. 43.

23 D. Kosáry, "Absolutisme éclairé – tendence nobiliaire éclairée," in *Les Lumières en Hongrie, en Europe Centrale et en Europe Orientale* (Actes du troisième colloque de Matrafüred, Budapest, 1977), p. 41.

24 Cited in J. Michalski, "Sarmatyzm a europeizacja Polski w XVIII wieku," in *Swojskość i cudzoziemszczyzna w dziejach kultury polskiej* (Warsaw, 1973), p. 158.

25 *The Letters and Works of Lady Mary Wortley Montagu*, ed. Lord Wharncliffe, vol. 1 (London, 1887), p. 130.

26 Cited in G. Barany, "Hoping against hope: The Enlightened Age in Hungary," *American Historical Review* 76 (2) (1971), p. 339.

27 Cited in A. Walicki, *The Enlightenment and the Birth of Modern Nationhood* (Notre Dame, Ind., 1989), p. 108 with slight, linguistic changes.

28 Edmund Burke cited in R. H. Lord, *The Second Partition of Poland: A Study in Diplomatic History* (Cambridge, Mass., 1915), p. 445.

29 J. Macůrek, "The achievements of the Slavonic Congress," *The Slavonic Review* 26 (1947), p. 330.

30 J. Breuilly, *Nationalism and the State* (London, 1982), p. 374.

31 Cited in H. Kohn, *Prelude to Nation-States: The French and German Experience 1789–1815* (Princeton, NJ, 1967), pp. 91–2.

32 Cited in E. J. Hobsbawm, *The Age of Revolution 1789–1848* (London, 1962), p. 163.

33 E. Niederhauser, *The Rise of Nationality in Eastern Europe* (Budapest, 1982), p. 61.

34 Cited in A. Walicki, *The Enlightenment and the Birth of Modern Nationhood* (Notre Dame, Ind., 1989), p. 87.

35 Cited by P. Brock, "Polish Nationalism," in P. F. Sugar and I. J. Lederer (eds), *Nationalism in Eastern Europe* (Seattle, Wash., 1969), p. 317.

36 Cited in F. S. Wagner, "Széchenyi and the nationality problem in the Habsburg empire," *Journal of Central European Affairs* 20 (1960), p. 299.

37 Ibid., pp. 297 and 299.

38 Cited in J. Zacek, *Palacky: The Historian as Scholar and Nationalist* (Cambridge, 1970), p. 18.

39 Cited by M. Hroch, "Vlastenci bez národa," in *Naše živá i mrtvá minulost* (Prague, 1968), p. 107.

40 Cited in G. Barany, *Stephen Széchenyi and the Awakening of Hungarian Nationalism 1790–1841* (Princeton, NJ, 1968), p. 12.

41 Cited in S. H. Thomson, *Czechoslovakia in European History* (Princeton, NJ, 1953), p. 168.

42 S. Z. Pech, *The Czech Revolution of 1848* (Chapel Hill, NC, 1969), p. 334.

43 I. T. Berend and Gy. Ránki, *Economic Development in East-Central Europe in the 19th and 20th Centuries* (New York, 1974), p. 92.

44 I. T. Berend and Gy. Ránki, "Underdevelopment in Europe in the context of East–West relations in the 19th century," in *Etudes historiques hongroises 1980*, vol. 1 (Budapest, 1980), p. 700.

45 Cited in I. Deák, "Hungary," in H. Rogger and E. Weber (eds), *The European Right* (Berkeley, Calif., 1965), p. 368.

46 Szekfű cited in Z. Horváth, "The development of nationalism in the last decades of Dualism," *Acta Historica* 9 (1–2) (1963), p. 7.

47 Ferenc Deák cited in E. Pamlényi (ed.), *A History of Hungary* (Budapest, 1973), p. 320.
48 Cited in P. S. Wandycz, *The Lands of Partitioned Poland 1795–1918* (Seattle, Wash., 1974), p. 195.
49 Szekfű cited in Horváth, "Development," p. 11.
50 Antonín Hajn cited in B. Garver, *The Young Czech Party 1874–1901 and the Emergence of a Multi-Party System* (New Haven, Conn., 1978), p. 271.
51 Viktor Dyk cited in B. Loewenstein, "Český pravicový radikalismus a první světová válka," in *Naše živá a mrtvá minulost* (Prague, 1968), p. 165.
52 Cited in J. Kalvoda, *The Genesis of Czechoslovakia* (Boulder, Colo., 1986), p. 502.
53 Hans Roos, *A History of Modern Poland* (New York, 1966), p. 96.
54 Cited in Jiři Hochman, "President Eduard Beneš and the Soviet Alliance," *Kosmas* 5 (1) (1986), p. 21.
55 Zbigniew Załuski, *Finał 1945* (Warsaw, 1968), p. 17.
56 Cited in R. L. Garthoff, "Eastern Europe in the context of US–Soviet relations," in S. M. Terry (ed.), *Soviet Policy in Eastern Europe* (New Haven, Conn., 1984), p. 318.
57 Cited in V. Mastny, "Tradition, continuity and discontinuity in recent Czecho-Slovak history," in N. Lobkowicz and F. Prinz (eds), *Die Tschechoslowakei 1945–1970* (Munich, Vienna, 1978), p. 89.
58 I. Svitak, "The Prague Spring Revisited," in H. Brisch and I. Volgyes (eds), *Czechoslovakia: The Heritage of Ages Past: Essays in Memory of Josef Korbel* (Boulder, Colo., 1979), p. 164.
59 M. Hauner, "Prague Spring," in N. Stone and E. Stouhal (eds), *Czechoslovakia: Crossroads and Crises* (London, 1989), p. 208.
60 J. Holzer, "Solidarity's adventures in wonderland," in S. Gomułka and A. Polonsky (eds), *Polish Paradoxes* (London, 1990), p. 105.
61 J. K. Galbraith, "Which capitalism for Eastern Europe?," *Harper's Magazine* (April, 1990), p. 21.

CHRONOLOGICAL TABLES

Bohemia		Hungary	
c. 830	Moravian state		
863	Cyril and Methodius mission; Christianization	896	Magyar conquest
921	St Wenceslas		
		955	Battle of Augsburg (Lechfeld)
		972	Prince Géza baptized
1003	Bolesław the Brave of Poland in Prague	1000	St Stephen king
1038–9	Břetislav in Poland		
1085	Vratislav (king ad personam)	1077	St Ladislas I king
c. 1119–25	Kosmas Chronicle	1102	dynastic union with Croatia
1158	Vladislav II (king ad personam)	1142–62	Saxon settlements in Transylvania
		c. 1200	Anonymous Chronicle (Gesta)
		1222	Golden Bull of Andrew II
		1239	Cuman settlements
		1241–2	Tatar invasion
1254	Privilege to Jews of Přemysl Otakar	1251	Privilege to Jews of Béla IV
1278	Battle of Moravské Pole (Dürnkrut)	1267	county delegates in diet
		c. 1283	Kézai Chronicle
1306	last Přemyslid	1308	Charles Robert king
c. 1311	Dalimil Chronicle	1342	Louis the Great king
1348	Prague University		
1356	Golden Bull of Charles IV		
		1367	University in Pécs
		1370	Louis becomes king of Poland
		1387	Sigismund of Luxemburg king
1409	Kutná Hora decree		
1415	Hus burnt at Constance	1416	first Turkish attack
1419–34	Hussite wars	1420	Dalmatia lost
1438	Battle of Lipany	1437	peasant uprising in Transylvania
		1440	Władysław III of Poland king (Ulászló I)
		1444	Battle of Varna
		1446	Janós Hunyadi regent
1458	George of Poděbrady king	1458	Matthias Corvinus king
1471	Vladislav Jagiellonian king	1490	Vladislav Jagiellonian king (Ulászló II)
1500	Land ordinance of Vladislav	1514	Dózsa's uprising
		1515	Tripartitum of Werböczy

Poland		General	
		800	Charlemagne emperor
966	Baptism of Mieszko I	962	Otto I emperor
		987	Hugh Capet king of France
1000	Gniezno meeting		
1025	Bolesław the Brave king		
1038–9	Czech invasion	1054	Schism between West and East
1076	Bolesław the Bold king		
1079	St Stanislas murdered	1066	Battle of Hastings
c. 1116–19	Gallus Chronicle	1096	First Crusade
1138	Testament of Bolesław the Wrymouth		
1180	Łęczyca Privileges to the clergy	1200	University of Paris
1226	Teutonic Knights invited	1215	Magna Carta
1241	Battle of Legnica	1241	Hanseatic League
1264	Kalisz Privilege to Jews		
1308–9	Gdańsk conquered by Teutonic Knights	1309–77	Papacy in Avignon
1320	Władysław the Short king		
1333	Casimir the Great king	1337–1453	Hundred Years War
1364	Cracow University	1348	Black Death
1370	Louis the Great (of Hungary) king		
1374	Kassa (Koszyce) Privilege		
1385	Polish-Lithuanian Union of Krewo, Jogaila, and Jadwiga co-rulers	1396	Crusade of Nicopolis
1410	Battle of Grunwald		
1422–33	Neminem captivabimus charter		
1434	Władysław III king		
1447	Casimir the Jagiellonian king	c. 1450	Gutenberg's discovery of print
1454	Statutes of Nieszawa	1453	Constantinople falls to Turks
c. 1455–80	Długosz's history of Poland	1455–85	Wars of the Roses in England
1466	Peace of Toruń; recovery of Gdańsk (Danzig)	1492	Columbus discovers America; Spanish reconquest completed; expulsion of Jews and Moors
1473	Printing shop in Cracow		
1505	Nihil novi constitution		
1506	Sigismund the Old king		

Bohemia (contd)			Hungary (contd)	
		1515	Congress of Vienna	
		1516	Louis II king	
1526	Ferdinand Habsburg king	1526	Battle of Mohács; double election: Ferdinand and John Zápolya	
1548	Czech Brethren expelled	1520s	Military Border in Croatia	
1564	Maximilian king	1541	Turks occupy Buda	
		1566	The siege of Szigetvár	
		1570	Principality of Transylvania	
1575	Confessio Bohemica	1571	Stephen Báthory Prince of Transylvania	
1576	Rudolf II king			
1579–93	Kralice Bible	1591	Károlyi Bible	
		1591–		
		1606	Fifteen Years War	
		1604–6	Bocskai's war of independence	
		1606	Peace of Vienna; Peace of Zsitvatorok	
		1608	Matthias king	
1609	Letter of Majesty; Porovnaní			
1612	Matthias king			
1617	Ferdinand elected king	1613	Gábor (Gabriel) Bethlen prince of Transylvania	
1618	Defenestration of Prague			
1619	Ferdinand II deposed; Frederick of the Palatinate, king	1619	Ferdinand king; Bethlen's war against the Habsburgs	
1620	Battle of White Mountain; Frederick flees			
1627	Renewed land ordinance			
		1630	Geroge I Rákóczi prince of Transylvania	
1635	Peace of Prague	1635	University of Nagyszombat (Trnava)	
1637	Ferdinand III king	1638	Religious Union of Ungvár (Užhorod)	
		1648	George II Rákóczi prince of Transylvania	
1657	Leopold I king	1657	Failure of Rákóczi's Polish campaign	

Poland (contd)		General (contd)	
1514	Battle of Orsha	1515	Luther's 95 Theses
1525	Teutonic Knights secularized; Duchy of Prussia a vassal of Poland	1519	Charles V emperor
		1540	Jesuit order founded
1543	Copernicus' De Revolutionibus Orbium	1545–63	Council of Trent
1561	Incorporation of Livonia; Courland vassal state	1555	Peace of Augsburg
1563	Radziwiłł Bible		
1563–70	Northern War		
1564	Jesuits in Poland		
1569	Union of Lublin		
1570	Sandomierz religious accord	1572	Battle of Lepanto; Massacre of St Bartholomew in Paris
1573	Warsaw Confederation; Henry of Valois king		
1576	Stephen Báthory of Transylvania king		
1578	Wilno (Vilnius) University		
1587	Sigismund III (Vasa) king	1588	Spanish Armada against England
1595–6	Religious Union of Brest	1598	Edict of Nantes
		1604–13	Time of troubles in Russia
1605	Battle of Kircholm	1607	colony of Virginia founded
1606–7	Rokosz of Zebrzydowski		
1610	Battle of Klushino		
1619	Truce of Dyvilino	1618–48	Thirty Years War
1620	Battle of Tutora (Cecora)	1624	Richelieu in France
1621	Siege of Hotin (Chocim); peace with Turkey		
1629	Truce with Sweden		
1632	Władysław IV king	1632	Death of Gustavus Adolphus
1648	Khmelnytsky rising in the Ukraine; John Casimir king	1648	Peace of Westphalia
		1649–58	Cromwell's rule
1651	Battle of Berestechko		
1652	Liberum veto		
1654–7	War with Muscovy		
1655	Swedish invasion; defense of Częstochowa	1657–60	Prussia's sovereignty recognized

Bohemia (contd)		Hungary (contd)	
		1664	Battle of Szentgotthárd; Peace of Vasvár
		1667	Wesselényi (Zrinski–Frankopan) conspiracy
		1672	Kuruc struggles begin
		1678–86	Imre Thököly's principality
		1686	Buda liberated
		1687	Habsburg hereditary rule recognized
		1697	Transylvania under Habsburgs; Tokaj uprising
		1697– 1700	Uniate Church in Transylvania
		1703	Rákóczi war of independence begins
		1711	Peace of Szatmár
1720	Pragmatic Sanction	1721–3	Pragmatic Sanction (Croatia, Transylvania, Hungary accept separately)
1740	Maria Theresa queen	1740	Maria Theresa queen
1740–2	First Silesian war (Charles Albert of Bavaria elected king 1741)		
1744–5	Second Silesian War		
1754	First population census	1754	Custom tariff with Austria–Bohemia
1756–63	Third Silesian War		
		1765	Peasant uprising
		1767	Urbarium
1775	Peasant uprising; Urbarium	1777	University moved to Pest
1780	Joseph II king	1780	Joseph II king
1781	Toleration edict; abolition of personal serfdom	1781	Toleration edict
		1785	abolition of personal serfdom; first population census
		1786	peasant uprising in Transylvania

Poland (contd)		General (contd)	
1658	Anti-Trinitarians expelled		
1660	Peace of Oliwa		
1665–6	Rokosz of Lubomirski	1661–	age of Louis XIV
1667	Truce of Andrusovo (peace 1686)	1715	
1669	Michael Korybut (Wiśniowiecki) king		
1672–3	war with Turkey; Treaty of Buczacz; Battle of Hotin		
1674	John III (Sobieski) king		
1683	relief of Vienna by John III	1688	"Glorious Revolution"
1697	Augustus II (Wettin) king		
		1699	Peace of Karlowitz (Karlovci)
1700	Northern War begins	1700–21	Northern War
1704	Stanislas (Leszczyński) king	1701–14	War of the Spanish Succession
1710	Augustus II restored as king		
1715	Confederation of Tarnogród		
1717	The Silent Sejm		
1724	Toruń religious riot		
1733	Augustus III king (Leszczyński re-elected and defeated)	1733–8	War of the Polish Succession
1741	Collegium Nobilium	1740–8	War of the Austrian Succession
		1756–63	Seven Years War
		1761	Rousseau's Social Contract
1765	Knights' School		
1768–72	Confederation of Bar	1769	Watt's steam engine
1772	first partition by Russia, Prussia, and Austria		
1773	Commission of National Education	1773	Jesuit order dissolved
1775	Permanent Council	1774	Treaty of Kuchuk Kainardji
		1775–83	American War of Independence
		1776	American Declaration of Independence
1788–92	Great Sejm	1789	French Revolution
1791	Constitution of May 3		

283

Bohemia (contd)		Hungary (contd)	
1790	Leopold II king	1790	Leopold II king
1792	Francis I king	1792	Francis I king
		1795	Martinovics conspiracy
		1802	Hungarian National Museum
		1809	Györ defeat of noble levies
1818	National Museum		
1824	Kollár's *Daughter of Glory*		
		1825	Vörösmarty's *Zalán's Flight*; Hungarian Academy of Sciences
		1830	Széchenyi's *Credit*
1831	Matice Česká	1831	The "cholera" uprising
1834–9	Jungmann's Czech–German dictionary		
1835	Ferdinand V king	1835	Ferdinand V king
1836	Palacký's *History*	1836–7	National Museum constructed
1837	Šafařik's *Slav Antiquities*	1837	Kossuth arrested
1848	Slav Congress in Prague (June); Prague bombarded; Franz Joseph king (Dec.)	1848	revolution in Pest (March); Batthyány cabinet (April); National Defense Committee of Kossuth (Sept.); Jelačić's defeat at Pákozd (Sept.); Francis Joseph king (Dec.)
		1849	Declaration of Independence (April); capitulation of Világos (Aug.)

Poland (contd)		General (contd)	
1792	Confederation of Targowica; Polish–Russian War	1792–7	War of the First Coalition
1793	second partition by Prussia and Russia		
1794	Kościuszko insurrection		
1795	third partition (Russia, Prussia, Austria)		
1797	Dąbrowski legions in Italy	1797	Treaty of Campo Formio
1800	Society of Friends of Learning in Warsaw	1798– 1801	War of the Second Coalition
		1804	Napoleon emperor
1806–7	Napoleon's "First Polish campaign"	1806	end of the Holy Roman Empire
1807–13	Duchy of Warsaw		
1809	Austrian war with the Duchy		
1811–23	peasants in Prussian Poland emancipated		
1812	"Second Polish campaign"	1812	invasion of Russia
		1814–15	Congress of Vienna
1815	"Congress Kingdom" and independent Republic of Cracow created	1815	Battle of Waterloo
1816	Warsaw University		
1822	Mickiewicz's Ballads and Romances		
1828	Bank Polski		
1830	November uprising	1830	July Revolution in Paris
1846	Cracow revolution and peasant jacquerie		
1848	uprising in Prussian Poland (April); emancipation of peasantry in Galicia; Cracow and Lwów (Lemberg) bombed; Warsaw–Vienna railroad	1848	February Revolution in Paris; Spring of Nations

Bohemia (contd)		Hungary (contd)	
		1867	Compromise (Ausgleich)
1868	Declaration of State Rights	1868	Nagodba (accord) with Croatia; law on minorities
1871	Eighteen Articles	1871	National Gallery
1882	Czech Charles University	1875–90	K. Tisza government
1883	National Theater opened		
1890	"Punktace"		
1891	Czech Academy		
1893	Omladina trials		
1896	Fifth Curia in Cisleithenia	1896	Millennium
		1903–5	I. Tisza cabinet
1905	strikes	1905	Constitutional crisis
1907	universal manhood suffrage in Cisleithenia; Masaryk involved in Zagreb trials	1907	Černova massacre; Zagreb trials
1908	Neo-Slav Congress in Prague	1913–17	I. Tisza government
1914	outbreak of First World War	1914	outbreak of First World War
1916	Czechoslovak National Council abroad; Declaration of loyalty of Reichsrat deputies (Nov.); Charles king	1916	new Independence Party of M. Károlyi; Charles king
1917	decree on Czechoslovak army in France	1917	M. Esterházy and S. Wekerle cabinets

286

Poland (contd)		*General (contd)*	
1851	customs abolished between Russia and Congress Kingdom		
1863–4	January uprising	1861–5	Civil War in America
1864	emancipation of peasants in Kingdom	1866	Austro–Prussian War
1867	autonomous Galicia		
		1870	Franco–Prussian War
		1871	German Empire
		1878	Congress of Berlin
1873	Academy of Sciences in Cracow	1882	Triple Alliance
1886	Colonization Commission in Prussian Poland	1894	Franco–Russian alliance
1892	Polish Socialist Party founded		
1893	National League founded; Social Democratic Party organized		
1896	Fifth curia in Cisleithania		
1905–7	revolution in Congress Kingdom	1904–5	Russo–Japanese war
		1905	Russian Revolution
1906–7	school strikes in Prussian Poland	1908	Austro-Hungary annexes Bosnia–Herzegovina; Young Turkish revolution
		1912–13	Balkan Wars
1914	outbreak of First World War; Supreme National Committee (NKN) in Galicia; legions formed	1914	outbreak of First World War
1915	German–Austrian occupation of Congress Kingdom		
1916	Two Emperors' Manifesto		
1917	Piłsudski imprisoned in Magdeburg (July); Polish army in France; National Polish Committee of Dmowski in Paris (Aug.); Regency Council in Congress Kingdom (Oct.)	1917	Wilson's peace without victory speech (Jan.); February Revolution in Russia; October Revolution in Russia

Czechoslovakia (contd)		Hungary (contd)	
1918	Czechoslovak–bolshevik clash in Cheliabinsk (May); Pittsburgh Declaration; recognition of Czechoslovak National Council as allied government (June–Sept.); Declaration of Czechoslovak independence in Prague and Turčiansky Sv. Martin (Oct.); Masaryk president	1918	Károlyi's National Council (Oct.); revolution: Károlyi government (Oct.); Belgrade armistice (Nov.); republic proclaimed (Nov.)
1919	armed clash with Poles in Teschen	1919	Presidency of Károlyi (Jan.–March); Soviet Republic (March–Aug.); Horthy enters Budapest (Nov.)
1920	Red–Green coalition cabinet; constitution and elections	1920	elections; Horthy regent; Treaty of Trianon
1920–1	Little Entente		
		1921	two coups of Charles fail; Habsburgs dethroned
1921–6	All-National coalition cabinet	1921–31	Bethlen government
		1922	elections
1924	alliance with France	1924	League of Nations loan
1925	elections		
1926–9	Gentlemen's coalition cabinet	1926	Upper House restored; elections
1927	Masaryk re-elected president		
1929	elections; broad coalition cabinet; Tuka trial	1930	Independent Smallholders Party
1932	Zvolen meeting of Slovak populists	1931	elections
1933	Organizational Pact of the Little Entente; Nitra meeting of Slovak populists	1932–6	Gömbös government
1934	Masaryk re-elected president	1934	Rome Protocols

Poland (contd)		*General (contd)*	
1918	Lublin government; Pił-sudski returns to Warsaw; Chief of State (Nov.)	1918	Wilson's Fourteen Points (Jan.); Treaty of Brest–Litovsk (March); Emperor Charles's Federalist Manifesto (Oct.); armistice of November 11
1918–19	uprising in Prussian Poland; Polish–Ukrainian struggle		
1919	Paderewski cabinet; Little Constitution	1919	Peace Treaty of Versailles (June); Peace Treaty of St Germain (Sept.)
1919–20	Polish–Soviet War		
1920	Battle of Warsaw; East Prussian plebiscites		
1921	March Constitution; Treaty of Riga (March); Upper Silesian plebiscite; alliance with France and Romania	1921	NEP in Russia
1922	Narutowicz president; assassinated; Wojciechowski president	1922	Treaty of Rapallo; fascist march on Rome
1923	Witos's right-center government	1923	Ruhr crisis
1924	Grabski reforms; Bank Polski; building of Gdynia	1925	Locarno
1926	Piłsudski's *coup d'état*		
1926–39	Mościcki president		
1928	elections		
1929	center–left bloc	1929	Wall Street Crash; the Depression
1930	"pacifications" in Eastern Galicia		
1931	Brześć trial		
1932	non-aggression treaty with USSR		
		1933	Hitler chancellor
1934	non-aggression declaration with Germany		

Czechoslovakia *(contd)*		*Hungary (contd)*	
1935	elections; success of Sudeten Germans; Henlein's Sudetendeutsche Partei; pact with USSR (May); Masaryk's resignation; Beneš president; Hodža cabinet (Nov.–Dec.)	1935	elections
		1936	Darányi government
1938	Henlein's Six Point Program (April); May crisis; Munich Conference (Sept.); Žilina Czech–Slovak accord (Oct.); Hácha president	1938	Györ program; First Vienna Award (Nov.)
1939	Germans enter Prague; Protectorate (March); Slovak state and constitution; German reprisals in Prague (Nov.); Beneš National Committee recognized in the West	1939	joins Anti-Comintern Pact; Carpatho-Ukraine occupied (March); elections
1940	Britain recognizes "Provisional Czechoslovak government"; Czechoslovak–Polish Declaration (Nov.)	1940	Second Vienna Award (Aug.); joins Tripartite Pact (Nov.)
1941	Beneš–Sikorski accord; recognition as government de jure	1941	Attack on Yugoslavia (April); at war with USSR (June)
1941–2	Heydrich governor in Protectorate		
1942	Polish–Czechoslovak Agreement (Jan.); Britain repudiates Munich; Heydrich killed; Lidice massacre (May)	1942	bloodbath at Novi Sad (Jan.); I. Horthy vice-regent (Feb.)
		1942–4	Miklós Kállay government
1943	German "transfer" negotiated; National Council in Slovakia; Czechoslovak–Soviet alliance signed in Moscow (Dec.)	1943	defeat at Voronezh (Jan.); secret negotiations with Western Allies (Sept.); battle near Debrecen; Horthy deported; Szálasi premier (Oct.)
1944	National Slovak uprising (Aug.–Oct.)	1944	Germans occupy Hungary (March); Jewish deportations (May–July); Red Army on Hungarian soil (Sept.)

	Poland (contd)		General (contd)
1935	April Constitution; Pił-sudski's death (May); elections (Sept.)		
1936	peasant strikes	1936–9	Spanish Civil War
		1936	remilitarization of the Rhineland (March)
1937	Camp of National Unity		
1938	elections	1938	Anschluss of Austria (March); Munich Conference (Sept.)
1939	alliance with Britain; German invasion (1 Sept.); Soviet invasion (17 Sept.); Polish government in France, then in Britain	1939	Ribbentrop–Molotov Pact (Aug.); outbreak of Second World War (Sept.)
1940–1	mass deportations to USSR	1940	Fall of France; Battle of Britain
1941	Sikorski–Maisky Pact; Polish army in Soviet Union	1941	Germany invades USSR (June); Atlantic Charter (Aug.); Japanese attack on Pearl Harbor (Dec.)
1942	declaration on union with Czechoslovakia	1942	Battle of Stalingrad
1943	Katyn murders discovered (April); Sikorski's death (July); Mikołajczyk premier; uprising in Warsaw ghetto (April)	1943	Teheran Conference
1944	Soviet army on prewar Polish territory (Jan.); Lublin Manifesto (July); Warsaw uprising (Aug.–Oct.); Arciszewski premier in London	1944	Allied landing in Normandy

Czechoslovakia (contd)		*Hungary (contd)*	
1945	coalitión government with communists; Košice program (April); Prague uprising (May)	1945	armistice in Moscow (Jan.); Red Army in Budapest (Feb.); land reform (March); provisional government (April); Tildy government (Nov.); elections (Nov.)
1946	elections	1946	Paris Peace Treaty; Tildy president
		1947	Smallholders' trials (Jan.–Feb.); F. Nagy and Varga in exile; elections (Aug.)
1948	communists in power (Feb.); Gottwald president; Socialist Party absorbed; transitional constitution	1948	socialists absorbed
		1948–56	Rákosi in power
1949	member of Council for Mutual Economic Assistance	1949	member of Council for Mutual Economic Assistance; trial of Cardinal Mindszenty (Feb.); trial of Rajk. (June); constitution of People's Republic
		1950	government–Catholic hierarchy accord
1952	show trials (Slánský, Clementis *et al.*)		
		1953–5	Nagy and the "new course"
1955	Warsaw Treaty Organization	1955	Warsaw Treaty Organization; Hungary in United Nations
		1956	Revolution (Oct.–Nov.)
1957	Novotný in power	1956–87	Kádár in power
1960	Socialist Republic; Council for Mutual Economic Cooperation	1960	Council for Mutual Economic Cooperation activated
		1966	New Economic Mechanism
1968	Prague Spring; Soviet and bloc intervention		

292

Poland (contd)		General (contd)	
1945	NKVD arrests sixteen underground leaders (March); withdrawal of recognition of Polish government in London; recognition of "Provisional Government of National Unity" (July)	1945	Yalta Conference (Feb.); German surrender (May); Potsdam Conference (July); atomic bomb dropped on Hiroshima; Japan surrenders (Aug.)
1946	referendum		*Hungary (contd.)*
1947	elections	1947	Marshall Plan (June); Paris Peace Treaties; Cominform (Sept.)
1948	Socialist Party absorbed	1948	Soviet break with Tito
1949	member of Council of Mutual Economic Assistance	1949	North Atlantic Treaty Organization; Council of Europe
1950	Warsaw Treaty Organization; state–church *modus vivendi*	1950–3	Korean War
1952	constitution of People's Republic		
1953–6	Cardinal Wyszyński imprisoned	1953	death of Stalin
1955	member of Warsaw Treaty Organization	1955	Austrian Treaty
1956	Poznań events (June); "Polish October"	1956	20th Party Congress; Khrushchev and de-Stalinization
1956–70	Gomułka in power		
		1962	Cuban missile crisis
		1965–73	Vietnam War
		1967	European Community; Arab–Israeli War (June)
1968	March events		

Czechoslovakia (contd)		*Hungary (contd)*	
1969	federalization; Husák in power		
1973	Munich Accord invalidated		
		1976	Cardinal L. Lékai primate
1977	Charter 77; Cardinal Tomášek primate		
1987	Husák resigns		
1989	"Velvet revolution"	1989	re-burial of Nagy (June); Party–opposition talks and accord
1990	General and presidential elections; Havel president; papal visit (April)	1990	elections (April); Antall premier; stock exchange reopened
1991	Withdrawal of Soviet troops	1991	Visegrád Summit (Feb.); papal visit (Aug.); withdrawal of Soviet troops
1992	Treaty with Germany (May); elections; Havel resigns (July)		
1993	Separation into Czech and Slovak republics (Jan. 1); Havel elected president of Czech Republic		

Poland (contd)		General (contd)	
1970	treaty with West Germany; rising in Baltic ports (Dec.)		
1970–80	Gierek in power		
		1975	Helsinki Accord
1976	workers' risings; KOR created		
		1978	election of Pope John Paul II
1979	first papal visit		
1980	Birth of Solidarność		
1981	Death of Cardinal Wyszyński; General Jaruzelski in power; martial law (Dec.)	1981	Attempt at assassination of the pope
1983	second papal visit		
1984	murder of Father Popiełuszko		
		1985	Gorbachev in power in USSR; *perestroika* and *glasnost*
1987	third papal visit		
1989	round table negotiations (Feb.–April); elections (June); Mazowiecki premier (Aug.)	1989	collapse of communism in East Central Europe; Berlin Wall dismantled
1990	local elections (June); presidential elections (Dec.); Wałęsa president	1990	unification of Germany
1990–1	treaties with Germany		
1991	fourth papal visit; Bielecki premier (Jan.)	1991	war in the Middle East; dissolution of Warsaw Treaty Organization and Council of Mutual Economic Assistance; disintegration of and war in Yugoslavia; emergence of Community of Independent States (CIS) in former USSR
1992	Olszewski premier (Jan.); withdrawal of Soviet troops; Suchocka premier (July)	1992	Bill Clinton elected president of USA (Nov.)

BIBLIOGRAPHY

The works listed below are, with some exceptions, limited to those written in English. The list is highly selective, and serves only as a guide. Bibliographies and other reference works are not included. The only historical atlas of East Central Europe is now in the process of being published as Volume XI of *A History of East Central Europe*, edited by P. F. Sugar and D. Treadgold (Seattle, Wash., 1974–).

GENERAL

Most of East Central European histories cover all the region, the Balkans included. Oscar Halecki, *Borderlands of Western Civilization* (New York, 1952) is superior to the newer Leslie C. Tihany, *A History of Middle Europe from the Earliest Times to the Age of the World Wars* (New Brunswick, NJ, 1976), while Francis Dvornik, *The Slavs in European History and Civilization* (New Brunswick, NJ, 1962) treats the period from the thirteenth to the eighteenth centuries and includes Russia. Antoni Mączak, Henryk Samsonowicz, and Peter Burke (eds), *East Central Europe in Transition from the Fourteenth to the Seventeenth Century* (Cambridge and Paris, 1985) is a collection of specialized studies. More popular is Robin Okey, *Eastern Europe 1740–1980* (Minneapolis, Minn., 1982). Alan Palmer, *The Lands Between: A History of East Central Europe since the Congress of Vienna* (New York, 1970) is useful. E. Garrison Walters, *The Other Europe: Eastern Europe to 1945* (Syracuse, NY, 1987) is somewhat elementary. R. A. Kann and Z. V. David, *The Peoples of the Eastern Habsburg Lands 1526–1918* (Seattle, Wash., 1984), the short study by Victor S. Mamatey, *Rise of the Habsburg Empire 1526–1815* (Huntington, NY, 1978), and Victor Tapié's excellent *The Rise and Fall of the Habsburg Monarchy* (New York, 1971) are most relevant.

A sociological interpretation is provided by Aleksander Gella, *Development of Class Structure in Eastern Europe: Poland and her Southern Neighbors* (New York, 1989). See also Daniel Chirot (ed.), *The Origins of Backwardness in Eastern Europe: Economics and Politics from the Middle Ages until the Early Twentieth Century* (Berkeley, Calif., 1989).

Some pertinent documents can be found in Stephen Fischer-Galati (ed.), *Man, State and Society in East European History* (New York, 1970) and in A. J. Bannan and A. Edelenyi (eds), *Documentary History of Eastern Europe* (New York, 1970). More limited in scope, but more valuable are: C. A. Macartney (ed.), *The Habsburg and Hohenzollern Dynasties in the Seventeenth and Eighteenth Centuries* (London, 1970), and Manfred Kridl, Władysław Malinowski, and Józef Witlin (eds), *For Your Freedom and Ours: Polish Progressive Spirit through the Ages* (New York, 1943). A revised and extended version edited by Krystyna Olszer was published in 1980. A volume that complements it is: M. B. Biskupski and J. S. Pula (eds), *Polish Democratic Thought from the Renaissance to the Great Emigration* (Boulder, Colo., 1970).

Among the relatively numerous histories of Poland, W. F. Reddaway *et al.*, *The Cambridge History of Poland*, 2 vols (Cambridge, 1941, 1950) reflects the prewar scholarship and Stefan Kieniewicz *et al.*, *History of Poland* (Warsaw, 1979) provides the postwar academic thought. Norman Davies, *God's Playground: A History of Poland*, 2 vols (New York, 1981) and *The Heart of Europe: A Short History of Poland* (New York, 1984) are particularly worth mentioning. Adam Zamoyski, *The Polish Way: A Thousand-year History of the Poles and their Culture* (New York, 1988) should appeal to the general reader. J. K. Fedorowicz (ed.), *A Republic of Nobles: Studies in Polish History to 1864* (Cambridge, 1982) brings together essays by specialists. Piotr S. Wandycz, *United States and Poland* (Cambridge, Mass., 1980) is designed to acquaint the American reader with the essentials of Polish history. J. Jedruch, *Constitutions, Elections and Legislatures of Poland 1493–1977* (Washington, DC, 1982) is a useful reference.

Hungary is almost as well served as Poland with the major postwar volume of Ervin Pamlenyi (ed.), *A History of Hungary* (Budapest, 1973); Péter Hanák *et al.*, *One Thousand Years: A Concise History of Hungary* (Budapest, 1988); the prewar Domokos Kosáry, *A History of Hungary* (Cleveland, Ohio, 1941), and C. A. Macartney, *Hungary: A Short History* (Edinburgh, 1962). The newest addition is the first-rate Peter F. Sugar (ed.), *A History of Hungary* (Bloomington, Ind., 1990).

The best survey of Czech and Slovak history, despite its age, is R. W. Seton-Watson, *A History of the Czechs and Slovaks* (London, 1943). S. Harrison Thomson, *Czechoslovakia in European History* (Princeton, NJ, 1953) is more of an essay. Kamil Krofta, *A Short History of Czechoslovakia* (New York, 1934) and Josef Polišenský, *History of Czechoslovakia: An Outline* (London, 1947) are hardly more than surveys. There is a brief comparative survey by Frederick G. Heymann, *Poland and Czechoslovakia* (Englewood Cliffs, NJ, 1966).

Stanko Guldescu contributed *History of Medieval Croatia* (The Hague, 1964) and *The Croatian-Slavonian Kingdom 1526–1792* (The Hague, 1970). Stephen Gazi, *A History of Croatia* (New York, 1973) is more popular. For a survey of the Slovak past see Jozef Lettrich, *History of Modern Slovakia* (New York, 1955). There is no scholarly history of Lithuania in English. C. R. Jurgela, *History of the Lithuanian Nation* (New York, 1948) is hardly satisfactory. Orest Subtelny, *Ukraine: A History* (Toronto, 1988) is the most recent synthesis. There is no comprehensive study of the Germans in East Central European history. Salo Baron, *A Social and Religious History of the Jews*, 18 vols (New York, 1952–83) has sections that deal with East Central Europe. Bernard Weinryb, *The Jews of Poland: A Social and Economic History of the Jewish Community in Poland from 1100 to 1800* (Philadelphia, Pa, 1972) is excellent, as is the essay by Aleksander Hertz, *Jews in Polish Culture* (Evanston, Ill., 1988). Randolph L. Brahan, *Hungarian Jewish Studies* 2 vols (New York, 1966) contains much useful material and so does William O. McCagg, *A History of Habsburg Jews* (Bloomington, Ind., 1989).

INTRODUCTION: WHAT'S IN A NAME?

The pioneering work by Oscar Halecki, *The Limits and Divisions of European History* (New York, 1950) refers to earlier debates. A more recent one is Jenő Szűcs, *The Three Historical Regions of Europe* (Acta Historica Academiae Scientiarum Hungaricae, vol. 29 (2/4), Budapest, 1983). A debate about the identity of the region can be found in Timothy Garton Ash, "Does Central Europe exist?," *New York Review of Books* (9 Oct. 1986), pp. 45–52; in several volumes of the periodical *Cross Currents* (notably in 1982); and in a special issue of *Daedalus* (Winter 1990). Two thought-provoking contributions are Ferenc Fehér, "On making Central Europe," *EEPS*, vol. 3, no. 3 (1989), pp. 412–47 and Stanley Z. Pech, "New avenues in Eastern European history," *Canadian Slavonic Papers* vol. 10, no. 1 (1968), pp. 3–18. A pamphlet published by the American Historical Association, R. V. Burks, *East European History: An Ethnic Approach* (Washington, DC, 1973) is elementary.

1 THE MEDIEVAL HERITAGE

F. Graus, K. Bosl, F. Seibt, M. M. Postan, A. Gieysztor, with an introduction by Geoffrey Barraclough, *Eastern and Western Europe in the Middle Ages* (New York, 1970) provides a general overview. For the origins see F. Dvornik, *The Making of Central and Eastern Europe*, 2nd edn (Gulf Breeze, Fla, 1974). Specific issues such as feudalism, capitalism, medieval economy, demography, or growth of towns are discussed by Hungarian and Polish specialists in the earlier cited volume *East Central Europe in Transition*.

Two studies by Marian Małowist, "The problem of inequality of economic development in Europe in the later Middle Ages," *Economic History Review*, 2nd series, vol. 19, no. 1 (1966), pp. 15–28 and "Problems of the growth of the national economy of Central Eastern Europe in the late Middle Ages," *Journal of European Economic History*, vol. 3 (1974), pp. 319–57 are valuable. Most other works on socio-economic problems are in French or German, an exception being Stanisław Russocki, "The parliamentary systems in 15th century Central Europe," *Poland at the 14th International Congress of Historical Sciences in San Francisco* (Wrocław, 1975), pp. 7–21.

The number of English-language studies in medieval history is rather limited. One can mention Erik Fügedi, *Castle and Society in Medieval Hungary 1000–1437* (Studia Historica Academiae Scientiarum Hungaricae, no. 187, Budapest, 1986); A. Komjathy, "Hungarian Jobbágyság in the fifteenth century," *East European Quarterly*, vol. 10, no. 1 (1970), pp. 77–111; and Bela Vardy, G. Grosschmid, and L. S. Domonkos (eds), *Louis the Great King of Hungary and Poland* (Boulder, Colo, 1986). Works dealing with the Hussite period are more numerous. They include: Howard Kaminsky, *A History of the Hussite Revolution* (Berkeley, Calif., 1967); F. M. Bartoš (prepared by John M. Klassen), *The Hussite Revolution 1424–1437* (Boulder, Colo, 1986); F. G. Heymann, *John Žižka and the Hussite Revolution* (Princeton, NJ, 1955); Matthew Spinka, *John Hus and the Church Reform* (Hamden, Conn., 1966), and his *John Hus: A Biography* (Princeton, NJ, 1968). More specialized is Peter Brock, *The Political and Social Doctrines of the Unity of the Czech Brethren in the Fifteenth and Early Sixteenth Century* (The Hague, 1957). There are two books on George of Poděbrady: Otakar O. Odlozilik, *The Hussite King: Bohemia in European Affairs 1440–71* (New Brunswick, NJ, 1965), and F. G. Heymann, *George of Bohemia: King of Heretics* (Princeton, NJ, 1965).

For medieval Poland see Zygmunt Wojciechowski, *Mieszko I and the Rise of* the Polish State (Toruń, 1936), Paul Knoll, *The Rise of the Polish Monarchy: Piast Poland in East Central Europe 1320–70* (Chicago, 1972), Paweł Jasienica, *Piast Poland* (New York, 1985) and Oscar Halecki, *Jadwiga of Anjou and the Rise of East Central Europe* (Boulder, Colo, 1991).

2 THE CHALLENGE OF THE MODERN AGE

Jan Białostocki, *The Art of the Renaissance in Eastern Europe* (New York, 1976), Samuel Fiszman (ed.), *The Polish Renaissance in the European Context* (Bloomington, Ind., 1988), H. B. Segel (ed.), *Renaissance Culture in Poland: The Rise of Humanism 1470–1543* (Ithaca, NY, 1989), and E. Fügedi and Gy. Székely (eds), *La Renaissance et la Reforme en Pologne et en Hongrie* (Budapest, 1963) offer useful comparisons. Important too are: Dražen Budiša, "Humanism in Croatia" and Marianna D. Birnbaum, "Humanism in Hungary," in Albert Rabil, Jr (ed.), *Renaissance, Humanism, Foundations, Forms and Legacy*, 2 vols (Philadelphia, PA, 1988), vol. 2, pp. 265–334. George H. Williams, *The Radical Reformation* (Philadelphia, PA, 1962) and R. J. W. Evans, "Calvinism in East Central Europe: Hungary and her neighbours 1540–1700," in Menna Prestwick (ed.), *International Calvinism 1541–1715* (New York, 1985) bring important contributions. The monumental Ambroise Jobert, *De Luther à Mohila; La Pologne dans la crise de la Chrétienté 1517–1648* (Paris, 1974), explores the complex religious and political connections. See also the somewhat controversial Oscar Halecki, *From Florence to Brest 1439–1596* (Rome, 1958).

Important works are: Janusz Tazbir, *State without Stakes: Polish Religious Toleration in the Sixteenth and Seventeenth Century* (New York, 1973); Wiktor Weintraub, "Tolerance and intolerance in Old Poland," *Canadian Slavonic Papers*, vol. 13 (1971), pp. 21–43; Maria Bogucka, "Towns in Poland and the Reformation: analogies and differences with other countries"; and Stanisław Grzybowski, "The Warsaw Confederation of 1573 and other acts of religious toleration in Europe," *Acta Poloniae Historica*, vol. 40 (1979), pp. 55–96. A short and useful treatment is Jaroslav Mezník, "Religious toleration in Moravia in the 16th century," *Kosmas*, vol. 3–4 (1984–5), pp. 109–23.

The debate about the "second serfdom" and the parting of the ways between West and East has been affected by Marxist historiography and recently by the controversial work of Immanuel Wallerstein, *The Modern World System: Capitalist Agriculture and the Origins of the European World Economy in the Sixteenth Century* (New York, 1974). Multiple studies include: Zsigmond Pach, *The Role of East Central Europe in International Trade*, Studia Historica Academiae Scientiarum Hungaricae, vol. 70 (Budapest, 1970), and his "The shifting of international trade routes in the 15–17 centuries," *Acta Historica*, vol. 14 (1968), pp. 87–319; S. Hoszowski, "L'Europe centrale devant la révolution des prix, XVI et XVII siècles," *Annales: Economies, sociétés, civilisation*, vol. 16 (1961), pp. 441–56; and Jerzy Topolski, "Sixteenth-century Poland and the turning points in European economic development," in the earlier cited Fedorowicz, *A Republic of Nobles*, pp. 70–90.

Jerome Blum, "The rise of serfdom in Eastern Europe," *American Historical Review*, vol. 72, no. 4 (1957), pp. 807–36 is now somewhat dated. Jerzy Topolski, "The manorial–serf economy in Central and Eastern Europe in the 16th and 17th centuries," *Agricultural History*, vol. 48 (1974), pp. 341–52 and the symposium on neo-serfdom in *Slavic Review*, vol. 34, no. 2 (1975), pp. 225–78 – especially the contributions of Andrzej Kamiński and László Makkai – are stimulating. David Prodan, "The origins of serfdom in Transylvania," *Slavic Review*, vol. 49, no.

1 (1990), pp. 1–17, and Josef Macek, "The emergence of serfdom in the Czech lands," *East Central Europe*, vol. 9, nos 1–2 (1982), pp. 7–23, and Anton Špiesz, "Czechoslovakia's place in the agrarian development of Middle and East Europe in modern times," *Studia Historica Slovaca*, vol. 6 (1969), pp. 7–62, question clichés and highlight the differences within the region.

Jaroslaw Pelenski (ed.), *State and Society in Europe from the Fifteenth to the Eighteenth Century* (Warsaw, 1985) and the more comparative in approach S. Russocki, "Les Structures politiques de l'Europe des Jagellons," *Acta Poloniae Historica*, vol. 39 (1979), pp. 101–42, Gottfried Schramm, "Polen-Böhmen-Ungarn: Übernationale Gemeinsamkeiten in der politischen Kultur des späten Mittelalters und der frühen Neuzeit," *Przegląd Historyczny*, vol. 76, no. 3 (1985), pp. 417–37, and I. Banac and F. E. Sysyn (eds), *Concepts of Nationhood in Early Modern Eastern Europe* (Harvard Ukrainian Studies, vol. X, nos 3/4, Cambridge, Mass., 1986) are very useful. A brilliant synthesis is R. J. W. Evans, *The Making of the Habsburg Monarchy 1550–1700* (Oxford, 1979). Informative are Vera Zimányi, *Economy and Society in Sixteenth and Seventeenth Century Hungary 1526–1650*, Studia Historica, vol. 188 (Budapest, 1987), and Kálmán Benda, "Hungary in turmoil 1580–1620," *European Studies Review*, vol. 8 (1978), pp. 281–304. The most recent is R. J. W. Evans and T. V. Thomas (eds), *Crown, Church and Estates: Central European politics in the sixteenth and seventeenth century* (London, 1991).

Harry E. Dembkowski, *The Union of Lublin: Polish Federalism in the Golden Age* (Boulder, Colo, 1982) and Andrzej Wyczański, "The problem of authority in sixteenth-century Poland: an essay in reinterpretation," in Fedorowicz (ed.), *A Republic of Nobles*, pp. 91–108, are well worth reading, as is Antoni Mączak, "The conclusive years: the end of the sixteenth century as the turning point of Polish history," in E. J. Kouri and Tom Scott (eds), *Politics and Society in Reformation Europe: Essays for Sir Geoffrey Elton on his 65th Birthday* (London, 1987), pp. 516–32.

3   THE SEVENTEENTH-CENTURY CRISIS

Several books listed above are also relevant for this chapter. Much of the polemical writings on the crisis is summarized in Theodore E. Rabb, *The Struggle for Stability in Early Modern Europe* (New York, 1975). Subsequent collective works include Geoffrey Parker and Lesley M. Smith (eds), *The General Crisis of the Seventeenth Century* (London, 1978) and Peter Clark (ed.), *The European Crisis of the 1650s* (London, 1985). An attempt to relate the crisis to East Central Europe is Orest Subtelny, *Domination of Eastern Europe: Native Nobilities and Foreign Absolutism 1500–1715* (Toronto, 1986). Economic and social issues are discussed, among others, in Zs. P. Pach, "Diminishing share of East-Central Europe in the 17th century international trade," *Acta Historica*, vol. 16 (1970), pp. 289–305, and in Krystyna Kuklińska, "Central European towns and the factors of economic growth in the transition from stagnation to expansion between the seventeenth and eighteenth centuries," *Journal of European Economic History*, vol. 11 (1982), pp. 105–15.

The most recent study of the great conflict is Geoffrey Parker, *The Thirty Years War* (London, 1984); the most provocative and stimulating is Josef V. Polišenský, *The Thirty Years' War and the Crisis of the Seventeenth Century* (Berkeley, Calif., 1972). His article "The Thirty Years' War: Problems of Motive, Extent and Effect," *Historica*, vol. 14 (1967), pp. 77–90, is well worth reading. O. Odlozilik, "The nobility of Bohemia 1620–1740," and V. S. Mamatey, "The

Battle of the White Mountain as myth in Czech history" appeared in *East European Quarterly*, respectively vol. 7, no. 1 (1973), pp. 15–30, and vol. 15, no. 3 (1981), pp. 335–45. Komenský was the object of several studies, to mention Matthew Spinka, *John Amos Comenius* (Chicago, 1943) and Vratislav Busek (ed.), *Comenius* (Ann Arbor, Mich., 1972). Connections between the Czech tragedy of the seventeenth century and the present are discussed by Peter Z. Schubert, "Resurgence of the Wallenstein theme in recent Czech literature," *Cross Currents*, vol. 3 (1983), pp. 231–8.

Poland's involvement in the seventeenth-century crisis has produced considerable literature, notably J. A. Gierowski, "The international position of Poland in the seventeenth and eighteenth centuries," in above-cited J. K. Fedorowicz (ed.), *A Republic of Nobles*, pp. 218–38, W. Czapliński, "Polish seym in the light of recent research," *Acta Poloniae Historica*, vol. 22 (1970), pp. 182–92, and Andrzej Kamiński, "The *Szlachta* of the Polish-Lithuanian Commonwealth and their government," in Ivo Banac and Paul Bushkovitch (eds), *The Nobility in Russia and Eastern Europe* (Yale Concilium, New Haven, Conn., 1983), pp. 14–45.

For the Ukrainian problem, see Andrzej Kamiński, "Polish-Lithuanian Commonwealth and its citizens (Was the Commonwealth a stepmother for Cossacks and Ruthenians?)," in Peter J. Potichnyj (ed.), *Poland and Ukraine. Past and Present* (Edmonton, Alberta, 1980), pp. 32–57, and "The Cossack experiment in Szlachta democracy in the Polish-Lithuanian Commonwealth: the Hadiach (Hadziacz) Union," *Harvard Ukrainian Studies*, vol. 1, no. 2 (1977), pp. 178–97. Frank E. Sysyn, *Between Poland and the Ukraine: the Dilemma of A. Kysil 1600–1653* (Cambridge, Mass., 1985) deserves mention. George Vernadsky, *Bohdan, Hetman of Ukraine* (New Haven, Conn., 1941) has not been yet replaced by a more recent study.

Z. Wójcik, "Poland and Russia in the 17th century," *Poland at the 14th International Congress of Historical Sciences in San Francisco* (Wrocław, 1975), pp. 113–33, and Peter B. Brown, "Muscovy, Poland, and the seventeenth century crisis," *Polish Review*, vol. 28, nos 3–4 (1982), pp. 55–69 are significant.

A. R. Várkonyi, *Historical Personality, Crisis and Progress in 17th Century Hungary*, Studia Historica Academiae Scientiarum Hungaricae, vol. 71 (Budapest, 1970) brings together a good deal of valuable material. D. G. Kosáry, "Gabriel Bethlen, Transylvania in the XVIIth century," *Slavonic Review*, vol. 17 (1938–9), pp. 162–73, and Béla Köpeczi, "Ferenc Rákóczi II," *The New Hungarian Quarterly*, vol. 61 (1976), pp. 39–57, are among the few biographies in English.

4 ENLIGHTENED ABSOLUTISM OR ENLIGHTENED LIBERTY?

R. R. Palmer, *The Age of the Democratic Revolution*, 2 vols (Princeton, NJ, 1959–64) devotes more attention to East Central Europe than most Western studies. The series *Les Lumières en Hongrie, en Europe Centrale et en Europe Orientale* (Budapest, Paris, 1972–84) contain much valuable material, for instance, Domokos Kosáry, "Absolutisme éclairé – tendence nobiliaire éclairée," vol. 3, pp. 39–46. Kosáry also contributed "Enlightenment and liberalism in Hungary," in Gy. Ránki (ed.), *Hungary and European Civilization* (Budapest, 1989), pp. 1–9. See also B. Köpeczi, "Lumières et nation en Europe Centrale et Orientale," *Etudes historiques hongroises 1980*, vol. 1 (Budapest, 1980) pp. 381–402.

H. Marczali, *Hungaria in the Eighteenth Century* (Cambridge, 1910) and Béla K. Kiraly, *Hungary in the Late Eighteenth Century: The Decline of Enlightened*

Despotism (New York, 1969) are basic. Peter Sugar contributed "The influence of the Enlightenment and the French Revolution in 18th century Hungary," *Journal of Central European Affairs*, vol. 17 (1958), pp. 331–5 and George Barany wrote "Hoping against hope: the enlightened age in Hungary," *American Historical Review*, vol. 76, no. 2 (1971), pp. 319–57.

Robert J. Kerner, *Bohemia in the Eighteenth Century* (New York, 1932) has not been superseded. Useful are: George J. Svoboda, "Recent trends in historical research on seventeenth and eighteenth century Bohemia," *East Central Europe*, vol. 7, no. 1 (1980), pp. 89–96, K. Klima, "Mercantilism in the Habsburg monarchy – with special reference to the Bohemian lands," *Historica*, vol. 11 (1965), pp. 95–120, and William E. Wright, *Serf, Seigneur, and Sovereign: Agrarian Reform in 18th Century Bohemia* (Minneapolis, Minn., 1966). Herman Freudenberger, "Industrialization in Bohemia and Moravia in the eighteenth century," *Journal of Central European Affairs*, vol. 19 (1960), pp. 347–56, and *The Waldstein Woolen Mill: Noble Entrepreneurship in 18th Century Bohemia* (Boston, Mass., 1963) deserve mention.

Andrzej Walicki, *The Enlightenment and the Birth of Modern Nationhood: Polish Political Thought from Noble Republicanism to Tadeusz Kościuszko* (Notre Dame, Ind., 1989) is thought-provoking. The two French classics are: Jean Fabre, *Stanislas-Auguste Poniatowski et l'Europe des lumières* (Paris, 1952) and A. Jobert, *Magnats polonais et physiocrates français 1767–1774* (Dijon, 1941). Important are: Witold Kula, "L'Histoire économique de la Pologne du 18e siècle," *Acta Poloniae Historica*, vol. 4 (1961), pp. 133–45; Daniel Stone, *Polish Politics and National Reform 1775–1778* (Boulder, Colo, 1976); Jörg K. Hoensch, *Sozialverfassung und Politische Reform. Polen im vorrevolutionären Zeitalter* (Cologne, 1973), and Zofia Libiszowska, "American thought in Polish political writings of the Great Diet," *Polish–American Studies*, vol. 1 (1976), pp. 41–58. Jan S. Kopczewski, *Kościuszko and Pulaski* (Warsaw, 1976) is a popular text that has not superseded M. Haiman, *Kościuszko: Leader and Exile* (New York, 1946).

Herbert H. Kaplan, *The First Partition of Poland* (New York, 1962) may be read jointly with J. Topolski, "Reflections on the first partition of Poland, 1772," *Acta Poloniae Historica*, vol. 27 (1973), pp. 89–104. The classic by Robert H. Lord, *The Second Partition of Poland* (Cambridge, Mass., 1915) remains important. Jerzy Łojek, "The international crisis of 1791: Poland between the triple alliance and Russia," *East Central Europe*, vol. 2, no. 1 (1975) pp. 1–63, is controversial.

5 AND 6   THE AGE OF LIBERAL NATIONALISM, AND FROM COMPROMISE TO INDEPENDENCE

The number of English language books dealing with the region in the nineteenth and twentieth centuries is much larger than for the earlier periods. They include the competent survey by Jörg Hoensch, *A History of Modern Hungary 1867–1986* (London, 1989), the stimulating and controversial Andrew C. Janos, *The Politics of Backwardness in Hungary 1825–1945* (Princeton, NJ, 1982), or R. F. Leslie (ed.), *The History of Poland since 1863* (Cambridge, 1980). Limited to the nineteenth century is Piotr S. Wandycz, *The Lands of Partitioned Poland 1795–1918*, 2nd printing with corrections (Seattle, Wash., 1984).

For the crucial problems of nationalism and national revival see P. F. Sugar and I. J. Lederer (eds), *Nationalism in Eastern Europe* (Seattle, Wash., 1869); the factual Emil Niederhauser, *The Rise of Nationality in Eastern Europe* (Budapest, 1982); and R. Sussex and J. E. Eade (eds), *Culture and Nationalism in Nineteenth-Century Eastern Europe* (Columbus, Ohio, 1984). Theoretical studies comprise

Jan Chlebowczyk, *On Small and Young Nations in Europe* (Wrocław, 1980) and Miroslav Hroch, *Social Preconditions of National Revival in Europe* (Cambridge, 1985). Raymond Pearson, *National Minorities in Eastern Europe 1848–1944* (New York, 1983) grapples less successfully with these difficult matters. Harry R. Ritter, "Friedrich Engels and the East European nationality problem," *East European Quarterly*, vol. 10, no. 2 (1976), pp. 137–52, and Keith Hitchins (ed.), *Studies in East European Social History* (Leiden, 1977) are pertinent. See also Stanley Z. Pech, "Right, Left and Centre in Eastern Europe 1860–1940," *Canadian Journal of History*, vol. 16, no. 2 (1981), pp. 237–62, and his "Political parties in Eastern Europe 1848–1939," *East Central Europe*, vol. 5, no. 1 (1978), pp. 1–38. Nationality problems in the Habsburg monarchy are the subject of a special issue of the *Austrian History Yearbook*, vol. 3 (1967). A. Sked, *The Decline and Fall of the Habsburg Empire 1815–1918* (New York, 1989) and Robert A. Kann, *The Habsburg Empire: A Study of Integration and Disintegration* (New York, 1957) are stimulating. A useful overview is B. Király, "The emancipation of the serfs of East Central Europe," *Antemurale*, vol. 15 (1971), pp. 63–85.

For Bohemia see Peter Brock and H. Gordon Skilling (eds), *The Czech Renascence of the Nineteenth Century* (Toronto, 1976), J. Havránek, *The Czechs: the Nationality Problem in the Habsburg Monarchy* (Prague, 1966), and J. F. Zacek, *Palacký: The Historian as Scholar and Nationalist* (The Hague, 1970). An entire issue of *East European Quarterly*, vol. 15, no. 1 (1981) is devoted to Palacký.

The Spring of Nations is covered, among others, by F. Fejtő (ed.), *The Opening of an Era 1848* (New York, 1966), and Lewis Namier, *1848: The Revolution of the Intellectuals* (New York, 1964). Parts of Hans Kohn, *Pan-Slavism* (rev. edn, New York, 1960) are relevant. Essential are: Stanley Pech, *The Czech Revolution of 1848* (Chapel Hill, NC, 1969), and L. D. Orton, *The Prague Slav Congress of 1848* (Boulder, Colo, 1975). S. B. Kimball, *Czech Nationalism: A Study of the National Theater Movement* (Urbana, Ill., 1964), Bruce M. Garver, *The Young Czech Party 1874–1901* (New Haven, Conn., 1978), and Paul Vyšný, *Neo-Slavism and the Czechs 1896–1914* (Cambridge, 1977) deserve attention. Wilma A. Iggers, "The flexible national identities of Bohemian Jewry," *East Central Europe*, vol. 7, no. 1 (1980), pp. 39–48 is informative. Among the most important works on Tomáš Masaryk are: Roman Szporluk, *The Political Thought of Thomas G. Masaryk* (Boulder, Colo, 1981); Eva Schmidt-Hartmann, *Thomas G. Masaryk's Realism: Origins of a Czech Political Concept* (Munich, 1984), and H. Gordon Skilling, "The rediscovery of Masaryk," *Cross Currents*, vol. 3 (1983), pp. 87–112. The collective work of S. Winters, R. B. Pysant, and Harry Hanak (eds), *T. G. Masaryk 1850–1937*, 3 vols (New York, 1989) is the most ambitious one in English.

George Barany, *Stephen Széchenyi and the Awakening of Hungarian Nationalism 1791–1841* (Princeton, NJ, 1968) may be supplemented by shorter pieces in the special issue of the *Journal of Central European Affairs*, vol. 20, no. 3 (1960). István Deák, *The Lawful Revolution: Louis Kossuth and the Hungarians 1848–49* (New York, 1979) is a must. Béla Király, *Ferenc Deák* (Boston, Mass., 1975) and G. Szabad, *Hungarian Political Trends between the Revolution and the Compromise 1848–1867* (Budapest, 1977) are useful. For social issues see Peter I. Higas, "The peasants of Hungary between revolution and compromise," *East European Quarterly*, vol. 19, no. 2 (1983), pp. 191–200, and Péter Hanák, "The bourgeois-ification of the Hungarian nobility – reality and utopia in the 19th century," *Etudes historiques hongroises*, vol. 2 (1985), pp. 401–21. See also William O. McCagg, *Jewish Nobles and Geniuses in Modern Hungary* (Boulder, Colo, 1972) and his "The role of the Magyar nobility in modern Jewish history," *East European Quarterly*, vol. 20, no. 1 (1986), pp. 41–53.

The classic of L. Eisenman, *Le Compromis Austro-hongrois de 1867* (Paris, 1904) remains valid, but P. Hanák, "Hundred years of Ausgleich," *New Hungarian Quarterly*, vol. 8, no. 27 (1967), pp. 17–31 brings a more recent interpretation. G. Vermes, *István Tisza. The Liberal Vision and Conservative Statecraft of a Magyar Nationalist* (Boulder, Colo, 1985); A. Horváth, "The development of nationalism in the last decades of dualism," *Acta Historica*, vol. 8, nos 1–2 (1963), pp. 1–37; and another classic, R. W. Seton-Watson, *Corruption and Reform in Hungary* (London, 1911) are important. See also Peter Brock, *The Slovak National Awakening* (Toronto, 1976) and Keith Hitchins, *The Idea of a Nation: The Romanians of Transylvania 1691–1849* (Bucharest, 1985).

An extensive bibliography on nineteenth-century Poland can be found in the earlier-cited Wandycz, *The Lands of Partitioned Poland*. Among more recent titles are: Andrzej Walicki, *Philosophy and Romantic Nationalism: The Case of Poland* (Oxford, 1982), and Tadeusz Łepkowski, "La Formation de la nation polonaise moderne dans les conditions d'un pays démembré," *Acta Poloniae Historica*, vol. 19 (1968), pp. 18–36. M. Kukiel, *Czartoryski and European Unity 1770–1861* (Princeton, NJ, 1955) provides a broad picture. S. Kieniewicz, *The Emancipation of the Polish Peasantry* (Chicago, Ill., 1969), Henryk Wereszycki, "Polish insurrections as a controversial problem in Polish historiography," *Canadian Slavonic Papers*, vol. 9 (1967), pp. 98–121, and Stanislaus A. Blejwas, *Realism in Polish Politics: Warsaw Positivism and National Survival in Nineteenth Century Poland* (New Haven, Conn., 1984) deal with crucial issues. Stefan Kieniewicz, "The Polish intelligentsia in the 19th century," in Keith Hitchins (ed.), *Studies in East European Social History*, 2 vols (Leiden, 1977), vol. 1, pp. 121–34, is important. R. F. Leslie, *Polish Politics and the Revolution of November 1830* (London, 1956) and his *Reform and Insurrection in Russian Poland 1856–1863* (London, 1963) are marred by somewhat one-sided interpretations. Many aspects of the 1863 insurrection are discussed in a special commemorative issue of *Antemurale*, vols 7–8 (1963).

For developments in Prussian Poland see, among others: William W. Hagen, *Germans, Poles and Jews. The Nationality Conflict in the Prussian East 1772–1914* (Chicago, Ill., 1980), Richard Blanke, *Prussian Poland in the German Empire 1871–1900* (Boulder, Colo, 1981) and Lech Trzeciakowski, *The Kulturkampf in Prussian Poland* (Boulder, Colo, 1990). There is a recent study by Andrei S. Markovits and Frank E. Sysyn (eds), *Nationbuilding and the Politics of Nationalism: Essays on Austrian Galicia* (Cambridge, Mass., 1982). Alfred E. Senn, *The Emergence of Modern Lithuania* (New York, 1959) provides some nineteenth-century background. For the great Polish leaders see Alvin M. Fountain III, *Roman Dmowski: Party, Tactics, Ideology 1895–1907* (Boulder, Colo, 1980) and Wacław Jędrzejewicz, *Piłsudski: A Life for Poland* (New York, 1982).

The impact of the Industrial Revolution on East Central Europe is examined, among others, by Iván Berend and György Ránki, *Economic Development in East Central Europe in the 19th and 20th Centuries* (New York, 1974); *The European Periphery and Industrialization 1780–1914* (Cambridge, Paris, 1982); and "Underdevelopment in Europe in the context of East–West relations in the 19th century," *Etudes historiques hongroises*, vol. 1 (Budapest, 1980), pp. 689–709. See also Witold Kula, "Some observations on the Industrial Revolution in Eastern European countries," *Ergon: Kwartalnik Historii Kultury Materialnej*, vol. 6, nos 1–2 (1958), pp. 239–48; John Komlos, *The Habsburg Monarchy as a Customs Union* (Princeton, NJ, 1983); L. Katus, "Economic growth in Hungary during the age of dualism," *Studia Historica*, vol. 62 (1970), pp. 35–127; J. Purš, "The Industrial Revolution in the Czech lands," *Historica*, vol. 2 (1960), pp. 183–272; Arnošt Klima, "Industrial growth and entrepreneurship in the early stages of industrialization in the Czech lands," *Journal of European Economic History*, vol. 6, no. 3 (1977), pp. 549–74. For the Congress Kingdom see Jerzy Jedlicki, "State industrial economy in the Kingdom of Poland in the 19th century," *Acta Poloniae Historica*, vol. 18 (1968), pp. 221–37.

The numerous studies on the First World War range from Wiktor Sukiennicki, *East Central Europe during World War I*, 2 vols (Boulder, Colo, 1984), with emphasis on Poland and the former lands of the Commonwealth, through the somewhat revisionist J. Kalvoda, *The Genesis of Czechoslovakia* (Boulder, Colo, 1986) to the brief but informative István Deák, "The decline and fall of Habsburg Hungary 1914–1918," in Iván Völgyes (ed.), *Hungary in Revolution 1918–19* (Lincoln, Nebr., 1971), pp. 10–30, and A. Siklós, *Revolution in Hungary and the Dissolution of the Multinational State 1918*, Studia Historica, vol. 189 (Budapest, 1988).

7 THE DIFFICULT INDEPENDENCE

The interwar period is covered by the classic Hugh Seton-Watson, *Eastern Europe between the Wars 1918–41* (3rd edn, Hamden, Conn., 1962); Joseph Rothschild, *East Central Europe between the Two World Wars* (Seattle, Wash., 1974); the somewhat more popular Antony Polonsky, *The Little Dictators: The History of Eastern Europe since 1918* (Boston, Mass., 1975); and C. A. Macartney and A. W. Palmer, *Independent Eastern Europe: A History* (London, 1962). This last book is particularly useful for international relations, as are Henry L. Roberts, *Eastern Europe: Politics, Revolution and Diplomacy* (New York, 1970), and Stephen Borsody, *The Tragedy of Central Europe* (rev. edn, New Haven, Conn., 1980). J. Żarnowski (ed.), *Dictatorship in East Central Europe 1918–39* (Wrocław, 1983) follows a comparative approach. Ezra Mendelsohn, *The Jews of East Central Europe between the Wars* (Bloomington, Ind., 1983) is more satisfactory than the only book on the Germans: A. Komjathy and R. Stockwell, *German Minorities and the Third Reich: Ethnic Germans of East Central Europe* (New York, 1980). For economics – the earlier-mentioned Berend and Ránki work on the nineteenth and twentieth centuries apart – M. C. Kaser and E. A. Radice (eds), *The Economic History of Eastern Europe 1919–75* (Oxford, 1985–) is the most ambitious undertaking. Leszek A. Kosiński, "Population censuses in East-Central Europe in the twentieth century," *East European Quarterly*, vol. 5, no. 3 (1971), pp. 279–301 brings together a great deal of important data. John A. Lukacs, *The Great Powers and Eastern Europe* (New York, 1953) is somewhat chaotic.

On individual countries: V. S. Mamatey and R. Luža (eds), *A History of the Czechoslovak Republic 1918–48* (Princeton, NJ, 1973); Věra Olivová, *The Doomed Democracy: Czechoslovakia in a Disrupted Europe 1914–38* (London, 1972); Josef Korbel, *Twentieth Century Czechoslovakia: The Meaning of its History* (New York, 1977); and Edward Taborsky, "Triumph and disaster of Eduard Beneš," *Foreign Affairs*, vol. 36 (1958), pp. 669–84 are particularly important. Eugen Steiner, *The Slovak Dilemma* (Cambridge, Mass., 1973), and Alice Teichová, *The Czechoslovak Economy 1918–1980* (New York, 1988) must be mentioned. For the German minority see especially J. W. Bruegel, *Czechoslovakia before Munich* (Cambridge, 1973).

István Deák, "Historical foundations: the development of Hungary from 1918 until 1945," in Klaus-Detlev Grothusen (ed.), *Ungarn* (Südosteuropa-Handbuch, V, Göttingen, 1987), pp. 36–66, offers a brilliant short treatment. C. A. Macartney, *October Fifteenth: A History of Modern Hungary 1929–45*, 2 vols (Edinburgh,

1956–7) is rich in details and interpretations. Gy. Juhász, *Hungarian Foreign Policy, 1919–45* (Budapest, 1979) presents a balanced picture. N. Katzburg, *Hungary and the Jews: Policy and Legislation 1920–1943* (Ramat-Gan, 1981) should be consulted. I. T. Berend and Gy. Ránki, *The Hungarian Economy in the Twentieth Century* (New York, 1983) is standard.

M. K. Dziewanowski, *Poland in the 20th Century* (New York, 1977), and R. M. Watt, *Bitter Glory: Poland and its Fate 1918–39* (New York, 1979) are surveys. The best is Antony Polonsky, *Politics in Independent Poland 1921–1939* (Oxford, 1972) except for foreign policy issues. For the latter, by way of introduction, see Piotr Wandycz, *Polish Diplomacy 1914–45* (M. B. Grabowski Lecture, London, 1988), and Jan Karski, *The Great Powers and Poland 1919–1945* (Lanham, NY, 1985). Z. Landau and J. Tomaszewski, *The Polish Economy in the 20th Century* (London, 1985) offers a counterpart to those for Hungary and Czechoslovakia listed above. Among works on the Jews of interwar Poland, H. M. Rabinowicz, *The Legacy of Polish Jewry* (New York, 1965), and Jerzy Tomaszewski, "Some methodological problems of the study of Jewish history in Poland between the two world wars," *Polin: A Journal of Polish–Jewish Studies*, vol. 1 (1986), pp. 163–75 deserve mention. S. Horak, *Poland and her National Minorities 1919–39* (New York, 1961) is not a balanced treatment.

International affairs are represented by many studies. Among those on the formation of Poland and Czechoslovakia and the 1919–20 Peace Treaties, T. Komarnicki, *Rebirth of the Polish Republic* (London, 1957), K. Lundgreen-Nielsen, *The Polish Problem at the Paris Peace Conference* (Odense, 1979), B. Király, P. Pastor, and I. Sanders (eds), *War and Society in East Central Europe, vol. VI: Essays on World War I: Total War and Peacemaking, A Case Study on Trianon* (New York, 1982) and D. Perman, *The Shaping of the Czechoslovak State* (Leiden, 1962) stand out. P. Wandycz, *Soviet–Polish Relations 1917–21* (Cambridge, Mass., 1969), Norman Davies, *White Eagle, Red Star* (New York, 1972) and M. K. Dziewanowski, *Joseph Piłsudski: A European Federalist* (Stanford, Calif., 1969) deal with Eastern problems, and P. Wandycz, *France and her Eastern Allies 1919–25* (Minneapolis, Minn., 1962) and *The Twilight of French Eastern Alliances 1926–36* (Princeton, NJ, 1988) discuss the French system in East Central Europe. G. F. Campbell, *Confrontation in Central Europe* (Chicago, 1975) analyzes Czechoslovak relationships with the Weimar Republic. Books on Munich could fill several shelves. Elizabeth Wiskemann, *Germany's Eastern Neighbours: Problems relating to the Oder–Neisse Line and the Czech Frontier Regions* (Oxford, 1956) places the German–Czech–Polish relationship in a wider perspective. A. M. Cienciala, *Poland and the Western Powers 1938–39: A Study in the Interdependence of Eastern and Western Europe* (London, Toronto, 1968) remains important.

For the Second World War, see Vojtech Mastny, *The Czechs under Nazi Rule: The Failure of National Resistance 1939–42* (New York, 1971); Radomír Luźa, *The Transfer of the Sudeten Germans* (New York, 1964); Yeshayahu Jelinek, *The Paris Republic: Hlinka's Slovak People's Party, 1939–45* (Boulder, Colo, 1976); and E. Taborsky, *President Eduard Beneš Between East and West 1938–1948* (Stanford, Calif., 1981).

M. D. Fenyo, *Hitler, Horthy and Hungary: German–Hungarian Relations 1941–44* (New Haven, Conn., 1972); S. D. Kertesz, *Diplomacy in a Whirlpool. Hungary between Nazi Germany and Soviet Russia* (South Bend, Ind., 1953); and J. Czebe and T. Pethö, *Hungary in World War II: A Military History of the Years of War* (Budapest, 1946) are among the more important. Józef Garliński, *Poland in the Second World War* (London, 1985) provides a survey, while Stefan Korbonski, *The Polish Underground State 1939–1945* (Boulder, Colo, 1978) offers a useful guide. Jan Ciechanowski, *The Warsaw Rising* (Cambridge, 1975) is controversial, while J. K. Zawodny, *Death in the Forest: The Story of the Katyn Forest Massacre* (Notre Dame, Ind., 1962) is pioneering. See also Sarah Meiklejohn Terry, *Poland's Place in Europe: General Sikorski and the Origin of the Oder–Neisse Line 1939–43* (Princeton, NJ, 1983) and Jan T. Gross, *Polish Society under German Occupation* (Princeton, NJ, 1979).

The Holocaust has a large literature, but there is no fully satisfactory overall treatment for Poland. István Deák, "The incomprehensible Holocaust," *The New York Review of Books*, vol. 36, no. 14 (1989), pp. 63–72 can serve as a balanced introduction. Among leading authors W. Bartoszewski, L. Dobroszycki, I. Gutman, N. Tec, L. Dawidowicz, and K. Moczarski have to be mentioned.

R. L. Braham, *The Politics of Genocide: The Holocaust in Hungary*, 2 vols (New York, 1981) provides an extensive treatment, and the multivolume *The Jews of Czechoslovakia: Historical Studies and Surveys* (Philadelphia, PA, 1984) has vol. 3, edited by Avigdor Dagan, devoted to the Holocaust and its aftermath.

8 THE HARD ROAD TO FREEDOM

Survey-type books on East Central Europe or the individual countries under communist rule, as well as specialized works by sociologists, economists, and political scientists are abundant. Those that stand out comprise: Zbigniew Brzezinski, *The Soviet Bloc: Unity and Conflict* (rev. edn, New York, 1967), and F. Fejtő, *History of the Peoples' Democracies: Eastern Europe since Stalin* (New York, 1971). M. Drachkovitch (ed.), *East Central Europe: Yesterday, Today, Tomorrow* (Stanford, Calif., 1982), and William E. Griffith (ed.), *Central and Eastern Europe: The Opening Curtain?* (Boulder, Colo, 1989) are useful. F. Fehér, "Eastern Europe's long revolution against Yalta," *EEPS*, vol. 2, no. 1 (1988), pp. 1–34 is thought-provoking. Joseph Rothschild, *Return to Diversity: A Political History of East Central Europe since World War II* (New York, 1989) provides a survey that may be read jointly with Gale Stokes (ed.), *From Stalinism to Pluralism: A Documentary History of Eastern Europe since 1945* (New York, 1991). Karen Dawisha, *Eastern Europe, Gorbachev and Reform, the Great Challenge*, 2nd edn (Cambridge, 1990), and Charles Gati, *The Bloc that Failed: Soviet–East European Relations in Transition* (Bloomington, Ind., 1990) are excellent.

See also Paul Marer and J. M. Montias, *East European Integration and East–West Trade* (Bloomington, Ind., 1980); Zygmunt Bauman, "Intellectuals in East Central Europe: continuity and change," *EEPS*, vol. 1, no. 2 (1987), pp. 162–86; and Paul Lendvai, *Anti-Semitism without Jews: Communist Eastern Europe* (New York, 1971).

For the individual countries: Norman Stone and Eduard Stouhal (eds), *Czechoslovakia: Crossroads and Crises 1918–88* (New York, 1989); Edward Taborsky, *Communism in Czechoslovakia 1948–1960* (Princeton, NJ, 1961); and Zdeněk Suda, *Zealots and Rebels: A History of the Ruling Communist Party of Czechoslovakia* (Stanford, Calif., 1980) are particularly useful. Charles Gati, *Hungary and the Soviet Bloc* (Durham, NC, 1985) and B. Kovrig, *Communism in Hungary. From Kun to Kadar* (Stanford, Calif., 1979) deserve attention. For Poland see: Hansjakob Stehle, *The Independent Satellite: Society and Politics in Poland since 1945* (New York, 1965); M. K. Dziewanowski, *The Communist Party of Poland. An Outline of History* (2nd edn, Cambridge, Mass., 1976); Jan de Weydenthal, *The Communists of Poland: An Historical Outline* (Stanford, Calif., 1986); and Richard F. Staar, *Poland 1944–1962: The Sovietization of a Captive People* (New

Orleans, La, 1962). Adam Bromke, *Poland's Politics: Idealism vs Realism* (Cambridge, Mass., 1967) is provocative.

The communist takeover of the region is the subject of Hugh Seton-Watson, *The East European Revolution* (2nd rev. edn, London, 1952) and Jerzy Tomaszewski, *The Socialist Regimes of East Central Europe: Their Establishment and Consolidation 1944–67* (London, 1989). For the coup of Prague see especially K. Kaplan, *The Short March: The Communist Takeover in Czechoslovakia 1945–48* (London, 1987) and the older J. Korbel, *The Communist Subversion of Czechoslovakia 1938–48* (Princeton, NJ, 1959); for Poland see the unusual Teresa Torańska, *"Them"*. *Stalin's Polish Puppets* (New York, 1987) and Krystyna Kersten, *The Establishment of the Communist Rule in Poland 1943–48* (Berkeley, Calif., 1991).

V. Mastny, *Russia's Road to the Cold War 1941–45* (New York, 1979) and Bennett Kovrig, *The Myth of Liberation: East Central Europe in U.S. Diplomacy and Politics* (Baltimore, Md, 1973) are particularly relevant.

For the 1956 Polish October and its aftermath see Nicholas Bethell, *Gomulka, his Poland, his Communism* (New York, 1969); Frank Gibney, *The Frozen Revolution* (New York, 1959) – there are also good books on the same subject by Flora Lewis, S. L. Shneiderman, and Konrad Syrop – A. Micewski, *Cardinal Wyszyński: A Biography* (San Diego, Calif., 1984), and Jakub Karpiński, *Count-Down: The Polish Upheavals of 1956, 1968, 1970, 1976, 1980* (New York, 1982). The most important studies and accounts of the Hungarian Revolution of 1956 include: F. Fehér and A. Heller, *Hungary 1956 Revisited: The Message of a Revolution: A Quarter of a Century After* (Winchester, Mass., 1983); P. Kesckemeti, *The Unexpected Revolution* (Stanford, Calif., 1961); B. Király, B. Lotze, and N. F. Dreisziger (eds), *The First War between Socialist States: The Hungarian Revolution of 1956 and its Impact* (New York, 1984); B. Király and P. Jones (eds), *The Hungarian Revolution of 1956 in Retrospect* (New York, 1978); Tibor Méray, *Thirteen Days that Shook the Kremlin* (New York, 1958); Miklós Molnár, *Budapest 1956* (London, 1968); and F. Vali, *Rift and Revolt in Hungary* (Cambridge, Mass., 1961). For later years see W. F. Robinson, *The Pattern of Reform in Hungary* (New York, 1973).

For the 1968 events in Czechoslovakia see Galia Golan, *The Czechoslovak Reform Movement: Communism in Crisis 1962–68* (New York, 1971) and *Reform Rule in Czechoslovakia: The Dubček Era 1968–69* (New York, 1973); Jiri Valenta, *Soviet Intervention in Czechoslovakia 1968: Anatomy of a Decision* (Baltimore, MD, 1979) which may be read together with E. J. Czerwinski and J. Piekalkiewicz (eds), *The Soviet Invasion of Czechoslovakia: Its Effects on Eastern Europe* (New York, 1972). V. V. Kusin, *The Intellectual Origins of the Prague Spring* (New York, 1971) and his *From Dubček to Charter 77* (New York, 1978) are especially important. The most comprehensive study may well be G. Gordon Skilling, *Czechoslovakia's Interrupted Revolution* (Princeton, NJ, 1977) whose *Charter 77 and Human Rights in Czechoslovakia* (London, 1981) also shows great insights.

Among the numerous works on the Polish Solidarity and its antecedents see A. Bromke and J. W. Strong (eds), *Gierek's Poland* (New York, 1973); Keith J. Lepak, *Prelude to Solidarity: Poland and the Politics of the Gierek Regime* (New York, 1988); J. J. Lipski, *KOR: The History of the Workers' Defense Committee in Poland 1976–81* (Berkeley, Calif., 1985); Timothy Garton Ash, *The Polish Revolution* (London, 1983); Neal Ascherson, *The Polish August* (New York, 1981); Jadwiga Staniszkis, *Poland's Self-Limiting Revolution* (Princeton, NJ, 1984); Alain Touraine, F. Dubet, Michel Wieviorka, and Jan Strzelecki, *Solidarity: Poland 1980–81* (Cambridge, 1983); and Lawrence Weschler, *The Passion of Poland: From Solidarity through the State of War* (New York, 1984). Also important are: J. Tischner, *The*

Spirit of Solidarity (San Francisco, Calif., 1984) and A. Michnik, *Letters from Prison and Other Essays* (Berkeley, Calif., 1985). Lech Wałęsa, *A Way of Hope* (New York, 1987) is rather disappointing. Books by P. Raina, L. Labedz, A. Brumberg, Kemp-Welsh D. Singer, and R. Laba are of varying importance and quality. A history of Solidarity by J. Holzer exists only in a German translation: *Solidarität* (Munich, 1985).

It is too early for scholarly monographs on the events of 1989–90 in East Central Europe, but T. Garton Ash, *The Magic Lantern: The Revolution of '89 Witnessed in Warsaw, Budapest, Berlin and Prague* (New York, 1990) deserves the title of *the* chronicler of the upheaval. Ralf Dahrendorf, *Reflections on the Revolution in Europe* (New York, 1990) is well worth reading.

INDEX